New Directions in Economic Geography

NEW HORIZONS IN REGIONAL SCIENCE

Series Editor: Philip McCann, *Professor of Economics, University of Waikato, New Zealand and Professor of Urban and Regional Economics, University of Reading, UK*

Regional science analyses important issues surrounding the growth and development of urban and regional systems and is emerging as a major social science discipline. This series provides an invaluable forum for the publication of high-quality scholarly work on urban and regional studies, industrial location economics, transport systems, economic geography and networks.

New Horizons in Regional Science aims to publish the best work by economists, geographers, urban and regional planners and other researchers from throughout the world. It is intended to serve a wide readership including academics, students and policymakers.

Titles in the series include:

New Directions in Economic Geography

Edited by

Bernard Fingleton

Reader in Geographical Economics, University of Cambridge, UK

NEW HORIZONS IN REGIONAL SCIENCE

Edward Elgar

Cheltenham, UK • Northampton, MA, USA

Published by
Edward Elgar Publishing Limited
Glensanda House
Montpellier Parade
Cheltenham
Glos GL50 1UA
UK

Edward Elgar Publishing, Inc.
William Pratt House
9 Dewey Court
Northampton
Massachusetts 01060
USA

A catalogue record for this book
is available from the British Library

Library of Congress Cataloguing in Publication Data

New directions in economic geography / edited by Bernard Fingleton.
       p. cm. — (New horizons in regional science)
    Includes bibliographical references and index.
    1. Economic geography. I. Fingleton, B. (Bernard), 1949–   II. Series.
    HF1025.N55   2007
    330.9—dc22   2006017902

ISBN 978 1 84542 373 5

Printed and bound in Great Britain by MPG Books Ltd, Bodmin, Cornwall

Contents

Contributors

Alvaro Angeriz, Cambridge Centre for Economic and Public Policy, Department of Land Economy, University of Cambridge, 19 Silver Street, Cambridge, CB3 9EP, UK. aa314@cam.ac.uk.

Steven Brakman, Department of Economics, University of Groningen, PO Box 800, 9700 AV, Groningen, the Netherlands. s.brakman@rug.nl.

Fabio Cerina, Centro Richerche Economiche Norde Sud (CRENoS) (Centre for North South Economic Research), Università degli Studi di Cagliari, Viale Fra Ignazio, 78 - 09123, Cagliari, Italy. fcerina@unica.it.

John Dewhurst, School of Social Sciences, University of Dundee, Dundee, DD1 4HN, Scotland. j.h.l.dewhurst@dundee.ac.uk.

Alessio D'Ignazio, University of Cambridge, UK and University of Rome 'La Sapienza', Italy. ad398@cam.ac.uk.

Bernard Fingleton, Department of Land Economy, University of Cambridge, 19 Silver Street, Cambridge, CB3 9EP, UK. bf100@cam.ac.uk.

Ugo Fratesi, Department of Management, Economics and Industrial Engineering, Politecnico di Milano, piazza Leonardo da Vinci 32, 20133 Milan, Italy and CERTeT, Università Bocconi, Milan, Italy. ugo.fratesi@polimi.it.

Harry Garretsen, Utrecht School of Economics, Utrecht University, Vredenburg 138, 3511 BG Utrecht, the Netherlands. H.Garretsen@ econ. uu.nl.

Emanuele Giovannetti, Department of Economics, University of Verona, Italy. giovannetti@cantab.net.

Philip McCann, Department of Economics, University of Waikato, Private Bag 3105, Hamilton, New Zealand, and Department of Economics, University of Reading, Whiteknights, Reading, RG6 6AW, UK. pmccann @waikato.ac.nz and p.mccann@reading.ac.uk.

John S.L. McCombie, Cambridge Centre for Economic and Public Policy, Department of Land Economy, University of Cambridge, 19 Silver Street, Cambridge, CB3 9EP, UK. jslm2@hermes.cam.ac.uk.

Gianmarco I.P. Ottaviano, Department of Economics, University of Bologna, Strada Maggiore, 45 – 40125 Bologna, Italy. ottavian@economia. unibo.it.

Francesco Pigliaru, Centro Richerche Economiche Norde Sud (CRENoS) (Centre for North South Economic Research), Università degli Studi di Cagliari, Viale Fra Ignazio, 78 – 09123, Cagliari, Italy. pigliaru@unica.it.

Paul Plummer, School of Geographical Sciences, University of Bristol, Bristol, BS8 1SS, UK. paul.plummer@bristol.ac.uk.

Mark Roberts, Cambridge Centre for Economic and Public Policy, Department of Land Economy, University of Cambridge, 19 Silver Street, Cambridge, CB3 9EP, UK. mr10013@cam.ac.uk.

Andrés Rodríguez-Pose, Department of Geography and Environment, LSE, Houghton Street, London WC2A 2AE, UK. a.rodriguez-pose@ lse.ac.uk.

Eric Sheppard, Department of Geography, University of Minnesota, Minneapolis, MN 55455, USA. shepp001@umn.edu.

Anna Soci, Department of Economics, University of Bologna, Strada Maggiore, 45 – 40125 Bologna, Italy. soci@spbo.unibo.it.

Introduction

Bernard Fingleton

The body of theory known as new economic geography (NEG) is first and foremost an outcome of the creative imagination of economists and not geographers, although one could easily be misled by the name commonly attributed[1] to this branch of economics. Indeed, it is not stretching the truth too far to claim that it is primarily a creation of a 'single' cohort of prominent economists,[2] the most notable among them being Paul Krugman, and it in part due to Krugman's status that the economics profession sat up and took note of this new development in economic theory, which is rooted in the theoretical systems of mainstream economics, particularly international trade theory, in which Krugman and Venables in particular have substantial reputations. As one might expect, this reinterpretation of what economic geography is, should or could be, sent shock waves throughout the community of economic geographers proper, and invoked some ardent criticism from within the geography profession. Probably the most prominent and notable critique, which received widespread coverage in a popular economics magazine[3] with a global circulation, was that of Ron Martin (1999), a geographer here at Cambridge, whose often cited work lists many of the limitations of this new approach to economic geography. Within the economics profession itself, not everyone was happy with the new turn of events, which put space centre stage in a way that had never before been possible. For example, there was serious criticism of the theoretical assumptions underpinning the NEG by Peter Neary in his article written in 2001.

None the less, and because of or despite these limitations, NEG has spurred both geographers and economists to new heights, in some cases to develop modifications to the theory so as to circumnavigate the criticisms that have been made, in other cases as a reaction to their concerns with what NEG has to offer and the direction in which it is steering. For others it is because NEG is viewed as a new and exciting sub-discipline of economics, despite the protestations of geographers and others that it is something of a reinvention of the wheel, albeit with extra analytical rigour and formalism. An outcome of all this activity is a revitalization of the interface between geography and economics, with new theories and analytical methods coming on-stream fast in the literature. Books have been published that attempt to see a way forward for economic geography, most notably *The Oxford Handbook of Economic Geography* (Clark, Feidman and Gertler, 2000), which is written principally from the geographers' perspective, whereas, for instance, *An Introduction to Geographical Economics* and the *Handbook of Urban and Regional Economics, Volume 4* (Henderson and Thisse, 2004), have a fairly exclusively economics emphasis. New journals have been established. *The Journal of Economic Geography* is dedicated to establishing a dialogue between geographers and economists, and more recently *Spatial Economic Analysis*[4] has been inaugurated jointly by the Regional Studies Association and the Regional Science Association (British and Irish section), with a focus on spatial economics and spatial econometrics.

This book is a constructive contribution to this interactive process: it is written by sympathetic and open-minded economists interested in economic geography, economists who were also trained as economic geographers, and economic geographers proper, all of whom are broadly characterized as having a natural affinity to, or interest in, NEG, but who want to take our understanding of economic geography beyond the restricted perspective offered by current NEG theory and practice. Therefore, to some extent, the book can be seen as a constructive critique of NEG, wishing to take economic geography forward in new directions in the aftermath of the initial wave of theory, and which sees a continuing role for theoretical and empirical contributions to the science of spatial economic analysis. The intention is to offer middle ways that build on, rather than destroy, the advances made by NEG, by helping to tear down the walls and perhaps shake the foundations, and rebuilding in the light of collective experience, wisdom and insight. This was the tenor of some of my own recent papers (Fingleton, 2000, 2004), which called for a 'third way', a call that is echoed in the work of like-minded colleagues (for example, Rodriguez-Pose, 1998; Sjoberg and Sjoholm, 2002). Where this 'third way' parts company with many geographers is that it treats economic geography as an essentially scientific endeavour. By 'scientific endeavour' I mean collective action in which communicable theories are constructed, and ultimately rejected, transcending culture, language, time and space. Hence the preferred approach is to set up a clearly defined model, hypothesizing explicit relationships and interactions, in order to cast light on a complex reality. Where 'the third way' parts company with what remains of traditional NEG is the emphasis it gives to realism; in other words, important variables are not assumed away because they get in the way of formal modelling, but are incorporated because at the end of the day theory is about explaining reality, and is somewhat sterile and fairly useless when treated as an end in itself. Useful theory leads to a model that will tell us what will, could or would happen at point X on the surface of the earth at time T; the more precise this prediction is, the more useful is the theory and model generating it. Although they had to start somewhere, much of NEG theory, as set out in the classic exposition by Fujita et al. (1999), is distinctly unreal and only potentially useful; much of this book tries to use, or evaluate the usefulness of, NEG theory. We therefore start with an introductory outline of some initial (unreal) NEG concepts in Chapter 1 before progressing swiftly in various new directions, as befits a book entitled *New Directions in Economic Geography*.

CHAPTER 1

Chapter 1 outlines some of the economic theory that underpins NEG, and illustrates the theory in two ways. One is a simulation that takes the reduced forms consistent with a simple version of NEG theory and attempts to apply it to the data for regions of Great Britain. On the whole the model works; it is possible to replicate reality even via this simple model, which assumes so much and excludes many of the very important variables that are known to determine, for example, wage rates. The data do seem to match the short-run equilibrium outcomes from the NEG model. This highlights an important direction for future research, which is that just because we can fit a model does not mean that the theory underpinning the model is true, or indeed it does not mean that the fitted model is superior to another (untested) model with a different theoretical basis, which may outperform the model in question. Hence the message we get from this 'successful' exercise in calibration is that we should not get too excited by a good statistical fit! The second example in Chapter 1 looks at the long-run rather than short-run dynamics of the NEG model, switching from the 36 regions of Great Britain to the much more manageable two: core and periphery. This artificial landscape evolves towards polarization or symmetry, depending on the conditions. The examples follow those in Fujita, et al. (1999), but with a different graphical flavour.

CHAPTER 2

This chapter raises the issue of observational equivalence between the two main classes of 'new economic geography' (NEG) models based on factor mobility and vertical linkages. The issue is illustrated in terms of two recent versions of those models, whose analytical solvability reveals that the two classes share the same fundamental structure and therefore the same equilibrium properties. Accordingly, they lead to the same key empirical predictions. This calls for additional theoretical efforts to embed the two classes of models in richer set-ups where new endogenous variables react differently depending on which class is given the dominant role.

CHAPTER 3

This is a first attempt to fully test the NEG theory against a competing theory derived from urban economics. Both theories have much in common, for example, they are underpinned by the Dixit-Stiglitz theory of monopolistic competition, but they also differ. Most notably, the NEG theory has explicit transport costs and the urban economic theory has none. Both empirical models need to allow for additional covariates to obtain a reasonably good approximation to the data, which comprises nominal wage rates across 200 EU regions. The outcome is that the two competing hypotheses are non-nested, meaning that one is not simply a restricted version of the other, comprising a subset of its explanatory variables, and accordingly, the analysis uses a methodology appropriate to the testing of non-nested hypotheses. The principal finding is that NEG theory, as manifest in the reduced form equation, is no better than urban economic theory as a predictor of wage rate variations. In fact, the data supports both theories, without producing a knockout blow that dismisses one entirely, or allows one to be completely convinced by the other. Clearly, the version of NEG adopted here is not very adequate. This chapter is one of several that show NEG theory, on its own, to be of limited value as a realistic model.

CHAPTER 4

This chapter is an attempt to take estimates based on NEG models one step further. A crucial distinction between NEG and its predecessor, the new trade theory, is that (small) changes in the key model parameters can lead to (large) changes in agglomeration if an economy is close to the so-called break points. Once estimates of key model parameters are available, the question becomes what do these estimates imply in practice? Is it possible, for instance, to use the empirical evidence to find out whether or not the EU is close to such a break point at the current level of economic integration? The answer to this question is obviously important for policy-makers. The authors try to find an answer, and by doing so they also show how difficult it is to answer this question. Their confrontation of NEG empirics with NEG theory points to some serious limitations of current NEG research.

CHAPTER 5

This chapter is divided into two parts. In the first part, the authors review the main results of a typical 'new economic geography and growth' (NEGG) model (Baldwin and Martin, 2003) and assess the contribution of this literature to the issue of long-run income gaps between countries. In the second part they discuss the robustness in some results of these models, which are directly linked to important policy implications, and they show that these results crucially depend on very restrictive values of some parameters of the model. In particular, depending on the different values of the degree of love for variety and the elasticity of substitution between traditional and manufacturing goods, their analytical examples reveal that: (1) when trade is costly enough the symmetric equilibrium might not be stable when capital is also perfectly mobile; (2) the rate of growth might depend on the geographical allocation of industries when spillovers are also global and, (3) when industrial firms are concentrated in only one region, countries might not grow at the same rate in real terms.

CHAPTER 6

This chapter focuses on the Achilles heel of NEG modelling: the assumption of iceberg transport costs. The main idea in the chapter is that iceberg transport costs are not a very realistic way to model transport costs, and yet are an essential element of NEG theory. The reason why they are unrealistic is that iceberg transport costs, as they are represented in explicitly spatial versions of new economic geography models, do not allow for any economies of distance and of scale in the transportation of either goods or information. Nor do they allow for possible variations in distance cost structures between inputs and outputs, and particularly those associated with information transactions costs. In contrast to the dynamics and equilibria that are the outcome of assuming iceberg transport costs, research on location production models suggests that stable locational equilibrium conditions are impossible with transport costs exhibiting economies of scale, even in conditions where transport costs exhibit economies of distance. Some progress is possible using alternatives, for example, a power function that at least captures economies of distance, calling into question whether we are really ever going to obtain satisfactory empirical models with the NEG theory as presently formulated.

CHAPTER 7

This chapter investigates the relationship between the size of an area and the extent of its industrial specialization, pointing to the need for caution in drawing conclusions about NEG-related characteristics from aggregate regional data. Much recent literature in regional economics and NEG suggests that certain patterns of industrial specialization, and by implication, regional trade, will be empirically evident within the spatial economy. In particular, renewed theoretical interest in the role played by agglomeration economies in determining the patterns of regional specialization, has also led to the development of new empirical efforts aimed at identifying such agglomeration effects. However, a fundamental point that has been largely overlooked in the literature on agglomeration is the fact that the outcomes of these empirical exercises may themselves also be affected by our chosen spatial units of analysis.

As such, it is necessary to be rather cautious where empirical evidence is used to support theoretical arguments of agglomeration externalities. In order to discuss the relationship between the size of a region and its level of specialization, the authors analyse UK sectoral employment data at a variety of different levels of spatial aggregation. This allows them to distinguish the effect of regional size on measures of industrial specialization from those related to agglomeration economies. The overall findings of the analysis do confirm that regional specialization is indeed generally inversely related to the size of a region, as well as to the position of the area within the urban hierarchy. However, it is also necessary to be aware of the fact that this relationship is not only non-monotonic, but also that this relationship may be subject to the issues raised by the modifiable unit area problem. These results therefore require us to be very careful and cautious when interpreting empirical results of sectoral specialization and diversity as evidence of various types of agglomeration economies.

CHAPTER 8

The immediate target for criticism in Chapter 8 is not NEG per se but some of the assumptions and methods relating to the traditional neoclassical growth model, most notably that stemming from Barro and Sala-i-Martin's (1991) work on convergence, which 'has spawned a mini-industry of research into cross-regional productivity differences predicated on a Solow-Swan type framework'. It is therefore, by implication, also critical of standard theoretical assumptions used in NEG. The authors argue that relatively little, if anything, is known about whether cross-regional differences in productivity growth in the EU are attributable to spatial differences in the efficiency with which factors are employed or spatial disparities in the rate of technical change. Indeed, the theoretical framework typically used as the backdrop for empirical research in this area assumes that all regions are technically efficient and that technology is a pure public good. That is to say, the framework typically used is an 'old' neoclassical growth framework that implicitly assumes that all regions are not only operating on their production functions, but that they share the *same* production function. This being the case, spatial differences in productivity are purely attributable to spatial differences in labour productivity emanating from differences in the capital intensity of production. Likewise, spatial differences in rates of productivity growth take the form of spatial differences in labour productivity growth attributable to different regions being in different degrees of (steady-state) disequilibrium.

To overcome some of these limitations, the chapter uses the non-parametric technique of data envelopment analysis (DEA) to calculate productivity growth using the Malmqüist index of total factor productivity (MTFP) change, which is subsequently decomposed into indices of efficiency change and technical change. Analysis of these results reveals that over the crucial period of deepening EU integration, 1986–2002, the average region fell substantially further behind Europe's 'best practice' manufacturing frontier, recording a drop in relative efficiency of 24 per cent. It further reveals important spatial patterns in the distribution of the MTFP change index and levels of technical efficiency.

CHAPTER 9

Recent debates in economic geography have raised profound questions about the ways in which we both conceptualize spatial economic systems and use empirical evidence to support our explanations. Everyone agrees that we need to confront ideas with empirical evidence. But, there exists a broad range of views as to what this might mean in practice. Increasingly, and with varying degrees of success, theoretical claims are being confronted with empirical evidence using the tools of conventional spatial econometrics. Whilst sharing a commitment to mathematical and statistical reasoning, the authors put these tools to a different use. Their approach to understanding the evolving economic landscape emphasizes the self-destabilizing nature of competitive dynamics in capitalist economies, raising the possibility of perpetual out-of-equilibrium spatio-temporal dynamics. While it has been possible to describe processes underlying this instability, empirical analysis of these theories has been scarce. In this chapter, the authors take a preliminary step in rectifying the paucity of econometric testing by outlining an empirical methodology that draws on, and extends, recent developments in the qualitative econometrics of non-linear dynamic systems. This involves extending and adapting the mathematical and statistical tools of symbolic and coding dynamics to complex spatio-temporal dynamics. When combined with a Bayesian model selection strategy, they argue that this permits the empirical comparison of some of the claims of NEG with those of *regional political economy*.

CHAPTER 10

This chapter reviews the literature on foreign direct investment (FDI) and tries to relate the empirical findings to theoretical structures, notably NEG. Numerous empirical results reveal FDI as a relevant and important aspect of economic reality that lacks a unified theoretical explanation. The chapter considers the possibility that NEG could help in throwing light on the mechanisms at work in FDI. Space – both in its physical and economic meaning – must play a decisive role in the decision made by firms about where they should locate or re-locate. Unfortunately, thus far, little effort has been made to incorporate something more than the flavour of NEG theory into FDI's theoretical and empirical framework. The suggestion is that future research should abandon the macro-view of FDI and focus on detailed firm-studies and micro-data, with a greater emphasis on the spatial elements, and that NEG should interplay more and more with trade theory to become more adaptable to the needs of FDI-related research.

CHAPTER 11

This chapter gives empirical evidence to support the view that even in the seemingly spaceless world of global information exchange, occurring at the speed of light over the Internet, with minimal transactions costs related to distance, proximity matters. While it may be true that as a result of the Internet, geographical proximity may matter less, what remains important is connectivity and language affinity. The chapter introduces the debate on the effects of ICT on the relevant notion of distance, either related to geographical or virtual dimensions, and discusses the role of trust and reputation in situations characterized by repeated incomplete contracts, as is manifest in industrial districts. It also provides a brief description of the main forms of interconnection on the Internet, with a special focus on the nature of peering agreements. Then the authors discuss the rationale for observing agglomeration in the peering decision, and provide an econometric analysis of peering decisions within three relevant Euro-IX members' Internet exchange points. This is linked to NEG by the discussion of how ICT exerts two opposite effects on the agglomeration: a weakening of the centrifugal forces, and a shift in the centre of gravity of the centripetal forces, focusing agglomeration around virtual locations. Despite the seemingly almost zero transactions costs that seem to be an integral feature of the world of ICT, the authors conclude that, nevertheless, proximity matters. This is believed to be due to the role that proximity still plays in reducing the transaction costs of monitoring and punishing deviant behaviour, which is important within an industry where cooperation is essential for the efficient traffic exchange that is required for universal Internet connectivity.

CHAPTER 12

This chapter addresses the question, 'Why have the returns of European structural policies been below the ambitious goal of economic and social cohesion?' Interestingly, and in line with recent developments in the application of NEG, despite its largely normative and policy-oriented focus, the authors use an NEG theoretical framework as a backcloth to their explanation. They find that the excessive emphasis on infrastructure and, to a lesser extent, on business support, may be contributing to a greater concentration of economic activity in the core at the expense of the periphery, a trend that does not seem to be compensated by the positive returns from investment in human resources in a period of low labour mobility.

NEG models provide some potential explanation for this. Investment in transport infrastructure, in particular, is contributing to greater economic agglomeration, making any change to the present equilibrium situation somewhat difficult. Moreover, improving the transport infrastructure can itself be a reason for increasing agglomeration and disparities. NEG models show how infrastructure linking different regions usually tends to favour those regions endowed with a stronger productive fabric, and thus tends to further reinforce agglomeration. This also helps explain why expenditure in human capital, which is intended to provide local economies with better skills and overcome some of the endowment shortcomings of the periphery, has evidently been the only element of policy to provide significant and durable growth effects in Objective 1 regions.

NOTES

1. A less controversial alternative is 'geographical economics', as used in the book by Brakman, Garretsen and van Marrewijk (2001).
2. The authors of classic text, *The Spatial Economy: Cities, Regions and International Trade*, namely Masahisa Fujita, Paul Krugman and Anthony Venables.
3. *The Economist*, 11 March 1999.
4. I am the Editor.

REFERENCES

Baldwin, R. and P. Martin (2003), 'Agglomeration and regional growth', *Discussion Paper 3960*, Centre for Economic Policy Research, London.

Barro, R.J. and X. Sala-i-Martin (1991), 'Convergence across states and regions', *Brookings Papers on Economic Activity*, **1**: 107–82.

Brakman, S., H. Garretsen and C. van Marrewijk (2001), *An Introduction to Geographical Economics*, Cambridge: Cambridge University Press.

Clark, G.C., M.P. Feldman and M.S. Gertler (2000), *The Oxford Handbook of Economic Geography*, Oxford: Oxford University Press.

Fingleton. B. (2000), 'Spatial econometrics, economic geography, dynamics and equilibrium: a third way?', *Environment & Planning A*, **32**: 1481–98.

Fingleton, B. (2004), 'Some alternative geo-economics for Europe's regions', *Journal of Economic Geography*, **4**: 389–420.

Fujita, M., P.R. Krugman and A.J. Venables (1999), *The Spatial Economy: Cities, Regions, and International Trade*, Cambridge, MA: MIT Press.

Henderson, V. and J.F. Thisse (eds) (2004), *Handbook of Regional and Urban Economics*, North-Holland: Elsevier.

Martin, R. (1999), 'The new "geographical turn" in economics: some critical reflections', *Cambridge Journal of Economics*, **23**: 65–91.

Neary, J.P. (2001), 'Of hype and hyperbolas; introducing the new economic geography', *Journal of Economic Literature*, **39**: 536–61.

Rodriguez-Pose, A. (1998), *Dynamics of Regional Growth in Europe: Social and Political Factors*, Oxford: Oxford Clarendon Press.

Sjoberg O. and F. Sjoholm (2002), 'Common ground? Prospects for integrating the economic geography of geographers and economists', *Environment and Planning A*, **34**: 467–86.

1. New economic geography: some preliminaries

Bernard Fingleton

1.1 INTRODUCTION

The aim of this chapter is to illustrate important principles underlying 'new economic geography' (NEG) as a lead in to the varieties of economic geography on display in subsequent chapters. The classic work on NEG is Fujita, Krugman and Venables (1999), and this should, of course, be consulted for a fuller and more detailed account. The emphasis here is on explaining some of the normally taken-for-granted ideas and assumptions for newcomers to this field. While the theory outlined here is well known, what is new about this chapter is the empirical application of NEG theory to real data for the UK regions, and the way in which the dynamics have been illustrated.

1.2 MICRO ASSUMPTIONS

An essential feature of NEG is the way increasing returns to scale emerge from microeconomic foundations. Economists and geographers have long been aware of the significance of increasing returns for spatial differentiation, and it is the basis of dynamic models of cumulative causation that were the precursors to the NEG.[1] In elemental versions of NEG theory it is the consumer's love of variety that is important as the determinant of increasing returns to scale. Our starting point is therefore a utility function in which there are two types of good, which we denote by M and C produced by M industries and C industries. We assume the Cobb-Douglas form, in which M is a composite index of goods produced under monopolistic competition. We use C to denote the consumption of goods characterized by a competitive market structure, with no internal increasing returns to scale:

$$U = M^{\theta} C^{1-\theta}. \tag{1.1}$$

In this equation, $0 < \theta < 1$ determines the relative importance of M and C goods to utility (it is the consumer's expenditure share on M goods). The quantity of the composite good M is a function of the separate varieties $m(i)$, where i ranges from 1 to x, where x is the number of varieties. To show this, we use a constant elasticity of substitution (CES) subutility function for M, so that:

$$M = \left[\sum_{i=1}^{x} m(i)^{(\sigma-1)/\sigma} \right]^{\sigma/(\sigma-1)} = \left[\sum_{i=1}^{x} m(i)^{\frac{1}{\mu}} \right]^{\mu} \tag{1.2}$$

in which $m(i)$ denotes the quantity of variety i, there are x varieties and σ is the elasticity of substitution between any two varieties. Since under monopolistic competition at equilibrium $m(i)$ is a constant across all i varieties, then we can state that $M = x^{\mu}m(i)$ so that M is not simply the sum of all x varieties, but its value also reflects the added bonus to be obtained from more variety (unless μ approaches closely to 1, in which case the elasticity of substitution of M products:

$$\sigma = \frac{\mu}{\mu - 1}$$

tends to infinity, so that there is then no benefit from variety). Under the theory, σ is also equal to the price elasticity of demand, measuring the proportional change in quantity demanded divided by the proportional change in price. More precisely, it is the derivative of quantity with respect to price divided by the ratio of quantity to price. Using this price elasticity is one of the main advantages arising from using the Dixit-Stiglitz model of monopolistic competition. It simplifies the theoretical analysis. Every firm has the same price elasticity of demand.

The consumer is assumed to wish to maximize U subject to total income being equal to Y, and we can treat this as two separate maximization problems, for M and for C, because preferences are separable and the subutility function is homothetic in $m(i)$. In plain English, separability means that we can partition M and C and treat them independently, and this allows two-stage budgeting, so that the consumer creates an optimal budget for each separable subgroup. Homothetic preferences ensure that consumers with different incomes but faced with the same prices, demand goods in the same proportions. In other words, the ratios of goods demanded depend only on relative prices and not on income. If a consumer chooses with a ratio $m(1)/m(2)$, then the same ratio will apply as his or her income increases. The slope of the indifference curve, the marginal rate of substitution, remains constant. This is a useful simplifying assumption since a single preference function applies across the whole range of income levels. If preferences are identical across consumers and are homothetic, then aggregate demand depends only on prices and aggregate income. If we take the first partial derivatives of the preference function, and their ratios depend only on the ratios of the arguments of the function, not their levels, then this ensures that the preference function is homothetic.

Let us consider the problem of choosing the $m(i)$ quantities so that the cost of the composite M is at a minimum. In other words, we wish to minimize $\sum_{i=1}^{x} p_i m(i)$ subject to the constraint given as (1.1). The minimization involves a Lagrangian function:

$$L = \sum_{i=1}^{x} p_i m(i) + \Lambda \left[M - \left\{ \sum_{i=1}^{x} m(i)^{(\sigma-1)/\sigma} \right\}^{\sigma/(\sigma-1)} \right] \tag{1.3}$$

and the first order conditions are the derivatives of L, with respect to $m(i)$ and the Lagrangian multiplier Λ, set equal to zero, hence:

$$\frac{\partial L}{\partial m(i)} = p_i - \Lambda \left[\sum_{i=1}^{x} m(i)^{(\sigma-1)/\sigma} \right]^{\frac{1}{\sigma-1}} m(i)^{\frac{-1}{\sigma}} = 0 \tag{1.4}$$

and:

$$\frac{\partial L}{\partial \Lambda} = M - \left[\sum_{i=1}^{x} m(i)^{(\sigma-1)/\sigma} \right]^{\sigma/(\sigma-1)} = 0. \tag{1.5}$$

Assume, somewhat heroically, that there are only three firms, hence $x = 3$ rather than an extremely large number as we would normally assume. In this rather artificial circumstance we can then produce a simplified version of equation (1.4) for the case where $i = 1$, hence:

$$p_1 - \Lambda \left[m(1)^{\frac{1}{\mu}} + m(1)^{\frac{1}{\mu}} + m(1)^{\frac{1}{\mu}} \right]^{\mu-1} m(1)^{\frac{1}{\mu}-1} = 0$$

with equivalent equations for $i = 2$ and $i = 3$. Equation (1.5) becomes:

$$M - \left[m(1)^{\frac{1}{\mu}} + m(1)^{\frac{1}{\mu}} + m(1)^{\frac{1}{\mu}} \right]^{\mu} = 0.$$

It is possible to isolate Λ giving:

$$\Lambda = p_1 \left[m(1)^{\frac{1}{\mu}} + m(2)^{\frac{1}{\mu}} + m(3)^{\frac{1}{\mu}} \right]^{1-\mu} m(1)^{1-\frac{1}{\mu}}$$

with equivalent expressions using $i = 2$ and $i = 3$. Since each of the three expressions has Λ in common, then it follows that, for $i = 1$ and $i = 2$, and with:

$$k = \left[m(1)^{\frac{1}{\mu}} + m(1)^{\frac{1}{\mu}} + m(1)^{\frac{1}{\mu}} \right]^{1-\mu}$$

$$\Lambda p_1 k m(1)^{1-\frac{1}{\mu}} = \Lambda p_2 k m(2)^{1-\frac{1}{\mu}}$$

so that:

$$\frac{p_1}{p_2} = \frac{\Lambda k m(2)^{1-\frac{1}{\mu}}}{\Lambda k m(1)^{1-\frac{1}{\mu}}} = \left[\frac{m(2)}{m(1)} \right]^{1-\frac{1}{\mu}} = \left[\frac{m(1)}{m(2)} \right]^{\frac{1}{\mu}-1}$$

$$m(1) = \left[\frac{p_2}{p_1} \right]^{\frac{1}{1-\frac{1}{\mu}}} m(2)$$

and generally, with varieties i and j:

$$m(i) = \left[\frac{p_j}{p_i} \right]^{\sigma} m(j). \tag{1.6}$$

Equation (1.6) simply tells us that the quantity of variety i is a function of the quantity of variety j and the relative prices of i and j. So if we now return to equation (1.2) the expression for the composite quantity M can now be rewritten as a function of quantities and prices for each variety, and this allows us to collect together prices as an entity to show how, given a unit of M, it gives the overall cost of its purchase. In other words, this collection of prices is the price index G, which is a measure of the minimum cost of buying a unit of the composite quantity M.

More precisely, in order to obtain an expression for G, we substitute for $m(i)$ in equation (1.2), and collect together price and quantity terms relating to i outside the summation, giving:

$$M = \left[m(i)^{\frac{1}{\mu}} \sum_j \left\{ \frac{p_i}{p_j} \right\}^{\frac{\sigma}{\mu}} \right]^{\mu} = \left[m(i)^{\frac{1}{\mu}} p_i^{\frac{\sigma}{\mu}} \sum_j p_j^{-\frac{\sigma}{\mu}} \right]^{\mu}.$$

For our $x = 3$ example, this is equivalent to:

$$M = \left\{ m(1)^{\frac{1}{\mu}} p_1^{\frac{\sigma}{\mu}} \left[p_1^{\frac{-\sigma}{\mu}} + p_2^{\frac{-\sigma}{\mu}} + p_3^{\frac{-\sigma}{\mu}} \right] \right\}^{\mu} = m(1) p_1^{\sigma} G^{-\sigma}$$

$$G^{-\sigma} = [p_1^{1-\sigma} + p_2^{1-\sigma} + p_3^{1-\sigma}]^{\frac{\sigma}{\sigma-1}}$$

and more generally:

$$M = m(i) p_i^{\sigma} G^{-\sigma}$$

and from this the (compensated) demand function for variety i is:

$$m(i) = p_i^{-\sigma} G^{\sigma} M \qquad (1.7)$$

$$G = \left[\sum_{j=1}^{x} p_j^{1-\sigma} \right]^{\frac{1}{1-\sigma}} \qquad (1.8)$$

and it turns out that G is the minimum unit cost function for M.

To show this, let us assume that $M = 1$, and also that the total cost of this unit is the sum of the quantity demanded for each of the x varieties $m(i = 1, \ldots, x)$ multiplied by the price of each variety $p(i = 1, \ldots, x)$. So then from equation (1.7) with the total cost of $M = 1$ we obtain:

$$\sum_{i=1}^{x} m(i) p_i = \sum_{i=1}^{x} p_i p_i^{-\sigma} G^{\sigma} = G^{\sigma} \sum_{i=1}^{x} p_i^{1-\sigma} = G.$$

This can be seen if we rewrite this as:

$$G^{\sigma} \sum_{i=1}^{x} p_i^{1-\sigma} = G^{\sigma} \left[\sum_{i=1}^{x} p_i^{1-\sigma} \right]^{\frac{1-\sigma}{1-\sigma}} = G^{\sigma} G^1 G^{-\sigma} = G.$$

We have obtained the demand function (1.7), which relates the demand for variety i to the composite level M so that the cost of attaining that level is at a minimum. We have not, however, determined the level that M should be at. The decision problem is simply one of finding the values of M and C

that maximize equation (1.1), subject to the budget constraint that overall expenditure is equal to $GM + p^C C = Y$, in other words equals the unit cost for M, G, multiplied by the number of units M, plus the cost of a unit of C (p^C) times C, which is the number of C units. It is a standard result that the shares of the total budget will be equal to the coefficients θ and $1 - \theta$, so that $GM = \theta Y$ and $p^C C = (1 - \theta) Y$ and from these we obtain the values for M and C, and substituting M into equation (1.7) we obtain the uncompensated demand function:

$$m(i) = \theta Y p_i^{-\sigma} G^{\sigma - 1}. \tag{1.9}$$

With a compensated demand function, consumer utility remains constant as p_i rises, this being accomplished by a commensurate rise in consumer income, but when a price rise is not compensated by extra income to achieve the same utility level as before the price rise, we have an uncompensated demand function. This is the case here since a rise in the price of an M variety would reduce utility since the budget Y is a fixed quantity in equation (1.9).

Also, we can obtain the indirect utility function, which is the maximum utility that can be attained by spending the budget Y subject to prices p^C and G. We find this by substituting $M = \theta Y G^{-1}$ and $C = (1 - \theta) Y / p^C$ into $U = M^\theta C^{1 - \theta}$, which after some manipulation gives:

$$U = \theta^\theta (1 - \theta)^{1 - \theta} Y G^{-\theta} (p^C)^{\theta - 1}.$$

This expression contains an important quantity, the cost of living index $G^\theta (p^C)^{1 - \theta}$, since while utility will increase directly with income Y, it will be inversely related to prices as encapsulated by the cost of living index. The cost of living index, which we show below, will vary by location since prices vary by location, is fundamental for a proper evaluation of the wage differences across regions.

1.3   INTRODUCING TRANSPORT COSTS AND M FIRMS

Equation (1.8) shows that the price index is the same for all locations, but this is a gross oversimplification because different locations will incur different transport costs, so we need to have a separate price index for each location. We denote this by G_i^M, where i refers to region i and M indicates that the price index is specific to M goods. To show this, we assume that each variety is produced in a different region, and that each region will import non-home-produced M varieties from other regions, and if these are expensive this will increase the price index accordingly. The price of a good coming from region j will depend on its 'home price' plus the cost of transportation.

Thinking about consumers has helped us to develop expressions for cost of living indices and price indices, which are important in evaluating real versus nominal wage differences between regions. We now switch to a single city or region where transport costs are negligible to enable us to think about other background concepts.

First, we can simplify by setting 'home price' equal to the wage rate. We know from our theory of producer behaviour under monopolistic competition that, without any consideration of transport costs, price is equal to the wage rate at i multiplied by two constants, the marginal labour requirement (a) and returns to scale at equilibrium (μ). Hence there is a mark-up on marginal costs $w^M a$ equal to μ. To show that the mark-up equals μ, first consider the profit function of the M firm. Profits (π), equal to revenues minus costs, hence:

$$\pi = p_i m(i) - w^M(am(i) + s)$$

with price p_i times quantity sold $m(i)$ equals revenue. Wages (w^M) times labour (L) equals costs, and we assume a linear labour requirement function equal to $L = s + am(i)$, in which the marginal labour requirement is a, and the fixed labour requirement is s. The demand function (1.9) shows how the quantity demanded $m(i)$ changes with price. The demand for a variety $m(i)$ depends simply on the price of that variety and on constants Y and G and the fixed coefficients θ and σ, the price elasticity of demand. Since (1.9) is an uncompensated demand function, Y is constant. Also, although G depends on prices in all firms, we are in effect assuming here is that there is no strategic interaction involving the firms, in other words, the price set by one firm, since it is one of a large number of firms, has no effect on the pricing strategy of its competitors. The quantity demanded depends simply on its own price. Firms are said to be myopic when it comes to strategic interaction, and keep their output the same regardless of the price charged by their competitors.

We replace $m(i)$ in the profit equation and write the profits of the typical M firm at i in terms of prices, hence:

$$\pi = p_i \theta Y p_i^{-\sigma} G^{\sigma-1} - w^M(ap_i \theta Y p_i^{-\sigma} G^{\sigma-1} + s) \tag{1.10}$$

and differentiating π with respect to p, and setting $\delta\pi/\delta p$ equal to zero gives $p_i = w^M a\mu$.

The reason why μ equals the returns to scale at equilibrium is as follows. The number of workers per firm L at equilibrium is given by $L = s + s/(\mu - 1)$, since the output per firm $m(i)$ at equilibrium is equal to $s/a(\mu - 1)$. This is because at equilibrium the firm's total revenue equals total costs and profits are driven to zero, so no firms enter or exit the market. Total revenue equals price multiplied by output, in other words, total revenue equals $w^M a\mu m(i)$. Costs equal wages multiplied by labour requirement, hence costs are $w^M (s + am(i))$, and setting total cost equal to total revenue gives the equilibrium level of output $m(i)$. Define returns to scale at equilibrium as average costs ($a.c.$) divided by marginal costs ($m.c.$), where average costs are:

$$a.c. = \frac{L}{m(i)} = \frac{s + \dfrac{s}{\mu - 1}}{\dfrac{s}{a(\mu - 1)}} = a\mu$$

$m.c.$ is equal to a. Therefore $a.c./m.c. = \mu$.

Setting 'home price' equal to the wage rate means that we have to eliminate the constants, since we have shown that $p_i = w^M a\mu$. To do this we employ the same normalization as in Fujita et al. (1999), setting the units of a so that $a = 1/\mu$. This is possible because we can choose any units we want for the marginal labour requirement, so we choose them so that the product of the two constants is equal to 1.

1.4   ICEBERG TRANSPORT COSTS

We next look at how (basic) NEG handles transport costs. The term 'iceberg' transport cost function implies a southward drifting iceberg in the northern hemisphere, which is losing its mass at a constant proportional rate of melting per unit of distance. While we have established that we can replace p_j in equation (1.8) by the wage rate w_j^M, this still does not take account of the fact that the varieties of M are produced in different places and that transport costs are incurred. To accommodate wage rate variations across regions and the existence of transport costs, it is convenient to set the overall cost equal to the 'home price' or, as it is now, the 'home wage rate' multiplied by a factor that is directly related to the distance separating the region where the variety is produced from where it is consumed. It turns out that from an operational point of view, a useful multiplier is the term $e^{\tau_M D_{ij}}$, in which D_{ij} is the distance between producer region i and

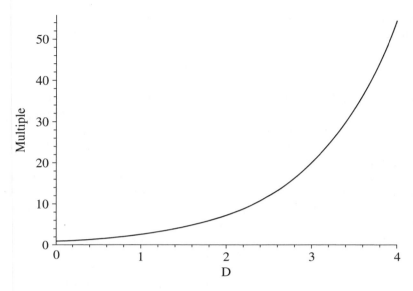

Figure 1.1   *The relationship between distance* D *and the (exponential) multiplier applied to the wage rate*

consumer region j, and τ_M is a scaling factor specific for M goods. We keep this extra parameter τ_M rather than choose units so that the distances D_{ij} are a convenient size since we will be introducing a similar function for C goods subsequently, and we prefer the option of allowing different multipliers but retaining the same distance metric. One convenient aspect of the multiplier $e^{\tau_M D_{ij}}$ is that when $D_{ij} = 0$, $e^{\tau_M D_{ij}} = 1$, so that for the variety produced in the region where it is consumed, the price is simply the wage rate. Otherwise, the price is greater. However, it is apparent that the function we have employed means that prices become exorbitantly large as distance increases, as shown by the following graph (Figure 1.1) ($\tau_M = 1$).

With exponential transport costs, the overall cost of a variety (home price plus transport costs) keeps on rising ever more steeply, since the M transport cost derivative with respect to D, $\tau_M e^{\tau_M D_{ij}}$, increases in D, with the second derivative equal to $\tau_M^2 e^{\tau_M D_{ij}}$, and we find that transport cost per unit of distance, $e^{\tau_M D_{ij}}/D_{ij}$, increases in distance. These characteristics of iceberg transport costs have been referred to as the 'Achilles heel' of NEG, as we demonstrate in Chapter 6 (see also Fingleton, 2005b; Neary, 2001 and McCann, 2005).

The virtue of the iceberg transport cost function is that it has the property that it maintains the constant elasticity of demand assumption that runs through the microeconomic theory underpinning the model. To see this, we need to return to the uncompensated demand function (1.9), but now substitute in what we are assuming for prices, which vary by region, hence:

$$m(i) = \theta Y_i (p_j^M e^{\tau_M D_{ij}})^{-\sigma} G_i^{\sigma-1} \qquad (1.11)$$

which is the demand in region i for a variety produced in j. To obtain region j's overall production we sum across all i regions, but we have to multiply by $e^{\tau_M D_{ij}}$ since this is the transport cost incurred in moving the variety produced at j to i. This means that production at j will be higher than the total consumption of variety j across regions, because some of j's production is absorbed by the cost of exporting to $i = 1 \ldots . R$. This kind of wastage in passage is reminiscent of the melting of the mass of the iceberg as it moves, with a constant fraction of output lost in transportation. Another analogy is a horse pulling a wagon that is transporting hay to market, but consuming a portion of the hay en route, so that the farmer's production exceeds what is sold at market (see von Thunen, 1826).

Observe that the price p_j^M increases by the factor $e^{\tau_M D_{ij}}$, regardless of the actual level of demand, and that this is a constant proportion of the overall price, as would be shown were we to plot the overall price (that is, including transport costs), and transport costs per se, against distance. This would show that the same share is taken by transport regardless of distance. Clearly, if the price at the point of origin is the constant p_j^M, then $e^{\tau_M D_{ij}}/p_j^M e^{\tau_M D_{ij}}$ will be a constant. Taking natural logs, the demand function (1.8) becomes:

$$\ln m(i) = \ln \theta + \ln Y_i - \sigma \ln p_j^M - \sigma \tau_M D_{ij} + (\sigma - 1) \ln G_i.$$

This function has a constant elasticity σ, which does not depend on transport costs $\tau_M D_{ij}$ and is the same across all varieties of M, and this is also true of the overall level of production of a variety at j, q_j^M, which is:

$$q_j^M = \sum_i^R m(i) e^{\tau_D D_{ij}} = \theta \sum_i^R Y_i (p_j^M)^{-\sigma} (e^{\tau_D D_{ij}})^{1-\sigma} G_i^{\sigma-1}. \qquad (1.12)$$

For C goods, the demand function is $(1 - \theta)\phi_i Y_i (p_j^C e^{\tau_C D_{ij}})^{-\eta} G_i^{\eta-1}$ and the constant elasticity is η.

1.5   THE PRICE INDEX

One other consideration is the fact that different regions will be the source of different numbers of M varieties, since they will have different productive capacities. Therefore a large region should carry more weight in the calculation of the price index than smaller regions. The number of varieties produced in region j is represented by λ_j, which is equal to the share in region j of the total supply of M workers. In our rewrite of equation (1.8) as equation (1.13) to take account of wages equalling prices, together with the impact of transport costs, we include λ_j to weight each region's contribution to the overall price index. Hence:

$$G_i^M = \left[\sum_j \lambda_j (w_j^M e^{\tau_M D_{ij}})^{1-\sigma} \right]^{\frac{1}{1-\sigma}}. \tag{1.13}$$

The reason why we can use the share λ_j in place of the actual number of varieties derives from the single city analogy. Assume that we endogenously determined the number of varieties x in the city by dividing the number of M workers overall by the number of M workers per firm at equilibrium, and since each M firm produces a different variety, the number that results is the number of varieties. Using the normalization that $a = 1/\mu$ means that the average cost equals 1, and the equilibrium number of workers per firm is $s\mu/(\mu - 1)$, which is the fixed labour requirement multiplied by the elasticity of substitution (see Fujita et al. 1999, equation [4.23]).

Just as we have normalized the marginal labour requirement a, we can also normalize the fixed labour requirement s. We can choose units so that s multiplied by the elasticity of substitution equals θ, in other words, the equilibrium number of workers per firm is equal to θ. This means that the equilibrium output per firm must also equal θ, because the average cost is equal to 1. This now brings us to the use of the proportions λ_j in equation (1.13). Remember that θ is also the coefficient of the Cobb-Douglas preference function given as equation (1.1), and we now also choose θ to equal the total number of M workers adding across all regions, since we can use any unit we wish for this total. It therefore follows that the number of M workers in region j is $\lambda_j \theta$ and the number of varieties is this number divided by the number of workers per firm, therefore the number of varieties is equal to λ_j.

1.6   INCOME AND THE WAGE EQUATION

We have gone into some detail explaining why equation (1.13) is as it is, and we next move on to explain the basis of equation (1.14), which shows that Y_j, the income in region j, is equal to the number of M workers in the region $(\lambda_j \theta)$ multiplied by the wage rate and the number of C workers in the region $(\phi_j(1 - \theta))$ multiplied by the C worker wage rate (w_j^C), with ϕ_j denoting the share in region j of the total supply of C workers. Since we are assuming that θ is equal to the total number of M workers adding across all regions, and also that $0 < \theta < 1$, then the total number of C workers must be $1 - \theta$:

$$Y_j = \theta \lambda_j w_j^M + (1 - \theta) \phi_j w_j^C. \tag{1.14}$$

We now have all the components necessary to explain what determines the level of M wages in region i, which is given as equation (1.15):

$$w_i^M = \left[\sum_j Y_j (G_j^M)^{\sigma-1} (e^{\tau_M D_{ij}})^{1-\sigma} \right]^{\frac{1}{\sigma}}. \tag{1.15}$$

Equation (1.15) is the famous wage equation that provides a focal point for empirical analysis (see, for example, Fingleton, 2005a, 2006). It states that M wages in region i will be higher if income Y_j is higher in other regions since high incomes, so long as they are not offset by high transport costs, boost market demand for region i's goods. Also, since the elasticity of substitution of M products $\sigma > 1$, wages will be boosted by higher price indices G_j^M (remember we are talking about nominal wages here). A high price index in region j indicates that there are less varieties sold in region j, since as we see from equation (1.8) the price index is inversely related to the number of varieties, so that as x increases the price index diminishes, and this means that if region j has a low number of varieties there is less domestic competition for goods produced by firms from region i. Also, as the elasticity of substitution σ reduces, so does the downward impact of distance on demand and hence on i's wage rate, since remote regions will be less able to substitute for region i's goods and therefore region i will have greater access to their markets. However, the relationship between wages and this complex function of price levels, income and distance is not a linear one, increasingly high values of the quantity in square brackets produces less and less of an impact on the wage level. The question has to be asked, why this function?

In order to understand the construction of equation (1.15), we need to return to the demand function (1.9), (1.8) and the overall level of production of a variety at j, q_j^M given by equation (1.12). From this it follows that:

$$(p_j^M)^\sigma = \frac{\theta}{q_j^M} \sum_i Y_i (e^{\tau_D D_{ij}})^{1-\sigma} G_i^{\sigma-1}. \tag{1.16}$$

We have already obtained that the equilibrium output per variety is $q_j^M = \theta$, and the relationship between prices and wages was given above as $p_i^M = w^M a \mu$. We turn this around, using the normalization $a = 1/\mu$ to give an expression for the equilibrium wage rate for M workers in region i, which is:

$$w_i^M = \frac{p_i^M}{a\mu} = p_i^M$$

and so substituting for equilibrium output and equilibrium wages in equation (1.16) we again obtain:

$$w_i^M = \left[\sum_j Y_j (e^{\tau_D D_{ij}})^{1-\sigma} G_j^{\sigma-1} \right]^{\frac{1}{\sigma}}.$$

1.7 C FIRMS WITH TRANSPORT COSTS

The analysis up to this point has concentrated on M, the goods produced under monopolistic competition. We now turn to the C goods, which are produced under competitive market conditions. Among other things this means there are no internal increasing returns to scale in the production of C firms. As with M goods however, it is often reasonable to assume that C goods are differentiated so that each region has a different mix of varieties, and that transport costs (broadly defined) are incurred as C goods are traded across regions. It turns out that we can obtain equations for the C price index that looks very similar to the one we have derived for M, in other words:

$$G_i^C = \left[\sum_j \phi_j (w_j^C e^{\tau_C D_{ij}})^{1-\eta} \right]^{\frac{1}{1-\eta}} \qquad (1.17)$$

in which G_i^C s the price index for C in region i, ϕ_j is the share in region j of the total supply of C workers, w_j^C denotes C worker wages in region j, τ_C is the distance scaling factor for C, and η is the elasticity of substitution of C goods. The similarities between equations (1.17) and (1.13) indicate that the derivations have the same provenance; in both cases we commence with a CES function. However, while we can apply the equivalent to equation (1.2), since we are not assuming monopolistic competition, there is no added bonus as a result of extra varieties. Nevertheless, we can use the same line of argument from the CES function to the demand equations and hence through to equation (1.17).

The wage rate for C workers is:

$$w_i^C = \left[\sum_j Y_j (G_j^C)^{\eta-1} (e^{\tau_C D_{ij}})^{1-\eta} \right]^{\frac{1}{\eta}} \qquad (1.18)$$

which is again very similar to the M wage rate. To obtain this expression, following Fujita et al. (1999), we equate the C variety supply and C variety demand to obtain the price and hence wage rate. Supply of each variety is equivalent to the number of C workers in each region, since regions produce different varieties, which for region j is equal to $(1 - \theta)\phi_j$. Demand for variety i is a function of $(1 - \theta)\phi_i$, the delivered price in each region taking account of the cost of transport, the income level of each region and the C price index. More specifically, from the uncompensated demand function we find that demand for variety i is:

$$q_i^C = (1 - \theta)\phi_i(p_i^C)^{-\eta}\sum_j^R Y_j(e^{\tau_C D_{ij}})^{1-\eta}(G_j^C)^{\eta-1}$$

and equating supply and demand we have:

$$(1 - \theta)\phi_i = (1 - \theta)\phi_i(p_i^C)^{-\eta}\sum_j^R Y_j(e^{\tau_C D_{ij}})^{1-\eta}(G_j^C)^{\eta-1}$$

so that on rearranging and simplifying we have an equation for the price of C variety i. Also since the C varieties are produced under perfect competition, the price equals the marginal revenue, which equals the marginal cost. As in the discussion relating to equation (1.13), the marginal cost is the wage rate times the marginal labour requirement; there is no mark up on marginal cost as under monopolistic competition. This means that we take the wage rate as equal to price by choosing units of output so that the marginal labour requirement is equal to 1, hence:

$$w_i^C = p_i^C = \left[\sum_j^R Y_j(e^{\tau_C D_{ij}})^{1-\eta}(G_j^C)^{\eta-1}\right]^{\frac{1}{\eta}}.$$

1.8   REAL WAGES

Finally, let us now return to the wage rate for M workers, that is w_i^M. This is a nominal quantity, but we also need to calculate real wages in order to examine whether it is worth M workers migrating to a different region. After all, while wages may be higher in London, it is well known that the cost of living is also higher, and that will deter many from moving from the provinces to London. We obtain the real wage rate simply by dividing nominal wages by the cost of living index for each region. Earlier, we obtained the cost of living index as $G^\theta(p^C)^{1-\theta}$, but now we need to take account of the fact that we have subsequently introduced regional differences in both M prices and in C prices. Hence, we have G_i^M, which is the price index for M in region i, and now G_i^C, which is the price index for C in region i. Our revised cost of living index therefore becomes $(G_i^M)^\theta(G_i^C)^{1-\theta}$ and therefore we divide our nominal M wages by this index to give real M wages ω_i, hence:

$$\omega_i = w_i^M(G_i^M)^{-\theta}(G_i^C)^{\theta-1}. \tag{1.19}$$

In contrast, in the most elemental version of NEG, the wage rate for C workers w_i^C is assumed to be constant across regions, since trade in C does not incur transport costs. We can think of this as the situation that occurs when $\tau_C = 0$, so that $e^{\tau_C D_{ij}} = 1$ in equations (1.17) and (1.18) and hence the price index $G_i^C = 1$ and $w_i^C = 1$ for all regions, hence:

$$\omega_i = w_i^M(G_i^M)^{-\theta}. \tag{1.20}$$

1.9 AN APPLICATION WITH MANY REGIONS

This section shows how the model outlined above can be operationalized. The results and data given here are taken and adapted from Fingleton (2005b). The simulation is centred around five non-linear simultaneous equations, equations (1.15) and (1.18) for M and C wages (w_i^M and w_i^C), equations (1.13) and (1.17) for M and C prices (G_i^M and G_i^C), and equation (1.14) for income (Y_i). Additionally, as shown by equation (1.19), nominal M wages and the M and C price indices determine real M wages (ω_i). In contrast to Fingleton (2005b), we initially adhere to the simplest exposition of NEG given by Fujita et al. (1999), so that $\tau_C = 0$ and the M sector is taken here as manufacturing. In other words, the C sector comprises all other sectors of the economy, and the assumption is that trade between regions for these sectors is costless, possibly because they are more concerned with moving information than goods, possibly because the lack of bulk in comparison with manufactured goods makes transport costs a negligible part of their overall costs.

A numerical solution to the non-linear simultaneous equations is based on known or assumed values for the exogenous variables and parameters. In the short run it is assumed that the share of C workers in each region (ϕ_j), and the share of M workers (λ_j) is exogenous, although in the long run these might change as workers respond to real wage differences. We also

Table 1.1   Basic data

Variable Region	ϕ_i	λ_i	Share of Emp. C Activities	Share of Emp. M Activities	Actual Wage (*actualw*)
Tees_Valley_and_Durham	0.0152	0.0215	0.7995	0.2005	0.7909
Northumb._et_al.	0.0218	0.0232	0.8417	0.1583	0.7957
Cumbria	0.0074	0.0105	0.7989	0.2011	0.8024
Cheshire	0.0175	0.0197	0.8335	0.1665	0.8744
Greater_Manchester	0.0435	0.0506	0.8292	0.1708	0.8437
Lancashire	0.0209	0.0336	0.7782	0.2218	0.8119
Merseyside	0.0204	0.0174	0.8690	0.1310	0.8396
East_Riding	0.0118	0.0220	0.7524	0.2476	0.7944
North_Yorkshire	0.0130	0.0108	0.8722	0.1278	0.8107
South_Yorkshire	0.0184	0.0237	0.8150	0.1850	0.7847
West_Yorkshire	0.0360	0.0449	0.8192	0.1808	0.8259
Derbyshire	0.0295	0.0450	0.7878	0.2122	0.8181
Leics.	0.0249	0.0440	0.7623	0.2377	0.8173
Lincolnshire	0.0090	0.0122	0.8063	0.1937	0.7458
Hereford_et_al.	0.0192	0.0268	0.8019	0.1981	0.8388
Shrops.	0.0218	0.0366	0.7706	0.2294	0.7884
West_Midlands_(county)	0.0428	0.0670	0.7831	0.2169	0.8564
East_Anglia	0.0357	0.0398	0.8353	0.1647	0.8356
Bedfordshire	0.0291	0.0254	0.8663	0.1337	0.9767
Essex	0.0244	0.0229	0.8578	0.1422	0.9104
Inner_London	0.1036	0.0339	0.9454	0.0546	1.0000
Outer_London	0.0726	0.0416	0.9080	0.0920	1.0000
Berkshire_et_al.	0.0455	0.0365	0.8759	0.1241	1.0337
Surrey	0.0494	0.0289	0.9064	0.0936	0.9616
Hants.	0.0323	0.0287	0.8642	0.1358	0.9118
Kent	0.0234	0.0203	0.8669	0.1331	0.8661
Gloucester_et_al.	0.0396	0.0414	0.8441	0.1559	0.8717
Dorset	0.0185	0.0186	0.8492	0.1508	0.8042
Cornwall	0.0068	0.0049	0.8878	0.1122	0.6807
Devon	0.0159	0.0150	0.8576	0.1424	0.7521
West_Wales	0.0226	0.0314	0.8028	0.1972	0.7700
East_Wales	0.0182	0.0216	0.8261	0.1739	0.8242
North_East_Scot.	0.0111	0.0082	0.8849	0.1151	0.9162
Eastern_Scotland	0.0345	0.0320	0.8589	0.1411	0.8161
South_West_Scot.	0.0381	0.0362	0.8562	0.1438	0.8230
Highlands_and_Islands	0.0058	0.0034	0.9063	0.0937	0.7663

need appropriate values for the expenditure share of M goods θ, the M transport cost function, and the elasticity of substitution σ for the M goods. Tables 1.1 and 1.2 give the values assumed for this simulation.

In order to solve the simultaneous equations, an iterative process is used. In round 1, the first step involves estimating the income variable Y on the

Table 1.2   Short-term equilibrium – without C transport costs: endogenous
           variables

Variable Region	G_i^M	G_i^C	W_i^M	W_i^C	ω_i	Y_i
Tees_Valley_and_Durham	1.3630	1.0000	0.9027	1.0000	0.8616	0.0158
Northumb._et_al.	1.4212	1.0000	0.9175	1.0000	0.8703	0.0217
Cumbria	1.4005	1.0000	0.8962	1.0000	0.8520	0.0077
Cheshire	1.2571	1.0000	0.9647	1.0000	0.9321	0.0177
Greater_Manchester	1.2393	1.0000	0.9711	1.0000	0.9403	0.0443
Lancashire	1.2786	1.0000	0.9388	1.0000	0.9047	0.0225
Merseyside	1.2941	1.0000	0.9440	1.0000	0.9081	0.0198
East_Riding	1.3243	1.0000	0.9155	1.0000	0.8777	0.0131
North_Yorkshire	1.3150	1.0000	0.9231	1.0000	0.8859	0.0126
South_Yorkshire	1.2583	1.0000	0.9614	1.0000	0.9288	0.0191
West_Yorkshire	1.2498	1.0000	0.9600	1.0000	0.9284	0.0371
Derbyshire	1.2541	1.0000	0.9739	1.0000	0.9414	0.0317
Leics.	1.2993	1.0000	1.0132	1.0000	0.9741	0.0279
Lincolnshire	1.3493	1.0000	0.9443	1.0000	0.9028	0.0093
Hereford_et_al.	1.3035	1.0000	1.0042	1.0000	0.9650	0.0204
Shrops.	1.2719	1.0000	0.9768	1.0000	0.9422	0.0239
West_Midlands_(county)	1.2637	1.0000	1.0077	1.0000	0.9729	0.0465
East_Anglia	1.4116	1.0000	1.0124	1.0000	0.9613	0.0364
Bedfordshire	1.3673	1.0000	1.0717	1.0000	1.0225	0.0288
Essex	1.4385	1.0000	1.0611	1.0000	1.0047	0.0244
Inner_London	1.3942	1.0000	1.1330	1.0000	1.0778	0.0938
Outer_London	1.3983	1.0000	1.1320	1.0000	1.0764	0.0688
Berkshire_et_al.	1.3638	1.0000	1.0780	1.0000	1.0289	0.0446
Surrey	1.4597	1.0000	1.0931	1.0000	1.0327	0.0467
Hants.	1.4577	1.0000	1.0531	1.0000	0.9951	0.0319
Kent	1.5070	1.0000	1.0579	1.0000	0.9947	0.0231
Gloucester_et_al.	1.3909	1.0000	1.0316	1.0000	0.9817	0.0401
Dorset	1.4892	1.0000	0.9901	1.0000	0.9326	0.0185
Cornwall	1.7545	1.0000	0.9116	1.0000	0.8378	0.0064
Devon	1.5633	1.0000	0.9577	1.0000	0.8955	0.0157
West_Wales	1.3681	1.0000	0.9231	1.0000	0.8806	0.0235
East_Wales	1.3353	1.0000	0.9548	1.0000	0.9142	0.0185
North_East_Scot.	1.7903	1.0000	0.9645	1.0000	0.8837	0.0106
Eastern_Scotland	1.4746	1.0000	0.9756	1.0000	0.9203	0.0340
South_West_Scot.	1.4542	1.0000	0.9696	1.0000	0.9165	0.0376
Highlands_and_Islands	1.8356	1.0000	0.9312	1.0000	0.8500	0.0054
Parameter values	$\sigma = 8$	$\tau_M = 10$	$\tau_C = 0$	$\theta = 0.1502$		

basis of (initially) randomly allocated values of the wage rates w_i^M and w_r^C. In the second step, the initial estimates of Y values are combined with price indices G_i^M and G_i^C to recalculate the wage rates for M and C workers, although in round 1 there are no estimated G values available from an earlier round and so they are set equal to 1. Finally, the third step of round 1 allows more sensible estimates of G_i^M and G_i^C based on the round 1 wage rates. Round 2 and subsequent rounds repeat the pattern of round 1, but using the estimates of the preceding round. A check is made at the end of each round to see if the values of the endogenous variables G_i^M, G_i^C, w_i^M, w_i^C, ω_i and Y_i have reached steady state. Note that although we allow G_i^C and w_i^C to vary, since the routine is a general one, the fact that $\tau_C = 0$ ensures that they each take the value 1.

Each successive iteration invariably causes successive differences in these endogenous variables to become smaller and smaller. While the differences never go to zero, they do become very small, as, therefore, does the sum across regions of the squared differences, such as $\Sigma_i(w_{it}^M - w_{it-1}^M)^2$, in which t and $t - 1$ here denote successive iterations. We terminate the iterations when this sum of squares calculated for each endogenous variable is less than 10^{-7} simultaneously.

In Table 1.1 I have given real data relating to the 36 NUTS 2 regions[2] of Great Britain (see Figure 1.2). The main consideration concerns assumptions about unknown elasticity of substitution σ, which has been chosen to equal 8 so as to maximize the correlation (equal to 0.8482) between M wages w_i^M, normalized so that London equals 1, and actual wages, having first set Inner London wages equal to Outer London wages, so as to avoid a 'bonus effect' associated with the City of London, which is largely concerned with banking and finance rather than with manufacturing. Of course, there will be other factors determining wage levels also, but it is interesting that even with such a simple adjustment, a high level of correlation can be attained. Wage rates by NUTS 2 region are taken from the year 2000 results[3] of the New Earnings Survey, which is a very large annual survey carried out by the UK's Office for National Statistics. The survey data consist of gross weekly pay[4] for male and female full-time workers irrespective of occupation. In order to calculate transport costs, I use an inter-regional distance matrix, with quantities D_{ij} for regions i and j. Table A1.1 in the Appendix gives coordinates of the approximate region centres on which these distances are based. These are simply straight-line distances, since it is considered unnecessary to use great circle distances within a small area such as Great Britain. One alternative would be to replace straight-line distances with time distances between regions (McCann, 2005; McCann and Shefer, 2004), but in practice this would be rather difficult to implement, since travel times would undoubtedly vary with mode of transport,

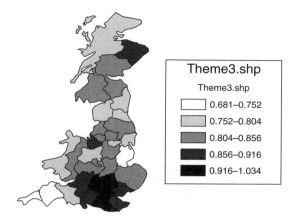

Figure 1.2   Relative wage rates in Great Britain

technology, infrastructure and congestion conditions, and require major and perhaps difficult-to-sustain simplifying assumptions.

The *M* activities are the manufacturing subsectors taken from the UK's 1992 Standard Industrial Classification, as described in Table A1.2 in the Appendix. The *C* activities are all other groups. Given these definitions, it is possible to calculate the shares of employment in either *C* or *M* activities, ϕ_i and λ_j, for each NUTS 2 region for the year 2000[5] (see Table 1.1). The overall share of total employment in 2000 that is engaged in *M* activities is taken as the expenditure share of *M* goods (θ), which also equates to the total *M* workers ($1 - \theta$ is the total *C* workers) measured on a scale such that the overall number of workers is equal to 1.

Figure 1.2 (and Tables 1.1 and 1.2) shows that the actual wage data reach a peak in Berkshire just to the west of London, followed by relatively high values in London and in the rest of the South East of England. Wages are lower in the more peripheral areas, apart from North East Scotland and Cheshire, where wages reach about 90 per cent of London levels. The simulated wage levels w_i^M (Figure 1.3) show a similar distribution, again with highest values in the South East of England, and with a fairly regular decline with distance from London. Figure 1.4 shows that that relative[6] income or demand (Y_i) is concentrated in the major conurbations. Given that they are generated by a very simple model, neither the simulated w_i^M distribution nor the Y_i appears completely unreasonable. Figure 1.5 gives the price index for *M* activities, showing that there exists a much lower *M* price index in Central and Northern areas characterized by a greater density of manufacturing activity than in the extremes of North and South, as shown by the share of employment in *M* in Table 1.1. This price index

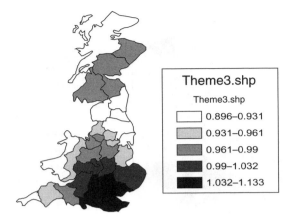

Figure 1.3   Simulated M *wages*

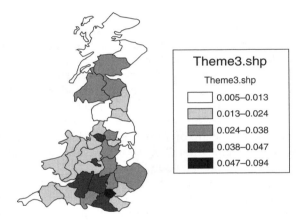

Figure 1.4   Income distribution by region

distribution in theory reflects the impact of competition on prices, but it may well also represent the externalities associated with the geographical clustering of activities.

The pattern of real *M* wages (ω_i) given by equation (1.20) is shown by Table 1.2 and Figure 1.6. This shows that the effect of a lower *M* price index in the Midlands and North West of England is not sufficient to compensate for the relatively low nominal wages compared with the South East, so that real wages in the South East remain relatively high despite a higher overall cost of living. It appears that, for the *M* worker, it would be beneficial to gravitate towards the South-Eastern corner of Britain, leading

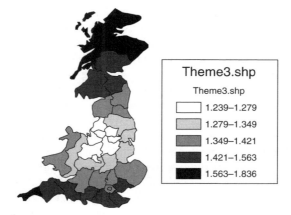

Figure 1.5   The price index for M

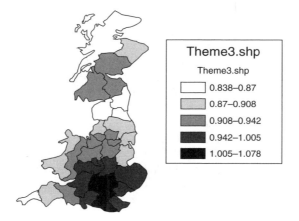

Figure 1.6   The real wage distribution

to a long-run equilibrium. However, in the short-term, with which we are concerned, this is assumed to have not yet happened and real wage differences remain unaltered by any migration that might occur in the long run. Of course, there are many real obstacles to such a long-run equilibrium being achieved, but in the next section we proceed as though the only factor to consider is real wage differences. Finally, it should be emphasized that the simulation exercise carried out here is one of several possible alternatives. In Fingleton (2005b), the model incorporates transport costs for both *C* and *M*, and it is necessary to consider the values of two elasticities of substitution, σ and η, that maximize the level of correlation between actual and simulated wage levels. Also in that paper, M is assumed to be group 7 of the UK's 1992 Standard Industrial Classification, which consists of real estate activities, renting machinery/equipment, etc., computing and related activities, research and development, other business activities, etc. Moreover, the focus of that paper is competing claims of an exponential versus power transport cost function. The aim of the current section is to illustrate some new simulations under alternative simplifying assumptions that equate to the simplest version of NEG given by Fujita et al. (1999).

In Table 1.3 the analysis is extended by also allowing transport costs for C goods. We therefore assume that $\tau_C = 10$ and it follows that setting the elasticity of substitution $\eta = 10$ and $\sigma = 10$ retains quite a high level of correlation (0.8209) between the mean predicted wages $(0.5\,w_i^M + 0.5\,w_i^C)$ and actual wages, as indicated by Figure 1.7. The reason why the predicted wage has equal weights for C and M sectors, even though we know the shares of the C and M sectors are unequal (see Table 1.1) is because the sectoral share of the respondents to the New Earnings Survey will not necessarily be equal to the Table 1.1 shares, and so weighting on this basis may induce bias in the predicted wage. The elasticities $\eta = 10$ and $\sigma = 10$ were obtained by an iterative search to maximize the Pearson product moment correlation between predicted and actual wage levels. The range of the search and the relationship between elasticities and correlations are given by the correlation surface in Figure 1.8 (using the method of McConalogue, 1970, fitted to a 10 by 10 matrix of correlations), which shows a clear maximum at more or less this point. Table 1.3 clearly shows how Inner London is predicted to have the highest nominal C wages as well as the highest M wages, and there is a clear price competition effect due to the concentration of C in Inner London, so that G_i^C is much lower in Inner London than elsewhere, thus enhancing the utility gained from high wage levels. The combined wage gives London the highest wages. Real M wages, in this case given by equation (1.19), are also highest in London, again suggesting that on the basis of real M wages alone, workers will migrate towards London. In this case, the short-run equilibrium that we have illustrated here will be disturbed by the fact that the constant M shares of Table 1.1 will no longer be constant. For simplicity we continue to assume that C workers are immune to real wage differences between regions.

1.10   TWO REGIONS, DYNAMICS AND LONG-RUN EQUILIBRIA

In this section consideration is given to the long-run implications of short-run real wages differences as outlined above. While we have written the model out in a general form so as to accommodate more than two regions, we focus

Table 1.3 Short-term equilibrium – with C transport costs: endogenous variables

Variable Region	G_i^M	G_i^C	W_i^M	W_i^C	ω_i	Y_i	Combined w_i
Tees_Valley_and_Durham	1.2236	1.3567	0.8548	0.9272	0.6400	0.0147	0.8910
Northumb._et_al.	1.2617	1.3478	0.8715	0.9206	0.6532	0.0201	0.8961
Cumbria	1.2629	1.3866	0.8441	0.9053	0.6174	0.0070	0.8747
Cheshire	1.1603	1.2693	0.9144	0.9838	0.7302	0.0173	0.9491
Greater_Manchester	1.1412	1.2545	0.9214	0.9956	0.7450	0.0438	0.9585
Lancashire	1.1693	1.3004	0.8893	0.9659	0.6949	0.0216	0.9276
Merseyside	1.1917	1.2968	0.8964	0.9642	0.7001	0.0191	0.9303
East_Riding	1.2066	1.3451	0.8686	0.9370	0.6564	0.0123	0.9028
North_Yorkshire	1.2027	1.3237	0.8742	0.9489	0.6700	0.0119	0.9116
South_Yorkshire	1.1599	1.2778	0.9104	0.9790	0.7229	0.0186	0.9447
West_Yorkshire	1.1478	1.2685	0.9102	0.9869	0.7284	0.0363	0.9486
Derbyshire	1.1599	1.2707	0.9227	0.9816	0.7361	0.0309	0.9521
Leics.	1.2166	1.2621	0.9700	0.9676	0.7728	0.0269	0.9688
Lincolnshire	1.2491	1.3377	0.8989	0.9290	0.6789	0.0087	0.9140
Hereford_et_al.	1.2174	1.2675	0.9589	0.9664	0.7611	0.0196	0.9626
Shrops.	1.1810	1.2775	0.9269	0.9727	0.7342	0.0231	0.9498
West_Midlands_(county)	1.1773	1.2490	0.9611	0.9856	0.7763	0.0455	0.9734
East_Anglia	1.3198	1.2719	0.9883	0.9406	0.7727	0.0344	0.9644
Bedfordshire	1.2996	1.2184	1.0423	0.9697	0.8471	0.0279	1.0060
Essex	1.3637	1.2377	1.0395	0.9491	0.8277	0.0232	0.9943
Inner_London	1.3310	1.1576	1.1153	1.0000	0.9434	0.0937	1.0576
Outer_London	1.3344	1.1594	1.1145	0.9984	0.9411	0.0686	1.0564
Berkshire_et_al.	1.2962	1.2098	1.0481	0.9755	0.8574	0.0435	1.0118
Surrey	1.3878	1.2067	1.0769	0.9630	0.8738	0.0451	1.0199
Hants.	1.3757	1.2470	1.0311	0.9431	0.8147	0.0303	0.9871
Kent	1.4258	1.2501	1.0436	0.9339	0.8185	0.0217	0.9887
Gloucester_et_al.	1.3051	1.2532	1.0006	0.9530	0.7935	0.0383	0.9768
Dorset	1.3791	1.3083	0.9648	0.9146	0.7316	0.0171	0.9397
Cornwall	1.5621	1.4221	0.9078	0.8413	0.6293	0.0055	0.8745
Devon	1.4216	1.3452	0.9393	0.8921	0.6925	0.0142	0.9157
West_Wales	1.2389	1.3386	0.8844	0.9332	0.6684	0.0221	0.9088
East_Wales	1.2305	1.3106	0.9098	0.9467	0.7008	0.0176	0.9283
North_East_Scot.	1.5592	1.3777	0.9414	0.8476	0.6711	0.0092	0.8945
Eastern_Scotland	1.3091	1.3009	0.9314	0.9270	0.7156	0.0316	0.9292
South_West_Scot.	1.2943	1.2986	0.9276	0.9313	0.7149	0.0352	0.9294
Highlands_and_Islands	1.6067	1.4209	0.9125	0.8266	0.6307	0.0046	0.8695
Parameter values	$\sigma = 10$	$\tau_M = 10$	$\tau_C = 10$	$\theta = 0.1502$	$\eta = 10$		

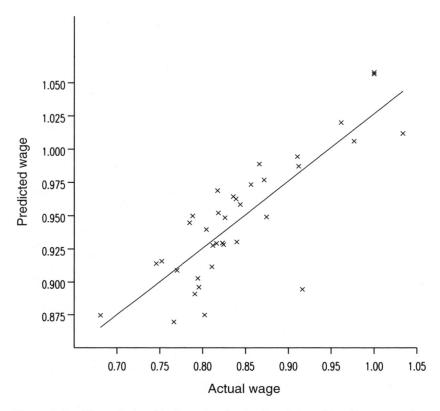

Figure 1.7   The relationship between the predicted (combined) wage and actual wage

on the very simple two-region case. Let us call the regions South (region 1) and North, and look at the short-term equilibrium that results. First we need to allocate some values to the parameters, so we assume $\theta = 0.4$, $\sigma = 5$ and $\eta = 10$ (these are special only because they are the ones used by Fujita et al., 1999). We choose distances D_{ij} and τ_M and τ_C so that the resulting multiplicative factors $e^{\tau_M D_{ij}}$ and $e^{\tau_C D_{ij}}$ are as follows $e^{\tau_M D_{12}} = e^{\tau_M D_{21}} = 1.8$ and $e^{\tau_C D_{12}} = e^{\tau_C D_{21}} = 1.2$ and $e^{\tau_M D_{11}} = e^{\tau_M D_{22}} = 1$, $e^{\tau_C D_{11}} = e^{\tau_C D_{22}} = 1$. So we are assuming that the effect of distance on transport costs is stronger for M goods than C goods. Also, there is an equal share of C workers in each region since $\phi_1 = 0.5$ and $\phi_2 = 0.5$ but $\lambda_1 = 0.8$ and $\lambda_2 = 0.2$ so there is a heavier preponderance of M workers in the South. The short-run equilibrium is given in Table 1.4. We also include real M wages ω_i as a contrast to the nominal wages w_i^M.

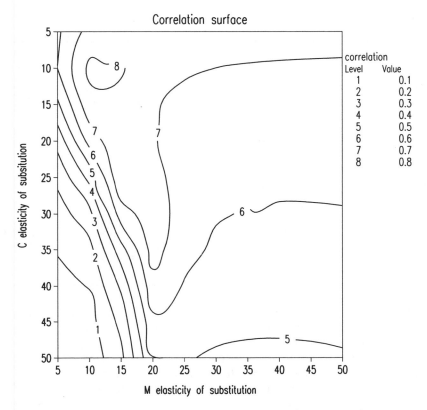

Figure 1.8 *The correlation surface for alternative elasticities of substitution*

Table 1.4 *Equilibrium income, wages and prices for two regions, $\sigma = 5$*

Variable Region	G_i^M	G_i^C	W_i^M	W_i^C	ω_i	Y_i
South	1.04434854	1.10379693	0.99069911	1.05295901	0.91763632	0.63291142
North	1.52261005	1.06635399	1.16940773	1.00000000	0.95102086	0.39355262
Parameter values	$\theta = 0.4$	$e^{\tau_M D_{ij}} = 1.8$	$e^{\tau_C D_{ij}} = 1.2$	$\phi_1 = 0.5$	$\lambda_1 = 0.8$	$\eta = 10$

Table 1.4 shows the short-term equilibrium values of our endogenous variables, using C wages in the North as a numeraire. We clearly need to change some parameters to show how they affect the equilibrium, although it is apparent that the preponderance of M workers in the South has had

Table 1.5   Equilibrium income, wages and prices for two regions, σ = 2

Variable Region	G_i^M	G_i^C	W_i^M	W_i^C	ω_i	Y_i
South	1.13217983	1.10852185	1.03503952	1.05889593	0.92585883	0.64888143
North	1.59235481	1.06699068	1.00703812	1.00000000	0.80414449	0.38056305
Parameter values	$\theta = 0.4$	$e^{\tau_M D_{ij}} = 1.8$	$e^{\tau_C D_{ij}} = 1.2$	$\phi_1 = 0.5$	$\lambda_1 = 0.8$	$\eta = 10$

Table 1.6   Equilibrium income, wages and prices for two regions, θ = 0.9

Variable Region	G_i^M	G_i^C	W_i^M	W_i^C	ω_i	Y_i
South	1.12326231	1.15088892	1.07019269	1.11654489	0.95044261	0.82636598
North	1.41406836	1.07176392	1.01024997	1.00000000	0.73450657	0.23184499
Parameter values	$\sigma = 5$	$e^{\tau_M D_{ij}} = 1.8$	$e^{\tau_C D_{ij}} = 1.2$	$\phi_1 = 0.5$	$\lambda_1 = 0.8$	$\eta = 10$

the effect that the income level (Y_i) in the South is higher. Even though most of M is located in the South, M wages, both nominal and real, are higher in the North. Let us now see (Table 1.5) what happens to the endogenous variables if we reduce the elasticity of substitution so that $\sigma = 2$, keeping all other values the same. As a result the South's income has increased, and that of the North decreased, and M wages in the South are now higher than those of the North. By reducing the elasticity of substitution of M varieties, the dominance of the larger economy (South) has increased, as a result of economies of scale becoming more important.

Increasing consumer preference for M varieties by raising θ from 0.4 to 0.9 has a similar effect to switching income to the South, where most M varieties produced under increasing returns are located, and also has the effect of increasing real M wages in the South so that, compared with the results in Table 1.4, they are now above the North's wage rate. This is shown in Table 1.6.

We have seen two distinct types of equilibrium, one with higher real M wages in the North, the other with higher real M wages in the South. It is questionable whether these short-term equilibria will hold in the long run, since the higher wages will attract workers and distort what we have thus far assumed to be a stable distribution of M workers across regions (we are assuming that C workers' wage differences do not induce migration). For example, suppose that the real wage gap in Table 1.6 had the effect, over a long period of time, of causing λ_1 to increase, let us say by 0.1. As Table 1.7

Table 1.7 Equilibrium income, wages and prices for two regions, $\lambda_1 = 0.9$

Variable Region	G_i^M	G_i^C	W_i^M	W_i^C	ω_i	Y_i
South	1.10541781	1.16884097	1.08059743	1.14425745	0.97210742	0.93249679
North	1.57082148	1.07335649	0.99661023	1.00000000	0.65907785	0.13969492
Parameter values	$\sigma = 5$	$e^{\tau_M D_{ij}} = 1.8$	$e^{\tau_C D_{ij}} = 1.2$	$\phi_1 = 0.5$	$\theta = 0.9$	$\eta = 10$

Table 1.8 Equilibrium income, wages and prices for two regions, $e^{T_M D_{ij}} = 1.2$

Variable Region	G_i^M	G_i^C	W_i^M	W_i^C	ω_i	Y_i
South	1.08993965	1.16889358	1.08102737	1.14434253	0.98491035	0.93284930
North	1.24175067	1.07336084	0.99316588	1.00000000	0.81155130	0.13938493
Parameter values	$\sigma = 5$	$\lambda_1 = 0.9$	$e^{\tau_C D_{ij}} = 1.2$	$\phi_1 = 0.5$	$\theta = 0.9$	$\eta = 10$

shows, the outcome is to make the real wages gap even wider, therefore potentially causing an even greater concentration of mobile M workers and income in the South.

Before we explore this cumulative causation process in more detail, let us first examine what happens if transport costs become lower and trade becomes easier, after all, one might expect this to be an outcome of technological progress and the lowering of barriers to trade. Table 1.8 shows that the effect of lower M transport costs is to make real wage rates converge. At first sight it appears that easier access will reverse the tendency towards polarization that we encountered above, but actually things are not so simple!

We can also play with transport costs for C varieties, but in order to reveal the dual effect of both C and M variety transport costs in a way that is most revealing, let us assume that we commence with a symmetric distribution of M activity, which is equally divided between North and South, but then disturb this slightly so that $\lambda_1 = 0.499$. What Table 1.9 shows us is that while the number of M activities in the South is (slightly) less than in the North, real wages in the South are also (slightly) lower than in the North, so there is no incentive for workers to migrate from North to South and cause the number of M activities to increase to regain symmetry. It is convenient to denote the transport costs associated with the M sector by TM, and the transport costs associated with the C sector by TC. It is possible to explore the implications of different combinations of M and C transport costs to see if particular combinations suggest a movement back

Table 1. 9   Equilibrium income, wages and prices for two regions, $\lambda_1 = 0.499$

Variable Region	G_i^M	G_i^C	W_i^M	W_i^C	ω_i	Y_i
South	1.077753	1.058705	0.999767	0.999658	0.932616	0.499167
North	1.077423	1.05895	0.99989	1	0.932866	0.500662
Parameter values	$\sigma = 5$	$e^{\tau_M D_{ij}} = 1.2$	$e^{\tau_C D_{ij}} = 1.2$	$\phi_1 = 0.5$	$\theta = 0.7$	$\eta = 10$

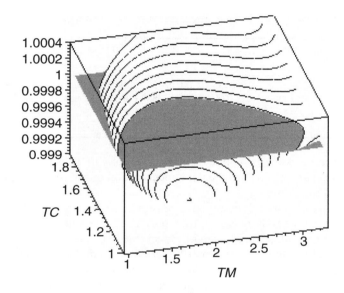

Figure 1.9   Real wages ratio as a function of TM *and* TC *($\theta = 0.7$)*

to symmetry or not. In fact, we do this for a whole range of different combinations of $TM = e^{\tau_M D_{ij}}$ and $TC = e^{\tau_C D_{ij}}$ and the resulting pattern turns out to be quite a remarkable one, for it is approximated very closely indeed by a cubic surface, namely Figure 1.9. This was obtained by calculating the short-term equilibrium (as in Table 1.8), initially for $TM = 1$ to 10, and for $TC = 1$ to 10, giving 100 real wage ratios. After some mild experimentation with the upper limits for TM and TC (each experiment giving 100 real wage ratios) to reveal where the real wage ratios in the vicinity of 1 occurred, we obtain Figures 1.9 and 1.10, which show the real wage ratio surface.

Figures 1.9 and 1.10 show the variation in the real wage ratio with TC and TM, indicating transport cost combinations that will cause the restoration

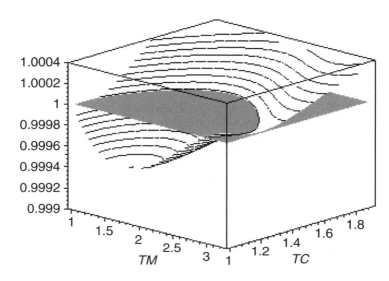

Figure 1.10   An alternative view of Figure 1.9

of symmetry and those that see its destruction. Our 3D picture reminds us of a crater with a lake, with the surface of the lake equal to the plane where the real wage ratio is exactly 1. We shall ignore the fact that the crater is open along one side, since despite this imperfection we still like the picture our crater analogy conjures up in our minds. Symmetry will be destroyed whenever transport costs put the regions in the depths of the crater below the surface of the lake, but if transport costs are such that we are on dry land on the upper slopes of the crater, then our deviation from symmetry will be corrected, so there we are at a stable equilibrium point. For example, the real wage ratio of Table 1.9 falls below the lake surface, where there is no inherent tendency to revert to symmetry. This is typical of the combination of low *TC* and very low *TM*, and suggests that falling transport costs will lead to polarized, uneven development.

Figures 1.9 and 1.10 show that as we climb out of the lake and cross the shoreline we move from where the equilibrium is an unstable one, to higher transport cost combinations that create the stable equilibrium; on the dry ground above the lake the slight disturbance from symmetry will tend to be rectified by a higher real wage ratio. In locating the shoreline we are identifying empirically what Fujita et al. (1999) refer to as the break (of symmetry) points.

The location of the break points depends on the model's parameter values. For instance, if we repeat the above exercise, but with the sole change that $\theta = 0.4$, we obtain Figures 1.11 and 1.12.

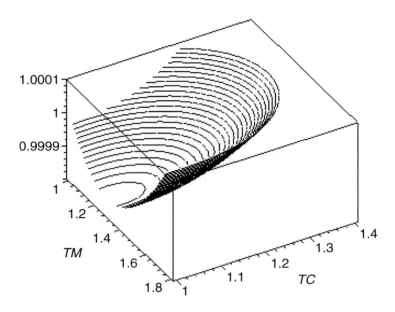

Figure 1.11   Real wage ratios (θ = 0.4)

In Figure 1.11 we have emptied the crater, while in Figure 1.12 we change our viewpoint, but the basic morphology is as in the previous figures, although there is one essential difference, the position of the shoreline has changed. It is now apparent that one emerges on dry ground much sooner as a result of the change in the θ parameter. This can be seen in the view given by Figure 1.12, where the shoreline (break point) along the $TC = 1$ line occurs at about $TM = 1.63$, whereas it is close to 3 when $θ = 0.7$. While our method of locating the break points where this happens is a little unsophisticated, and one should refer to Fujita et al. (1999) for an analytical approach, it is appealing that both give the same result.

Fujita et al. 1999, equation [5.28] gives a formula that locates the break point (when there are no C varieties transport costs) at the value:

$$TM = \left[\frac{\left\{ θ + \frac{σ-1}{σ} \right\} \{1 + θ\}}{\left\{ \frac{σ-1}{σ} - θ \right\} \{1 - θ\}} \right]^{\frac{1}{σ-1}}$$

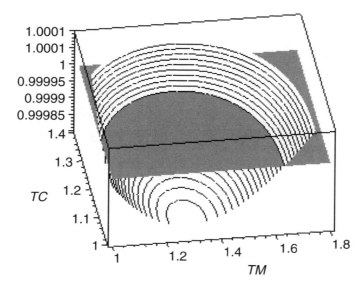

Figure 1.12 Real wage ratios (θ = 0.4): alternative view

which is equal to 1.6266. More complex mathematics are given to obtain the locus of points equivalent to our shoreline. The analytical equation for *TM* points to another active parameter, the elasticity of substitution of *M* products σ. If we reduce the elasticity of substitution, we will be assuming that increasing returns are a more powerful force, and this means that for any given transport cost combination, real wages will tend to be higher in the region with the larger concentration of *M* production. Figure 1.13 shows the crater and lake configuration comparable to Figure 1.12 but with one change, the elasticity of substitution σ now takes the value 4 rather than 5 as above. If we use the formula above to calculate the position of the shoreline for *TC* = 1, we find that it equals 1.972. The previous break point at *TM* = 1.6266 is now below the lake's surface, where symmetric equilibrium is unstable. We can therefore see that reducing the elasticity of substitution in effect raises the level of the lake surface and therefore widens the area in which symmetry is under threat. It turns out that as σ approaches the lower bound of $(1 - θ)^{-1}$ then the break point approaches infinity, no part of the landscape is above water! This is known as the black hole condition.

Up to this point we have examined what happens when we start from a position of symmetry with both *C* and *M* workers evenly divided between South and North, and perturb that situation slightly to see what happens

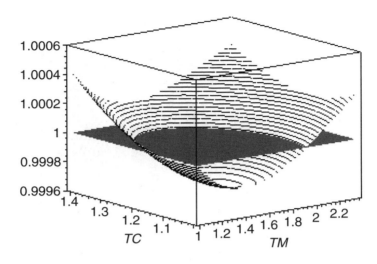

Figure 1.13   Real wage ratios (θ = 0.4, σ = 4)

to the real wage ratio. We have found that when transport costs are low both for *C* and *M* varieties, there is an inherent tendency for the initial slight asymmetry to increase, since real *M* wages in the South will be lower than in the North, where *M* is already more concentrated as a result of the perturbation, and this will encourage even more *M* workers to migrate to the North. We now look at what happens if we start from the alternative perspective of a polarized economic landscape, so that all *M* is concentrated in the South. We retain the assumption that *C* workers are evenly divided between North and South. Is there any possibility of this being an unstable equilibrium and that over time the economy will become symmetrical, or will the polarized landscape exist forever?

Our analysis is based on the same parameter values as were used to create Figure 1.14, but the real wage ratios are calculated assuming $\lambda_1 = 1$, so that all *M* workers are concentrated in the South. We therefore have to treat the *M* wages in the North as the potential wages that would be paid, if there were any workers there to earn them! Figure 1.15 is the outcome. To retain our topological analogy, we think of the picture as comprising an island, with a hill, set in an ocean. The fact that the hill is rather steep, in truth vertical, along one side, is not unrealistic, it simply reminds us of the steep cliffs one encounters on remote crags off the west coast of Ireland! Figure 1.15 shows that for a situation in which there are no *C* transport costs (the *TC* = 1 axis) the wage ratio goes to 1 at about *TM* = 2.4. Below this level of transport costs we are on dry land where the real wage ratio is

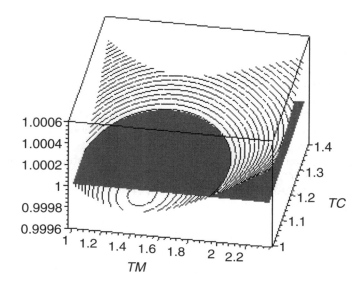

Figure 1.14   Real wage ratios (θ = 0.4, σ = 4): alternative view

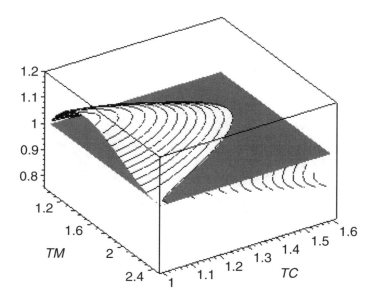

Figure 1.15   Real wage ratios (θ = 0.4, σ = 4): polarized landscape

above 1, meaning that the South's dominant position (remember we are starting out from a position in which all M activity is in the South) will be reinforced. Moving further along the TM axis beyond $TM = 2.4$ means that we have crossed the shoreline and are underwater; in such locations there is an inherent tendency for agglomeration to weaken. It is possible to conjecture that beyond the shoreline there will be migration by M workers from the South to the higher real wages on offer in the North, so the South's dominant status will be threatened. In Fujita et al. (1999) terminology, this is the sustain point. Figure 1.15 also shows that the larger are TC transport costs, the less likely it will be that the economy will be stuck in a polarized state, and once TC is greater than about 1.5, no amount of M transport cost reduction will be able to preserve the South's dominant position as the sole producer of M varieties. In this region we are in open sea and the shoreline can only be reached by reducing TC for some sensible values of TM. Notice also that, as is most apparent from Figure 1.16, with TC in the range 1 to about 1.5, agglomeration is also at risk for very low TM values, indicating that it is only at intermediate transport costs that an initially polarized economy will remain so.

On the high ground of the island, real M wages are higher in the South than in the North, thus reinforcing agglomeration in the South. Imagine

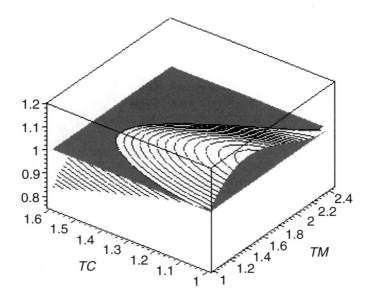

Figure 1.16   Real wage ratios ($\theta = 0.4$, $\sigma = 4$): polarized landscape (alternative perspective)

that agglomeration was partial rather than total, so that, taking an arbitrary share, say 85 per cent rather than 100 per cent of *M* was in the South. Now we might find that the balance was still in favour of the South, but the real wage ratio was very close to 1. Reducing the amount of agglomeration slightly more, we might now find that real wages now favoured the North, thus causing further reduction of agglomeration, and so on (remember the shoreline in Figure 1.15 applies to the case where there is complete agglomeration). In other words, there will be some share at which the real wage ratio will be exactly equal to 1, and which is therefore an equilibrium, although it will be an unstable equilibrium. Likewise, we can envisage another unstable equilibrium point for the parallel scenario relating to complete agglomeration in the North. The shares at which this occurs are not in fact arbitrary, but depend on the transport costs. As we move closer to the break point, the shares of these unstable equilibria move closer to symmetry, so that at and below the break point, symmetry is the single unstable equilibrium.

Let us next explore what happens when economies of scale become stronger. We anticipate that the enhanced benefits of agglomeration will make it less likely for the presence of *C* variety transport costs to make inroads into the dominant position of the South, so that, for *TC* = 1 for instance, with stronger increasing returns, polarization will be maintained at a higher value of *TM*. We can make this comparison by retaining all the parameter values of Figure 1.16, with the exception that the elasticity of substitution σ is now only equal to 3. Figure 1.17 is the outcome, which on comparison with Figure 1.16, shows what amounts to a fall in sea level, with the shoreline retreating to expose a bigger island.

Figure 1.18 shows the vertical view of Figures 1.13 and 1.15 combined. The inner region with the low *TC* and *TM* values is that part of the crater landscape that is below the lake surface; it is the region where a slight deviation from symmetry causes equilibrium to be destroyed; it is the region of unstable equilibrium. Assuming the black-hole condition does not prevail, there exists an outer boundary to this inner zone, the locus of break points. Consider next the outer boundary of the dark shaded zone; this is the locus of sustain points. Beyond this outer boundary we are off the hill of dry land and agglomeration begins to be unsustainable as an equilibrium. The fascinating thing about this diagram is that it shows that either agglomeration or symmetry can occur at the same parameter values! For *TM* and *TC* values in the grey zone between the break point and sustain point, we have stable equilibrium if the point of departure is symmetry, or stable equilibrium if the point of departure is polarization. Therefore, the starting point determines the kind of equilibrium, starting from symmetry we return to symmetry and starting from agglomeration we return to agglomeration; agglomeration in the South if the starting point is agglomeration in the

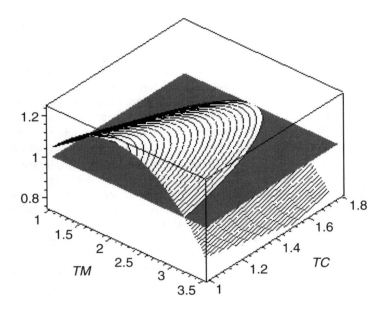

Figure 1.17   Real wage ratios ($\theta = 0.4$, $\sigma = 3$): polarized landscape

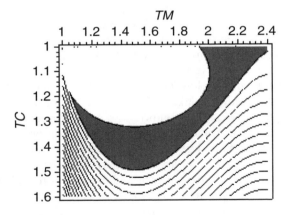

Figure 1.18   Figure 1.13 combined with 1.15

South, and agglomeration in the North if the starting point is agglomeration in the North. In addition, there are two unstable equilibria for each pair of values *TC* and *TM* within this grey area, where real *M* wages are equal in both South and North, but there is asymmetry. There is one unstable equilibrium point where the South has the majority but not all of *M* production, at which a slight deviation, so that the South's share becomes even larger, pushes real South wages higher and therefore agglomeration occurs in the South, and where a slight deviation in favour of the North pushes real wages in the North above those of the South. The other unstable equilibrium point of the grey area is where the North has the majority but not all of M, with similar consequences.

For lower transport costs, within the locus of break points, symmetry is an unstable equilibrium, since only slight deviation from symmetry causes polarization or agglomeration to occur. There are two stable equilibria within this zone, agglomeration in either the South or the North, depending on the starting position. In contrast, symmetry is the stable equilibrium with higher transport costs, beyond the locus of sustain points. In this zone, if agglomeration is the starting point, agglomeration breaks down (we are off the island of high ground beneath the waves). If symmetry is the starting point, it remains intact (we are on dry ground outside the deep water of the crater lake).

It is apparent that as technology or political changes reduce the barriers to trade, so that there is a movement from bottom right to top left of Figure 1.18, we will see a process of agglomeration occurring in the economic landscape. At bottom right, with high transport costs, then immobile C workers ensure that demand cannot be served by agglomeration, transport is too expensive to deny production of M in both South and North. At the other extreme, near the top left-hand corner of Figure 1.18, low transport costs ensure than the South's C workers can be served by concentrating production in the North, or if production is concentrated in the South this can serve the North also. However, as Figure 1.18 shows, very low TM and very low TC also induce symmetry rather than polarization. At the left-hand edge of the figure, we see that there is a thin wedge where the zone of symmetry (in which agglomeration is unsustainable and symmetry is unbroken) goes to $TM = 1$ and $TC = 1$. What is happening here is that C transport costs are effective in causing the immobile C workers to be supplied locally with M, since if M was agglomerated there would be high transport costs importing C varieties to the agglomeration but no overriding effect from agglomeration economies as would occur with higher TM. Finally, while we have worked with specific parameter values, these observations are quite general, as shown by Fujita et al. (1999).

1.11 CONCLUSION

This chapter is intended as a basic introduction to NEG, focusing on underlying assumptions and showing by example what NEG implies.

It considers both short- and long-run equilibria, exploring the implications for wage levels across regions of Great Britain, and looking, in a hypothetical two-region context, at the long-run equilibria that emerge from real wage differences and migration in response to these wage differences.

The analysis is necessarily partial and incomplete, for example, it does not consider Venables (1996), extended in Krugman and Venables (1995) and simplified by Ottaviano and Robert-Nicoud (2006) (see also Robert-Nicoud, 2006). In these versions, rather than labour migration, agglomeration is the outcome of inter-sector labour mobility and input–output (or vertical) linkages between firms. In this context, Fujita et al. (1999) also drive the dynamics by increasing demand based on technical progress rather than by falling trade costs. Overall, the chapter does not attempt to explore the many new developments and directions in NEG research. Apart from what is provided in this volume, a good survey is given by Fujita and Mori (2006), who comprehensively summarize new theoretical developments, and describe related empirical work. The picture they paint is that new NEG theory will be guided more by empirical analysis than was old NEG, will take on board other paradigms such as insights from urban economics and the increasingly recognized significance of worker heterogeneity and alternative market and organizational structures, will acknowledge the fundamental importance of technological externalities such as knowledge generation and transmission and will move away from conventional representations of iceberg transport costs towards more realistic formulations. It appears that economic geography is about to take another turn, this time towards increasing realism and applicability, while remaining within the mathematical and economic foundations laid down over recent decades. Although Fujita and Mori (2006) don't mention it, it is highly likely that econometrics will come to the fore as a way of testing the real value of NEG theory, and not simply by fitting reduced forms deriving from NEG, but in the form of more rigorous tests involving the comparison of competitor models with fundamentally different theoretical positions (see, for example, Fingleton, 2004b, 2005a, 2006; Head and Mayer, 2004). This competition between theories is seen as the acid test of the worth of NEG theory, and is fundamental for the healthy progress of geographical economics, leading towards a better understanding of the real world.

APPENDIX

Table A1.1   Data for the distance matrix

Coordinates Region	x	y
Tees_Valley_and_Durham	0.4840	0.6305
Northumb._et_al.	0.4827	0.6490
Cumbria	0.4654	0.6365
Cheshire	0.4577	0.6014
Greater_Manchester	0.4625	0.6045
Lancashire	0.4618	0.6155
Merseyside	0.4513	0.6044
East_Riding	0.4900	0.6013
North_Yorkshire	0.4821	0.6149
South_Yorkshire	0.4770	0.5984
West_Yorkshire	0.4740	0.6077
Derbyshire	0.4732	0.5914
Leics.	0.4710	0.5715
Lincolnshire	0.4872	0.5837
Hereford_et_al.	0.4524	0.5704
Shrops.	0.4531	0.5857
West_Midlands_(county)	0.4590	0.5762
East_Anglia	0.4927	0.5598
Bedfordshire	0.4739	0.5553
Essex	0.4861	0.5456
Inner_London	0.4723	0.5418
Outer_London	0.4727	0.5407
Berkshire_et_al.	0.4623	0.5522
Surrey	0.4672	0.5309
Hants.	0.4523	0.5339
Kent	0.4820	0.5296
Gloucester_et_al.	0.4443	0.5508
Dorset	0.4312	0.5400
Cornwall	0.3943	0.5357
Devon	0.4151	0.5398
West_Wales	0.4277	0.5849
East_Wales	0.4382	0.5799
North_East_Scot.	0.4929	0.7031
Eastern_Scotland	0.4682	0.6747
South_West_Scot.	0.4554	0.6655
Highlands_and_Islands	0.4680	0.7083

Table A1.2   Manufacturing subsectors defined as M activities

---

15: Manuf. food products and beverages
16: Manuf. tobacco products
17: Manuf. textiles
18: Manuf. apparel; dressing/dyeing fur
19: Tanning/dressing of leather, etc.
20: Manuf. wood/products/cork, etc.
21: Manuf. pulp, paper and paper products
22: Publishing, printing, repro recorded media
23: Manuf. coke, refined petroleum products
24: Manuf. chemicals and chemical products
25: Manuf. rubber and plastic goods
26: Manuf. other non-metallic products
27: Manuf. basic metals
28: Manuf. fabricated metal products, etc.
29: Manuf. machinery and equipment nec.
30: Manuf. office machinery and computers
31: Manuf. electrical machinery/apparatus nec.
32: Manuf. radio, tv/communications equipment
33: Manuf. medical, precision instruments, etc.
34: Manuf. motor vehicles, trailers, etc.
35: Manuf. other transport equipment
36: Manuf. furniture; manufacturing nec.
37: Recycling

Note: nec = not elswhere classifed.

NOTES

1. For related but strictly non-NEG theory and empirics, see Abdel-Rahman and Fujita (1990); Bernat (1996); Ciccone and Hall (1996); Fingleton (2001, 2003, 2004a); Fingleton and McCombie (1998); Fujita and Thisse (2002); Harris and Lau (1998, 1999); Huriot and Thisse (2000); Quigley (1998); Rivera-Batiz (1988).
2. The NUTS 2 regions are used by the European Commission for statistical and administrative purposes.
3. Available on the Nomis (labour market statistics) website.
4. For ease of analysis the observed wage rates are scaled so that Inner London is equal to 1.
5. Available on the Nomis website.
6. The levels reflect the fact that the total number of workers in Great Britain has been set equal to 1.

REFERENCES

Abdel-Rahman, H. and M. Fujita (1990), 'Product variety, Marshallian externalities and city size', *Journal of Regional Science*, **30**: 165–83.

Bernat, A. (1996), 'Does manufacturing matter? A spatial econometric view of Kaldor's laws', *Journal of Regional Science*, **36**: 463–77.

Ciccone, A. and R.E. Hall (1996), 'Productivity and the density of economic activity', *American Economic Review*, **86**: 54–70.

Fingleton, B. (2001), 'Equilibrium and economic growth: spatial econometric models and simulations', *Journal of Regional Science*, **41**: 117–48.

Fingleton, B. (2003), 'Increasing returns: evidence from local wage rates in Great Britain', *Oxford Economic Papers*, **55**: 716–39.

Fingleton, B. (2004a), 'Some alternative geo-economics for Europe's regions', *Journal of Economic Geography*, **4**: 389–420.

Fingleton, B. (2004b), 'Testing the new economic geography. A comparative analysis based on EU regional data'. Paper presented at conference on *New Economic Geography – Closing the Gap Between Theory and Empirics*, Hamburg Institute of International Economics, Germany.

Fingleton, B. (2005a), 'Beyond neoclassical orthodoxy: a view based on the new economic geography and UK regional wage data', *Papers in Regional Science*, **84**: 351–75.

Fingleton, B. (2005b), 'Towards applied geographical economics: modelling relative wage rates, incomes and prices for the regions of Great Britain', *Applied Economics*, **37**: 2417–28.

Fingleton, B. (2006), 'The new economic geography versus urban economics: an evaluation using local wage rates in Great Britain', forthcoming in *Oxford Economic Papers*, **58**: 501–30.

Fingleton, B. and J. McCombie (1998), 'Increasing returns and economic growth: some evidence for manufacturing from the European Union regions', *Oxford Economic Papers*, **50**: 89–105.

Fujita, M. and T. Mori (2006), 'Frontiers of the new economic geography', *Papers in Regional Science*, **84**: 377–405.

Fujita, M. and J.-F. Thisse (2002), *Economics of Agglomeration*, Cambridge: Cambridge University Press.

Fujita, M., P.R. Krugman and A.J. Venables (1999), *The Spatial Economy: Cities, Regions and International Trade*, Cambridge, MA: MIT Press.

Harris, R.I.D. and E. Lau (1998), 'Verdoorn's Law and increasing returns to scale in the UK regions, 1968–91: some new estimates based on the cointegration approach', *Oxford Economic Papers*, **50**: 201–19.

Harris, R.I.D. and E. Lau (1999), 'Verdoorn's Law and increasing returns to scale: country estimates based on the cointegration approach', *Applied Economics Letters*, **6**: 29–33.

Head, K. and T. Mayer (2004), 'The empirics of agglomeration and trade', in V. Henderson and J.-F. Thisse (eds), *The Handbook of Regional and Urban Economics. vol. IV*, North Holland: Elsevier.

Huriot, J.-M. and J.-F. Thisse (eds) (2000), *Economics of Cities*, Cambridge: Cambridge University Press.

Krugman, P. and A. Venables (1995), 'Globalization and the inequality of nations', *Quarterly Journal of Economics*, **110** (4): 857–80.

McCann, P. (2005), 'Transport costs and new economic geography', *Journal of Economic Geography*, **6**: 1–14.

McCann, P. and D. Shefer (2004), 'Location, agglomeration and infrastructure', *Papers in Regional Science*, **83**: 177–96.

McConalogue, D.J. (1970), 'A quasi-intrinsic scheme for passing a smooth curve through a discrete set of points', *Computer Journal*, **13**: 392–6.

Neary, J.P. (2001), 'Of hype and hyperbolas: introducing the new economic geography', *Journal of Economic Literature*, **XXXIX**: 536–61.

Ottaviano, G. and F. Robert-Nicoud (2006), 'The "genome" of NEG models with vertical linkages: a positive and normative synthesis', *Journal of Economic Geography*, **6**: 113–9.

Quigley, J.M. (1998), 'Urban diversity and economic growth', *Journal of Economic Perspectives*, **12**: 127–38.

Rivera-Batiz, F. (1988), 'Increasing returns, monopolistic competition, and agglomeration economies in consumption and production', *Regional Science and Urban Economics*, **18**: 125–53.

Robert-Nicoud, F. (2006), 'Agglomeration and trade with input–output linkages and capital mobility', *Spatial Economic Analysis*, forthcoming.

Venables, A.J. (1996), 'Equilibrium location of vertically linked industries', *International Economic Review*, **37**: 341–59.

Von Thunen, J.H. (1826), *Der Isolierte Staat in Beziehung auf Landwirtschaft und Nationalökonomie*, Berlin, translated by Carla M. Wartenberg (1966), *The Isolated State: An English Edition of Der Isolierte Staat*, Pergamon Press.

2. Models of 'new economic geography': factor mobility vs. vertical linkages

Gianmarco I.P. Ottaviano

2.1 INTRODUCTION

This chapter presents a theoretical contribution to the empirical testing of 'new economic geography' (henceforth, NEG) models.[1] At the moment such testing is generally crippled by identification problems due to two types of observational equivalence. The first type concerns the comparison between the implications of NEG models and those of alternative models mainly based on technological externalities ('between-equivalence'). The second type concerns the comparison between the implications of NEG models based on vertical linkages among firms and those on NEG models based on factor mobility ('within-equivalence').

The focus of the chapter is on within-equivalence. Its meaning is described in Section 2.2 by comparing the two most popular simple NEG models due to Krugman (1991) and Krugman and Venables (1995). These models deal with labour mobility and input–output linkages respectively. The relevance of within-equivalence is usually not fully understood. A possible explanation is that models with vertical linkages are typically very difficult to deal with analytically. This has not only hampered the exploitation of their full analytical potential but has also concealed their observational equivalence with models based on factor mobility. For this reason, Section 2.2 compares the analytically solvable versions of Krugman (1991) and Krugman and Venables (1995) as proposed by Forslid and Ottaviano (2003) and Ottaviano and Robert-Nicoud (2005) respectively. Closed form solutions reveal the fundamental equivalence of the equilibrium and stability properties of the two types of models.

These equivalence results raise doubts on the possibility of empirically testing the relative relevance of labour mobility and vertical linkages in driving the evolution of the economic landscape. In the wake of Ottaviano and Pinelli (2005) Section 2.3 shows how the observational equivalence of those simple models can be circumvented by casting them within a richer encompassing framework that pays tribute to the central role of land use in urban economics. Section 2.4 concludes.

2.2   THE OBSERVATIONAL EQUIVALENCE OF SIMPLE NEG MODELS

The two theoretical blueprints of NEG are the models proposed by Krugman (1991) and Krugman and Venables (1995). These models are sometime called 'core-periphery' (CP) and 'vertical-linkages' (VL) models respectively. In the former model, agglomeration forces arise in the presence of labour mobility; in the latter, in the presence of input–output linkages among firms.

Notwithstanding their different logic, when it comes to empirical predictions, the two models happen to be observationally equivalent. This feature has passed virtually unnoticed for a while due to the impossibility of finding analytical solutions. Recently it has been highlighted by Baldwin et al. (2003) and it is best illustrated through the analytically solvable versions of the original models. Forslid and Ottaviano (2003) achieve analytical solvability in the CP model by introducing skill heterogeneity between workers, by making the fixed costs of production relatively skill-intensive and by coupling a higher level of skills with higher inter-regional labour mobility. For this reason, their model is called the 'footloose entrepreneurs' (FE) model. Ottaviano and Robert-Nicoud (2005) obtain analytical solvability in the VL model by confining input–output linkages to the fixed costs of production. By analogy with the former case, their model has been dubbed the FEVL model.

Comparing the modified models with the corresponding original versions shows that they exhibit the same qualitative properties. Comparing the two modified versions with each other shows that they are homomorphic, that is, the FEVL and FE models exhibit the same equilibrium and stability properties.[2] This can be shown following Baldwin et al. (2003).

2.2.1   Factor Mobility

The basic structure of the FE model is the same as the CP model. In the CP model there are two regions, North and South. Northern variables bear no label whereas southern ones are labelled by an asterisk. Each region has two factors of production (entrepreneurs or human capital H and unskilled workers L) and two sectors (industry M and agriculture A). While factor H is inter-regionally mobile, factor L is not and is evenly distributed across regions. The A-sector is perfectly competitive. It supplies a homogeneous good, which is freely traded, under constant returns to scale. Unskilled labour L is its only input and it is inter-regionally immobile. In particular, A-sector unit cost is $a_A w_L$ where w_L is the reward to L. The M-sector is monopolistically competitive and produces a horizontally differentiated good under increasing returns to scale using H as its only input. Increasing returns are captured by a linear cost function with fixed and variable costs. Specifically, the total cost of producing x units of a variety of the M-good is $w(F + a_m x)$ where w is the reward to H. Differently from the A-good, inter-regional trade in manufactures is inhibited by frictional barriers. While it is costless to ship M-goods to local consumers, in order to sell one unit in the other region an M-firm must ship $\tau \geq 1$ units.

In the FE model the only departure from this framework is the assumption that fixed and variable costs in manufacturing are undertaken in terms of H and L respectively rather than both being incurred in the H only. This leads to total costs equal to $wF + w_L a_M x$. The fixed cost can be interpreted as stemming from R&D activities or headquarter services, which naturally makes it relatively skill-intensive.

The rest of the FE model is the same as in the CP. The representative consumer in each region has preferences consisting of a CES subutility defined over M-varieties nested in a Cobb-Douglas upper-tier function that also includes consumption of A. For expositional purposes, it is useful to take a logarithmic transformation:

$$U = \ln C; \quad C \equiv C_M^\mu C_A^{1-\mu}, \quad C_M \equiv \left(\int_{i=0}^{n+n^*} c_i^{1-1/\sigma} di \right)^{\frac{1}{1-1/\sigma}}; \quad 0 < \mu < 1 < \sigma \quad (2.1)$$

where C_M and C_A are, respectively, consumption of the M composite and consumption of A. Moreover, n and n^* are the number (mass) of North and South varieties, μ is the expenditure share on M-varieties, and σ is the constant elasticity of substitution between M-varieties.

Regional supplies of L as well as the global supply of H are fixed at $L^w/2$ and H^w, respectively. However, the inter-regional distribution of H is endogenous with H flowing to the region with the highest real reward. In particular, migration is governed by the ad hoc migration equation:

$$\dot{s}_H = (\omega - \omega^*)(1 - s_H)s_H; \quad s_H \equiv \frac{H}{H^w}, \quad \omega \equiv \frac{w}{P}, \quad P \equiv p_A^{1-\mu} \left(\int_{i=0}^{n+n^*} p_i^{1-\sigma} di \right)^{\frac{\mu}{1-\sigma}}$$

$$(2.2)$$

where s_H is the share of entrepreneurs in the north, H is their northern supply, ω and ω^* are the northern and southern real skilled wages, w is the northern nominal return to H, and P is the northern exact price index associated with C_M; p_A is the price of A and p_i is the price of M-variety i. Analogous definitions hold for southern variables.

2.2.2 Equilibrium Conditions

Utility optimization yields a constant division of expenditure between M and A, and CES demand functions for M-varieties, which may be written as:

$$c_j \equiv \frac{p_j^{-\sigma}\mu E}{\displaystyle\int_{i=0}^{n+n^*} p_i^{1-\sigma}di}; \quad E = wH + w_L L \tag{2.3}$$

where E is regional expenditure. As usual in monopolistic competition, free and instantaneous entry drives pure profits to zero. That is why E includes only factor income. Demand for A is $C_A = (1-\mu)E/p_A$.

On the supply side, in sector A perfect competition leads to marginal cost pricing, that is, $p_A = a_A w_L$ and $p_A^* = a_A w_L^*$. In addition, costless trade in A equalizes northern and southern prices and thus indirectly equalizes L wage rates in the two regions: $w_L = w_L^*$.[3] In the M-sector, profit-maximizing firms set prices as a constant mark-up $1/(1-1/\sigma)$ over marginal costs, inclusive of trade costs in the case of distant sales. Thus, the ratio of the price of a northern variety in its local and export markets is τ. Summarizing these equilibrium-pricing results, we have:

$$p = \frac{w_L a_M}{1 - 1/\sigma}, \quad p^* = \frac{\tau w_L a_M}{1 - 1/\sigma}, \quad p_A = p_A^* = w_L = w_L^* \tag{2.4}$$

Similar pricing rules hold for southern firms.

The total number of firms in each region is pinned down by factor endowments and technology. To see this, consider that any active firm demands F units of H. Thus, H-factor market clearing implies that the equilibrium number of firms is:

$$n = H/F. \tag{2.5}$$

Given (2.4) operating profit π is the value of sales divided by σ. Moreover, due to free entry, π just covers the fixed entry cost F, so $px/\sigma = wF$. Then the equilibrium scale of firms equals:

$$\bar{x} = wF(\sigma - 1)/(w_L a_M) \tag{2.6}$$

which is increasing with the ratio between H and L rewards.

In equilibrium, the market for northern *M*-varieties must clear. Since firm output is given by (2.6), demand (2.3) allows one to write the market clearing condition for a typical northern variety as:

$$p\bar{x} = R; \quad R \equiv \frac{w_L^{1-\sigma}\mu E}{nw_L^{1-\sigma} + \phi n^* w_L^{*1-\sigma}} + \frac{\phi w_L^{1-\sigma}\mu E^*}{\phi n w_L^{1-\sigma} + n^* w_L^{*1-\sigma}} \quad (2.7)$$

where *R* is revenue and $\phi = \tau^{1-\sigma}$ measures the 'freeness' of trade that rises from $\phi = 0$ (with infinite trade costs) to $\phi = 1$ with zero trade costs (with $\tau = 1$). A condition analogous to (2.7) has to hold for a typical southern variety . Finally, the market of good *A* also has to clear. Since this good is freely traded, that happens when its demand and supply match for the whole economy:

$$(1 - \mu)(E + E^*) = 2L/p_A. \quad (2.8)$$

Thanks to Walras's law one of the three market clearing conditions can be dropped as it is granted by the remaining two. To exploit the symmetry of the model it is natural to drop the *A*-sector condition. Then, condition (2.7) and its southern equivalent can be solved together to express *w* and *w** as explicit functions of *H* and *H**. For this reason they are called 'wage equations'.

2.2.3 Choice of Numeraire and Units

Appropriate normalizations and a careful choice of the numeraire good can be used to get rid of parameters that have no bearing on the final results. First, if *A* is taken as numeraire and the units of *A* are chosen such that $a_A = 1$, free trade in *A* implies the equilibrium price of *A* and the wages of *L* satisfy $p_A = w_L = w_L^* = 1$. Moreover, if *M* is measured in units such that $a_M = (1 - 1/\sigma)$, the equilibrium prices of *M*-varieties become $p = w_L = 1$ and $p^* = \tau w_L = \tau$, with associated equilibrium firm size, becomes equal to $\bar{x} = wF\sigma$. Second, if *F* is normalized to 1, then $\bar{x} = w\sigma$, $n = H$ and $n^* = H^*$. These results simplify the *M*-sector market-clearing condition (2.7). The fact that $n = H$ and $n^* = H^*$ cleanly stress the connection between migration and industrial relocation. Finally, choosing the units of *H* such that its world endowment H^w equals unity also pins down the world number of varieties at unity ($n + n^* = 1$).

To sum up, the equilibrium values with these normalizations become:

$$p = w_L = 1, \quad p^* = \tau w_L = \tau, \quad \bar{x} = w\sigma, \quad \bar{x}^* = w^*\sigma, \quad p_A = p_A^* = w_L = w_L^* = 1,$$

$$n + n^* = H + H^* = 1, \quad n = H = s_H = s_n, \quad n^* = H^* \quad (2.9)$$

where s_H and s_n are the North's shares of H^w and n^w respectively. Note that, instead of writing s_H for the northern share of H^w, now one can equivalently write H, s_n or n.

2.2.4 Spatial Equilibria

We are now ready to determine the equilibrium distribution of the mobile skilled workers, and hence of firms, between North and South. A spatial equilibrium is reached when no skilled worker wants to change his or her location. In terms of the migration equation (2.2), that happens when $\dot{s}_H = 0$. By inspection, (2.2) shows that there are two types of candidates for spatial equilibria. To the first type belong 'core-periphery' outcomes that correspond to $s_H = 1$ and 0. To the second type belong 'interior' outcomes that correspond to values of s_H such that $\omega = \omega^*$ but $0 < s_H < 1$. Given the symmetry of the set-up, it is clear that $\omega = \omega^*$ at the symmetric outcome $s_H = 0.5$, so that $s_H = 0.5$ is always a spatial equilibrium. However, it may be not the only one.

To see whether there are other interior equilibria the first step is to use (2.7) and (2.9) to write the wage equations of the two regions after substituting for the chosen normalizations:

$$w\sigma = \frac{\mu(wn + L)}{n + \phi n^*} + \frac{\phi\mu(w^*n^* + L)}{\phi n + n^*}, \quad w^*\sigma = \frac{\phi\mu(wn + L)}{n + \phi n^*} + \frac{\mu(w^*n^* + L)}{\phi n + n^*}$$

(2.10)

where the definitions of E and E^* given in (2.3) have been used. Being linear in wages, the wage equations can be easily solved for w and w^* as functions of n and n^*:

$$w = \frac{\mu L}{\sigma - \mu} \frac{2\sigma\phi n + [(\sigma + \mu)\phi^2 + (\sigma - \mu)]n^*}{\sigma(n + \phi n^*)(\phi n + n^*) - \mu(1 - \phi^2)nn^*}$$

(2.11)

and

$$w^* = \frac{\mu L}{\sigma - \mu} \frac{2\sigma\phi n^* + [(\sigma + \mu)\phi^2 + (\sigma - \mu)]n}{\sigma(n + \phi n^*)(\phi n + n^*) - \mu(1 - \phi^2)nn^*}.$$

(2.12)

The second step is to use the values of w and w^* to write the real wage difference $\omega - \omega^*$ as:

$$\omega - \omega^* = \ln\left(\frac{\phi n + \psi(\phi)n^*}{\psi(\phi)n + \phi n^*}\right) + \frac{\mu}{\sigma - 1}\ln\left(\frac{n + \phi n^*}{n^* + \phi n}\right)$$

(2.13)

where $\psi(\phi) \equiv [(\sigma + \mu)\phi^2 + (\sigma - \mu)]/(2\sigma)$. Recalling that $n^* = 1 - n$ and $n = s_n = s_H$, expression (2.13) gives the real wage difference $\Omega \equiv \omega - \omega^*$ as an explicit function of the share s_H of firms in the North. As expected $n = 0.5$ is always a solution of $\Omega = 0$.

The third step is to show that Ω changes concavity at most once. Indeed, it is readily established that the sign of its first derivative $d\Omega/ds_H$ depends on the sign of its quadratic numerator and therefore changes sign at most twice. Together with the fact that Ω always equals zero at $s_H = 0.5$, this implies that it crosses the horizontal axis either once or (no less and no more than) three times. That is, either $s_H = 0.5$ is the only zero of Ω or there are (no more and no less than) two other zeros. Due to symmetry, when they exist the two additional zeros must be symmetric around $s_H = 0.5$. Thus, the model exhibits either one or three or five spatial equilibria, corner solution included.

2.2.5 Stability Analysis

The NEG literature traditionally relies on informal tests to find two threshold levels of trade costs below which the symmetric equilibrium becomes unstable and the full agglomeration outcome becomes stable.[4] Such informal tests identify the stability conditions of the symmetric and core-periphery outcomes respectively as:

$$\frac{d(\omega - \omega^*)}{ds_H}\bigg|_{sym} < 0, \quad \omega_{CP} > \omega_{CP}^* \tag{2.14}$$

where *sym* and *CP* indicate evaluation at $s_H = 0.5$ and $s_H = 1$, respectively. The value of ϕ at which the first condition in (2.14) holds with equality is called the 'break' point, ϕ^B. The value of ϕ at which the second condition holds with equality is called the 'sustain' point, ϕ^S.

Differencing (2.13) with respect to s_H and evaluating the derivative at $s_H = 0.5$ reveals that the symmetric equilibrium becomes unstable for trade costs such that the corresponding values of ϕ are lower than the 'break' point:

$$\phi^B = \frac{(\sigma - \mu)(\sigma - 1 - \mu)}{(\sigma + \mu)(\sigma - 1 + \mu)}. \tag{2.15}$$

By inspection the 'break' point is a decreasing function of μ and increasing function of σ. Indeed, a larger expenditure share on manufacturing μ strengthen the agglomeration forces, which implies that the symmetric equilibrium is stable for a smaller range of trade costs. A larger σ works in the opposite direction since it implies a lower mark-up in the M-sector and thus lowers agglomeration forces. Note that a value of μ larger than $\sigma - 1$ makes ϕ^B negative. In this case ϕ cannot be smaller than ϕ^B and the symmetric equilibrium is always unstable for any parameter values. This situation is ruled out by imposing the so-called 'no-black-hole' condition, which prevents the symmetric equilibrium from always being unstable irrespective of the extent of trade freeness. The exact condition is $\mu < \sigma - 1$.

As to the core-periphery equilibrium, this cannot be sustained for trade costs above the 'sustain' point, which is given by trade costs for which Ω evaluated at $s_H = 0$ (or $s_H = 1$) equals zero:

$$2\sigma(\phi^S)^{1 - \frac{\mu}{\sigma - 1}} - (\sigma + \mu)(\phi^S)^2 - \sigma + \mu = 0. \qquad (2.16)$$

It can be shown that ϕ^S cannot be larger than ϕ^B (see Baldwin et al., 2003 for details). This implies that the model displays 'hysteresis' in location when trade freeness rises above the 'sustain' point: once the dispersed equilibrium is reached, trade freeness has to rise further above the 'break' point before such equilibrium disappears.

To summarize, the symmetric equilibrium is stable only for sufficiently low levels of trade freeness, specifically for $\phi < \phi^B$, and core-periphery outcomes are stable only for sufficiently high levels of trade freeness, specifically for $\phi > \phi^S$. Hence, for $\phi < \phi^S$, $n = 0.5$ is the only spatial equilibrium of (2.2) and it is stable. For $\phi > \phi^B$, $n = 0.5$, $n = 0$ and $n = 1$ are all spatial equilibria but only the core-periphery ones are stable. Finally, for $\phi^S < \phi < \phi^B$, there are five spatial equilibria. Two are core-periphery outcomes and are stable, two are interior asymmetric equilibria and are unstable and the last one is the symmetric outcome and it is also stable. These results are summarized in Figure 2.1 where the equilibrium values of s_n are depicted on the vertical axis as a function of trade freeness ϕ reported on the horizontal axis. Arrows point at stable equilibria.

2.2.6 Vertical Linkages

In the FE models, agglomeration arises because the relative sizes of regional markets are endogenously determined by the migration decisions of workers as a larger market attracts firms (demand linkage), thus offering workers a cheaper access to M-varieties (cost-of-living linkage). An alternative reason why regional market size can be endogenous is the presence of input–output linkages among firms: what is output for one firm is input for another and vice versa. In this respect, the entry of a new firm in a certain region not only increases the intensity of competition between

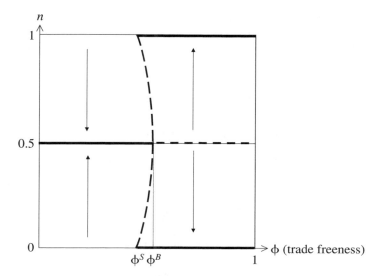

Figure 2.1   Observational equivalence in FE and FEVL models

parallel firms (market crowding effect). It also increases the size of the market of upstream firms (demand linkage) and decreases the costs of downstream firms (cost linkage).

This can be shown using the FEVL model, which considers the same set-up as the FE model with two crucial modifications. First, there is only one factor of production, simply labour L, which is in equal and fixed supply in the two regions: $L = L^* = L^W/2$. Labour can freely move between sectors within the same region but it is geographically immobile. As in the FE model, this factor is used in both sectors to fulfil the marginal input require-ments, a_A and a_M. Second, the fixed cost of manufacturing is incurred in a composite input consisting of labour and the differentiated varieties of the M-good. For simplicity, the composite input is assumed to be Cobb-Douglas in L and C_M with shares $1 - \mu$ and μ respectively. This way, con-sumers and firms devote the same shares of expenditures to manufactures.

Using the same normalizations as in the FE model, the corresponding total cost function for a typical northern firm is given by $FP/\eta + w_L a_M x$, where P is the price index defined in (2.2) and $\eta = \mu^\mu(1 - \mu)^\mu$. Setting again $a_A = 1$ and $a_M = (1 - 1/\sigma)$, free trade in the agricultural good yields $p_A = w_L = w_L^* = 1$, $p = w_L = 1$ and $p^* = \tau w_L = \tau$. Accordingly, the maximized profit of a northern firm is:

$$\Pi = \sigma x - P/\eta. \tag{2.17}$$

Intermediate demand implies that expenditures on manufactures now stem not only from consumers but also from firms:

$$\mu E = \mu(Y + nP/\eta) \tag{2.18}$$

where Y is consumers' income inclusive of firms' profits Π:

$$Y = L/2 + n\Pi = L/2 + n(\sigma x - P/\eta) \tag{2.19}$$

with the second equality granted by (2.17). Then, substituting (2.19) into (2.18) yields:

$$\mu E = \mu(L/2 + n\sigma x). \tag{2.20}$$

Recalling (2.7), market clearing in northern manufactures requires:

$$x = \frac{\mu E}{n + \phi n^*} + \frac{\phi \mu E^*}{\phi n + n^*} \tag{2.21}$$

which, by (2.20), can be rewritten as:

$$x = \frac{\mu(L^W/2 + \sigma n x)}{n + \phi n^*} + \frac{\phi \mu(L^W/2 + \sigma n^* x^*)}{\phi n + n^*} \tag{2.22}$$

with a symmetric equation holding for the South:

$$x^* = \frac{\mu(L^W/2 + \sigma n^* x^*)}{\phi n + n^*} + \frac{\phi \mu(L^W/2 + \sigma n x)}{n + \phi n^*}. \tag{2.23}$$

Equations (2.22) and (2.23) can be solved to obtain x and x^* as explicit functions of the numbers of active firms n and n^*. Standard derivations give $x = w/\sigma$ and $x^* = w^*/\sigma$ as reported in (2.11) and (2.12) respectively.

We are now ready to analyse the entry decision of firms in the two regions. As in (2.2), we assume that agents are short-sighted: firms enter when current profits are positive and exit when they are negative. Specifically, their flow is regulated by the following simple ad hoc adjustments:

$$\dot{n} = n\,\Pi(n, n^*), \quad \dot{n}^* = n^*\,\Pi(n, n^*) \tag{2.24}$$

where:

$$\Pi(n, n^*) = \sigma x - P/\eta = \frac{\mu L}{\sigma - \mu} \frac{2\sigma\phi n + [(\sigma + \mu)\phi^2 + (\sigma - \mu)]n^*}{\sigma(n + \phi n^*)(\phi n + n^*) - \mu(1 - \phi^2)nn^*}$$

$$- \frac{1}{\eta(n + \phi n^*)^{\mu/(\sigma-1)}} \tag{2.25}$$

with symmetric expressions holding for the South. Therefore, the dynamics of the FEVL model are described by two differential equations. With respect to the FE model, the FEVL model cannot be reduced to a unique differential equation.

In a spatial equilibrium no firm wants to enter or exit the regional markets. Accordingly, given (2.24), a spatial equilibrium arises for $0 < n < 1$ when $\Pi(n,n^*) = \Pi^*(n,n^*) = 0$. It arises at $(n,n^*) = (n_0,0)$, with $n_0 > 0$, when $\Pi(n_0,0) = 0$ and $= \Pi^*(n_0,0) < 0$ or at $(n,n^*) = (0,n_0)$, with $n_0 > 0$, when $\Pi(0,n_0) < 0$ and $\Pi^*(0,n_0) = 0$. As in the FE model, equilibria may be multiple, so their stability properties are crucial.

Consider first an agglomerated configuration with all active firms in one region, say $(n,n^*) = (n_0,0)$. As just discussed, this is a stable spatial equilibrium for (2.24) if and only if $\Pi(n_0,0) = 0$ and $\Pi^*(n_0,0) < 0$. On the one side, it is readily verified that the former requirement is met for n equal to:

$$n_0 = \left(\frac{\mu/\sigma}{1 - \mu/\sigma}\eta L^W\right)^{\frac{1}{1-\mu/(\sigma-1)}}. \tag{2.26}$$

On the other, the latter is met when:

$$\frac{1 - \mu/\sigma + (1 + \mu/\sigma)\phi^2}{2\phi^{1-\mu/(\sigma-1)}} - 1 < 0 \tag{2.27}$$

which implies that the condition for agglomeration to be a stable spatial equilibrium in the FEVL model is the same as in the FE model. Specifically, ϕ has to be larger than the sustain point ϕ^S as defined in (2.16).

Turning to interior equilibria, Ottaviano and Robert-Nicoud (2005) prove that the loci $\Pi(n,n^*) = 0$ and $\Pi^*(n,n^*) = 0$ always cross at least once and no more than thrice. In particular, they always cross at the symmetric outcome in which n and n^* are both equal to:

$$n_{0.5} = \frac{n_0}{[2^{1-\sigma}(1 + \phi)^\mu]^{1/(1-\sigma+\mu)}}. \tag{2.28}$$

Therefore, while the number of active firms with agglomeration (n_0) is invariant to trade barriers, the number of those active in the symmetric equilibrium ($n_{0.5}$) is not. Moreover, they also show that the symmetric equilibrium is stable as long as $\phi < \phi^B$ as defined in (2.15). Thus, the FEVL and FE models share the same sustain point (ϕ^S), the same break point (ϕ^B), and the same no-black-hole condition $\mu < (\sigma - 1)$.

All this implies that, once we define $s^H \equiv n/(n + n^*)$, Figure 2.1 also depicts the equilibrium and stability properties of the FEVL model. Hence, the two models are observationally equivalent. The only difference is that, as already mentioned, whereas the total number of firms is independent from trade barriers in the FE model, it is not in the FEVL model. In particular, under the no-black-hole condition, (2.28) reveals that $n_{0.5}$ is an increasing function of ϕ. The freer trade is, the larger the number of active firms: trade integration fragments the market. Moreover, when that condition holds, under symmetry the number of active firms in each country is larger than the total number of firms under agglomeration ($n_{0.5} > n_0$). Therefore, differently from the FE frameworks, in the FEVL model agglomeration defragments the market and reduces product variety.

2.3   A RICHER ENCOMPASSING MODEL

The equivalence results of the previous section cast a shadow on the possibility of checking whether labour mobility or vertical linkages drive the agglomeration of economic activities if one believes in NEG models. Such impasse can be circumvented by embedding the two alternative models within a richer encompassing framework. In the wake of Ottaviano and Pinelli (2005) that can be achieved by extending the model of Redding and Venables (2004) through the introduction of labour mobility and land à la Hanson (1998) and Helpman (1998). In the tradition of urban economics, the extended framework recognizes the centrality of land use in the spatial economy.

Consider an economy consisting of $i = 1, \ldots, R$ regions. On the demand side, in region j the representative worker consumes a set of horizontally differentiated varieties and land services ('housing'). His or her utility function is:

$$U_j = (X_j)^\mu (L_j)^{1-\mu}, 0 < \mu < 1 \tag{2.29}$$

where L_j is land consumption and:

$$X_j = \sum_{i=1}^{R} \left\{ \int_0^{n_i} [x_{ij}(z)]^{\frac{\sigma-1}{\sigma}} dz \right\}^{\frac{\sigma}{\sigma-1}} = \sum_{i=1}^{R} \left(n_i x_{ij}^{\frac{\sigma-1}{\sigma}} \right)^{\frac{\sigma}{\sigma-1}} \tag{2.30}$$

is a CES quantity index of the $\Sigma_{i=1}^{R} n_i$ varieties available in region j with x_{ij} labelling the consumption in region j of a typical variety produced in region i. The associated exact CES price index is:

$$P_j = \sum_{i=1}^{R} \left\{ \int_0^{n_i} [p_{ij}(z)]^{1-\sigma} dz \right\}^{\frac{1}{1-\sigma}} = \sum_{i=1}^{R} \left(n_i p_{ij}^{1-\sigma} \right)^{\frac{1}{1-\sigma}} \qquad (2.31)$$

where p_{ij} is the delivered price in region j of a typical variety produced in region i. In the above expressions the second equality exploits the fact that in equilibrium, quantities and prices are the same for all varieties produced in country i and consumed by country j.

Utility maximization then gives the demand in j for a typical variety produced in i:

$$x_{ij} = p_{ij}^{-\sigma} E_j P_j^{\sigma-1} \qquad (2.32)$$

where E_j is expenditures on X_j, which is a fraction μ of income I_j, while $\sigma > 1$ is both the own and the cross-price elasticity of demand.

On the supply side, each variety is produced by one, and only one, firm under increasing returns to scale and monopolistic competition. In so doing, the firm employs labour, land and, as intermediate input, the same bundle of differentiated varieties that workers demand for consumption. This is the FEVL component of the encompassing framework. Specifically, in region i the total production cost of a typical variety is:

$$TC_i = P_i^{\alpha} r_i^{\beta} w_i^{\gamma} c_i (F + x_i), \quad \alpha, \beta, \gamma > 0, \quad \alpha + \beta + \gamma = 1 \qquad (2.33)$$

where x_i is total output, r_i and w_i are land rent and wage, while c_i and $c_i F$ are marginal and fixed input requirements respectively. Trade faces frictional costs: for one unit of any variety to reach destination when shipped from region i to region j, $\tau_{ij} > 1$ units have to be shipped. Hence:

$$x_i = \sum_{j=1}^{R} x_{ij} \tau_{ij}. \qquad (2.34)$$

Firm profit maximization yields the standard CES mark-up pricing rule:

$$p_i = \frac{\sigma}{\sigma - 1} P_i^{\alpha} r_i^{\beta} w_i^{\gamma} c_i, \quad p_{ij} = \tau_{ij} p_i. \qquad (2.35)$$

Free entry then implies that in equilibrium, firms are just able to break even, which happens when they operate at scale $\bar{x} = (\sigma - 1)F$. Together with (2.32) and (2.35) that allows us to write the free entry condition in region i as:

$$(\text{FE}) \ \bar{x} \left(\frac{\sigma}{\sigma - 1} r_i^\beta w_i^\gamma c_i \right)^\sigma = MA_i SA_i^{\frac{\alpha\sigma}{\sigma - 1}}$$

where $MA_i = \Sigma_{j=1}^R \tau_{ij}^{1-\sigma} E_j P_j^{\sigma-1}$ is the 'market access' of region i. This is a measure of customer and competitor proximity ('demand linkages') that predicts the quantity a firm sells given its production costs. The term $SA_i = P_i^{1-\sigma} = \Sigma_{j=1}^R n_j p_j^{1-\sigma} \tau_{ji}^{1-\sigma}$ is, instead, the 'supplier access' of region i, a measure of supplier proximity. This inversely predicts the prices a firm pays for its intermediate inputs ('cost linkages') and a worker pays for his or her consumption bundle ('cost-of-living linkages') when located in a certain region.

As in the FE model, workers work and consume in the region where they reside and select their residence freely. This implies that in equilibrium they are indifferent about location as they would achieve the same level of indirect utility V wherever located.[5] Given the chosen utility, if we further assume that the land of a region is owned by locally resident landlords, free mobility then gives:[6]

$$(\text{FM}) \ \frac{w_i}{SA_i^{\frac{\mu}{1-\sigma}} r_i^{1-\mu}} = V.$$

After log-linearization, conditions (FE) and (FM) are depicted in Figure 2.2, which measures the logarithm of regional nominal wages (w) along the vertical axis and the logarithm of regional land rents (r) along the horizontal one. Downward sloping lines are derived from (FE) and depict the combinations of wages and rents that make firms indifferent about regions. Their downward slope reflects the fact that firms can break even in different regions provided that higher wages correspond to lower rents and vice versa. Upward sloping lines are derived from (FM) and depict the combinations of wages and rents that make workers indifferent about regions. Their upward slope reflects the fact that workers can achieve the same utility ('real wage') in different regions provided that higher rents correspond to higher wages and vice versa.

The exact positions of the two lines depend on regional market access and supplier access. Better market access (larger MA) shifts FE up, increasing both wages and land rents. Better supplier access (larger SA) shifts both FE and FM up, also increasing rents. The effect on wages is, instead,

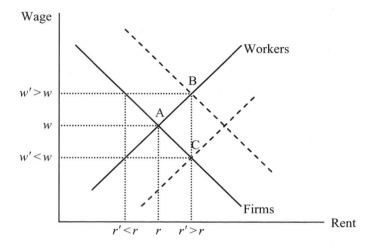

Figure 2.2   Identification in the encompassing model

ambiguous: they increase (decrease) if the shift in FE dominates (is dominated by) the shift in FM.

This theoretical ambiguity makes it pointless to try to disentangle the effects of *MA* and *SA* on equilibrium wages and rents. One can instead check whether their combined effect is indeed positive on rents as predicted by both FE and FEVL models. More interestingly, one can also check whether the combined effect of *MA* and *SA* is positive or negative on wages, which would point at a dominant impact on firms (point B) or on workers (point C) respectively. Demand and cost linkage would dominate in the former case as predicted by the FEVL model; cost-of-living linkages in the latter as predicted by the FE model. Alternatively one can reach similar conclusions by looking at the net migration flows of workers and the net birth rates of firms rather than at the changes in land rents. The reason is that, since land values capitalize the attractiveness of a place, land rents rise also because net immigration and net firm creation increase the demand for land.

2.4   CONCLUSION

This chapter has raised the issue of observational equivalence between the two big classes of NEG models, respectively based on factor mobility and vertical linkages. The issue has been illustrated in terms of two recent models, the FE and FEVL models, whose analytically solvability reveals that the two classes of models share the same fundamental structure and therefore the same equilibrium properties. Accordingly, they lead to the same empirical predictions.

Observational equivalence calls for additional efforts to extract different empirical predictions from different theoretical models. This chapter has presented an example of the way this can be achieved by embedding the two classes of models in a richer set-up where a new endogenous variable (land rent) reacts differently to changes in market access and supplier access depending on whether factor mobility or vertical linkages play a dominant role.

NOTES

1. See Fujita, Krugman and Venables (1999) and Baldwin et al. (2003) for detailed theoretical surveys.
2. Robert-Nicoud (2005) builds on this result to show that the CP and VL models are also homomorphic.
3. This is so insofar as the A-good is produced everywhere. This happens when no country alone can satisfy world demand. The exact condition requires $\alpha < \sigma/(2\sigma - 1)$. This is assumed to hold henceforth.
4. The results of informal tests in the FE model are confirmed by formal local stability analysis (Ottaviano, 2001).
5. With respect to the FE and FEVL models, in the encompassing framework the presence of land prevents core-periphery outcomes. That is, all spatial equilibria are interior but some may not be symmetric.
6. This assumption is made only for analytical convenience. What is crucial for what follows is that the rental income of workers, if any, is independent of locations and, thus, it does not affect the migration choice. The alternative assumptions of absentee landlords or balanced ownership of land across all cities would also serve that purpose.

REFERENCES

Baldwin, R., R. Forslid, Ph. Martin, G. Ottaviano and F. Robert-Nicoud (2003), *Economic Geography and Public Policy*, Princeton, NJ: Princeton University Press.

Forslid, R. and G.I.P. Ottaviano (2003), 'Trade and location: two analytically solvable cases', *Journal of Economic Geography*, **3**: 229–40.

Fujita, M., P. Krugman and A.J. Venables (1999), *The Spatial Economy: Cities, Regions and International Trade*, Cambridge, MA: MIT Press.

Hanson, G. (1998), 'Market potential, increasing returns, and geographic concentration', *NBER Working Paper No. 6429*.

Helpman, E. (1998), 'The size of regions', in D. Pines, E. Sadka and I. Zilcha (eds), *Topics in Public Economics. Theoretical and Applied Analysis*, Cambridge: Cambridge University Press.

Krugman, P. (1991), 'Increasing returns and economic geography', *Journal of Political Economy*, **99**: 483–99.

Krugman, P.R. and A.J. Venables (1995), 'Globalization and the inequality of nations', *Quarterly Journal of Economics*, **60**: 857–80.

Ottaviano, G.I.P. (2001), 'Monopolistic competition, trade and endogenous spatial fluctuations', *Regional Science and Urban Economics*, **31**: 51–77.

Ottaviano, G.I.P. and D. Pinelli (2005), 'Market potential and productivity: evidence from Finnish regions', University of Bologna, mimeo.

Ottaviano, G.I.P. and F. Robert-Nicoud (2005), 'The "genome" of NEG models with vertical linkages: a positive and normative synthesis', *Journal of Economic Geography*, **6**: 113–39.

Redding, S. and A. Venables (2004), 'Economic geography and international inequality', *Journal of International Economics*, **62**: 53–82.

Robert-Nicoud, F. (2005), 'The structure of simple "New Economic Geography" models (or, On identical twins)', *Journal of Economic Geography*, **5**: 201–34.

3. Testing the 'new economic geography': a comparative analysis based on EU regional data

Bernard Fingleton

3.1 INTRODUCTION

Interest in economic geography has been stimulated by the introduction of a formal general equilibrium 'new economic geography' (NEG) theory in which increasing returns to scale are an outcome of each agent solving a clearly defined economic problem within the context of a monopolistic competition market structure (Dixit and Stiglitz, 1977). Recents books, notably Fujita, Krugman and Venables (1999) and Brakman, Garretsen and van Marrewijk (2001), have helped to popularize these developments in geographical economics, and despite some cautious reactions (Neary, 2001), on the whole, NEG theorizing has been reasonably widely appreciated among the broader economics and regional science community, helping to establish at a formal level the role of increasing returns, which had long been seen as a key to understanding the spatial concentration of economic activity. Initially, theoretical developments were at the cutting edge of research activity, but more recently we have seen a growing literature aimed at operationalizing and testing NEG (see, for example, Combes and Lafourcade, 2001, 2004; Forslid, Haaland and Midelfart Knarvik, 2002; Combes and Overman, 2003; Head and Mayer, 2003; Rice and Venables, 2003; Redding and Venables, 2004). Among this literature is analysis relating to the so-called wage equation, which links nominal wages to market access or potential,[1] and which was initially studied by Hanson (1997, 1998) and more latterly by Roos (2001), Brakman, Garretsen and Schramm (2002), Mion (2003) and Niebuhr (2004). The present chapter also follows this strand of analysis.

This recent rigorous empirical work has raised some questions about the operationalization, scope and relevance of NEG theory, and in this heightened wave of constructive criticism, I follow Head and Ries (2001) and Davis and Weinstein (2003) by going beyond NEG model fitting, calibration and parameter estimation to examine the success of NEG in the face of a competing explanation. Although Leamer and Levinsohn's (1994) advice is to 'estimate don't test', it is this kind of direct confrontation that is seen as the acid test of whether a theory can be accepted as the superior explanation of empirical reality. In this spirit, the present chapter, building on the work in Fingleton (2003, 2005), confronts NEG with an alternative (simpler) model derived largely from the literature of urban economics (what is referred to as the UE model), to see which of the two provides a better explanation of variations in nominal wage rates across 200 EU regions.

Of course, it is somewhat artificial to consider the two theories as entirely separate. There is a developing literature in which the tenets of UE-style theory are embodied within NEG theory, given the growing acceptance of their relevance. Prominent examples of this hybrid style are Krugman and Venables (1995) and Venables (1996) who focus on intersectoral linkages; de Vaal and van den Berg (1999), who incorporate producer service linkages into an NEG model; and Redding and Venables (2004) and Amiti and Cameron (2004), who also give theory and estimates embodying intermediate inputs. However, for the purposes of exposition and clarity we retain a clear distinction between the two theories in our analysis below.

One issue of particular importance here is the fact that the two competing hypotheses are non-nested, meaning that one is not simply a restricted version of the other, comprising a subset of the explanatory variables. There is a wide literature on the most appropriate way to test non-nested hypotheses, which is not straightforward, and in this chapter I initially use the J test, in which fitted values of the competing model are added as a covariate to the maintained hypothesis model. The resulting t-ratio has a non-standard distribution so I use bootstrapping (following Davidson and MacKinnon, 2002a) in order to obtain appropriate reference distributions for the test statistic. Further evidence about the respective contributions of NEG and UE is provided by an artificial nesting model (ANM), which takes inspiration from the work of Davidson and MacKinnon (1993) and Hendry (1995), which combines both the UE and NEG perspectives in a single empirical model.

To summarize, in Section 3.2 of the chapter I briefly set out the basis of the relevant theoretical relationship coming from NEG theory, namely the wage equation linking nominal wages to market potential. Section 3.3 is concerned with an outline of the competing UE hypothesis. In Section 3.4, additional covariates are introduced as a necessary requirement for unbiased estimation, and in Section 3.5, estimation methods are considered and the initial model estimates presented. Section 3.6 describes the J test results, and Section 3.7 the results from using the ANM. Section 3.8 concludes.

## 3.2	THE NEG MODEL

The wage equation (3.1) is one of the set of simultaneous equations that are given by Fujita, Krugman and Venables (1999, pp. 53–5) that define the basic NEG theory. It links nominal wages (w_i^M) in the monopolistically competitive sector M to market access (P_i), where i denotes region. Note that this is a short-run equilibrium relationship based on an assumption that the migration response (say) to real wage differences is slow compared with the instantaneous entry and exit of firms in the M sector (usually taken to be industry) so that profits are immediately driven to zero. It is only in the very long run that we would expect movement to a stable long-run equilibrium resulting from labour migration:

$$w_i^M = P_i^{\frac{1}{\sigma}} \tag{3.1}$$

$$P_i = \sum_r Y_r (G_r^M)^{\sigma-1} (\bar{T}_{ir})^{1-\sigma}. \tag{3.2}$$

Equation (3.2) shows that P for region i depends on income levels, (Y_r), M prices (G_r^M) and transport costs from region i to r $(\bar{T}_{ir})$, where $\sigma > 1$ is the elasticity of substitution of M varieties, summing across all regions including i. The competitive sector C (normally characterized as 'agriculture') consists of goods that are freely transported and produced under constant returns, so that C wages w_i^C are constant across regions. We assume iceberg transport costs of the form:

$$\bar{T}_{ir} = e^{\tau \ln D_{ir}} \tag{3.3}$$

in which D_{ir} is the straight-line distance between regions i and r. Since some of the regions are quite large, it is infeasible to assume that internal distances are zero. The problem of internal distance estimation was first considered by Stewart (1947), whose solution underlies the convention (Head and Mayer, 2003) that $D_{ii} = 2/3 \sqrt{area_i / \pi}$ in which $area_i$ is area i's area in square miles.

The use of natural logarithm of distance rather than distance per se implies a power function, since $e^{\tau \ln D_{ir}} = D_{ir}^{\tau}$. This function is preferred because it is frequently seen to be superior in gravity model estimation of trade flows. I am unable to explore the most appropriate functional form or estimate τ because of the lack of trade data for small regions, so $\tau = 0.1$ is chosen by assumption. However, it seems reasonable in that it implies that if $D_{ir} = 100$ miles, the delivered price increases by a factor of 1.58, compared with, for example, a factor of 3.16 that would result from assuming

$\tau = 0.25$, which appears to be a very large increase over a relatively short distance. Also, with $\tau = 0.25$ we see that market potential P is very similar to the employment density E that is at the core of the competing UE model, so that both the competing reduced forms are very similar. Moreover, the NEG model with $\tau = 0.25$ causes the values of P for each region to be very much influenced by D_{ii}, and therefore P will be subject to the assumptions used to define D_{ii}.

The M price index G_i is given by:

$$G_i^M = \left[\sum_r \lambda_r (w_r^M e^{\tau \ln D_{ir}})^{1-\sigma} \right]^{\frac{1}{1-\sigma}} \qquad (3.4)$$

in which the number of varieties produced in region r is represented by λ_r, which is equal to the share in region r of the total supply of M workers. Income in region r is:

$$Y_r = \theta \lambda_r w_r^M + (1 - \theta)\phi_r w_r^C. \qquad (3.5)$$

In order to estimate equation (3.3), I use the share of C workers in each region (ϕ_r), and the share of M workers (λ_r), and the expenditure share of M goods (θ) is taken as the overall share of total employment in 2000 that is engaged in M activities, assuming also that θ is also the total M workers and $1 - \theta$ is the total C workers using a suitable metric that equates the overall number of workers to 1.

The conventional assumption[2] is that industry is the M sector and 'agriculture' is the competitive (C) sector, where agriculture means all other sectors in which there is no trade cost, so that under basic NEG theory C goods are freely transported and produced under constant returns, and C wages w_i^C are constant across regions. Monopolistic competition on the other hand implies the production of differentiated varieties under internal increasing returns to scale, with very many myopic producers and no strategic interaction between firms. However, the notion that this market structure applies to industry has been questioned by Neary (2001), who argues that oligopoly may be a better description for industry, with relatively few firms and strategic interaction such as the erection of barriers to entry. Accepting that industry may not be well described by the monopolistic competition market structure, I make an initial simplifying assumption that 'industry' is competitive, with constant returns to scale and prices set on world markets. By industry I mean all sectors other than market services, in other words, non-market services, agriculture, construction, energy and manufacturing. On the other hand I make the assumption that it is the market service sector that is better described by monopolistic competition, although, of course, there are numerous exceptions.

The idea here is that the urban economy is typified by many small service firms producing differentiated varieties under internal increasing returns to scale. This choice is also based on the precedence set in the earlier UE literature (Rivera-Batiz, 1988; Abdel-Rahman and Fujita, 1990). The assumption is that with free entry and exit to the sector and profits continually being driven to zero, there are numerous start-ups so that fixed start-up costs are a prominent part of many firms' costs structure, and their small equilibrium size means that internal economies do not become negligible. For example, assume that typical firm t has a single input, labour (L), so that its total cost function is $L = s + am(t)$ in which the fixed labour requirement is s and the marginal labour requirement a, and the equilibrium output is $m(t)$. Although as $m(t)$ increases, returns to scale (defined as average cost divided by marginal cost) fall asymptotically to 1, typically $m(t)$ is small. Hence, it seems reasonable to choose a 'sector' typified by small firms using labour as a predominant input, firms freely entering and leaving the market and competitive pressure giving a zero profit equilibrium. However, the assumption that market services are the M sector and 'industry' is the C sector is not crucial to the results or arguments of the chapter. It turns out that when we assume instead that the M sector is 'industry', and market services are the C sector, very similar estimates are obtained that do not alter the conclusions.

Defining the M sector enables us to obtain quantities for ϕ_r, λ_r and θ, but in order to calculate equation (3.1) it is also necessary to have data on wage rates w_i^M in the M sector and wages w^C for the C sector. Unfortunately these data are not available, and I have therefore used the overall wage level (w_i^o) as a proxy for w_i^M (see Figure 3.1). The basis of the empirical analysis is therefore annual compensation by NUTS 2 region, data that are produced by Cambridge Econometrics (CE) using the EUROSTAT REGIO database and EUROSTAT national accounts. In the theory, C wages do not vary with region, and I approximate them by assuming that $w^C = MEAN(w_r^o)$. Allowance is made subsequently for the measurement errors these assumptions introduce into our analysis.

For the UK part of the EU compensation data, I use a more credible source of compensation data, namely the New Earnings Survey (NES)[3], giving regional weekly wage rates in pounds sterling. This follows from the fact that the compensation in euros provided in the CE database is an exact linear function of total GVA per worker, so I prefer to replace this by the direct survey data of the NES. Compatibility with the other EU regions was achieved by multiplying each region's NES wage rate by the ratio of overall UK annual euro compensation per employee to the UK

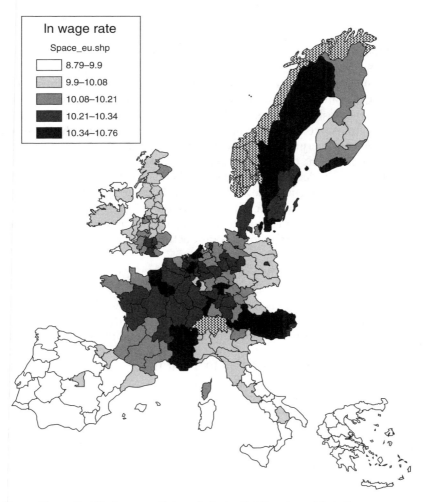

In wage rate

Space_eu.shp

- ☐ 8.79–9.9
- ▨ 9.9–10.08
- ▨ 10.08–10.21
- ▨ 10.21–10.34
- ■ 10.34–10.76

Note: The spotted black area on the map indicates that there is no data in these areas.

Figure 3.1 Wage rates by EU NUTS 2 regions

overall weekly wage rate.[4] The resulting euros wage data for UK regions gives a total UK wage bill that is exactly equal to the total in the CE data-base. In fact, using the entire CE compensation dataset has a negligible effect on the results obtained. In exactly the same way, the German compensation data for NUTS 2 regions is obtained by scaling the NUTS 1 region wage by the ratio of the output per worker in the NUTS 1 and NUTS 2 regions.

3.3 THE UE MODEL

The UE model is the same as that set out in Fingleton (2003), following Rivera-Batiz (1988); Abdel-Rahman and Fujita (1990) and Ciccone and Hall (1996), so in order to save space I simply sketch its main features here. The model again divides the economy into an M and a C sector, with the same characteristics as outlined above, and under the model the M sector provides inputs to C's production, which have the effect that, subject to congestion effects, internal scale economies in the M sector translate into external economies to the C sector that are increasing in the density of economic activity. This then leads to a reduced form with wages as a function of the density of employment in the area, and thus in this way we have a competing (UE) hypothesis for regional wage variation.

To see this in a little more detail, assume that the production technology for the C sector is a Cobb-Douglas production function:

$$Q = (E(C)^\beta I^{1-\beta})^\alpha L^{1-\alpha} = [f(E)]^\alpha L^{1-\alpha} \qquad (3.6)$$

in which L is land, $E(C)$ is the level of C labour units, $E = E(C) + E(M)$, and I is the level of composite services (I) derived from the M sector, determined by a CES sub-production function under monopolistic competition. Production is per unit of land, hence $L = 1$, and from this it is possible to show (Fujita and Thisse, 2002, p. 102) that the level of C production is defined by the total number of labour units E (in both C and M sectors), in this case per unit area, thus:

$$Q = (E(C)^\beta I^{1-\beta})^\alpha = \phi E^\gamma \qquad (3.7)$$

in which ϕ is a function of other constants and γ is the elasticity where:

$$\gamma = \alpha[1 + (1 - \beta)(\mu - 1)]. \qquad (3.8)$$

Equation (3.7) therefore, captures increasing returns to the density of activity given by E, reflecting the increased variety of M services, so long as $\gamma > 1$. In equation (3.8) $\mu > 1$ reflects the market power of the M firms and defines the elasticity of substitution and price elasticity of demand, so that a larger value of μ means that there are larger internal returns to scale and lower elasticities, leading to a larger value for γ. Equation (3.8) shows that whether or not we see increasing returns ($\gamma > 1$) depends on services being sufficiently important to final production, which is indexed by the magnitude of $\beta < 1$, and on the amount of internal scale economies to producer services ($\mu > 1$). It also depends on congestion effects ($1 - \alpha < 1$) being sufficiently small so as not to overcome the other two factors (Ciccone and Hall, 1996).

The direct comparability of the UE and NEG models depends on both acting as competing explanations for nominal wage rates. For the UE model, the wage rate is the outcome of assuming an equilibrium allocation of production factors so that the coefficient α is equal to the share of Q that goes to E (rather than the other factor L), in other words using standard equilibrium theory and equating the wage rate to the marginal product of labour, we obtain:

$$w = \frac{\alpha Q}{E} \tag{3.9}$$

Substituting into equation (3.7), we obtain:

$$\ln(w) = \ln(\alpha\phi) + (\gamma - 1)\ln(E). \tag{3.10}$$

It is apparent that the UE hypothesis makes no reference to market potential (see Figure 3.2), which depends on transport costs, transport cost mediated price index variations and income variations across regions. The position of a region in relation to other regions is of no consequence, and it is the internal conditions within each region that are important. Both theories depend on Dixit-Stiglitz monopolistic competition theory, but the M variety elasticity of substitution $\sigma = \mu/(\mu - 1)$ only enters the UE reduced form (3.10) via the 'returns to scale' parameter γ; in contrast in NEG σ appears in various ways. It is both the coefficient on P in the reduced form (3.1), and it also determines P, crucially controlling the magnitude of distance cost effects via $\bar{T}_{ir}^{1-\sigma}$.

3.4   THE EXTENDED MODEL SPECIFICATIONS

In modelling the wage data, under NEG theory market access (P) is the principal explanatory variable, but there are also other ancillary effects that also need to be taken account of in order to allow unbiased estimation. Similarly, under UE theory the wage rates depend primarily on the density of employment (Figure 3.3) (E), but will in practice depend also on other factors. I assume that for both hypotheses one of the principal causes of wage rate differences between regions is regional variation in labour efficiency, which is assumed to depend on schooling (S) and on technical skills (T) acquired at the place of work. In the analysis below

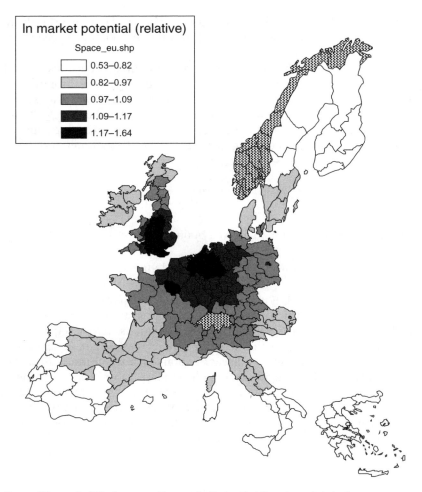

Note: The spotted black area on the map indicates that there is no data in these areas.

Figure 3.2   Market potential

I therefore include the variables S and T to capture efficiency variations across the EU regions.

The schooling variable S is the share of the population aged 25–59 with a high level of educational attainment in 1999, as provided for EU NUTS 2 regions by Eurostat's Labour Force Survey (see Figure 3.4). The technical skill variable T is represented by the International Patent Classification patents per capita (averaged over 1985–95) by EU NUTS 2 region that is

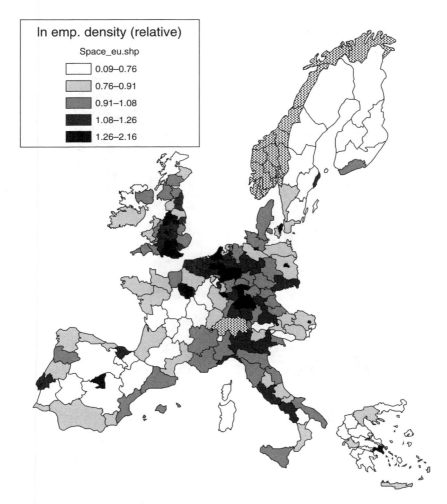

Note: The spotted black area on the map indicates that there is no data in these areas.

Figure 3.3 Employment density

available from REGIO, which broadly reflects regional variations in R&D activity and therefore workers with computing and information technology skills (Figure 3.5). Full technical details of data availability, definitions and methodologies are given in the *Regions: Statistical Yearbook* published by the Office for Official Publications of the European Communities. First I discuss in more detail what these variables imply by comparing them with supplementary data available for the United Kingdom.

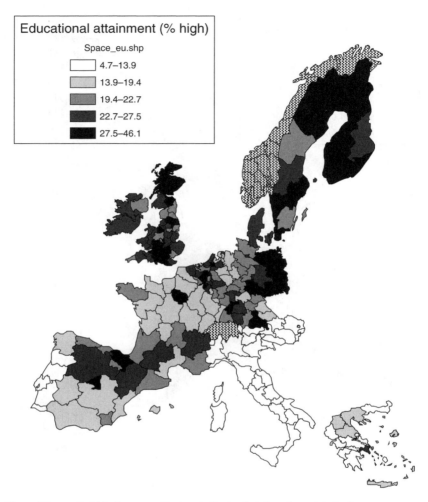

Note: The spotted black area on the map indicates that there is no data in these areas.

Figure 3.4 Educational attainment

Pan-European educational attainment measures are undoubtedly subject to variations due to varying national standards. Moreover, there may be doubt that the labour force survey data measures educational attainment with sufficient accuracy. In fact, we get a good indication of the quality of the data used by comparing it with UK census data on the proportion of the population (aged 18 and over) with no educational qualifications.[5] The (Pearson product moment) correlation between the 1991 NUTS 2 census

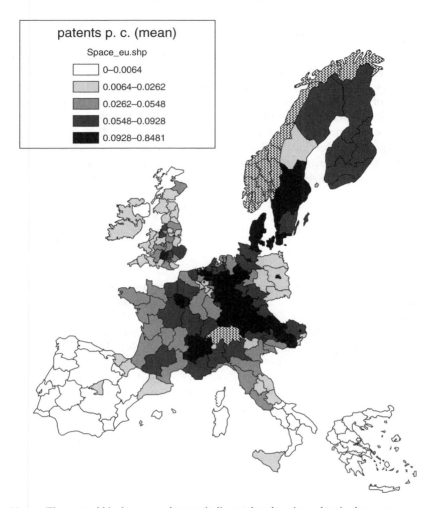

patents p. c. (mean)

Space_eu.shp

☐ 0–0.0064
▨ 0.0064–0.0262
▨ 0.0262–0.0548
▨ 0.0548–0.0928
■ 0.0928–0.8481

Note: The spotted black area on the map indicates that there is no data in these areas.

Figure 3.5   Patents per capita

data on the shares with no qualifications and the NUTS 2 level pan-European labour force survey data indicator (S) is equal to -0.948.

Similarly, our interpretation of IPC patents per capita as a proxy for T is supported by a fairly strong correlation ($r = 0.654$) at the UK NUTS 2 level, with the location quotient based on data from the year 2000 annual business enquiry employee analysis for the two-digit sectors 72 (computing and related activities) and 73 (research and development). The assumption is that the workers in these sectors have a high level of computing and related skills, which enhances their efficiency.

I also assume that there are various national-level factors relating to differences between countries in labour efficiency, which I capture by country-specific dummy variables. However, these dummy variables undoubtedly also represent the net effect of various other country-specific effects, such as any remaining differences in employment law and minimum wages, working hours regulations and exchange rates, and so on, so that the national dummies are in effect catch-all variables helping to account for a large portion of the variance in wage rates and hopefully ruling out mis-specification bias due to omitted variables. The final specifications are therefore:

$$\text{H1:NEG } \ln w^0 = b_0 + b_1 \ln P + b_2 S + b_3 T + dummies + \xi \qquad (3.11)$$

$$\text{H2:UE } \ln w^0 = c_0 + c_1 \ln E + c_2 S + c_3 T + dummies + \psi. \qquad (3.12)$$

There are other wage equation specifications that these can be related to. For instance, analysing data for smaller area units than the NUTS 2 regions used here, one may wish to explicitly include the effects of commuting in the model, as in Fingleton (2003, 2005), allowing the level of worker efficiency in an area to depend on workers resident outside the local area. More generally, a wage equation falls out from the version of NEG theory developed by Helpman (1998) and Hanson (1998). While this has essentially the same micro-foundations as Fujita et al. (1999), a non-tradable consumption good (housing services) replaces the perfectly traded competitive sector (or 'agriculture' in Fujita et al., 1999). Brakman, Garretsen and Schramm (2004) develop this approach, creating reduced forms quite similar to equation (3.11), including district-specific control variables (dummies) comparable to the variables S, T and the dummy variables used here. With regard to equation (3.12), similar specifications are the outcome of adding variables equivalent in effect to S, T and the dummy variables to the basic UE specification, linking wage rates with employment density. Combes, Duranton and Gobillon. (2004) for example, exploit a large database to control for worker skill differences, emphasizing the effect of endogenous interactions (skilled workers attracted to high wages as well as high wages dependent on skilled workers) and the role of amenity difference between areas.

Clearly there are other variables that could be introduced to sharpen the models or replace the variables actually used. For instance Niebuhr (2004) uses the share of total population with qualifications or work experience in science and technology occupations, and also introduces variables such as local amenities (climate etc.), sectoral composition (GVA shares in markets services, etc.) and border effects. For instance, it might be argued that technological externalities have been omitted, with the exception of the inclusion of congestion effects in the UE model. There is a growing body of evidence that other un-priced factors will also affect productivity and wage rates, notably as a result of spillover effects relating to knowledge and its enhanced rate of generation and transmission (see, for example, Audretsch and Feldman, 1996 and Breschi and Lissoni, 2001). The essential idea here is that firms investing in knowledge production will be unable to capture the benefits of their investment completely, which will spill over as external economies to other free-riding firms employing skill-enhanced job-migrants. I therefore assume that the presence of a high proportion of workers who are associated with research and development, knowledge generation and production and transmission, as represented by the variables S and T, will be associated with additional externalities that boost labour efficiency levels and wage rates, capturing in an indirect way the more elusive technological externalities associated with knowledge flows. These spillovers are likely to be primarily confined within local labour market areas within the EU, since job-migration is much easier than household migration, for various cultural and economic reasons.

3.5. INITIAL MODELS: ESTIMATION METHODS AND RESULTS

Table 3.1 shows the 2sls estimates of the NEG model, augmented by labour efficiency variables and the catch-all country dummies. To obtain these, an assumed value of $\sigma = 12$ has been used to construct P_i. Alternative assumptions give similar results, but this assumption maximizes the level of fit of this model over the range of alternatives assumed. A smaller value for σ results in a 'flatter' market potential surface, which has less explanatory power when faced with the wage rate surface (see Figures 3.1, 3.2). The higher the value of σ, the higher the trade costs and the more undulating is the market potential surface, which at the extreme (say $\sigma = 20$) looks very similar to the employment density surface, so it is very difficult to disentangle their relative influences as they are effectively the 'same' model. To save space these alternative estimates, and corresponding (inconsistent) OLS estimates have not been reported, but similar results to those presented here are obtained. The R-squared and correlation of observed and fitted values indicate that the model as designated here provides a reasonably accurate account of the observed data.

The instruments used in the first stage of 2sls are the exogenous variables in the model, in other words the variables S and T and D_i^c, which is the country dummy for country i, so there are 14 of these for 15 countries. As

Table 3.1   NEG and UE model estimates

Parameter	2sls Estimates[a]		2sls Estimates[a]
	NEG model[e] $\sigma = 12$		UE model[e]
Constant (b_0)	9.9567		10.0873
	(97.19)		(133.98)
Log mkt.pot. (ln P_i)	0.1418	Emp. density	0.0798
($b_1 = 1/\sigma$)	(3.72)	ln E (c_1)	(3.49)
Schooling S_i (b_2)	0.0130		0.0090
	(7.98)		(3.90)
Tech.know. T_i (b_3)	0.3642		0.1784
	(3.59)		(1.30)
Error variance (Ω^2)	0.009189		0.01071
R-squared[c]	0.9570		0.9316
Correlation[b]	0.9414		0.9316
Degrees of freedom	182		182
Residual autocorrelation[d] (z)	0.1746		1.091

Notes:
a.   These models also include 14 national dummy variables, but these estimates are of limited interest and have been omitted.
b.   The square of the Pearson product moment correlation between observed and fitted values of the dependent variable.
c.   Given by var ($\hat{Y}$)/var (Y), where Y is the dependent variable.
d.   The Anselin and Kelejian (1997) test for residual correlation with endogenous variables and without endogenous lag, using the contiguity matrix.
e.   Defining M as manufacturing and construction (or 'industry') and all other sectors as C produces fitted values that are almost identical to those given by this model, with the Pearson product moment correlation coefficient equaling 0.9998.

is standard practice in spatial econometrics (Kelejian and Robinson, 1993 and Kelejian and Prucha, 1998), extra instruments are obtained by using the first and second spatial lags of the exogenous variables. The exogenous spatial lags WS, WT and WD_i are the result of multiplying variable S, T and D_i^c by the standardized contiguity matrix[6] W, which is derived from the 200 by 200 contiguity matrix W^*, hence:

$$W_{ij}^* = 1, \quad i \longleftrightarrow j$$

$$W_{ij}^* = 0, \textit{ otherwise}$$

$$W_{ij} = \frac{W_{ij}^*}{\sum_j W_{ij}^*} \tag{3.13}$$

in which $\leftrightarrow$ indicates that regions i and j are contiguous. In other words, cell i of vector WS, for example, is the weighted average of S in regions that are contiguous to region i, with weights equal to the reciprocal of the number of regions contiguous to i. The second spatial lags are the result of multiplying the first spatial lags by W, hence these are $W^2 S$, $W^2 T$ and $W^2 D_i^c$. The resulting 2sls estimates are given in Table 3.1.

Table 3.1 shows that the estimated value $\hat{\sigma} = 1/0.1418 = 7.0522$. This differs from the assumed value of 12 used to construct P_i, but 12 lies within the approximate 95 per cent confidence interval of 4.59 to 15.25 for $\hat{\sigma}$.

The results of fitting the competing model H2:UE given by equation (3.12) are also given in Table 3.1. The 2sls estimates are obtained in almost precisely the same way as for the NEG model, but in this case it is employment density (E) that is instrumented to allow for any endogeneity caused by employment levels depending on wage rates. I use the same set of instruments as for equation (3.11). The coefficient estimate $\hat{c}_1 = 0.0798$ means that $\hat{\gamma} = 1.0798$, implying increasing returns to scale. The estimated elasticity on employment density $\gamma - 1$ indicates that doubling city density causes wages to rise by about $\ln(2^{0.0798}) = 5.5$ per cent. Overall, Table 3.1 shows that H2:UE performs almost equally as well as H1:NEG in explaining the variation in wage rates.

3.6.   PRELIMINARY ANALYSIS : THE J TEST
RESULTS

The two competing models of Table 3.1 both account for almost the same proportion of wage rates variance, and both show that either $\ln P$ or $\ln E$ are significant. However, the hypotheses are non-nested, in other words the explanatory variables of one are not a subset of the explanatory variables of the other, so it is not possible to simply test the models by restricting parameters. In general, with non-nested hypotheses, inferential methods used to test nested hypotheses becomes inappropriate (Cox, 1961, 1962; Pesaran, 1974; Pesaran and Deaton, 1978). In order to overcome this problem, I initially use the comparatively simple[7] Davidson and MacKinnon (1981, 1982) J test applied to 2sls estimation. This involves estimating the H2:UE model to obtain fitted values $\ln \hat{w}_{UE}^o$, which are then added as an auxiliary variable to the maintained H1:NEG model, giving equation (3.14). If the coefficient on the added variable is not significantly different from expectation under the maintained hypothesis, then we do not reject H1. However, the non-symmetry of the test means that rejecting H1 does not imply that H2 is true, and vice versa. It could turn out that both H1 and H2 are falsified. We also need to test the opposite case, first estimating H1:NEG to obtain the fitted values $\ln \hat{w}_{NEG}^o$, which then becomes an auxiliary variable under the maintained H2:UE model, as in equation (3.15):

$$\ln w^o = b_0 + b_1 \ln P + b_2 S + b_3 T + b_4 \ln \hat{w}_{UE}^o + dummies + \xi \quad (3.14)$$

$$\ln w^o = c_0 + c_1 \ln E + c_2 S + c_3 T + c_4 \ln \hat{w}_{NEG}^o + dummies + \psi. \quad (3.15)$$

One problem with this approach is that the reference distributions for the t-ratios on the auxiliary fitted variables $\ln \hat{w}_{NEG}^o$ and $\ln \hat{w}_{UE}^o$ are unknown, and not simply $N(0,1)$, which tends to over-reject the null. Fan and Li (1995), Godfrey (1998), MacKinnon (2002) and Davidson and MacKinnon (2002a, b) suggest the bootstrap J test to obtain a better measure of the true size of the J test, and this has been suggested by Godfrey (1983) and Pesaran and Weeks (1999) for non-nested linear regressions estimated[8] by 2sls. Taking H1:NEG as the maintained hypothesis, for example, I first use 2sls to fit equation (3.14) to obtain:

$$\hat{J}_1 = \frac{\hat{b}_4}{s.e.(\hat{b}_4)} \quad (3.16)$$

and then refer this statistic to its reference distribution obtained by resampling the residuals[9] under the maintained hypothesis.

The left hand side of Table 3.2 gives the result of fitting equation (3.14), with $\sigma = 12$ and with $\ln \hat{w}_{UE}^o$ the outcome of fitting equation (3.12) (as summarized by the 2sls estimates in Table 3.1). For the reference distribution I randomly re-sample with replacement from the vector of residuals produced by the maintained hypothesis H1:NEG. To achieve this, commencing with the equation (3.11) estimates, I calculate the 2sls residual vector $\hat{\xi} = \ln \hat{w}^o - \ln w^o$ and resample this B^* times to give $\hat{\xi}_B$, where $B = 1 \ldots B^*$ denotes the bootstrap sample number. From this I calculate, for $B = 1 \ldots B^*$, $\ln w_B^o = A\hat{b} + \hat{\xi}_B$, in which A is an n by k matrix with columns 1, $\ln P$, S, T and the 14 country dummies and $\hat{b}$ is the k by 1 vector of 2sls estimates given by Table 3.1, plus the coefficients for the country dummies. First the resulting vectors $\ln w_B^o (B = 1 \ldots B^*)$ are used as the dependent variable to estimate the UE model equation (3.12) by 2sls, which provides fitted values $\ln \hat{w}_B^o$. Second I obtain the set of B^* t-ratios ($\hat{J}_1 s$) by introducing $\ln \hat{w}_B^o$ (in place of $\ln \hat{w}_{UE}^o$) as the ancillary variable in equation (3.14), which is estimated by 2sls. The $B^* \hat{J}_1 s$ are an appropriate reference distribution for testing the significance of the t-ratio given as 6.92 in Table 3.2.

Figure 3.6 shows the $\hat{J}$ reference distribution for $B^* = 999$, which clearly illustrates how the t or $N(0,1)$ distribution would lead to over-rejection of the maintained hypothesis. The reference distribution has a mean equal

Table 3.2   J test results: NEG and UE as maintained hypothesis

Parameter Maintained	2sls Estimates NEG model $\sigma = 12$		2sls Estimates UE model $\sigma = 12$
Constant (b_0)	3.6272		−0.8090
	(3.97)		(−0.45)
Log mkt.pot. ($\ln P_i$)	0.0883	Emp. density	0.0550
($b_1 = 1/\sigma$)	(2.35)	$\ln E\,(c_1)$	(2.51)
Schooling $S_i\,(b_2)$	0.0037		−0.0051
	(1.81)		(−1.59)
Tech.know. $T_i\,(b_3)$	0.1120		−0.2336
	(1.07)		(−1.60)
$\ln \hat{w}^o{}_{UE}\,(b_4)$	0.6240	$\ln \hat{w}^o{}_{NEG}\,(C_4)$	1.0623
	(6.92)		(6.01)
Error variance (Ω^2)	0.008582		0.009522
R-squared	0.9681		0.9730
Correlation	0.9456		0.9398
Degrees of freedom	181		181

to 2.367 and variance equal to 3.990, hence 6.92 would be an extreme occurrence under the maintained hypothesis. We therefore have quite strong evidence that H1:NEG should be rejected:

$$\hat{J}_2 = \frac{\hat{c}_4}{s.e.(\hat{c}_4)}. \tag{13.17}$$

While we have rejected H1 using H2, this does not imply that H2 is true, and it is entirely possible that H2 could be rejected by H1, in which case neither NEG nor UE would be acceptable. In order to test this proposition, I therefore treat H2:UE as the maintained hypothesis and look at the significance of $\ln \hat{w}^o_{NEG}$ in equation (3.15), where $\ln \hat{w}^o_{NEG}$ is the vector of fitted values given by equation (3.11). The resulting estimates of equation (3.15) are in the right-hand side of Table 3.2. This shows the outcome produced by adding the fitted values $\ln \hat{w}^o_{NEG}$ given by Table 3.1 ($\sigma = 12$).

The $\hat{J}_2$ reference distribution is obtained using the same method as for $\hat{J}_1$. In this case we generate residuals from which to randomly resample under the maintained UE hypothesis from $\ln w^o_B = A\hat{b} + \hat{\Psi}_B$, in which A is an n by k matrix with columns 1, $\ln E$, S, T and the 14 country dummies and $\hat{b}$ is the k by 1 vector of estimates given by Table 3.1. Hence, the vectors $\ln w^o_B (B = 1 \ldots B^*)$ lead to the $\hat{J}_2$ reference distribution. For $\sigma = 12$, the $\hat{J}_2$ reference distribution is given in Figure 3.7; this has a mean equal to 6.100 and variance equal to 2.218, so the observed t-ratio of 6.01 is very close to

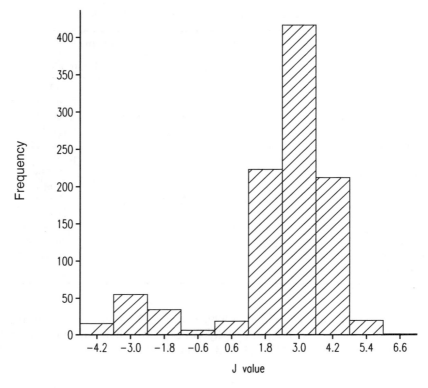

Figure 3.6 The $\hat{J}_1$ reference distribution: NEG is the maintained hypothesis

the expected value and with an upper tail probability of 0.588 could have been generated by randomly re-sampling the residuals from the maintained model.

To summarize the J test analysis, the evidence I have presented thus far suggests that the UE model is capable of falsifying the NEG model, but the NEG model does not have additional explanatory power given to the UE model, and therefore does not falsify it. We next look for supplementary evidence from the ANM.

3.7   RESULTS OBTAINED USING THE ARTIFICIAL NESTING MODEL

The rival NEG and UE models are non-nested, and so do not have the property that constraining some parameters to zero reduces from one to the

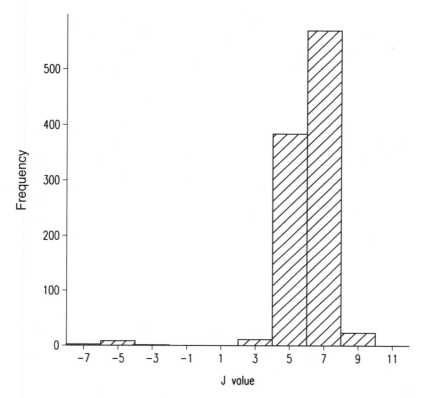

Figure 3.7 The $\hat{\jmath}_2$ *reference distribution: UE is the maintained hypothesis*

other, as would be typical of nested models. In order to achieve some analytical tractability for non-nested models, Hendry (1995) advocates an assumed data generating rocess[10] (DGP), of which non-nested rival models are special cases. The problem of deciding between the rivals is approached by looking at whether any one of the rivals encompasses the DGP, where to encompass a model means that its results can be explained by the encompassing model. If model A encompasses the DGP, then it explains the results of the DGP. Since the DGP nests model B, the DGP explains the data generated by model B. The inference is that model A explains model B.

Building on these ideas, I use the term artificial nesting model (ANM) to describe an empirical model that nests the rival NEG and UE models, and test whether there is a loss of information in restricting the ANM and reducing to either of the UE and NEG models. Rather than theoretically distinct hypotheses, with the ANM we assume that wage rates depend jointly on market potential (P_j), producer services input linkages (density of employment E_i) and on labour efficiency, together with the national effects represented by the country dummies. This is referred to as an artificial model since it is simply an empirical construct, it presages the development of formal theory that combines these separate perspectives:

$$\ln w^o = d_0 + d_1 \ln P + d_2 \ln E + d_3 S + d_4 T + dummies + u. \quad (3.18)$$

The left-hand side of Table 3.3 shows 2sls estimates assuming $\sigma = 12$. The indication is that both market potential and employment density are significant, and there is a highly significant schooling effect, although T_i is insignificant. However, the presence of significant residual spatial autocorrelation suggests some kind of mis-specification error. We choose to handle this by means of GMM (generalized method of moments) estimation (Kelejian and Prucha, 1999). Therefore, the model is the ANM as described above but with the added error process:

$$u = \lambda W u + \zeta$$

$$E(\zeta) = 0, \text{var}(\zeta) = \bar{\omega}^2.$$

For the purposes of estimation, we replace the potentially endogenous variables P_i and E_i by their non-stochastic exogenous instruments, and take care to base the estimation of the spatial autoregressive parameter λ and the square root of the error variance $\bar{\omega}$ on the appropriate 2sls residuals, which define the sample moments used for estimation. These allow unconstrained non-linear least squares estimation and an iterative solution with, at each iteration, the estimator of λ allowing calculation of the feasible GLS estimator of the vector of coefficients d. The estimator of $\bar{\omega}$ also allows estimation of the asymptotic variance-covariance matrix and therefore approximate t-ratios for the estimated d. The non-linear estimation uses a modified Newton-Raphson method, which is suitable for minimizing any non-linear function and this depends on numerical differences, so there is no need to specify derivatives. There is no variance estimator available to test the null $\lambda = 0$, but we obtain an informal indication by simulation methods. The method involves combining the GMM parameter estimates from Table 3.3 and the regressors, but also adding on an error term equal to $(I - \hat{\lambda} W)^{-1} v$, sampling at random from the distribution $v \sim N(0, \bar{\omega}^2)$. Although not required for GMM estimation, we have to be specific about the form of the distribution to do this simulation. For iteration k, this produces a vector of values of the quasi-dependent variable y_k^* and GMM estimates are obtained for $k = 1 \ldots K$. Doing this for $K = 1000$ gives standard deviations, which are quite similar to those given in Table 3.3, as shown by Table 3.4. Now that we also have standard deviations for the K values of λ,

Table 3.3   ANM estimates ($\sigma = 12$)

Parameter	2sls Estimates	GMM Estimates Spatial Errors	ML Spatial Errors
Constant (b_0)	9.8845	9.9006	9.8937
	(93.56)	(93.76)	(89.32)
Log mkt.pot. (ln P_i)	0.1035	0.0981	0.1006
($b_1 = 1/\sigma$)	(2.55)	(2.45)	(2.38)
Emp. Density	0.0591	0.0552	0.0570
ln E (c_1)	(2.62)	(2.61)	(2.48)
Schooling S_i (b_2)	0.0093	0.0103	0.0098
	(4.36)	(5.05)	(4.48)
Tech.know. T_i (b_3)	0.1640	0.1449	0.1554
	(1.30)	(1.22)	(1.20)
Error parameter λ	----------	0.200957	0.09400
			(1.030)
Error variance (Ω^2)	0.009107	0.007958	0.009389
Log likelihood	----------	----------	182.8045
R-squared	0.9781	----------	----------
Correlation	0.9425	0.9428	0.9336
Degrees of freedom	181	180	180
Residual autocorrelation (z)	2.354	----------	----------

Table 3.4   Standard error estimates

Parameter	GMM Estimates ANM $\sigma = 12$
Constant (b_0)	9.9006
s.e. from Table 3.3	0.1056
1000 replications	0.1098
Log mkt.pot. (ln P_i)	0.0981
s.e. from Table 3.3	0.0400
1000 replications	0.04107
Emp. density	0.0552
s.e. from Table 3.3	0.0212
1000 replications	0.02235
Schooling S_i (b_2)	0.0103
s.e. from Table 3.3	0.0020
1000 replications	0.002098
Tech.know. T_i (b_3)	0.1449
s.e. from Table 3.3	0.1191
1000 replications	0.1230
Error parameter λ	0.200957
s.e. from Table 3.3	-------------
1000 replications	0.1292

and the ratio of λ to its standard deviation suggests that it is not significantly different from 0. Also given in Table 3.3 are maximum likelihood estimates, which also assume a normal distribution for ζ.

The results in the centre and on the right-hand side of Table 3.3 show that controlling for nuisance error autocorrelation does not make much difference to the results obtained. What we do find is that both market potential (P_i) and density of employment (E_i) retain their significance, and this allows us to conclude that market potential does not dominate the employment density effect. On the other hand, somewhat in contrast to the J test results, neither does employment density dominate market potential. It appears that we need both variables.

3.8   CONCLUSIONS

Usually one model is formulated and tested against data, and it is rarely if ever the case that competing models are tested against each other as in this chapter (see Fingleton, 2005, 2006). The contention in this chapter is that this is an appropriate way to proceed to rigorously test theory, and superior to simply calibrating models in an uncontested modelling environment. A successful theory should perform better when faced with data than do competing theories. In this chapter I show that an econometric model motivated by NEG theory accounts for a large proportion of the variation in wage rates across 200 NUTS 2 regions of the EU. However, it is also the case that a competing non-nested model based on UE theory performs equally as well in accounting for the data, and when we directly confront the two competing hypotheses, there is evidence that the NEG model is falsified by the UE model. This is the conclusion arrived at via preliminary investigations using the J test. However, under the ANM, both employment density and market potential show up as significant variables.

Overall, it appears that both UE theory and NEG theory have a lot to offer in explaining wage rate variations across the EU. The data supports both theories, without producing a knockout blow that allows one to dismiss one entirely, or be completely convinced by the other. Interestingly, a different conclusion is arrived at when more micro-level data are considered (Fingleton, 2006). In this case, an augmented UE model outperforms an NEG model of wage rate variations across local areas of Great Britain. This suggests that different scales of analysis call for different models. Additionally, the chapter also shows that efficiency variations are a significant factor, coming through particularly via the educational attainment variable, and also probably being picked up by the catch-all national dummy variables. These effects are omitted from basic NEG theory and from the standard form of UE theory as presented in much of the literature, presumably because they are somewhat messy facts that get in the way of theoretical elegance and are lacking explicit theoretical provenance. Although to save space other specifications omitting national dummies and the covariates are not reported, it is the case that reduced models such as these are seriously mis-specified. Even when the additional covariates are included, it is shown that both the purely NEG-driven and the purely UE-driven specifications are inadequate. The conclusion is that neither the NEG nor the UE theory provides a satisfactory account of the EU-wide data. When looking at the variegated patterns associated with these regions, there evidently is a need to incorporate the joint effects of market potential and of producer services input linkages, together with the effects of efficiency variations across regions, plus country dummies that are accounting for national differences across a range of variables. In the light of empirical evidence presented here, it appears that a new wave of more realistic hybrid models, combining elements of both NEG and UE theory, and allowing other covariates to have a role, will be a fruitful way to make progress in spatial economic analysis, and permit a fuller evaluation of the real explanatory power of our major contemporary theories.

NOTES

1. Harris (1954) was the first to use a variant of the market potential concept.
2. Manufacturing is assumed to have increasing returns to scale in many theoretical and applied papers, for example, Forslid et al. (2002) use evidence from the presence of scale economies in different industrial sectors provided by Pratten (1988).
3. This is an annual employer-based survey carried out by the Office of National Statistics. The data are gross weekly pay for male and female full-time workers irrespective of occupation, and are available on the NOMIS website (the Office for National Statistics' online labour market statistics database).
4. Equal to pounds per week times employment for each region to give the overall UK wage bill, then divided by total UK employment.
5. Unfortunately at the time of writing we only have access to the 1991 census data at the NUTS 2 level, which is a 10 per cent sample provided by the NOMIS database. In order to justify our correlation of S with 1991 UK census data, we observe that at a different level of spatial resolution the 1991 and 2001 censuses give essentially the 'same' distribution. Comparing the 1991 and 2001 shares with no qualifications for the 408 unitary authority and local authority districts in Great Britain, we find that while the average population share with no qualifications has fallen dramatically, there exists a strong linear correlation ($r = 0.872$) between the 1991 and 2001 census data sets.
6. This matrix is also used throughout for the spatial autocorrelation tests.
7. There is an extensive literature dedicated to non-nested hypothesis tests, including the Mizon and Richard (1986) encompassing test, although none are as straightforward as the J test.

8. Davidson and MacKinnon (2002a) show why bootstrapping the J test almost always works well compared with the ordinary J test, even when assumptions of normal errors and exogenous regressors do not hold.
9. Davidson and MacKinnon (2002a) recommend scaling the residuals by multiplying by $\sqrt{n/(n-k)}$, but with $n = 200$ and $k = 18$; this amounts to 1.048, which has a negligible effect.
10. This does not mean that the assumed DGP is the true mechanism generating the data, which remains unknown.

REFERENCES

Abdel-Rahman, H. and M. Fujita (1990), 'Product variety, Marshallian externalities and city size', *Journal of Regional Science*, **30**: 165–83.
Amiti, M. and L. Cameron (2004), 'Economic geography and wages', *Discussion Paper 4234*, Centre for Economic Policy Research, London.
Anselin, L. and H.H. Kelejian (1997), 'Testing for spatial error autocorrelation in the presence of endogenous regressors', *International Regional Science Review*, **20**: 153–82.
Audretsch, D.B. and M.P. Feldman (1996), 'R&D spillovers and the geography of innovation and production', *American Economic Review*, **86**: 630–40.
Brakman, S., H. Garretsen and M. Schramm (2002), 'The empirical relevance of the new economic geography: testing for a spatial wage structure in Germany', *CESifo Working Paper 395*, Munich.
Brakman, S., H. Garretsen, and M. Schramm (2004), 'The spatial distribution of wages: estimating the Helpman-Hanson model for Germany', *Journal of Regional Science*, **44**: 437–66.
Brakman, S., H. Garretsen and C. van Marrewijk (2001), *An Introduction to Geographical Economics*, Cambridge: Cambridge University Press.
Breschi, S. and F. Lissoni (2001), 'Localized knowledge spillovers vs innovative milieux: knowledge "tacitness" reconsidered', *Papers in Regional Science*, **80**: 255–73.
Ciccone, A. and R.E. Hall (1996), 'Productivity and the density of economic activity', *American Economic Review*, **86**: 54–70.
Combes, P.-P. and M. Lafourcade (2001), 'Transportation costs decline and regional inequalities: evidence from France', *Discussion Paper 2894*, Centre for Economic Policy Research, London.
Combes, P.-P. and M. Lafourcade (2004), 'Trade costs and regional disparities in a model of economic geography: structural estimations and predictions for France', Unpublished paper available from http://www.vcharite.univ-mrs.fr/combes/.
Combes, P.-P. and H. Overman (2003), 'The spatial distribution of economic activity in the EU', *Discussion Paper 3999*, Centre for Economic Policy Research, London.
Combes, P.-P., G. Duranton and L. Gobillon (2004), 'Spatial wage disparities: sorting matters!', *Discussion Paper 4240*, Centre for Economic Policy Research, London.
Cox, D.R. (1961), 'Tests of separate families of hypotheses', *Proceedings of the Fourth Berkeley Symposium on Mathematical Statistics and Probability*, **1**: 105–23.

Cox, D.R. (1962), 'Further results on tests of separate families of hypotheses', *Journal of the Royal Statistical Society B*, **24**: 406–24.

Davidson, R. and J. MacKinnon (1981), 'Several tests for model specification in the presence of alternative hypotheses', *Econometrica*, **49**: 781–93.

Davidson, R. and J. MacKinnon (1982), 'Some non-nested hypothesis tests and the relations among them', *Review of Economic Studies*, **49**: 551–65.

Davidson, R. and J. MacKinnon (1993), *Estimation and Inference in Econometrics*, Oxford: Oxford University Press.

Davidson, R. and J. MacKinnon (2002a), 'Bootstrap J tests of non-nested linear regression models', *Journal of Econometrics*, **109**: 167–93.

Davidson, R. and J. MacKinnon (2002b), 'Fast double bootstrap tests of non-nested linear regression models', *Econometric Reviews* , **21**: 419–29.

Davis, D.R. and D.E. Weinstein (2003), 'Market access, economic geography and comparative advantage: an empirical test', *Journal of International Economics*, **59**: 1–23.

de Vaal, A. and M. van den Berg (1999), 'Producer services, economic geography, and services tradability', *Journal of Regional Science*, **39**: 539–72.

Dixit, A. and J.E. Stiglitz (1977), 'Monopolistic competition and optimum product diversity', *American Economic Review*, **67**: 297–308.

Fan, Y. and Q. Li (1995), 'Bootstrapping J-type tests for non-nested regression models', *Economics Letters*, **48**: 107–12.

Feenstra, R.C. (1994), 'New product varieties and the measurement of international prices', *The American Economic Review*, **84**: 157–77.

Fingleton, B. (2003), 'Increasing returns: evidence from local wage rates in Great Britain', *Oxford Economic Papers*, **55**: 716–39.

Fingleton, B. (2005), 'Beyond neoclassical orthodoxy: a view based on the new economic geography and UK regional wage data', *Papers in Regional Science*, **84**: 351–75.

Fingleton, B. (2006), 'The new economic geography versus urban economics: an evaluation using local wage rates in Great Britain', *Oxford Economic Papers*, **58**: 501–30.

Forslid, R., J. Haaland and K.-H. Midelfart Knarvik (2002), 'A U-shaped Europe? A simulation study of industrial location', *Journal of International Economics*, **57**: 273–97.

Fujita, M. and J.-F. Thisse (2002), *Economics of Agglomeration*, Cambridge: Cambridge University Press.

Fujita, M., P.R. Krugman and A. Venables (1999), *The Spatial Economy: Cities, Regions, and International Trade*, Cambridge, MA: MIT Press.

Godfrey, L.G. (1983), 'Testing non-nested models after estimation by instrumental variables or least squares', *Econometrica*, **51**: 355–66.

Godfrey, L.G. (1998), 'Tests for non-nested regression models: some results on small sample behaviour and the bootstrap', *Journal of Econometrics*, **84**: 59–74.

Hanson, G.H. (1997), 'Increasing returns, trade, and the regional structure of wages', *Economic Journal*, **107**: 113–33.

Hanson, G.H. (1998), 'Market potential, increasing returns and geographic concentration', *NBER Working Paper 6429*, National Bureau of Economic Research.

Harris, C. (1954), 'The market as a factor in the localization of industry in the United States', *Annals of the Association of American Geographers*, **64**: 315–48.

Head, K. and T. Mayer (2003), 'The empirics of agglomeration and trade', *Discussion Paper 3985*, Centre for Economic Policy Research, London.

Head, K. and J. Ries (2001), 'Increasing returns versus national product differentiation as an explanation for the pattern of US-Canada trade', *American Economic Review*, **91**: 858–76.

Helpman, E. (1998), 'The size of regions', in D. Pines, E. Sadka and I. Zilcha (eds), *Topics in Public Economics. Theoretical and Applied Analysis*, Cambridge: Cambridge University Press.

Hendry, D.F. (1995), *Dynamic Econometrics*, Oxford: Oxford University Press.

Kelejian, H.H. and I.R. Prucha (1998), 'A generalized spatial two-stage least squares procedure for estimating a spatial autoregressive model with autoregressive disturbances', *Journal of Real Estate Finance and Economics*, **17**: 99–121.

Kelejian, H.H. and I.R. Prucha (1999), 'A generalized moments estimator for the autoregressive parameter in a spatial model', *International Economic Review*, **40**: 509–33.

Kelejian, H.H. and D.P. Robinson (1993), 'A suggested method of estimation for spatial interdependent models with autocorrelated errors, and an application to a county expenditure model', *Papers in Regional Science*, **72**: 297–312.

Krugman, P.R. and A.J. Venables (1995), 'Globalization and the inequality of nations', *Quarterly Journal of Economics*, **110**: 857–80.

Leamer, E.E. and J. Levinsohn (1994), 'International trade theory: the evidence', *NBER Working Paper 4940*, National Bureau of Economic Research.

MacKinnon, J. (2002), 'Bootstrap inference in econometrics', *Canadian Journal of Economics*, **35**: 615–45.

Mion, G. (2003), 'Spatial externalities and empirical analysis: the case of Italy', *Journal of Urban Economics*, **56**: 97–118.

Mizon, G.E. and J.-F. Richard (1986), 'The encompassing principle and its application to non-nested hypotheses', *Econometrica*, **54**: 657–78.

Neary, J.P. (2001), 'Of hype and hyperbolas: introducing the new economic geography', *Journal of Economic Literature*, **XXXIX**: 536–61.

Niebuhr, A. (2004), 'Market access and Regional Disparities', *HWWA Discussion Paper 269*, Hamburg Institute of International Economics.

Pesaran, H. (1974), 'On the general problem of model selection', *Review of Economic Studies*, **41**: 153–71.

Pesaran, M.H. and S. Deaton (1978), 'Testing non-nested non-linear regression models', *Econometrica*, **46**: 677–94.

Pesaran, M.H. and M. Weeks (1999), 'Non-nested hypothesis testing: an overview', Cambridge Working Papers in Economics 9918 Department of Applied Economics University of Cambridge.

Pratten, C. (1988), 'A survey of the economies of scale', in *Research on the Cost of Non-Europe Vol 2, Studies of the Economics of Integration*, Luxembourg: EC.

Redding, S. and A.J. Venables (2004), 'Economic geography and international inequality', *Journal of International Economics*, **62**: 53–82.

Regions: Statistical Yearbook (2003), Office for Official Publications of the European Communities.

Rice, P. and A.J. Venables (2003), 'Equilibrium regional disparities: theory and British evidence', *Regional Studies*, **37**: 675–86.

Rivera-Batiz, F. (1988), 'Increasing returns, monopolistic competition, and agglomeration economies in consumption and production', *Regional Science and Urban Economics*, **18**: 125–53.

Roos, M. (2001), 'Wages and market potential in Germany', *Jahrbuch für Regionalwissenschaft* (*Review of Regional Research*), **21**: 171–95.

Stewart, J.Q. (1947), 'Empirical mathematical rules concerning the distribution and equilibrium of population', *Geographical Review*, **37**: 461–85.

Venables, A.J. (1996), 'Equilibrium locations of vertically linked industries', *International Economic Review*, **37**: 341–59.

4. From theory to estimation and back: the empirical relevance of new economic geography

Steven Brakman and Harry Garretsen

4.1 INTRODUCTION

The development of new economic geography (NEG) in the past 15 years has renewed the interest among economists in the spatial distribution of economic activity.[1] NEG can best be seen as a natural extension of the new trade theory that was developed in the late 1970s and early 1980s. The small step taken by Krugman (1991), but the giant leap for the rest of the economics profession, was that in Krugman the assumption of factor immobility between countries or regions was dropped. This allowed factors of production to migrate to those locations where welfare or real income is maximized. As a result, it became possible to explain or endogenize the existence of agglomerations because the Krugman model gave rise to core-periphery equilibria.

For international trade theorists this was a novel approach because, traditionally, the whole field rested basically on two pillars: location does not matter in neo-classical Heckscher-Ohlin-type models, because without factor mobility the integrated equilibrium can be restored by trade alone (incentives for migration are absent), or factor mobility is simply ruled out by assumption, as in the new trade theory. Similarly, for urban and regional economists, the NEG approach was also novel to the extent that the latter is based on a general equilibrium approach, whereas the former by and large uses partial equilibrium models. Krugman's 1991 model led to an outburst of theoretical NEG papers in the 1990s, but although the theoretical progress was indeed quite substantial (see, for example, Fujita, Krugman and Venables, 1999; Fujita and Thisse, 2002; Baldwin et al., 2003), the need to provide some empirical corroboration for NEG models also became apparent. Neary (2001) concluded that NEG is interesting, but that convincing empirical evidence was still lacking. Since Neary (2001), however, much more empirical evidence as to the relevance of NEG has come to the fore. Although it is far too soon to derive clear conclusions from this work, two issues stand out (see also Head and Mayer, 2004). First, it is rather difficult to test or even to estimate NEG models, because empirical hypotheses derived from these models are often also consistent with other models. For example, the home market effect (HME) drives the incentive for factors of production to migrate to more attractive locations, but the HME is also a characteristic of the new trade theory. So, finding evidence for the HME by itself is not necessarily evidence of the relevance of NEG. Second, finding evidence for the relevance of NEG begs the question of how findings should be interpreted from the point of view of NEG theory once we move back from NEG empirics to NEG theory. One of the interesting characteristics of NEG is that (small) changes in the key model parameters, notably the level of transport costs, can lead to (large) changes in the degree of agglomeration if an economy is close to the so-called break points. How should one then interpret the empirical findings of the NEG research? Are the findings such that small (policy-induced) changes are able to change the existing spatial distribution of economic activity, or is it virtually impossible to do so?

The aim of this chapter is twofold. First, we discuss the progress in empirical research related to NEG and give an example based on one of the testable NEG hypotheses, the existence of a spatial wage structure. Our sample will consist of the EU NUTS 2 regions. Second, and more importantly for our present purposes, we will address the question as to whether and how our empirical findings can be interpreted with the use of the underlying NEG model. In doing so, it will become clear that, especially with respect to this issue, much more work remains to be done.

Our chapter is organized as follows. After a short reminder that the spatial distribution of economic activity across space is rather uneven in Section 4.2, Section 4.3 highlights the main distinguishing characteristics of NEG models that can be tested. The most important distinguishing characteristic, the relationship between trade costs and the degree of agglomeration, is the main topic for the remainder of the chapter. The equilibrium wage equation that we use as our main vehicle is derived and then estimated in Section 4.4. The 'Now, what's next?' question is answered in Sections 4.5 and 4.6. In Section 4.5 we briefly explain what the relationship between trade costs and agglomeration looks like in our underlying NEG model, and we then use this insight in Section 4.6 where we confront our estimations with this theoretical relationship. In Section 4.7 we discuss the limitations of our own and related NEG research. Section 4.8 concludes.

4.2   THE UNEVEN SPATIAL DISTRIBUTION: A QUICK REMINDER

Although the measurement of the spatial distribution of economic activity at an urban, regional or national level is not without problems we provide some evidence on the location of economic activity (Combes and Overman, 2004).[2] It only serves to remind us that economic activity is unevenly distributed across space. Out of many possible examples (and reflecting our own background as international economists), Figure 4.1 shows that countries that have a relatively high production density – countries that also have a relatively high population density – are concentrated in three core regions: Europe, Japan and the United States.

A similar picture emerges at lower levels of aggregation, that is, at the regional or the urban level: most people live where most activity takes place.[3] From observations like these some conclusions emerge:

- Economic activity is not homogeneously distributed across space.
- Core countries and regions have high levels of GDP per capita and also often have a relative high population density.
- Core countries and regions are located close to each other.
- These stylized facts hold for various geographical scales.

Once this has been concluded, the next obvious question becomes how to explain spatial patterns like these. In the past 200 years, dating back at least to Adam Smith's insights on the (international) division of labour, many models have been introduced to explain (parts) of these stylized facts (for an overview see Brakman, Garretsen and van Marrewijk, 2001).

One of the most recent attempts to shed light on the spatial distribution of economic activity is the NEG approach initiated by Krugman (1991). The novel aspect of the NEG approach was that Krugman allowed for factor mobility between two countries or regions in a specific new trade model that was also developed by him (Krugman, 1980). Central in the analysis of Krugman (1980) was that the larger country benefits from the so-called home market effect (HME). This HME implies, for a given distribution of production factors, that when transportation costs are present, the larger market is able to attract more than its proportional share of firms in imperfectly competitive markets. The larger region is the net exporter of goods produced under increasing returns to scale. The innovation of Krugman (1991) is that once factor mobility is allowed, the larger market is able to attract an ever-increasing number of firms and workers in the imperfectly competitive industry. The final result is a core-periphery structure in which all footloose production factors are concentrated in a single country

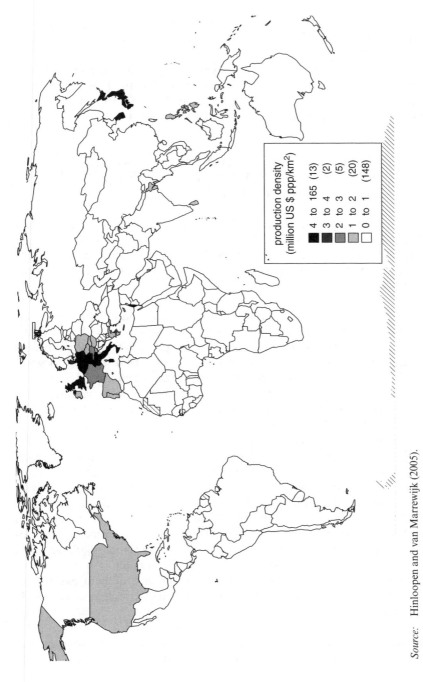

Source: Hinloopen and van Marrewijk (2005).

Figure 4.1   Concentration of economic activity

or region. This result depends on the specific parameters in the model, but in a qualitative sense, the Krugman (1991) model is able to explain some of the stylized facts presented above.

For a theory to be taken seriously, explaining stylized facts is, however, not enough. According to Neary (2001) NEG has to show its 'ultimate usefulness' by surviving empirical tests. This turns out to be rather problematic as we will show in the remainder of this chapter.

4.3 EMPIRICAL TESTING AND TESTABLE HYPOTHESES FROM NEG THEORY: FROM THEORY TO ESTIMATIONS

Empirical testing should first of all identify distinguishing characteristics of a specific theory. Head and Mayer (2004, p. 2616) identify five main characteristics – slightly reformulated by us – that are special for NEG and could be tested to explain the stylized facts like those illustrated by Figure 4.1:

1. The home market effect (HME): in the Krugman (1980) setting this implies that large regions will be home to a disproportional share of the imperfectly competitive industry. Such large markets are therefore, net exporters of industries characterized by increasing returns to scale. There are also two other possible consequences from the HME:
    a. The price version of the HME: a large market potential raises local factor prices in the core relative to the periphery. An attractive market with a strong HME will increase demand for factors of production and this raises factor rewards.
    b. The quantity version of the HME: a large market potential induces factor inflows from the small to the large market. Footloose factors of production will be attracted to those markets that pay relatively high real factor rewards. This leads to a process of circular causality.
2. At some critical level of transport or trade costs, a further reduction in transport costs induces agglomeration. This implies that more economic integration should at some point lead to (more) agglomeration of the footloose activities and factors of production.
3. Shock sensitivity: changes in the economic environment can trigger drastic and permanent changes in the spatial distribution of economic activity.

The recent literature on each of these effects separately is thoroughly surveyed by Head and Mayer (2004). In this chapter we will not try to provide a survey as well, but rather focus the combination of the HME effect (the price version) and the second characteristic. Interestingly, empirical research in NEG tends to focus on the HME, whereas in our view the second and third characteristics are in many ways far more essential for the NEG. *That is to say, agglomeration itself should be explained as a function of key parameter changes or other shocks to the economy.*

The first characteristic, the HME, simply states that the larger market is attractive for those workers or firms that are located there. This characteristic is at home in NEG models, but also in, for instance, the new trade models. So, finding evidence for an HME does not necessarily tell us something specific on the relevance of the NEG models, although it is a *conditio sine qua non*. Characteristics (1a) and (1b) describe the consequence for factors of production or factor prices once the HME is established. As explained in Fujita et al. (1999, p. 57), the equilibrium equations of the Krugman (1991) model give the following equation: $dY/Y = \alpha(dw/w) + \beta(dL/L)$, where Y is demand for the footloose sector, w is the wage rate in this sector, and L is employment in this sector, α and β are parameters.[4] It shows that an increase in the demand (Y) for the goods from the footloose sector not only causes employment changes (the quantity version of the HME), but also induces wage (w) changes (the price version of the HME). The latter increase takes away some of the location advances for new firms as the cost of production increases. Spatial equilibrium can thus be restored in three ways: employment changes, wage changes or combinations of both. As shown in Brakman, Garretsen and Schramm (2005), both effects are typically at work. Head and Mayer (2005) find, however, that the wage channel is the main route towards spatial equilibrium.

The three elements we have described so far are related to the NEG models, but the most important distinguishing elements are (2) and (3). The key idea of NEG is in our view that – small or temporary – changes in the economic environment, like a reduction in transport costs or a shock like an earthquake can have permanent effects with respect to the equilibrium distribution of economic activity.[5] This key NEG feature is not addressed by merely testing the existence of the HME. The characteristics (1), (1a) or (1b) in fact use a given distribution of economic activity as an explanatory variable that could explain trade patterns, the spatial distribution of workers or that of wages. The key contribution of NEG is the other way around: the spatial distribution of economic activity itself should be explained, simultaneously with the endogenous location of demand. A small change in economic integration could thus lead to changes in the spatial distribution of both, which, as said, can be catastrophic after a certain threshold is reached. Furthermore, if small changes can have large effects, one should be able to find permanent effects in the spatial distribution of economic activity and workers after large shocks.

In the remainder of this chapter we will concentrate on the main characteristic of the NEG models and show why it is rather difficult in the end to come up with convincing evidence for characteristic (2).[6] In doing so, the HME feature, and notably its price version, will serve as a starting point, but our analysis on the so-called spatial wage structure will only be a means to an end. We are really after the second feature of the above NEG list. We do this by taking NEG seriously and spelling out what we estimate, and in particular what the possible consequences are of these estimates, that is, can we determine whether or not a system of regions is on the brink of a drastic change or not. We do this by applying a general two-region NEG model due to Puga (1999) to the regions of the EU.

4.4   THE MODEL AND THE ESTIMATION RESULTS FOR THE WAGE EQUATION[7]

In this section we give a brief description of the model and focus on the derivation of the equilibrium wage equation in order to be able to test for this spatial wage structure (recall, the HME and its price version from the previous section). The model we use, Puga (1999), encompasses the two most important NEG models: the Krugman (1991) model with inter-regional labour mobility, and the Krugman and Venables (1995) model without inter-regional labour mobility. The model without inter-regional labour mobility is considered to be more relevant in an international context, because it is a stylized fact that labour is internationally less mobile than nationally. For the EU, however, it is not a priori clear if this is true in the long run. Economic integration could stimulate international labour mobility. In the context of NEG such a gradual change to more labour mobility can have serious implications, as we will discuss below. We will now introduce and summarize the basic set-up of the Puga model (for more details see, besides Puga (1999), Fujita et al. (1999, Chapter 14). After this introduction, we will provide an example of the actual estimation of the wage equation for the EU regions. In the next two sections, we will elaborate upon the relationship between trade costs and agglomeration in the Puga model (Section 4.5) and we will then combine the insights derived from our estimations and this relationship in Section 4.6 when confronting the estimation results with the underlying model and thereby address characteristic (2) from the NEG list of hypotheses as introduced in the previous section.

4.4.1 The Set-up of the Model and the Derivation of the Wage Equation

4.4.1.1 Demand

Assume an economy with two sectors, a numeraire sector (H), and a manufacturing (M) sector. As a short cut, one often refers to H as the agricultural sector to indicate that this industry is tied to a specific location. Every consumer in the economy shares the same, Cobb-Douglas, preferences for both types of commodities:

$$U = M^{\delta} H^{(1-\delta)}$$

The parameter δ is the share of income spent on manufactured goods. M is a CES subutility function of many varieties:

$$M = \left(\sum_{i=1}^{n} c_i^{\rho} \right)^{1/\rho}. \tag{4.1}$$

Maximizing the subutility subject to the relevant income constraint, that is, the share of income that is spent on manufactures, δE, gives the demand for each variety, j:

$$c_j = p_j^{-\varepsilon} I^{\varepsilon-1} \delta E \tag{4.2}$$

in which $I = [\Sigma_i (p_i)^{(1-\varepsilon)}]^{1/(1-\varepsilon)}$ is the price index for manufactures, $\varepsilon = 1/1 - \rho$ the elasticity of substitution and $E =$ income.

Firms also use varieties from the M sector as intermediate inputs. Assuming that all varieties are necessary in the production process and that the elasticity of substitution is the same for firms as for consumers, we can use the same CES-aggregator function for producers as for consumers, with the same corresponding price index, I. Given spending on intermediates, we can derive demand functions for varieties of producers that are similar to those of consumers.

Total demand for a variety, j, can now be represented as:

$$c_j = p_j^{-\varepsilon} I^{\varepsilon-1} Y \tag{4.3}$$

where Y is defined as $Y = \delta E + \mu npx^*$. The first term on the right-hand side of Y comes from consumers, representing the share of income E that is spent on all M-varieties. The second term on the right-hand side comes from firm demand for intermediate inputs. This is equal to the value of all varieties in a region, npx^*, multiplied by the share of intermediates in the production process, μ (see below).

4.4.1.2 Manufacturing supply
Next, turn to the supply side. Each variety, *i*, is produced according to the following cost function, $C(x_i)$:

$$C(x_i) = I^\mu W_i^{(1-\mu)}(\alpha + \beta x_i) \tag{4.4}$$

where the coefficients α and β describe the fixed and marginal input requirement per variety. The input is a Cobb-Douglas composite of labour, with price (wages) W, and intermediates, represented by the price index I. Maximizing profits gives the familiar mark-up pricing rule (note that marginal costs consists of two elements, labour and intermediates):

$$p_i(1 - \tfrac{1}{\varepsilon}) = I^\mu W^{(1-\mu)}\beta. \tag{4.5}$$

Using the zero profit condition, $p_i x_i = I^\mu W_i^{(1-\mu)}(\alpha + \beta x_i)$, and the mark-up pricing rule (4.5), gives the break-even supply of a variety *i* (each variety is produced by a single firm):

$$x_i = \frac{\alpha(\varepsilon - 1)}{\beta}. \tag{4.6}$$

4.4.1.3 Equilibrium with transportation costs in the two-region model
Furthermore, transportation of manufactures is costly. Transportation costs T are so-called iceberg transportation costs: $T_{12} > 1$ units of the manufacturing good have to be shipped from region 1 to region 2 for one unit of the good to actually arrive in region 2. Assume, for illustration purposes, that the two regions – 1 and 2 – are the only regions. Total demand for a product from, for example region 1, now comes from two regions, 1 and 2. The consumers and firms in region 2 have to pay transportation costs on their imports. This leads to the following total demand for a variety produced in region 1:

$$x_1 = Y_1 p_1^{-\varepsilon} I_1^{\varepsilon-1} + Y_2 p_1^{-\varepsilon}(T_{12})^{-\varepsilon} I_2^{\varepsilon-1}.$$

We already know that the break-even supply equals $x_1 = \alpha(\varepsilon - 1)/\beta$. Equating this to total demand gives (note that the demand from region 2 is multiplied by T_{12} in order to compensate for the part that melts away during transportation):

$$\frac{\alpha(\varepsilon - 1)}{\beta} = Y_1 p_1^{-\varepsilon} I_1^{\varepsilon-1} + Y_2 p_1^{-\varepsilon}(T_{12})^{1-\varepsilon} I_2^{\varepsilon-1}.$$

Inserting the mark-up pricing rule, (4.5), in this last equation and solving for the wage rate gives the two-region version of the wage equation in the presence of intermediate demand for varieties.[8] This version of the NEG model is also known as the vertical-linkages model, because this model introduces an extra agglomeration force: the location of firms has an impact on production costs. The wage equation for the two-region case can be stated as:

$$W_1 = Const.(I_1)^{\frac{-\mu}{(1-\mu)}}(Y_1 I_1^{\varepsilon-1} + Y_2(T_{12})^{1-\varepsilon} I_2^{\varepsilon-1})^{\frac{1}{\varepsilon(1-\mu)}} \qquad (4.6)$$

where the constant, *Const.*, is a function of (fixed) model parameters.

Similarly for the *n* region ($n=1, \ldots r$) case we arrive at the following equilibrium wage equation:

$$W_r = Const.\{I_r\}^{-\mu/(1-\mu)}[\Sigma_s Y_s I_s^{\varepsilon-1} T_{rs}^{(1-\varepsilon)}]^{\frac{1}{\varepsilon(1-\mu)}}. \qquad (4.7)$$

W_r is the region's *r* (nominal) wage rate, Y_s is expenditures (demand for final consumption and intermediate inputs), I_s is the price index for manufactured goods, ε is the elasticity of substitution for manufactured goods and T_{rs} are the iceberg transport costs between regions *r* and *s*.

Note that when we want to estimate wage equation (4.7) for our sample of NUTS 2 EU regions we need to come up with a specification of the transport costs T_{rs}. This will be done below. In particular, we will have to answer the question of how transport costs vary with the distance between regions. In the short run, when the spatial distribution of firms and labour is fixed, the model reduces to three equations with three unknowns (wages *W*, expenditures *Y* and the price index *I*). In the long run the spatial distribution of economic activity is endogenous because then footloose firms and, depending on the particular version of the model used, manufacturing workers, can move between sectors and regions.

4.4.2 Estimating the Wage Equation

Wage equation (4.7) will do for our empirical purposes, in the sense that it suffices to test for the relevance of the first NEG characteristic, the HME (the price version), by establishing whether or not there is a spatial wage structure: do wages fall the further one moves away from economic centres? In the short run when the spatial distribution of firms and workers is fixed, demand differences between regions will be fully reflected in regional wage differences. Or, in other words, regional differences in *real market access*, the term between [ ] in wage equation (4.7), or *supplier access*, $I^{-\mu/(1-\mu)}$, both of which are fixed in the short run, will result in regional wage differences. In the long run when firms and workers can move, these differences will also give rise to relocation of firms and workers (which amounts to saying that in the long run, real market and supplier access are endogenous).[9] All that matters for our empirical analysis is that wage equation (4.7) is the equilibrium wage equation and can be estimated. However, to learn more about the relationship between economic integration and agglomeration the wage equation will not do and we have to address the nature of the long-run equilibria. This will done in the next section. But first we present an example of estimating wage equation (4.7).

Before we can estimate wage equation (4.7) for our sample of EU NUTS 2 regions we have to specify the distance function (see the Appendix and Brakman, Garretsen and Schramm, 2005 for more information on the data used and various measurement and econometrical issues respectively). The distance function we use is $T_{rs} = TD_{rs}^{\gamma}$, where the parameters T, $\gamma > 0$ (Crozet, 2004). The size of the distance decay parameter γ needs thus to be estimated and we will let the data decide whether transport costs rise or fall more or less than proportionally with increased distance between r and s. The distance variable D_{rs} will be measured in km between NUTS 2 regions. The distance from a region r to itself, D_{rr} is measured as $0.667 \sqrt{area/\pi}$ in which area is the size of region r in km^2 (see Head and Mayer, 2000 for a discussion of this measure for internal distance). Given our specification for T_{rs} we can calculate the so-called freeness of trade $\phi_{rs} \equiv T_{rs}^{1-\varepsilon}$, see Section 4.5, for all combination of D_{rs} and D_{rr}. The price index (on which we have no data on the NUTS 2 level) is approximated following a method developed in Brakman et al. (2004), in which we express the price index in region r as an average of the wage in region r and the wages in centre regions corrected for the distance between region r and these centre regions.

Regional wages across Europe and its regions may, of course, differ for reasons that have nothing to do with the demand and cost linkages from the NEG literature. This leads us to another issue that needs to be addressed. Positive human capital externalities or (pure) technological externalities might also give rise to a spatial wage structure! These externalities imply that regions may simply differ in terms of their marginal factor productivity and this is something we would like to take into account when estimating the wage equation. Also, the physical and political geography of Europe might be a factor in explaining regional wage differences; these are the fixed endowments that are truly fixed geographically (Combes and Overman, 2004).

To take these alternative explanations for regional wage differences on board as control variables we proceeded as follows. We allow for labour productivity to differ across the EU regions. We cannot measure human or technological externalities separately (due to lack of relevant data on the NUTS 2 level). Relative marginal labour productivity is $[MPL_{EU}/MPL_r]$, where MPL_{EU} is the average real gross value-added per employee in the NUTS 2 regions and MPL_r is the real gross value-added per employee for region r. By allowing for MPL-differences the wage equation changes into:

$$W_r = \text{constant} \cdot \left(\frac{MPL_{EU}}{MPL_r}\right)^{(1-\varepsilon)/\varepsilon} I_r^{-\mu/(1-\mu)} \left[\sum_{s=1}^{R} Y_s(T_{rs})^{1-\varepsilon} I_s^{\varepsilon-1}\right]^{1/\varepsilon}$$

where, MPL = marginal productivity of labour in a specific region (indicated by the subscript).

The possibility that the physical geography (climate, elevation, access to waterways etc.) or the political geography (borders, country-specific institutional wage arrangements etc.) might also explain regional wage differences will be addressed below. As proxies for physical geography we will use for the NUTS 2 regions the mean annual sunshine radiation (in kWH/m²) and the mean elevation above sea level. We will also use dummy variables when a region borders the sea, has direct access to (navigable) waterways, or is a border region. To capture the possibility of country-specific determinants of wages (like the centralization of wage setting) we also use country dummies as control variables. The physical and political geography variables capture the fixed (= natural) features of the economic geography that may have a bearing on regional wages. By fixed we mean that these variables are not determined by the location decisions of mobile firms or workers.[10]

The log-transformation of the equilibrium wage equation gives the specification that, see wage equation below, has actually been used as the central wage equation in our estimations, and by adding physical and political geography control variables we thus end up with:

$$\log(W_r) = \text{constant} + \frac{1-\varepsilon}{\varepsilon \cdot (1-\mu)} \log\left(\frac{MPL_{EU+}}{MPL_r}\right) - \frac{\mu}{1-\mu} \log(I_r)$$

$$+ \frac{1}{\varepsilon \cdot (1-\mu)} \log\left[\sum_{s=1}^{R} Y_s(T_{rs})^{1-\varepsilon} I_s^{\varepsilon-1}\right] + \sum_i \beta_i Z_i \qquad (4.7')$$

where $(T_{rs})^{1-\varepsilon} = (TD_{rs})^{\gamma(1-\varepsilon)}$ and internal distance $D_{rr} = 0.667 \sqrt{area/\pi}$ in which area is the size of region r in km²; and Z_i = a set of additional control variables for each region that potentially consists of mean annual sunshine; mean elevation above sea-level; and dummy variables (country dummy, border-region dummy, access to sea dummy, access to navigable waterway dummy). For more information on the data used and the definition of variables see the Appendix.

What is immediately apparent from the wage equation is that the supplier access (SA) term is correlated with the real market access (RMA) term. The multi-collinearity between RMA and SA is discussed at length by Redding and Venables (2004) and Knaap (2004), and we follow these authors and opt thereby for RMA in our estimation (and thus eliminate the SA term). In addition, we have estimated wage equation (4.7') in levels and also, without the time-invariant control variables, in first differences. In doing so, we have also performed IV-estimations and used both non-linear least squares (NLS) and weighted least squares (WLS). In particular, when estimating in levels, the Glejser test indicated the presence of heteroscedasticity so we choose WLS. But for the sake of comparison (for instance, with Crozet, 2004) we also present the NLS regression. The sample period is 1992–2000. It is not our goal for this chapter to solve all these econometrical issues since the estimation of the wage equation is only a means to an end. The means is to arrive at 'reasonable' estimates for the substitution elasticity ε and the distance parameter γ to be able to infer the freeness of trade parameter that will guide us in our analysis of characteristic (2), the relationship between the transport costs, here the freeness of trade, and the degree of agglomeration in Section 4.6.

Table 4.1 gives the results of estimating equation (4.7') in levels. The first column gives the WLS results of estimating (4.7'). The second column does the same but now the estimation is the second stage of a 2SLS regression where, in the first stage regression, wages and income were regressed upon the exogenous controls Z, a time trend, and 1-period lagged wages or income. This is a 'first pass' way to instrument wages and income. The third column shows the estimation results for a 2SLS regression of wage equation (4.7') but now we use NLS instead of WLS. To save space we only show the estimation results for our two key variables (results for other variables and/or other specifications are available upon request).

The coefficient for the substitution elasticity is relatively high, but many studies find values in the range of 7–11 (see, for instance, Broda and Weinstein, 2004 for sector evidence for the United States, or Hanson and Xiang, 2004 for recent international evidence). The distance coefficient $\gamma < 1$, which indicates that transport costs increases less than proportionally with distance (see Crozet, 2004 for an opposite finding).[11]

To be able to show what the estimations mean for the relationship between economic integration and agglomeration (our holy grail in this chapter), we first need to go back to the underlying theoretical model as introduced in Section 4.1 and ask ourselves what the relationship between transport costs

Table 4.1 *Estimating wage equation (4.7'), 1992–2000 (t-values in parentheses)*

	Levels, WLS	Levels, 2SLS, WLS	Levels, 2SLS, NLS
Variable: ε	9.62	9.53	5.48
	(24.9)	(16.9)	(11.7)
Variable: γ	0.21	0.19	0.32
	(33.4)	(22.1)	(13.0)

Note: *t*-values for 2SLS have been corrected for the fact that fitted values for wages and income from the first stage regression are included in the second stage. Number of obs.: column 1: 1830; column 2: 1566.

(here, the freeness of trade) and the degree of agglomeration (characteristic [2] from the NEG list) looks like in our NEG model, Puga (1999).

4.5 FREENESS OF TRADE AND AGGLOMERATION: THE THEORETICAL BENCHMARK FOR THE ESTIMATION RESULTS

4.5.1 Inter-regional Labour Mobility: the Tomahawk[12]

NEG models with the same set-up as Puga (1999) predict that with inter-regional labour mobility economic integration will lead to complete agglomeration of the footloose agents in the end. The intuition behind this is simple and is illustrated, for the two-region case in Figure 4.2. Assume that there are two regions. Economic integration implies lower transportation costs. In Figure 4.2 this is a movement from left to right along the horizontal axis, from low to high φ's (more on the important role of φ below). The parameter φ is called the freeness of trade or 'phiness' of trade parameter (Baldwin et al., 2003) and, in terms of our model, is defined as $\varphi_{rs} \equiv T_{rs}^{1-\varepsilon}$. It is easy to interpret: $\varphi_{rs} = 0$ denotes autarky and the absence of economic integration, whereas $\varphi_{rs} = 1$ denotes free trade and full economic integration between regions r and s. In empirical work this gives an extra degree of freedom: one has to choose a functional form for T_{rs}. The vertical axis in Figure 4.1 shows the share of the footloose production factor in region 1.

Assume that the initial situation is one of autarky ($\varphi = 0$) and that (footloose) labour is equally distributed over the two regions, indicated by the horizontal solid line at 0.5. Because the regions are identical, this situation

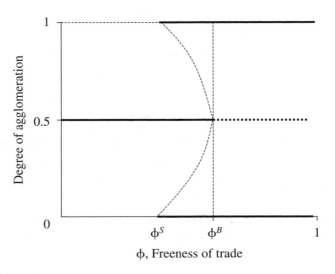

Figure 4.2   The tomahawk

is also a long-run equilibrium. This is why this situation is known as the symmetric or spreading equilibrium. What happens if the degree of economic agglomeration increases? Mobile workers have to decide whether relocating to the other region, say from region 1 to 2 (which becomes slightly larger than region 1), is beneficial for them. Initially, relocating is not beneficial because transportation costs are still quite high and relocating means that exporting from region 2 to region 1 is still too expensive. Furthermore, competition in region 2 increases. This implies that prices and wages in region 2 have to go down in order to be able to sell the break-even amount. A defecting worker will return to his or her original location. But if transportation costs decline beyond a certain point, the advantages of moving to region 2 outweighs the disadvantage of exporting to region 1. This stimulates further migration towards region 2 until all workers and firms have moved towards this region. Figure 4.2, the tomahawk figure, gives the theoretical relationship between economic integration φ and the degree of agglomeration.

As Figure 4.2 illustrates, the point where it becomes profitable to agglomerate is indicated by φ^B; in the literature this point is known as the so-called break point: the point where the symmetric equilibrium (degree of agglomeration $= 0.5$) is no longer a stable equilibrium (indicated by the dotted horizontal line). At this point the relocation decision of a worker means that others will follow, triggering a process of agglomeration. So, in our NEG model version with inter-regional labour mobility we either have perfect spreading or full agglomeration as a long-run equilibrium. Analysing the effects of increasing economic integration on agglomeration is now reduced to the question of where an economy is located on the horizontal axis in Figure 4.2, that is, one is interested in whether or not an economy is in actual fact to the left or to right of φ^B.[13] Where we are on the horizontal axis is an empirical question to which the estimations of the freeness of trade-parameter-based wage equation will give us the answer in Sections 4.4 and 4.5. Furthermore, the estimates for φ help us to infer φ^B.

Puga (1999, equation [16]) derives the following analytical solution for the break point for the two-region case (dropping subscripts r and s):

$$\phi^B = (T^{1-\varepsilon})^B =$$
$$\left[1 + \frac{2(2\varepsilon - 1)(\delta + \mu(1 - \delta))}{(1 - \mu)[(1 - \delta)(\varepsilon(1 - \delta)(1 - \mu) - 1] - \delta^2\eta}\right]^{(1-\varepsilon)/(\varepsilon-1)}. \quad (4.8)$$

The elasticity η is the elasticity of a region's labour supply from the H-sector to the manufacturing sector. If $\eta = 0$, no inter-sector labour mobility is possible, if $\eta = \infty$ there is perfect labour mobility between sectors, that is to say the inter-sectoral labour supply elasticity is infinite. In the latter case, wages in the manufacturing sector and the H-sector are identical until a region becomes specialized in manufactures. If $0 < \eta < \infty$, migration from the H-sector to the manufacturing sector can be consistent with a wage increase in *both* sectors. The inclusion of an upward-sloping labour supply function thus implies that the model is more general than Krugman (1991, where $\eta = 0$), or Krugman and Venables (1995, where $\eta = \infty$). Most importantly, if $0 < \eta < \infty$, the bang-bang long-run solutions as in the tomahawk model might disappear once we no longer allow for inter-regional labour mobility. This is discussed next.

4.5.2 No Inter-regional Labour Mobility: the Bell-shaped Curve

How relevant is the tomahawk for the analysis of EU integration and agglomeration? In international trade theory it is standard to assume that labour is mobile between sectors, but not across national borders. This assumption reflects the stylized fact that labour is less mobile across borders than within regions or countries. Without inter-regional labour mobility, agglomeration, however, is still possible. The absence of inter-regional labour mobility still allows agglomeration because of the presence of inter-mediate goods. Firms may find it to be advantageous to agglomerate because of intermediate input linkages; they want to be near the suppliers of these inputs: recall the discussion about the supplier access term in wage equation (4.7) from the previous section. The labour required to sustain the agglomeration of firms comes from the immobile H-sector. To persuade workers to move from the H-sector to the manufacturing sector, each firm has to offer workers in this sector a higher wage than the existing wage in this sector: the more inelastic labour supply is to manufacturing wages, the higher this wage offer has to be. Agglomeration in this class of NEG model, and opposed to the case where the tomahawk figure applies, is associated with increasing wage differences between regions. In the peripheral region, wages decrease, because once firms agglomerate in the more attractive region, labour that is released in the manufacturing sector increases labour supply in the agricultural sector.

The point to emphasize here is that (with $0 < \eta < \infty$) agglomeration drives up wages in the core region. This ultimately reduces the incentive for firms in the manufacturing sector to concentrate production in the region where manufacturing economic activity is agglomerated for a number of reasons. First, an increased demand for labour raises production costs in the region where manufacturing is concentrated. Second, the importance of being close to a specific market diminishes as transportation costs become less important due to increased economic integration, that is, when φ, the degree of economic integration, increases. Third, the peripheral region, with its lower wage rate, becomes more and more attractive.

Without inter-regional labour mobility the long-run relationship between the freeness of trade (economic integration) and agglomeration *might* look like Figure 4.3, which has aptly been called the bell-shaped curve by Head and Mayer (2004).[14] As in Figure 4.2 for the two-region case we have φ on the horizontal axis and the degree of agglomeration on the vertical axis. For low degrees of economic integration (to the left of φ^B_{low}) we have spreading, and, similar to the previous section, once economic integration passes the break point (here φ^B_{low}) a process of agglomeration starts. The main difference with the previous model, is that agglomeration can be partial and go along with inter-regional wage differences. If economic integration is pushed far enough, a second (!) break point, denoted φ^B_{high}, will be reached. From φ^B_{high} onwards we have renewed spreading, no agglomeration is left whatsoever and inter-regional wages will now be equal (because both regions will have the same number of manufacturing firms and an equally sized manufacturing sector).

The solutions for φ^B_{low} and φ^B_{high} are the (real) solutions to the quadratic equation in φ (Puga, 1999, equation [33]):

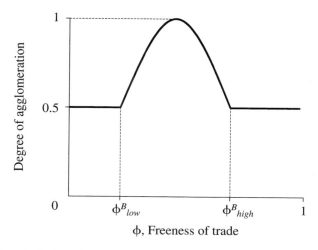

Figure 4.3   Bell-shaped curve

$$[\varepsilon(1+\mu)-1][(1+\mu)(1+\eta)+(1-\mu)\gamma]\varphi^2 - 2\{[\varepsilon(1+\mu^2)-1]$$
$$(1+\eta)-\varepsilon(1-\mu)[2(\varepsilon-1)-\gamma\mu]\}\varphi$$
$$+ (1-\mu)[\varepsilon(1-\mu)-1](\eta+1-\gamma)=0. \qquad (4.9)$$

If, depending on the exact parameter configuration for ε, γ, μ and η, these solutions exist, this expression gives us the two break points. To follow Head and Mayer (2004) we would like to answer the question for the case of the EU regions: 'Where in the bell are we?' Finally, and this must be emphasized, since the difference between the two classes of NEG models (Figure 4.2 versus Figure 4.3) only comes to the fore when we are dealing with long-run equilibria, the equilibrium wage equation (4.7) is at home in *both* classes of NEG models. This means that our estimations of the freeness of trade parameter φ based on the equilibrium wage equation can be confronted with the tomahawk figure as well as the above bell-shaped curve.

4.6   FROM ESTIMATIONS TO THEORY: φ FINALLY MEETS φ^B

Given the estimates we are now ready to confront our phi-estimations with the theoretical insights with respect to the relationship between economic integration and agglomeration. The starting point for our confrontation of our empirically grounded φ with the theoretical break points φ^B is that we take the NEG theory very seriously indeed.

Armed with our estimations for the structural parameters $\varepsilon = 9.53$ and $\gamma = 0.19$ for the EU NUTS 2 regions, we would like to know what these estimations imply when confronted with the tomahawk and bell-shaped figures, that is, when confronted with our NEG model. The break points φ^B for both the tomahawk and bell-shaped curve can be derived from equations (4.8) and (4.9). In order to be able to infer for any pair of regions r and s with bilateral distance D_{rs} the implied value for the freeness of trade parameter φ_{rs} based on our estimates for γ and ε, we have to take into consideration that the NUTS 2 regions are not of equal size and that therefore the internal distance D_{rr} matters to assess the freeness of trade between a region r and any other region s. This is why the associated value of φ_{rs} is in fact a measure of relative distance D_{rs}/D_{rr} and thereby of relative transport costs T_{rs}/T_{rr}.

We dub the break point φ^B_{labmob} for the version of the NEG model with inter-regional labour mobility; see equation (4.8). Given certain restrictions on the model parameters (see Puga, 1999, p. 315), this break point gives us the critical value of φ, below which the symmetric equilibrium (no agglomeration) is locally stable. If, however, $\varphi > \varphi^B_{labmob}$ we have complete agglomeration just like Figure 4.2 illustrates. Note, however, that due to presence of internal distance we thus have to adjust the definition of φ^B as follows, that is, we have to define the freeness of trade in terms of relative distance D_{rs}/D_{rr} (see Crozet, 2004, equation [16], p. 454 for a similar approach) and this holds for the break points in both the model with and without inter-regional labour mobility:

$$\phi^B = \left[\left[\frac{T(D_{rs})^\gamma}{T(D_{rr})^\gamma} \right]^{1-\varepsilon} \right]^B = \left[\left[\frac{D_{rs}}{D_{rr}} \right]^{\gamma(1-\varepsilon)} \right]^B. \qquad (4.10)$$

The break-condition (4.8) is not affected by our particular definition of the freeness of trade parameter as given in equation (4.10), and this is also true for the break-condition (4.9). For the bell-shaped curve depicted by Figure 4.3, and provided that equation (4.9) gives us two real solutions we know that $(\varphi^B_{low}$ and φ^B_{high} denote the first and second break point in Figure 4.2):

- For phi-values where $\varphi < \varphi^B_{low}$ or $\varphi > \varphi^B_{high}$ the spreading equilibrium is locally stable (there is no agglomeration).
- For phi-values where $\varphi^B_{low} < \varphi < \varphi^B_{high}$, the economy is on the bell part of the bell-shaped curve where the equilibria display (partial) agglomeration.

From equation (4.9) it is thus clear that the value of the two break points φ^B_{low} and φ^B_{high} do *not* as such depend on the specification of the transport costs function. Given, see equations (4.8) and (4.9), parameter values for μ, η, δ and ε, we can arrive at a specific value for the various break points φ^B. If we then use this in equation (4.10) and also plug in our estimates for ε and γ, we know the threshold value for the relative distance D_{rs}/D_{rr} that corresponds with the break point. Comparing this threshold with the actual relative distance between regions r and s provides information as to the spatial reach of agglomeration forces.

Before we can confront our estimation results with the break point conditions (4.8) and (4.9) and taking into account that the definition of the freeness of trade as given by equation (4.10), we thus finally need some benchmark numbers for the parameters μ, η, δ (given that we already have an estimate for ε). Recall that these four parameters suffice to yield the break points for the two models. For the last parameter we can start with our own estimations for the substitution elasticity (see Table 4.1). For the other three parameters we follow Puga (1999) and Head and Mayer (2004) and use as our benchmark values $\mu = 0.3$, $\eta = 200$, $\delta = 0.1$. It is important to keep in mind that the conclusions are, of course, sensitive to the choice of parameter values. Having said this, an extensive sensitivity analysis showed that our main conclusions hold up for a broad range of parameter values (not shown here but available upon request).

Table 4.2 gives for both the tomahawk and bell-shaped curve and for a number of alternative parameter values the break points φ^B_{low}, φ^B_{high}, and φ^B_{labmob} respectively. That is to say, these are the results for the break points when we apply the benchmark values for the four parameters to equations (4.8) and (4.9). Generally speaking it is true in both versions of the NEG model that the range of values of φ for which the symmetric equilibrium is stable, shrinks and, conversely, for which (partial) agglomeration is stable, expands whenever, ceteris paribus, μ, η, or δ get larger and/or ε gets smaller (see also Puga, 1999, equation [18]). The economic intuition for this is clear. If the importance of intermediate inputs in production increases (larger μ) it gets more attractive for firms to agglomerate in order to benefit from the intermediate cost and demand linkages between firms as explained in Section 4.3. If the elasticity of labour supply increases, firms will find that relatively low manufacturing wages can already persuade workers to move from the H-sector to the manufacturing sector. This decreases the strength of this congestion or spreading force. Also, a larger expenditure share of manufacturing goods benefits agglomeration because it increases the relevance of demand linkages. Finally, a lower value for the substitution elasticity stimulates agglomeration. Note, that this elasticity provides a measure of the (equilibrium) economies of scale,

Table 4.2   The break points for alternative parameter settings (benchmark parameter values in italic, including the estimated value for ε)

Key Parameters	φ^B_{low}	φ^B_{high}	φ^B_{labmob}
$\mu = 0.2$, $\eta = 200$, $\delta = 0.1$, $\varepsilon = 9.53$	0.55	0.77	0.20
$\mu = 0.2$, $\eta = 200$, $\delta = 0.1$, $\varepsilon = 4$	0.44	0.90	0.05
$\mu = 0.3$, $\eta = 200$, $\delta = 0.1$, $\varepsilon = 9.53$	0.30	0.89	0.11
$\mu = 0.2$, $\eta = 250$, $\delta = 0.1$, $\varepsilon = 9.53$	0.51	0.83	0.18
$\mu = 0.2$, $\eta = 200$, $\delta = 0.05$, $\varepsilon = 9.53$	0.55	0.77	0.33
$\mu = 0.1$, $\eta = 200$, $\delta = 0.05$ and $\varepsilon = 5$	symm	symm	0.52
$\mu = 0$, $\eta = 0$, $\delta = 0.1$ and $\varepsilon = 8$	symm	symm	0.65

Note: Symm indicates that the symmetric equilibrium is stable for all values of phi. The break points are derived for the case of $n = 2$ regions. In case $n < 2$, analytical solutions for the break points do not exist unless, see the Appendix in Puga, 1999, one sticks to the assumption of equidistance between all regions. See the main text for a further discussion of this issue.

where the economies of scale are measured as $\varepsilon/(\varepsilon - 1)$. A decrease of ε thus means an increased relevance of firm-specific increasing returns to scale, which boosts agglomeration.

Table 4.2 gives rise to the following three conclusions:

- First, the values for the various break points are indeed sensitive to the parameter settings even though the direction of change can thus be predicted.
- Second, it matters whether one chooses the model version with or without inter-regional labour mobility. As a rule, over the whole range of permissible φ's, $0 < \varphi < 1$, the agglomeration range is smaller (!) in the bell-shaped world than in the tomahawk world. Also, the symmetric equilibrium becomes unstable for lower values of φ. Hence, a process of economic integration gives rise more quickly to agglomeration in the model without inter-regional labour mobility.
- The third and, most important, conclusion relates to our set of benchmark parameter values (see Table 4.2), the empirical estimates for the freeness of trade parameter from Table 4.1 with the break-conditions (4.8) and (4.9). With $\mu = 0.3$, $\eta = 200$, $\delta = 0.1$ and $\varepsilon = 9.53$ (from Table 4.1, second column), we get from break-conditions (4.9) and (4.8) respectively that $\varphi^B_{low} = 0.30$, $\varphi^B_{high} = 0.89$ and, for the tomahawk, that $\varphi^B_{labmob} = 0.11$. Combining this with our estimates of $\gamma = 0.19$ and $\varepsilon = 9.53$ we can derive the critical or threshold relative

distance D_{rs}/D_{rr} that corresponds with each of these three break points.

From condition (4.9) or (4.8) we get values for φ^B and we also know, see equation (4.10), that $\varphi^B = [[D_{rs}/D_{rr}]^{\gamma(1-\varepsilon)}]^B$ and given our estimates for the distance parameter γ and the substitution elasticity ε we get the hypothetical relative distance that corresponds with the break point. More precisely we get for $\varphi^B{}_{low} = 0.30 \rightarrow D_{rs}/D_{rr} = 2.08$; $\varphi^B{}_{high} = 0.89 \rightarrow D_{rs}/D_{rr} = 1.07$; $\varphi^B{}_{labmob} = 0.11 \rightarrow D_{rs}/D_{rr} = 3.84$.

These results imply that the agglomeration does not extend further than one to four times the internal distance of a region. To see this, note that the average internal distance for the NUTS 2 regions is 42 km. With this value for internal distance D_{rr} we get from the perspective of region r a 'critical' or threshold external distance D_{rs} for the model underlying the bell-shaped curve of 87.3 km for $\varphi^B{}_{low}$ and 44.9 km for $\varphi^B{}_{high}$. This means that for any actual $D_{rs} > 87.3$ km we are on Figure 4.3 to the left of the first break point where spreading rules. Along similar lines, it is only when the actual $D_{rs} < 44.9$ km that spreading rules again. In between, that is, for 44.9 km $< D_{rs} < 87.3$ km, we are on the part of Figure 4.3 with (partial) agglomeration. For the tomahawk, Figure 4.2, the threshold external distance $D_{rs} = 161$ km. Here, the range or radius of agglomeration forces is thus somewhat stronger but still rather limited if one considers the fact that the distance between any pair of economic centres for the case of the EU NUTS 2 regions is often much larger than 161 km. Figure 4.4 summarizes our findings.[15] The conclusion about the rather limited spatial reach of agglomeration forces does not change when we substitute our benchmark parameter values for one of the other possibilities shown in Table 4.3. In most other cases and compared with our benchmark, the values for $\varphi^B{}_{low}$ and $\varphi^B{}_{labmob}$ are higher, which means that the threshold distance D_{rs}, beyond which agglomeration forces are no longer present, is even *lower* than for the set of benchmark parameter values.

Figure 4.4 summarizes our findings. The top panel of Figure 4.4 gives for our three respective break points the relative threshold distance D_{rs}/D_{rr} and the bottom panel does the same for the external distance D_{rs} under the assumption that the internal distance is 42 km.

To put our results into perspective, we estimated a simple market potential function (not shown here) to get some idea about what the centre regions are in our sample of EU+ regions. We list 39 regions with the highest market potential (we stopped when London entered the list). This is, of course, rather ad hoc but it nevertheless gives an indication as to what Figure 4.4 implies. For these 39 centre regions, the average distance to each other is 309 km (of these regions, the region Limburg in Belgium has the

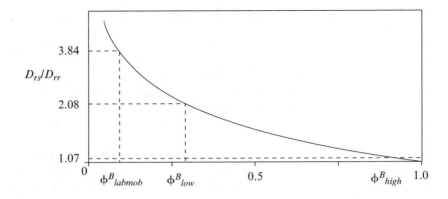

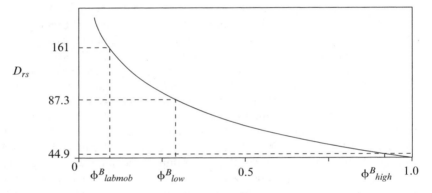

Note: Top panel: ε = 9.53, γ = 0.19; bottom panel: ε = 9.53, γ = 0.19, D_{rr} = 42 km.
Benchmark parameter values: μ = 0.3, η = 200, δ = 0.1.

Figure 4.4   Break points and threshold distances

lowest average distance to the other 38 regions: 220 km). Set against Figure
4.3 these distances imply that *on average*, agglomeration forces emanating
from a centre region *r* are too small or weak to affect other centre regions.
Another way to illustrate our results is to take one particular region like the
'most central' region, Limburg in Belgium (with D_{rr} = 18.5 km), or the
region with highest market potential, Nordrhein-Westfalen in Germany
(with D_{rr} = 69.4 km), and to calculate for these individual regions their
threshold distance D_{rs}. Also, for these two regions the spatial strength of
agglomeration forces is such that only a very limited number of the other
38 regions are affected. For the region of Nordrhein-Westfalen for instance,
seven (14) other regions fall within the reach of Nordrhein-Westfalen, that

is, have a distance to Nordrhein-Westfalen that is lower than the threshold D_{rs} that corresponds to φ^B_{low} (φ^B_{labmob}).

4.7 FROM THEORY TO ESTIMATIONS AND BACK: THE LIMITATIONS OF NEG

4.7.1 The Incompatibility Between a Multi-region World and a Two-region Model

To understand what we do and do not claim, it is important to be clear as to what we have done in Sections 4.4, 4.5 and 4.6. For our sample of NUTS 2 regions, we estimated the wage equation (4.7') in Section 4.4 and this helps us to arrive at the freeness of trade parameter for any region r with distances D_{rs} and D_{rr} in Section 4.6. Once we do this we can derive region-specific freeness of trade parameters. The NEG theory (the tomahawk and bell-shaped curve) from Section 4.5 gives us the break points, *but in fact only for the case of two regions!* Solutions for these break points for the case of $n > 2$ only exist for the case where distance is normalized (this is an innocent assumption to make as long as $n = 2$ but certainly no longer so when $n > 2$ because it means assuming equidistant regions).[16] In multi-region settings, concepts of symmetry or agglomeration become clouded. It is not clear, for example, how to call an equilibrium in which $n - 1$ regions have the same share of the manufacturing production but the nth region is larger: is this symmetry or agglomeration? Most importantly, however, the underlying assumption of equidistant regions is hard to maintain for $n > 2$ to start with. If one wants to analyze the long-run equilibria by means of a multi-region model, analytical solutions do not exist and one has to work with multi-region simulations (see Brakman, Garretsen and Schramm, 2005 for an example of these multi-region simulations).

Using our estimates for the substitution elasticity and the distance parameter from Table 4.1 we can calculate implied threshold distances between regions r and s at which a break point occurs. This implied distance is shown in Figure 4.4, and gives an idea about the geographical reach of agglomeration forces. Or stated differently, these differences 'indicate how far the agglomeration forces emanating from a region extend across space' (Crozet, 2004, p. 454). For a region r with an internal distance of D_{rr}, we arrive at the threshold distance D_{rs} at which the balance between agglomerating and spreading forces changes sign. We thereby establish in Figure 4.4 for any region r for both NEG models the radius (measured by D_{rs}) within which agglomeration or spreading forces dominate. This is, of course, a rather partial analysis and, rather problematically, it tries to force a two-region model upon the multi-region reality of the NUTS 2 regions. We set out on this enquiry into the relationship between transport costs (here, freeness of trade) and agglomeration because this relationship is in our view the defining feature of the NEG approach as we stated in Section 4.3 of this chapter. The conclusion must therefore be that in analytical terms it is at present rather difficult to ground NEG estimation results on NEG theory with respect to this key NEG relationship. One obvious way forward is to develop NEG models that can be tackled analytically too in a multi-region setting.

4.7.2   How to Pick Between the Two NEG Models?

The discussion so far begs the question, which of the two models is the most relevant? This leads us to another limitation of NEG research at present. A priori, our preference is with the second class of NEG models, in which labour is not mobile between regions. It implies less extreme agglomeration patterns (compare Figures 4.1 and 4.2). This seems more in line with the stylized facts for the EU and elsewhere. These models also incorporate the stylized fact that labour mobility is larger within countries than between countries. Having said this, we cannot dismiss the first of class of NEG models out of hand for basically three reasons:

- Both models assume wage flexibility. With wage rigidity (Faini, 1999; Puga, 2002) we return to the tomahawk figure because agglomeration by definition does not lead to a wage differential between regions and there will thus be no wage gap (and even no wage cost differential) between core and peripheral regions.
- Wage rigidity is larger within EU countries than between EU countries, this might be relevant in deciding which (regions versus countries) NEG model is relevant.
- Even though inter-regional labour mobility is relatively low in the EU (compared with for instance the United States), labour mobility is higher within than between countries and this might be relevant in deciding which class of NEG model applies for what geographical scale. Also, with increasing economic integration in the EU inter-regional labour mobility might increase in the future, which might make the world of the tomahawk curve more relevant.

Given the stylized facts on wage rigidity and labour (im)mobility within the EU and with the caveat about the usefulness of a two-region model in mind, does this mean that the 'bleak conclusions' of the tomahawk model as to the impact of ongoing economic integration on agglomeration are pervasive? No, not necessarily. One can think of alternative congestion forces for core regions besides higher wages that also give rise to a bell-shaped curve even with (!) inter-regional labour mobility. The best example is due to Helpman (1998) and Hanson (2001) where, instead of immobile workers (a non-traded input) we have a non-traded consumption good, in their case, housing, but one can think of various non-traded services of which the price rises when agglomeration increases. This can be looked upon as an example of agglomeration costs. Ottaviano, Tabuchi and Thisse (2002) show that such a non-traded good may act as a powerful dispersion force that acts a brake on agglomeration.[17] More fundamentally, however, is the issue that in order to be able to pick between NEG models, there is a need to develop NEG models that incorporate key features like the difference between inter-regional and international labour mobility within a single model (see Behrens et al., 2003, for a hopeful example). This might lead to additional testable hypotheses that allow for a better choice between various NEG agglomeration mechanisms.

4.7.3   Taking NEG Theory too Seriously

So far in this section we have argued that in order to make progress with the research on the empirical relevance of NEG we need better NEG models. But, there is also a danger of taking NEG theory too seriously. Two issues stand out in this respect. The first one is that NEG researchers should make better use of econometric insights from outside NEG proper and should make more use of new (micro) data sets that are increasingly becoming available. As to the former, see Combes and Overman (2004) and also Fingleton (2004). Spatial econometrics is a really powerful tool when it comes to the testing of spatial models like the NEG models. The second issue is that more testing as opposed to merely estimating NEG models is called for. In this chapter and in a rather implicit and ad hoc manner (see Section 4.4), we controlled for 'competing' explanations of a spatial wage structure by trying to control for fixed endowments and human capital or technological externalities in our wage equation (4.7'). A more direct testing of competing agglomeration or location theories would be a fruitful avenue for future research. Fingleton (2006) is the first to test an alternative model to describe the spatial distribution of wages – which he calls the urban economics (UE) model – explicitly against an NEG model. As these models are non-nested, he tests whether or not the fitted wages by an NEG model have additional explanatory power in a UE model (and vice versa). He finds that NEG has no additional explanatory power over his UE model. One implication of his research is that even though the inclusion of spatial linkages between regions or countries as emphasized by the NEG models is to be preferred from a theoretical point of view, this is not necessarily true when one engages in empirical research. In economic terms the spatial linkages can be quite weak, which means that the modelling of these linkages that complicates any attempt to analyse the model analytically, can be an unnecessary burden from an empirical point of view. Depending on the question and the geographical scale at hand, the general equilibrium nature of NEG models, where all locations are by definition interdependent, can be something of an theoretical overdose in the search for the empirical relevance of NEG. Here, less (theory) might be more (relevant).

4.8   CONCLUSIONS

Testing NEG models is difficult because many characteristics present in NEG models are also at home in alternative models, most notably the new trade models. In this respect the HME stands out. Showing that this effect is important in practice is, as such, not proof of the NEG. In fact, the main distinguishing characteristic of NEG is that the spatial distribution and the location of demand are simultaneously determined. The spatial distribution of economic activity can change catastrophically, even when changes in the economic environment – in the model represented by parameters – are small. The moment at which this happens is when an economy reaches a specific threshold – the so-called break points. This is special for NEG models, compared with alternative models that describe the spatial distribution of economic activity. It is therefore crucial to interpret the findings of estimates of NEG models in the light of these break points; is the economy on the brink of a catastrophic change or not?

This is the main topic of this chapter. We apply this idea to the EU and its regions. The EU is a good test case for this research, as economic integration has a long history in the EU. Economic integration increases, still we do not witness a catastrophic change. This is only consistent with NEG models if the EU has not passed its break point. We find some evidence that this indeed is the case. In terms of the NEG models the EU is still in the 'symmetric' equilibrium situation.

However, this conclusion is not without its problems:

- We draw this conclusion based on a theoretical model with only two regions/countries, and apply that to the EU (with many regions).
- Our conclusions are consistent with more than one variant of NEG models (with or without labour mobility between countries). These variants describe completely different worlds. This is problematic by itself.

- Alternative explanations are not tested, and there is some evidence that alternatives can also be important.

Although we highlighted that the evidence that shows the relevance of NEG models is compelling, we have also shown that much more work needs to be done. Not only are tests of NEG models against alternatives necessary, but also the translation of empirical estimates of NEG models into real world policy conclusions is only just beginning.

APPENDIX

Data Description

Nominal wage is defined as compensation of employees per worker (NUTS 2 level, except for Germany – NUTS 1). The measure of regional purchasing power is gross value-added (all sectors). Time series are nominalized by using the GVA series of Cambridge Econometrics, which are denominated in 1995 euros, and the price deflator of national GDP (AMECO database).

In the real market term RMA in the wage equation, we included the NUTS 1 regions of EU14 (= EU15 excluding Luxembourg) + Norway, Czech Republic, Poland, Hungary, Switzerland.

For wages we used the EU14 only. All wage, income and production data are taken from The European Regional Database (summer 2002 version) from Cambridge Econometrics.

Distance D_{rs} is in km.

A set of additional control variables for each NUTS 2 region that potentially consists of mean annual sunshine; mean elevation above sea-level; and dummy variables (country dummy, border region dummy, access to sea dummy, access to navigable waterway dummy). The variables mean annual sunshine radiation in kWh/m? (sunshine) and mean elevation above sea-level (in metres) are taken from the SPESP database (see http://www. mcrit.com/SPESP/SPESP_reg_ind_final% 20report.htm).

NOTES

1. In our own work we prefer the label '(new) geographical economics' but here we stick to the more commonly used label to denote the line of research that begins with Krugman (1991): new economic geography (NEG).

2. Combes and Overman (2004) show that the quality of the data is not optimal, and also list criteria for the ideal measure – not surprisingly, the optimal measure does not exist.
3. See, for instance, Barro and Sala-i-Martin (2004, Table 11.9) or Brakman, Garretsen, Gorter et al. (2005) for some evidence on the distribution of activity in European regions, and Gabaix and Ioannides (2004) for evidence on the distribution of city sizes.
4. This equation also shows why the findings on the HME show a highly variable pattern of estimated coefficients: both wages and employment changes should be accounted for, not only employment changes as in the strict version of the HME (Helpman and Krugman, 1985).
5. In that sense, characteristics (2) and (3) really amount to the same!
6. The research on the effects of large shocks is also very relevant but beyond the scope of this chapter. Work initiated by Davis and Weinstein (2002) relates the bombing shock of US strategic bombing of Japan during World War II to this issue. They find that the effects of the shock dissipate in time. It is, however, not clear to relate their findings explicitly to NEG; other models can not be ruled out. Closer to the predictions of NEG is the finding of Bosker et al. (2005): they find evidence for multiple equilibria in Germany after the strategic bombing campaign of the Allied forces of Germany during World War II, but also here explanations other than NEG are not ruled out.
7. Sections 4.4–4.6 are extended versions of related sections in Brakman, Garretsen and Schramm (2005).
8. The reason to derive a wage equation instead of a traditional equilibrium price equation is twofold. First, labour migration between regions is a function of (real) wages, second, data on regional wages are easier to obtain than regional manufacturing price data.
9. Whether or not in the long run both prices (here, wages) and quantities (here, mobile firms and workers) act as adjustment mechanisms, depends on the inter-sector elasticity of manufacturing labour supply (see Head and Mayer, 2004). With an infinite elastic labour supply all the adjustment has to come from the quantity side (and there will be no regional wage differences). In case, as we will assume too, of a positively sloped labour supply function to the relative (= manufacturing/agricultural) wage, at least part of the adjustment will come through regional wages.
10. This is why we decided not to use the regional production structure as a control variable. In NEG models this is clearly an endogenous variable. NEG models are all about the simultaneous determination of demand and production across regions.
11. Estimating in first differences (in 2SLS) instead of in levels, gave significant (and correctly signed) results for ε and γ too. But, more in line with Crozet, the substitution elasticity is much lower (between 2–3) and $\gamma > 1$ (around 1.8). Our concern here is, however, not so much the estimated coefficients as such but their compound effect on the freeness of trade parameter φ. In this respect, the first difference results yield a freeness of trade parameter that is very similar to the one based on the estimations in levels shown in Table 4.1.
12. Our discussion in this section is based on the two core NEG models as discussed in Puga (1999), but compare also Fujita et al. (1999, Chapters 4 and 5) with Chapter 14.
13. For the purpose of this chapter the sustain point, φ^S is deemed not relevant under the assumption that we are only interested in the case where we move from less to more economic integration, that is, we only move from left to right along the horizontal axis in Figure 4.2. The characteristics of break and sustain points are analysed in detail by, for example, Neary (2001); Robert-Nicoud (2004) and Ottaviano and Robert-Nicoud (2004).
14. It might but it need not; this depends on exact parameter configuration, see the Appendix in Puga (1999) or Robert-Nicoud (2004). The point to emphasize is that what really distinguishes Figure 4.3 from Figure 4.2 is that once agglomeration has arrived, the economy will stay in the agglomeration regime in Figure 4.2 as economic increases further whereas in Figure 4.3 for high levels of economic integration (high levels of φ) agglomeration will turn into (renewed) spreading. Here we assume that the latter possibility occurs with 'smooth', that is, partial agglomeration, equilibria as depicted in

Figure 4.3 but one can also come up with a double tomahawk (Robert-Nicoud, 2004, pp. 22–3) to depict this second possibility.

15. Our third conclusion is in line with the findings by Crozet (2004, Table 6). He conducts a similar analysis, the major difference being that the break point analysis is limited to the Krugman (1991) model (the break condition (4.8) with $\mu = \eta = 0$) and the fact that Crozet estimates his model for five EU countries (for each country separately).

16. Suppose that we stick to the assumption of equidistant regions for $n > 2$, then it can be shown (see Appendix in Puga, 1999) that the number of regions (n) enters the break conditions (4.8) and (4.9) as an additional parameter. For a large number of regions, like our sample of NUTS 2 regions, the result is that when n increases $\varphi^B \approx 0$, which means that the corresponding threshold distance D_{rs} also approaches 0 km. This would mean that for any real distance D_{rs} between any pair of regions we are always in the agglomeration regime. Symmetry is no longer viable (which is not very surprising in the sense that symmetry, every region having exactly a share of $1/n$ of the footloose production, is a rather stringent condition when n is large).

17. The key here for the possibility of (renewed) spreading at low trade costs (a large φ) arises in NEG models when the strength of the spreading or congestion forces do not fall when trade costs fall: 'with any . . . congestion force unrelated to trade costs, the equilibrium pattern of location will return to dispersion for some (low) trade costs threshold' (Head and Mayer, 2004, p. 2652).

REFERENCES

Baldwin, R., R. Forslid, Ph. Martin, G.I.P. Ottaviano and F. Robert-Nicoud (2003), *Economic Geography and Public Policy*, Princeton: Princeton University Press.

Barro, R.J. and X. Sala-i-Martin (2004), *Economic Growth*, Second Edition, Cambridge, MA: MIT Press.

Behrens, K., C. Gaigné, G.I.P. Ottaviano and J.-F. Thisse (2003), 'Interregional and international trade, seventy years after Ohlin', *Discussion Paper 4065*, Centre for Economic Policy Research, London.

Bosker, M., S. Brakman, H. Garretsen and M. Schramm (2005), 'Looking for multiple equilibria when geography matters: German city growth and the WWII shock', *CESifo Working Paper 1553*, Munich.

Brakman, S., H. Garretsen and M. Schramm (2004), 'The spatial distribution of wages: estimating the Helpman-Hanson model for Germany', *Journal of Regional Science*, **44**: 437–66.

Brakman, S., H. Garretsen, M. Schramm (2005), 'Putting new economic geography to the test: freeness of trade and agglomeration in the EU regions', *CESifo Working Paper 1566*, Munich.

Brakman, S., H. Garretsen, J. Gorter, A. van der Horst and M. Schramm (2005), *New Economic Geography, Empirics, and Regional Policy*, Den Haag: CPB Netherlands Bureau for Economic Policy Analysis, http://www.cpb.nl/nl/pub/cpbreeksen/bijzonder/56/bijz56.pdf.

Broda, C. and D. Weinstein (2004), 'Globalization and the gains from variety', *NBER Working Paper 10314*, National Bureau of Economic Research.

Combes, P.P. and H.G. Overman (2004), 'The spatial distribution of economic activities in the European Union', in J.V. Henderson and J.-F. Thisse (eds), *Handbook of Regional and Urban Economics: Cities and Geography*, North-Holland: Elsevier.

Crozet, M. (2004), 'Do migrants follow market potentials? An estimation of a new economic geography model', *Journal of Economic Geography*, **4**: 439–58.

Davis, D. and D. Weinstein (2002), 'Bones, bombs, and break points: the geography of economic activity', *American Economic Review*, **92**: 1269–89.

Faini, R. (1999), 'Trade unions and regional development', *European Economic Review*, **43** (2): 457–74.

Fingleton, B. (2004), 'Some alternative geo-economics for Europe's regions', *Journal of Economic Geography*, **4**: 389–420.

Fingleton, B. (2006), 'The new economic geography versus urban economics: an evaluation using local wage rates in Great Britain', *Oxford Economic Papers* (in press), paper first presented at the HWWA, Hamburg, 14/15 October, 2004: http://www.hwwa.de/Projekte/Forsch_Schwerpunkte/FS/EI/NEG/Paper%20Fingleton.pdf.

Fujita, M., P.R. Krugman and A. Venables (1999), *The Spatial Economy: Cities, Regions, and International Trade*, Cambridge, MA: MIT Press.

Fujita, M. and J.-F. Thisse (2001), 'Economics of agglomeration', in S. Brakman, H. Garretsen and M. van Marrewijk (eds), *Introduction to Geographical Economics*, Cambridge: Cambridge University Press.

Gabaix, X. and Y.M. Ioannides (2004), 'The evolution of city size distributions', in J.V. Henderson and J.-F. Thisse (eds), *Handbook of Regional and Urban Economics: Cities and Geography*, North-Holland: Elsevier.

Hanson, G.H. (2001), 'Market potential, increasing returns, and geographic concentration', mimeo, Graduate School of International Relations and Political Studies, UC San Diego (revised version of *NBER Working Paper 6429*, National Bureau of Economic Research, forthcoming *Journal of International Economics*).

Hanson, G.H. and C. Xiang (2004), 'The home market effect and bilateral trade patterns', *American Economic Review*, **94**: 1108–24.

Head, K. and Th. Mayer (2000), 'Non-Europe: the magnitude and causes of market fragmentation in Europe', *Weltwirtschaftliches Archiv*, **136**: 285–314.

Head, K. and Th. Mayer (2004), 'The empirics of agglomeration and trade', in J.V. Henderson and J.-F. Thisse (eds), *Handbook of Regional and Urban Economics: Cities and Geography*, North-Holland: Elsevier.

Head, K. and Th. Mayer (2005), 'Regional wage and employment responses to market potential in the EU', mimeo, Paris.

Helpman, E. and P. Krugman (1985), *Market Structure and Foreign Trade*, Cambridge, MA: MIT Press.

Helpman, E. (1998), 'The size of regions', in D. Pines, E. Sadka and I. Zilcha (eds), *Topics in Public Economics*, Cambridge: Cambridge University Press.

Hinloopen, J. and C. van Marrewijk (2005), 'Locating economic concentration', in S. Brakman and H. Garretsen (eds), *Location and Competition*, London/New York: Routledge Studies in Global Competition Series.

Knaap, T. (2004), 'Models of economic geography, dynamics, estimation and policy evaluation', PhD thesis, University of Groningen.

Krugman, P.R. (1980), 'Scale economics, product differentiation, and pattern of trade', *American Economic Review*, **70**: 950–59.

Krugman, P.R. (1991), *Geography and Trade*, Leuven/Cambridge: MIT Press.

Krugman, P. and A. Venables (1995), 'Globalization and the inequality of nations', *Quarterly Journal of Economics*, **110**: 857–80.

Neary, J.P. (2001), 'Of hype and hyperbolas: introducing the New Economic Geography', *Journal of Economic Literature*, **39**: 536–61.

Ottaviano, G.I.P. and F. Robert-Nicoud (2005), 'The "genome" of NEG models with vertical linkages: a positive and normative synthesis', *Journal of Economic Geography*, **6**: 113–39.

Ottaviano, G., T. Tabuchi and J.-F. Thisse (2002), 'Agglomeration and trade revisited', *International Economic Review*, **43**: 409–36.

Puga, D. (1999), 'The rise and fall of regional inequalities', *European Economic Review*, **43**: 303–34.

Puga, D. (2002), 'European regional policies in the light of recent location theories', *Journal of Economic Geography*, **2**: 372–406.

Redding, S. and A.J. Venables (2004), 'Economic geography and international inequality', *Journal of International Economics*, **62**: 53–82.

Robert-Nicoud, F. (2004), 'The structure of simple "New Economic Geography" models', *Discussion Paper 4326*, Centre for Economic Policy Research, London.

5. Agglomeration and growth in NEG: a critical assessment[1]

Fabio Cerina and Francesco Pigliaru

5.1 INTRODUCTION

There are sizeable and persistent per-capita income gaps across states and even across the regions of a rich integrated area such as the EU. With regard to regional inequality, one of the most prominent explanations stems from the idea that regions are highly specialized, and that productivity may differ across sectors. In Kaldor's influential explanation, trade can drive apart two almost identical regions by causing industry to agglomerate in one location. This mechanism has been modelled in several papers on endogenous growth and trade (for example, Lucas, 1988 and Grossman and Helpman, 1991). However, papers in this tradition do not take geography (that is, transport costs) into account. More recently, the development of the new economic geography (NEG) literature has extended the Grossman and Helpman approach to include explicit mechanisms of agglomeration. In this chapter we will assess the contribution of recent models of agglomeration and economic growth in relation to Kaldor's proposition. In the first part of the chapter we explain, compare and discuss the new approach. In particular, we:

- review how the mechanism leading to (catastrophic) agglomeration of the high-tech sector works and assess the existence of core results across different models;
- explain and discuss what the economic consequences of catastrophic agglomeration are for the core and for the periphery.

In the second part of the chapter we will assess the analytical robustness of some important results that may be of interest to policy-makers.[2] We will focus on the following: (1) the symmetric equilibrium is always stable when capital is perfectly mobile; (2) the geographical allocation of industries does not affect the growth rate of innovation when spillovers are global; (3) agglomeration can be growth-enhancing both for the core (where agglomeration takes place) and for the periphery. These results have strong implications for regional policy and therefore deserve closer scrutiny. We aim to show:

- that in its current analytical formulation these results are far from robust;
- that adopting a more general representation of consumers' preferences results in a less optimistic outlook regarding the consequences of agglomeration for the core and, above all, for the periphery.

The chapter is organized as follows: Section 5.2 analyses the contribution of some recent developments in new economic geography to the issue of long-run income gaps among countries, and the policy implications that can be drawn from the most important results coming from the so-called 'new economic geography and growth' (NEGG) literature. Section 5.3 discusses the robustness of some of these results and shows how their validity is restricted to a very narrow set of parameter values. Section 5.4 concludes.

5.2 NEG, GROWTH AND REGIONAL GAP

Kaldor famously wrote as far back as 1970:

> When trade is opened up between them, the region with the more developed industry will be able to supply the need of the agricultural area of the other region on more favourable terms: with the result that the industrial centre of the second region will lose its market and will tend to be eliminated. (Kaldor, 1970, p. 338)

But what conditions are really needed for this catastrophic agglomeration to occur? What are the consequences for the economy as a whole and for the periphery? Is there a case for regional policy? What kind of regional policy? In the following section, we focus on finding the answer that NEG provides to these questions. More precisely, our aim is to assess the contribution of NEG in understanding what the sources and the growth-effect of agglomeration will be and how much the periphery should worry about agglomeration. In order to do this, we focus on a typical NEGG model. We believe it is useful to stress some basic assumptions and some already known intermediate results because they will represent a benchmark for the second part of the chapter in which we will evaluate to what extent the policy implications of the NEG models are sensitive to small changes in the assumptions.

Our main references are Baldwin et al. (2003) and Baldwin and Martin (2003) who have supplied the most important results in this field. The original results are contained in Martin (1999); Baldwin and Forslid (1999, 2000a and 2000b); Martin and Ottaviano (1999 and 2001); Baldwin, Martin and Ottaviano (2001) and Bellone and Maupertuis (2003).[3]

NEGG models can be thought of as the results of the meeting between two different strands of literature: new growth theory (Romer, 1990; Grossman and Helpman, 1991) and new economic geography (Krugman, 1991; Krugman and Venables, 1995). Many of the most popular NEG models focus on labour and don't take into account the accumulation of physical or knowledge capital. These models are therefore not suited to explaining the growth process. In order to ensure that these models are capable of creating sustained growth, most NEGG models make use of an instrument that is typical of endogenous growth theory: they add a capital-producing sector, which makes capital stock endogenous. The introduction of this sector, which represents the key analytical difference from the standard CP (core-periphery) models, allows for an analysis (1) of how new economic activities emerge as a consequence of technological innovations; (2) of the way these economic activities decide to locate. In other words, by means of NEGG models, the creation and localization process of new firms can be considered as a unique process.

5.2.1 Model Structure and Intermediate Results

Most existing geography and growth models adopt international settings where the migration of workers across regions or countries is not allowed for. This is because, in the majority of cases, the introduction of workers' migration into an endogenous growth model under perfect foresight raises difficult problems.[4] Accordingly, we will focus on a framework in which labour is immobile across regions but a core-periphery outcome is still possible if particular assumptions are made about capital mobility.

Apart from the introduction of the capital-producing sector, the structure of NEGG models is almost identical to that of the most popular NEG models. The world is made up of two regions, North and South, both endowed with two factors: labour L and capital K. Three sectors are active in both regions: manufacturing M, traditional goods T and a capital-producing sector I. Regions are symmetric in terms of preferences, technology, transport costs and labour endowment. As already stated, labour is assumed to be immobile across regions but mobile across sectors within the same region.

As in the CP models, the usual Dixit-Stiglitz M-sector (manufactures) consists of differentiated goods but, in this context, fixed cost is expressed in terms of K. Each variety requires one unit of capital, which, according to the assumption on capital mobility, can be interpreted as an idea, a new technology, a patent, or machinery, etc. Production also entails a variable cost (a_M units of labour per unit of output). Its cost function, therefore, is $\pi + wa_M x_i$, where π is K's rental rate, w is the wage rate and x_i is total output of a typical firm.

Each region's K is produced by its I-sector, which produces one unit of K with a_I unit of labour. So the production and marginal cost function for the I-sector are, respectively:

$$\dot{K} = Q_K = \frac{L_I}{a_I} \tag{5.1}$$

$$F = wa_I. \tag{5.2}$$

Note that this unit of capital in equilibrium is also the fixed cost F of the manufacturing sector. As one unit of capital is required to start a new variety, the number of varieties and of firms at the world level is simply equal to the capital stock at the world level: $K + K^* = K^w$. We denote n and n^* as the number of firms located in the North and South respectively. As one unit of capital is required per firm we also know that: $n + n^* = K^{w*}$. However, depending on the assumptions we make on capital mobility, the stock of capital produced and owned by one region may or may not be equal to the number of firms producing in that region. In the case of capital mobility, the capital may be produced in one region but the firm that uses this capital unit may be operating in another region. Hence, when capital is mobile, the number of firms located in one region is generally different from the stock of capital owned by this region.

To individual I-firms, the innovation cost a_I is a parameter. However, following Romer (1990), endogenous and sustained growth is provided by assuming that the marginal cost of producing new capital declines (that is, a_I falls) as the sector's cumulative output rises. In the most general form, learning spillovers are assumed to be localized. The cost of innovation can be expressed as:

$$a_I = \frac{1}{AK^w}$$

where $A \equiv s_n + \lambda (1 - s_n)$ and $0 < \lambda < 1$ measures the degree of globalization of learning spillovers. The South's cost function is isomorphic, that is, $F^* = w^*/K^w A^*$ where $A^* = \lambda s_n + 1 - s_n$. Notice that, when learning spillovers are global ($\lambda = 1$), $A = A^* = 1$. In the model version we examine, capital depreciation is ignored.[5] Because the number of firms, varieties and capital units are equal, the growth rate of the number of varieties, on which we focus, is therefore:

$$g \equiv \frac{\dot{K}}{K}; \, g^* \equiv \frac{\dot{K}^*}{K^*}.$$

Finally, traditional goods, which are assumed to be homogeneous, are produced by the *T*-sector under conditions of perfect competition and constant returns. By choice of units, one unit of *T* is made with one unit of *L*. Basically, the traditional sector has no 'active' role in these models but its existence in both regions has a crucial role for some of the implications of this class of model.

5.2.1.1   Consumer choice
The representative consumer is infinitely-lived and has the following preferences:

$$U_t = \int_{t=0}^{\infty} e^{-\rho t} \ln Q_t dt; \, Q_t = C_M^{\mu} C_T^{1-\mu}; \, C_M = \left[\int_{i=0}^{K+K^*} c_i^{1-1/\sigma} di \right]^{\frac{1}{1-1/\sigma}} \quad (5.3)$$

where ρ is the rate of time preference, σ is the constant elasticity of substitution among varieties and the other parameters have their customary meaning. As usual, utility optimization can be thought of as a three-stage decision in which consumers first inter-temporally allocate their income between consumption and savings (according to a logarithmic utility function), then allocate consumption between manufacturing and traditional goods (according to a Cobb-Douglas utility function) and finally distribute manufacturing consumption across varieties (according to a CES utility function).

Intertemporal optimization implies that the time path of consumption expenditures E is driven by the standard Euler equation:

$$\frac{\dot{E}}{E} = r - \rho$$

with the interest rate r satisfying the no-arbitrage-opportunity condition between investment in the safe asset and capital accumulation:

$$r = \frac{\pi}{F} + \frac{\dot{F}}{F}$$

where π is the rental rate of capital and F its asset value, which, due to perfect competition in the *I*-sector, is equal to its marginal cost of production.

In the second stage, maximization of the Cobb-Douglas utility function means that a constant fraction of total northern consumption expenditure E falls on M-varieties with the rest spent on T:

$$P_M C_M = \mu E \tag{5.4}$$

$$p_T C_T = (1 - \mu) E \tag{5.5}$$

where p_T is the price of the traditional good and $P_M = [\int_{i=0}^{K+K^*} p_i^{1-\sigma} di]^{1/1-\sigma}$ is the Dixit-Stiglitz perfect price index for the manufactured goods.

Finally, in the third stage, the amount of M-goods expenditure μE is allocated across varieties according to the CES demand function for a typical M-variety $c_j = p_j^{-\sigma}/P_M^{1-\sigma} \mu E$, where p_j is variety j's consumer price. Southern optimization conditions are isomorphic.

5.2.1.2 Firms' choice

Due to perfect competition in the T-sector, the price of the agricultural good must be equal to the wage of the traditional sector's workers: $p_T = w_T$. Moreover, *as long as both regions produce some T*, the assumption of free trade in T implies that not only price, but also wages are equalized across regions. It is therefore convenient to choose home labour as numeraire so that:

$$p_T = p_T^* = w_T = w_T^* = 1.$$

Is it always the case that both regions produce some T? An assumption is actually needed in order to avoid complete specialization: a single country's labour endowment must be insufficient to meet global demand. Formally:

$$L^* = L < (1 - \mu)\frac{(E + E^*)}{p_T} = (1 - \mu)(E + E^*). \tag{5.6}$$

The purpose of making this assumption is to maintain the M-sector wages fixed at the unit value. Since labour is mobile across sector, as long as the T-sector is present in both regions, a simple arbitrage condition would suggest that wages of the two sectors cannot differ. Hence, M-sector wages are tied to T-sector wages, which, in turn, remain fixed at the level of the unit price of a traditional good. Therefore:

$$w_M = w_M^* = w_T = w_T = 1 \tag{5.7}$$

As we might easily conclude, (5.7) holds even when the M-sector disappears in one region. But it does not hold any longer in cases where there is full specialization. These cases are actually excluded a priori by (5.6). However, as we shall see later, Bellone and Maupertuis (2003) show that by removing this assumption, and therefore allowing for complete specialization to occur and for wages to diverge, has no particular consequences on the divergence-convergence scenario.

Since wages are uniform and all varieties' demand have the same constant elasticity σ, firms' profit maximization yields local and export prices that are identical for all varieties no matter where they are produced: $p = wa_M \frac{\sigma}{\sigma-1}$. Then, imposing the normalization $a_M = \frac{\sigma-1}{\sigma}$ and (5.7), we finally have:

$$p = w = 1 \tag{5.8}$$

As usual, since trade in M is impeded by iceberg import barriers, prices for markets abroad are higher:

$$p^* = \tau_p; \tau \geq 1.$$

With monopolistic competition, equilibrium operating profit is given by the value of sales divided by σ. Due to free entry, this profit is entirely absorbed by the fixed cost of production (the rental rate of capital π). Thus, market clearing conditions for each variety result in:

$$\pi = B\frac{\mu E^w}{\sigma K^w}; \; B = \left[\frac{s_E}{s_n + \phi(1-s_n)} + \frac{\phi(1-s_E)}{\phi s_n + (1-s_n)} \right] \tag{5.9}$$

$$\pi^* = B^*\frac{\mu E^w}{\sigma K^w}; \; B^* = \left[\frac{\phi s_E}{s_n + \phi(1-s_n)} + \frac{(1-s_E)}{\phi s_n + (1-s_n)} \right] \tag{5.10}$$

where $E^w = E + E^*$ is world total expenditure, $s_E = E/E^w$ is the North share of E^w and $\phi = \tau^{1-\sigma}$ measures the freeness of trade since trade gets freer as φ rises from 0 (prohibitive costs) to 1 (costless trade). Finally, considering the market clearing condition on M- and T-goods and the labour market, we conclude that a steady state, with constant growth rate in the number of varieties (and hence a constant number of R&D workers), will only exist if E^w is itself constant:

$$E^w = (2L - L_I - L_I^*)\frac{\sigma}{\sigma - \mu}. \tag{5.11}$$

5.2.2   Does Economic Growth Generate Agglomeration?

For the sake of simplicity, we shall answer this question by focusing on the case when spillovers are global ($\lambda = 1$). Allowing for localized learning spillovers will not change the nature of the answer to this question: if capital is immobile and trade is free enough, an increase in the rate of capital growth in one of the two regions leads to a core-periphery outcome in the high-growth region.

By using a Tobin q approach (Baldwin and Forslid, 1999 and 2000b), we know that the equilibrium level of investment (production in the I-sector) is characterized by the equality of the stock market value of a unit of capital (denoted with the symbol V) and the replacement cost of capital, F. With E and E^* constant in steady state, the Euler equation gives us $r = r^* = \rho$. Moreover, in steady state, the growth rate of the capital stock (or of the number of varieties) will be constant and will either be common ($g = g^*$ in the interior symmetric case) or North's g (in the core-periphery case).[6] In either case, the steady-state values of investing in new units of K are:

$$V_t = \frac{\pi_t}{\rho + g}; \ V^*_t = \frac{\pi^*_t}{\rho + g}$$

so that, using (5.9), (5.10), (5.2) and the labour market clearing condition,

$$q = B(s_E, s_n) \frac{\mu E^w}{(\rho + g)\sigma}$$

$$q^* = B^*(s_E, s_n) \frac{\mu E^w}{(\rho + g)\sigma}$$

in equilibrium $q = q^* = 1$ and therefore, using (5.11) and the fact that, both in the symmetric and the CP equilibrium we have $B(s_E, s_n) = B^*(s_E, s_n) = 1$, we can solve for the equilibrium rate of growth g:

$$g = \frac{2\mu L - (\sigma - \mu)\rho}{\sigma} \tag{5.12}$$

which tells us that *the geographical allocation of the I-sector does not influence the rate of growth g*. As we will see later, this is true only if the cost of innovation is the same across regions, that is, when learning spillovers are global. Given that $L_I > 0$ ($L^*_I > 0$), investment will be positive if and only if $q \geq 1 (q^* \geq 1)$. Hence, starting from a symmetric equilibrium when $s_n = s_E = 0.5$ and $q = q^* = 1$ we can study the linkage between growth

and agglomeration of economic activities by studying the behaviour of q
and q^* as s_n varies. We thus have:

$$\frac{\partial B(s_E, s_n)}{\partial s_E}\bigg|_{s_n = 0.5} = -\frac{\partial B^*(s_E, s_n)}{\partial s_E}\bigg|_{s_n = 0.5} = 2\left[\frac{1 - \phi}{1 + \phi}\right] > 0 \qquad (5.13)$$

$$\frac{\partial B(s_E, s_n)}{\partial s_n}\bigg|_{s_E, s_n = 0.5} = -\frac{\partial B^*(s_E, s_n)}{\partial s_n}\bigg|_{s_E, s_n = 0.5} = -2\left[\frac{1 - \phi^2}{1 + \phi^2}\right] < 0. \quad (5.14)$$

Equation (5.14) tells us that a production shifting in the North (that is, an increase in the number of firms located in the North) has, by itself, a negative effect: competition increases, sales and profit go down, the value of the firm becomes smaller than the replacement cost of capital and there is no more incentive to invest in the *I*-sector. The opposite happens in the South.

If this were the only mechanism at work, the system would go back to symmetry. But (5.13) suggests that the story does not finish here. In fact, things are different if an increase in s_n makes s_E increase also. In this case, production shifting ($\delta s_n > 0$) leads to demand shifting ($\delta s_E > 0$) and profits in the North may grow enough to offset the negative effect of competition. If so, the typical North *I*-sector firm now has the incentive to invest more, so s_n increases further. The symmetric equilibrium will then become unstable and catastrophic agglomeration of *I* and *M* starts to take place.

So, in order to have catastrophic agglomeration, we need to answer 'yes' to the following crucial questions: (1) Does production shifting lead to demand shifting? (2) Does production shifting lead to *enough* demand shifting? Identifying cases when the answer to both questions is 'yes' means recognizing the conditions under which catastrophic agglomeration takes place.

5.2.2.1 Does production shifting lead to demand shifting?

Given the structure of the model, the only case when the answer to this question is 'yes' is if we assume *capital to be immobile*. Analogously to other NEG models, catastrophic agglomeration is due to a circular causality characterized by both production and demand shifting, which reinforce each other. Production shifting takes the form of capital accumulation in one region (and de-accumulation in the other) and the demand shifting takes the form of an increase in permanent income in one region (and a decrease in the other) due to larger investment. With perfect capital mobility, firms' owners can decide where to locate production and profits are repatriated. Hence, production shifting does not lead to demand shifting.

By using (5.14), we can easily infer that, when capital is perfectly mobile, the symmetric equilibrium will be stable.[7] In fact, since with perfect mobility s_K does not change with s_n (production shifting does not affect the distribution of capital) a small increase in s_n will unambiguously lead to a decrease in the North's profits and an increase in the South's profits, so that firms are induced to go back in the South. The only active mechanism here is that, when more firms locate in the North, this increases competition there (and decreases it in the South).

By contrast, if capital is immobile, then firms cannot choose where to locate and firm owners are forced to invest in the region where they live ($s_n = s_K$). In this case, gains from capital ownership have to be spent in the region where production takes place. Hence, production shifting results in demand shifting, that is, a larger number of firms located in a region means that there will be a larger share of expenditure in the same region.

This happens because of a simple equilibrium relation between s_E and s_K. In equilibrium, when $q = q^* = 1$ we have the following:

$$s_E = \frac{E}{E^w} = \frac{L + \rho s_K}{2L + \rho} = \frac{1}{2} + \frac{\rho}{2L + \rho}\left(s_K - \frac{1}{2}\right) \tag{5.15}$$

that is, an increase in the North's share of capital increases its permanent income and leads therefore to an increase in its share of expenditure. Since, with capital immobility an increase in the North's share of firms corresponds to an increase in its share of capital ($s_n = s_K$), then, following a small increase in s_n the North's incentives to accumulate are now affected by another mechanism, that of demand linkages, which works on the opposite direction with respect to the competition effect (5.13).

We therefore need capital immobility to obtain a demand linkage effect from s_n to s_E. However, this necessary condition for cumulative causation to take place, is *not* sufficient.

5.2.2.2 Does production shifting lead to *enough* demand shifting?

Differentiating B we obtain the following:

$$dB(s_n, s_E) = \frac{\partial B}{\partial s_n} ds_n + \frac{\partial B}{\partial s_E} ds_E.$$

When capital is immobile and since $s_n = s_K$ and by (5.15) $ds_E/ds_n = \rho/(2L + \rho) > 0$, we will see that:

$$dB(s_n, s_E(s_n)) = \frac{\partial B}{\partial s_n} ds_n + \frac{\partial B}{\partial s_E} \frac{ds_E}{ds_n} ds_n.$$

In symmetry we have:

$$\left.\frac{dB(s_n, s_E(s_n))}{ds_n}\right|_{s_n = s_E = 0.5} = -\left.\frac{dB^*(s_n, s_E(s_n))}{ds_n}\right|_{s_n = s_E = 0.5}$$

$$= \underbrace{-2\left[\frac{1-\phi^2}{1+\phi^2}\right]}_{\text{market-crowding effect}} + \underbrace{2\left[\frac{1-\phi}{1+\phi}\right]\frac{\rho}{2L+\rho}}_{\text{demand-linked effect}}.$$

Following a small increase in s_n the North's profits increase, and so agglomeration takes place, whenever the market-crowding effect is offset by the demand-linked effect (which is absent in the case of perfect mobility). A quick examination reveals that this is the case when:

$$\phi > \frac{L}{L+\rho} = \phi_{CP}.$$

Hence, catastrophic agglomeration occurs if $ds_n > 0$ when transport costs are sufficiently low. It can be shown that, if the same condition holds, the CP equilibrium becomes stable.

As usual, both effects decrease as trade becomes freer. But the market-crowding effect decreases (in absolute value) faster than the demand-linked effect, so that, when transport costs are low enough, the latter offsets the former and symmetric equilibrium becomes unstable and CP outcome will be reached with probability 1.

To sum up, we can so far draw the following conclusions:

- *Capital immobility is a necessary and sufficient condition for economic integration (raising of φ) to generate catastrophic agglomeration.* No localized spillovers of knowledge are required for this result: although the cost of innovation is the same everywhere, a higher expenditure share in the core makes expected profits too low in the periphery.
- *When spillovers are global, the overall growth rate of the economy does not depend on the geographical allocation of economic activities.* While there is no inequality in the symmetric equilibrium, *permanent income levels in the core are higher than permanent income levels in the periphery* where, by definition, capital just disappears (asymptotically). However, this difference remains constant in equilibrium. Indeed:

● By terms of trade, *the growth rate of real income is the same across regions.* We will come back to this issue later.

5.2.3 Is Agglomeration Growth-enhancing?

We are now interested in the growth-effect of agglomeration. As we have already mentioned, for agglomeration of I- and M-sectors to be growth-enhancing, we need to modify the assumptions of the model presented above. Although introducing localized spillovers is not the only way that geography can affect growth,[8] this seems, to some extent, the most natural way.[9]

Within this class of models, localized spillovers (LS) means that the cost of R&D in one region depends only partially ($\lambda < 1$) on the other region's capital stock. Hence, innovation costs will also depend both on the stock *and* the allocation of overall capital stock. Therefore, taking into account that the wage rate is equal to 1, (5.2) becomes:

$$F = \frac{1}{AK^w}$$

where $A \equiv s_n + \lambda (1 - s_n)$. The South's expression for innovation costs is isomorphic.

From the viewpoint of geographical allocation equilibrium analysis, the main differences to note are that: (1) the symmetric equilibrium becomes unstable for even higher trade costs ($\phi_{cat} < \phi_{CP}$); (2) the level of trade costs that causes symmetric equilibrium to become unstable (ϕ_{cat}) no longer coincides with the level of trade costs where the CP equilibrium becomes stable ($\phi_{CP'}$). In particular $\phi_{cat} < \phi_{CP'} < \phi_{CP}$ and for $\phi_{cat} < \phi < \phi_{CP}$ two more interior stable equilibria emerge; (3) both ϕ_{cat} and ϕ_{CP} are increasing in λ so that if we are in a CP equilibrium and λ grows enough, the CP equilibrium becomes unstable and the system might go back to symmetry. A further difference regarding the nature of agglomeration is that while we still observe that a CP outcome (catastrophic agglomeration of the M-sector in only one region) will emerge if and only if capital is immobile, a full concentration of the I-sector may also occur when capital is perfectly mobile. Due to localized spillovers, in fact, it is less costly to innovate in the region with the highest number of firms. This implies that, because of perfect capital mobility, all the innovation will take place in the region with a higher number of firms. In any case, the other region will be able to simply buy (without trade costs) innovations or capital produced in the innovating region.

But, as far as policy rules are concerned, the most significant differences concern the issue of growth: *in an LS world the geographical allocation of* *manufacturing firms affects the global growth rate.* Using the optimal investment condition $q = q^* = 1$, we find that, in the symmetric equilibrium (for $s_n = 0.5$):

$$g_S = \frac{(1 + \lambda)\mu L - (\sigma - \mu)\rho}{\sigma}$$

while, in the CP outcome (when $s_n = 1$):

$$g_{CP} = \frac{2\mu L - (\sigma - \mu)\rho}{\sigma}.$$

The latter is identical to the solution when spillovers are global since, in the CP outcome, all innovators are located in the same region so that learning is not affected by the degree of localization λ. Since $\lambda < 1$, $g_{CP} > g_S$: when industry is spread across the two regions, spillovers are minimized, the cost of innovation is at its maximum and the global growth rate is at its minimum.

5.2.4 The Rate of Growth of Consumption and Real Income

NEGG models like those presented above are not able to explain differences in the long-run rate of growth of consumption and real income between core and peripheral regions: real GDP and consumption growth rates in the two regions are identical in both the GS and the LS cases. And, most importantly, real GDP and consumption growth rates are the same in the two regions in the interior equilibrium (where both are innovating) as well as in the CP equilibria (where only one is doing so). This is due to the fact that real growth stems from the constant fall in the price index that is driven by a continuously widening range of varieties and which is common to the two regions. The price index for manufactures can be rewritten as:

$$P_M = (s_n + (1 - s_n)\phi)^{\frac{1}{1-\sigma}} K^{w\frac{1}{1-\sigma}} \tag{5.16}$$

$$P_M^* = (\phi s_n + (1 - s_n))^{\frac{1}{1-\sigma}} K^{w\frac{1}{1-\sigma}} \tag{5.17}$$

where P_M^* is the price index for the South.

Taking the rate of growth in the steady state, where $\dot{s}_n = 0$ we find that:

$$\frac{\dot{P}_M}{P_M} = \frac{\dot{P}_M^*}{P_M^*} = \frac{1}{1-\sigma}\frac{\dot{K}^w}{K^w} = -\frac{g}{\sigma - 1}. \tag{5.18}$$

Hence, prices for manufactures decreases at the same rate in both regions, regardless of the transport costs and the equilibrium allocation of industries. But the global price level depends also on the price of the traditional good. Since the latter is our numeraire, the perfect price index associated to the second-stage Cobb-Douglas utility is then:

$$P = P_M^\mu; \ P* = P*_M^\mu$$

which, finally, gives us the following growth rate of prices:

$$\frac{\dot{P}}{P} = \frac{\dot{P}*}{P*} = -\frac{\mu g}{\sigma - 1}. \tag{5.19}$$

Once again, *the growth rate of global prices is the same across regions regardless of both transport costs and the geographical allocation of firms.*

Steady state nominal income in the two regions is the sum of labour income plus profit income and can be written as:

$$Y = L + \pi s_K K^w = L + B(\bar{s}_n, \bar{s}_E)\frac{\mu E^w}{\sigma}$$

$$Y* = L + \pi*(1 - s_n) K^w = L + B(\bar{s}_n, \bar{s}_E)\frac{\mu E^w}{\sigma}.$$

Given that s_n, s_E and E^w are constant in steady state, Y and $Y*$ are constant as well. The common long-run growth rate of real income is therefore:

$$\frac{\dot{Y}}{Y} - \frac{\dot{P}}{P} = \frac{\dot{Y}*}{Y*} - \frac{\dot{P}*}{P*} = \frac{\mu g}{\sigma - 1}. \tag{5.20}$$

We should stress that, since the long-run growth rate of real income is the same across countries regardless of the geographical allocation of industries, countries grow at the same real long-run rate even in CP equilibrium, where $s_n = 1$. In this case, although long-run nominal incomes differ:

$$Y = L + \frac{\mu E^w}{\sigma} \tag{5.21}$$

$$Y* = L. \tag{5.22}$$

The long-run growth rate of prices and real income are still represented by (5.19) and (5.20). In other words, while the *level* of real incomes can differ across regions, the growth rate can only differ in the medium term, that is, as the economy approaches its long-run equilibrium. In the long run, regional real income growth rates are identical.

As for consumption, in the CP equilibrium both regions display the following consumption levels:

$$Q_{CP} = \frac{E}{P} = \left(L + \frac{\mu E^w}{\sigma} - g \right) \frac{1}{P}$$

$$Q^*_{CP} = \frac{E^*}{P^*} = \frac{L}{P^*}$$

where $Q_{CP} > Q^*_{CP}$ but $\dot{Q}_{CP}/Q_{CP} = \dot{Q}^*_{CP}/Q^*_{CP} = \mu g/(\sigma - 1)$.

Why should it be so? Consider the CP equilibrium: although the South is completely specialized in the traditional sector and does not innovate or indeed make any investment of any kind, it experiences the same rate of growth as the North due to continual terms-of-trade gains. In other words, thanks to the technological progress in the industrial sector, the price index of the manufacturing goods decreases faster than the price of the agricultural good. This means that the relative value of the commodity in which the periphery specializes – agricultural goods – increases over time making the periphery's imports of manufacturing goods cheaper. As a result, the real income of the periphery grows, in the long run, at the same rate as the core. As we will see later, this result crucially depends on the particular functional forms chosen to represent individual preferences.

5.2.5   Main Results and Policy Implications

We now summarize the main results of the NEGG models, focusing on the periphery in the CP equilibrium. Results are summarized in Table 5.1.

What we first notice is that core results are not easy to identify: we have

Table 5.1   The main results of the NEGG models

	GS K-mob	GS K-imm	LS K-mob	LS K-imm
Cat. agglomeration in *I-M*	NO	YES	YES – NO	YES
Static losses for the periphery	NO	YES	NO	YES
Dyn. gains for the periphery	NO	NO	YES	YES
Dyn. losses for the periphery	NO	NO	NO	NO

too many cases that are based on extreme assumptions. These difficulties are well represented by the sharp contrast between the LS case with capital immobility and the GS case with capital mobility. So how much should a periphery worry about agglomeration in the core? Very little if the 'true' model is the one with capital mobility. First, when spillovers are global, the allocation of manufacturing industries and knowledge sectors is always stable so that there is no chance of a CP outcome occuring unless we start from such an initial condition. Second, when spillovers are localized, people should be only too happy to see their region's R&D sector disappear. With this sector being perfectly competitive, the periphery does not suffer any static or dynamic losses as a consequence of the agglomeration process of the *I*-sector. By contrast, the concentration of the entire *I*-sector in the other region allows for learning spillovers to be exploited at their maximum degree and, hence, the periphery *M*-sector and real income grow at the maximum speed.

If the 'true' model is instead the one with capital immobility, the outcomes are slightly less favourable for the periphery, albeit not tragic. When spillovers are global, the periphery suffers from a static loss due to the fact that, since the *M*-goods are produced only in the core, the periphery has to face a higher cost of living because trade costs are positive and this lowers its long-run permanent income level with respect to the symmetric equilibrium. On the other hand, when spillovers are localized, the periphery's worries for the static losses may or may not be offset by the dynamic gains achieved through the higher growth rate of knowledge. In both cases, the peripheral region will *not* suffer any dynamic losses following the agglomeration of the *M*- and the *I*-sector in the other region.

Hence, a policy-maker, who takes NEGG models seriously, can draw *two* main messages from these models' results:

- 'If you are interested in the long-run income of the periphery, do not worry *too much* about the agglomeration of the *M*-sector in the core.' As we can see from Table 5.1, and as we have analysed above, the periphery *never* suffers from dynamic losses in the long run since the rate of growth of its real income is *always* equal to that of the core region. From the dynamic viewpoint, in a GS world, agglomeration of the *M*-sector in the core is at most something about which the periphery can be indifferent. While, in an LS world, it might also be beneficial for the periphery because it allows for the real rate of growth, which is equal to that of the core, to be a maximum.
- 'In an LS world, be careful with policies aimed at keeping R&D activity in the periphery, since they could (1) harm the aggregate growth;

(2) harm the periphery.' Both messages seem to imply that regional inequalities might be the price to be paid in order to reach a higher aggregate growth and to maximize long-run welfare even in the periphery. If these implications turn out to be analytically robust (and empirically relevant), then the contribution of the NEG to the understanding of regional problems and policy would be highly valuable. But are they?

5.3 AGGLOMERATION AND GROWTH REVISITED

In the following sections we will show that the rather optimistic results of the NEGG models for the periphery become more pessimistic if the assumptions we are using are slightly changed. We then discuss the consequences of a slight variation in two parameters of this class of models: *the elasticity of substitution between manufacturing and traditional goods in the second-stage utility function* and the so-called *degree of love for variety*. Most (if not all) NEGG models: (1) make use of Cobb-Douglas (CD) second-stage instant utility function as in (5.3), which displays *unitary* elasticity of substitution between the two kinds of goods and (2) reduce the dimensionality of the parameter space by linking the marginal taste for an additional variety (what we call the 'love for variety' parameter) to another crucial parameter: the elasticity of substitution across varieties.[10] This choice allows for a number of results and important simplifications. First, with CD preferences the expenditure shares in the two kinds of goods remain fixed and hence they are not affected by changes in relative prices. A different (albeit constant) value of the elasticity of substitution between the two kinds of goods triggers some important mechanisms, which, although not easily tractable, cannot emerge with unitary elasticity of substitution. Second, the real growth rate of income and consumption crucially depends on the value of the love for variety parameter, which, in most NEG models[11] is fixed at $v = 1/\sigma - 1$.

It should be stressed here that our intention is not to build a model but rather to discuss the analytical source of some important (and optimistic) results of NEGG models and to provide some examples (not necessarily more restrictive and in most cases more general) in which such optimistic results for the periphery are not obtained. To this end, we first introduce the following preference structure for a representative consumer:

$$U_t = \int_{t=0}^{\infty} e^{-\rho t}\ln Q_t dt;\ \ Q_t = [\delta(n^{w^{v+\frac{1}{1-\sigma}}}C_M)^\alpha + (1-\delta)C_T^{\alpha}]^{\frac{1}{\alpha}};$$

$$C_M = \left[\int_{i=0}^{K+K^*} c_i^{1-1/\sigma} di \right]^{\frac{1}{1-1/\sigma}};$$

$$\alpha \leq 1. \tag{5.23}$$

The preference structure identified by (5.23) generalizes (5.3) in two directions. First, it considers a CES second-stage instant utility function. This functional form still displays a constant elasticity of substitution between M- and T-goods, yet in this case the elasticity of substitution is equal to $1/1-\alpha$, which can be greater or lower than unity (as in the CD case) according to whether α is respectively negative or positive. Under CES preferences specified here, the expenditure shares of the final goods are not fixed but depend on the price index of manufacturing goods.

Second, adopting the same approach as Dixit and Stiglitz (1975), Benassy (1996) and Smulders and van de Klundert (2003), the love for variety parameter v is explicitly considered. In the typical NEGG models it takes the value of $1/\sigma-1$ so that love of variety is intrinsically linked to the elasticity of substitution across varieties σ but in a more general context, love of variety need not to be tied to σ.

For $\alpha = 0$ we have a unit value of the elasticity of substitution between goods M and T and the resulting utility function $Q_t = (n^{w^{v+\frac{1}{1-\sigma}}} C_M)^\delta C_T^{1-\delta}$ is identical to the previous CD case except for the multiplicative term $n^{w^{v+\frac{1}{1-\sigma}}}$. For $v = \frac{1}{\sigma-1}$ and $\alpha = 0$ the utility function collapses to the previous case.

In what follows, we show how some important results of the NEGG models crucially depend on particular values of these parameters and are not robust to slight changes. In particular, we will show that, according to different values of v and α (1) *when trade is costly enough the symmetric equilibrium might not be stable even when capital is perfectly mobile*; (2) *the rate of growth might depend on the geographical allocation of industries even when spillovers are global*; and, (3) *in the CP outcome, countries might not grow at the same rate in real terms*.

5.3.1 Intermediate Results with CES Utility

Taking the T-good as numeraire, second-stage utility maximization leads to the following demand functions:

$$C_M = \frac{E}{P_M} \mu(n^w, P_M) \tag{5.24}$$

$$C_T = E(1 - \mu(n^w, P_M)) \tag{5.25}$$

where now the expenditure share for manufactures is given by:

$$\mu(n^w, P_M) = \frac{1}{1 + (n^{w\frac{1}{\sigma-1}-v}P_M)^{\frac{\alpha}{1-\alpha}}(\frac{1-\delta}{\delta})^{\frac{1}{1-\alpha}}}.$$

Notice that (5.24) and (5.25) differ from (5.4) and (5.5) in that the expenditure shares are not fixed. In particular, it's easy to see that when α is positive, the expenditure shares on M-goods tends to increase as the price index of the M-goods goes down. Substituting the expression for P_M with (5.16) and (5.17), we can write:

$$\mu(n^w, s_n, \phi) = \frac{1}{1 + (n^w)^{-\frac{\alpha v}{1-\alpha}}(s_n + (1-s_n)\phi)^{\frac{\alpha}{(1-\alpha)(1-\sigma)}}(\frac{1-\delta}{\delta})^{\frac{1}{1-\alpha}}} \qquad (5.26)$$

$$\mu^*(n^w, s_n, \phi) = \frac{1}{1 + (n^w)^{-\frac{\alpha v}{1-\alpha}}(\phi s_n + (1-s_n))^{\frac{\alpha}{(1-\alpha)(1-\sigma)}}(\frac{1-\delta}{\delta})^{\frac{1}{1-\alpha}}}. \qquad (5.27)$$

We can make a number of observations as a result of analysing these two expressions. First, when the elasticity of substitution between the two goods is different from 1 (that is, $\alpha \neq 0$), North and South expenditure shares differ ($\mu \neq \mu^*$) in correspondence to any geographical allocation of the manufacturing industry except for $s_n = 0.5$ (symmetric equilibrium). In particular, we find that:[12]

$$\alpha > (<)0 \Rightarrow \frac{\partial \mu}{\partial s_n} = \frac{\alpha(1-\phi)\mu(1-\mu)}{(1-\alpha)(\sigma-1)((s_n + (1-s_n)\phi))} > (<)0 \quad (5.28)$$

$$\alpha > (<)0 \Rightarrow \frac{\partial \mu^*}{\partial s_n} = \frac{\alpha(\phi-1)\mu^*(1-\mu^*)}{(1-\alpha)(\sigma-1)((s_n + (1-s_n)\phi))} < (>)0. \quad (5.29)$$

Hence, when $\alpha > 0$, production shifting in the North ($\partial s_n > 0$) leads to a relative increase in the southern price index for the M-goods because southern consumers have to buy a larger fraction of M-goods from the North, which are more expensive because of trade costs. Unlike the CD case, where this phenomenon had no consequences for the expenditure shares for manufactures, which remained constant across time and space, in the CES case, expenditure shares on M-goods are influenced by the geographical allocation of industries because they depend on relative prices and relative prices change with s_n.

Second, we have:

$$\alpha > (<) 0 \Rightarrow \frac{\partial \mu}{\partial \phi} = \frac{\alpha (1 - s_n) \mu (1 - \mu)}{(1 - \alpha)(\sigma - 1)((s_n + (1 - s_n)\phi))} > (<) 0 \quad (5.30)$$

$$\alpha > (<) 0 \Rightarrow \frac{\partial \mu^*}{\partial \phi} = \frac{\alpha s_n \mu^* (1 - \mu^*)}{(1 - \alpha)(\sigma - 1)((s_n + (1 - s_n)\phi))} > (<) 0 \quad (5.31)$$

so that, when $\alpha > 0$ economic integration gives rise to an increase in the expenditure share for manufactured goods in both regions. Obviously, the smaller the share of manufacturing firms already present in the North (South), the larger the increase in expenditure share for the M-good in the North (South).

Third, and more importantly, by calculations we obtain the following:

$$\alpha > (<) 0 \Rightarrow \frac{\partial \mu}{\partial n^w} = \frac{\alpha v}{1 - \alpha} \frac{(1 - \mu)\mu}{n^w} \geq (\leq 0)$$

$$\alpha > (<) 0 \Rightarrow \frac{\partial \mu^*}{\partial n^w} = \frac{\alpha v}{1 - \alpha} \frac{(1 - \mu^*)\mu^*}{n^w} \geq (\leq 0).$$

Therefore, when goods are good substitutes ($\alpha > 0$), and unless individuals do not love variety ($v > 0$), the expenditure share for the M-goods is in both regions an increasing function of the total number of varieties. In the analytical context of the NEGG models, this result (which is a feature of the CES utility function we have chosen) has highly unwelcome effects from the viewpoint of formalizing the dynamics of the model. However, although the dynamic properties of this model are highly complex, they are not complex enough to obscure the fact that, when v and α are strictly positive, the two regions might grow at a different real growth rate.

Moreover, it is worth noticing that when $v = 0$, which is simply a 'different' but 'equally restrictive' case with respect to the typical NEGG model,[13] μ and μ^* are both constant in steady state since they are no longer affected by the increase in the number of varieties ($\partial \mu / \partial n^w = \partial \mu^* / \partial n^w = 0$ when $v = 0$). Indeed, by eliminating the love for variety, the expenditure shares are only affected by the price index through the transport cost ϕ, which is our exogenous parameter, and through the allocation of industrial activitiy (s_n), which is constant along the balanced growth path.

In what follows, we will focus on three issues whose analysis leads to conclusions that are shown to be highly dependent on the value of the parameters α and v. In dealing with the first two issues (the stability properties of the symmetric equilibrium and the influence of geographical allocation in the growth rate of the technological progress) we will focus on the case where $v = 0$ and α may assume any positive value[14] between 0 and 1. When

looking at the growth differentials in the real income between the two countries (our third issue), a positive v is needed in order to obtain a positive
growth gap.

5.3.2 The Stability of the Symmetric Equilibrium when $v = 0$

The lack of love for variety allows us to focus on how a decline in transportation costs affects expenditure shares owing to a rise in real purchasing
power. When $v = 0$ we find:

$$\mu(s_n, \phi) = \frac{1}{1 + (s_n + (1 - s_n)\phi)^{\frac{\alpha}{(1-\alpha)(1-\sigma)}}(\frac{1-\delta}{\delta})^{\frac{1}{1-\alpha}}} \qquad (5.32)$$

$$\mu^*(s_n, \phi) = \frac{1}{1 + (\phi s_n + (1 - s_n))^{\frac{\alpha}{(1-\alpha)(1-\sigma)}}(\frac{1-\delta}{\delta})^{\frac{1}{1-\alpha}}}. \qquad (5.33)$$

By eliminating the love for variety we are able to maintain a version
of the typical assumption in NEGG models, which states that a
single country's labour endowment must be insufficient to meet global
demand. We are entitled to do this because, when $v = 0$ both μ and μ^*
cannot reach the unit value. This assumption should be modified as
follows:

$$L < ([1 - \mu(s_n, \phi)]s_E + [1 - \mu^*(s_n, \phi)](1 - s_E)) E^w$$

$$\forall (s_n, \phi) \in (0, 1) \subset R^2. \qquad (5.34)$$

Since s_E has to be constant by definition and even:

$$E^w(s_E, s_n, \phi) = \frac{(2L - L_I - L_I^*)\sigma}{s_E(\sigma - \mu(s_n, \phi)) + (1 - s_E)(\sigma - \mu^*(s_n, \phi))} \qquad (5.35)$$

is constant in steady state, (5.34) can be accepted without particular loss of
generality.

North and South profits respectively become:

$$\pi = \left[\frac{s_E}{s_n + \phi(1 - s_n)}\mu(s_n, \phi) + \frac{\phi(1 - s_E)}{\phi s_n + (1 - s_n)}\mu^*(s_n, \phi) \right] \frac{E^w}{\sigma K^w} \quad (5.36)$$

$$\pi^* = \left[\frac{\phi s_E}{s_n + \phi(1 - s_n)} \mu(s_n, \phi) + \frac{(1 - s_E)}{\phi s_n + (1 - s_n)} \mu^*(s_n, \phi) \right] \frac{E^W}{\sigma K^W}. \quad (5.37)$$

In the symmetric equilibrium, North and South expenditure shares are given by:

$$\mu(s_n, \phi)|_{s_n = 0.5} = \mu^*(s_n, \phi)|_{s_n = 0.5} = \frac{1}{1 + (\frac{1 + \phi}{2})^{\frac{\alpha}{(1 - \alpha)(1 - \sigma)}}(\frac{1 - \delta}{\delta})^{\frac{1}{1 - \alpha}}} \quad (5.38)$$

so that world expenditure is given by:

$$E^w(s_n, \phi)|_{s_n = 0.5} = \frac{(2L - L_I - L_I^*)\sigma}{\sigma - \mu(\frac{1}{2}, \phi)} \quad (5.39)$$

and profits can be written as:

$$\pi = \pi^* = \frac{(2L - g)}{K^w} \frac{\mu(\frac{1}{2}, \phi)}{\sigma - \mu(\frac{1}{2}, \phi)}.$$

What is the effect of production shifting in the North on profits? Using the above equations we find that:

$$\frac{\partial \mu(s_n)}{\partial s_n}\Bigg|_{s_n = s_E = 0.5} = -\frac{\partial \mu^*(s_n)}{\partial s_n}\Bigg|_{s_n = s_E = 0.5}$$

$$= 2\frac{1 - \phi}{1 + \phi}\frac{\alpha}{(1 - \alpha)(\sigma - 1)}\frac{(\frac{1 + \phi}{2})^{\frac{\alpha}{(1 - \alpha)(1 - \sigma)}}(\frac{1 - \delta}{\delta})^{\frac{1}{1 - \alpha}}}{1 + (\frac{1 + \phi}{2})^{\frac{\alpha}{(1 - \alpha)(1 - \sigma)}}(\frac{1 - \delta}{\delta})^{\frac{1}{1 - \alpha}}} > 0.$$

In words, production shifting leads to a relative increase in the southern price index of *M*-goods because southern consumers have to buy a larger fraction of *M*-goods from the North, which are more expensive because of trade costs. In the CD case, this phenomenon has no consequences on expenditure shares for manufactures that are exogenously fixed and remain constant across time and space. But in the CES case, expenditure shares on *M*-goods depend on relative prices and the latter change with the geographical allocation of industries. By a sort of home market effect, the decrease in southern demand is more than compensated for by the increase in northern consumers' demand. This change in relative demands will have some consequences for relative profits.

Let us start with the case of capital mobility where production shifting does not lead to a change in the regional allocation of capital (that is, generally, $s_n \neq s_K$). Therefore, the effect of production shifting in the North on relative profits can be written as:

$$
\left. \frac{\partial(\pi/\pi^*)}{\partial s_n} \right|_{s_n=s_E=0.5} =
$$

$$
\underbrace{2\frac{(1-\phi)^2}{(1+\phi)^2}\frac{\alpha}{(1-\alpha)(\sigma-1)}\left(\frac{1+\phi}{2}\right)^{\frac{\alpha}{(1-\alpha)(1-\sigma)}}\left(\frac{1-\delta}{\delta}\right)^{\frac{1}{1-\alpha}}}_{\text{price effect}} \underbrace{-\, 2\frac{(1-\phi)^2}{(1+\phi)^2}}_{\text{market-crowding effect}}
$$

If we compare this expression with (5.14), we can easily notice that, thanks to the change in μ, the negative influence of the market crowding effect is now mitigated (and might be offset) by a positive effect on profits, which was not present in the CD case. Unlike before, northern profits might increase because of the larger domestic demand of manufacturing goods due to the increase in the domestic expenditure share μ following a reduction in the domestic price index. This new agglomeration force, which we call *price effect*, vanishes as trade becomes freer at a speed that is *higher* than market-crowding effect.

The price effect offsets the market-crowding effect, and hence relative profits in the North increase after production shifting when:

$$
\left. \frac{\partial(\pi/\pi^*)}{\partial s_n} \right|_{s_n=s_E=0.5} > 0 : \phi < \phi_S(\alpha,\sigma,\delta) \tag{5.40}
$$

where

$$
\phi_S(\alpha,\sigma,\delta) = 2\left(\frac{\alpha}{(1-\alpha)(\sigma-1)}\right)^{\frac{(1-\alpha)(\sigma-1)}{\alpha}}(\frac{1-\delta}{\delta})^{\frac{\sigma-1}{\alpha}} - 1.
$$

This means that the symmetric equilibrium is stable *not* for any value of ϕ but only when ϕ is low enough. In other words, the presence of a new agglomeration force makes for a new possible scenario where symmetric equilibrium may be unstable even when capital is mobile. But unlike the case with capital immobility and CD preferences, the symmetric equilibrium is unstable for *low* values of ϕ, that is, when trade is costly enough. This might be considered to be a case of *stabilizing integration*. When trade is costly, production shifting in the North will result in a relevant reduction (increase) in North (South) prices, which leads to a relevant increase (reduction) in northern (southern) expenditure shares for the M-goods. In other words, as μ is positively influenced by s_n, northern consumers spend a larger fraction of their income on manufacturing goods. Northern profits benefit from such an increase in the domestic demand and if trade is costly enough this positive demand effect may offset the negative congestion effect and therefore increase the North's profits. As a consequence, southern firms have a further incentive to relocate their activities in the North and, as long as trade remains costly enough, this process leads to the disappearance of the industrial sector in the South and to a perfect concentration of the M-sector in the North. It is worth highlighting that, since the expenditure shares are fixed, this possibility was discarded in the CD case. Obviously, since half of the firms have southern owners (s_n may go to unity, but s_K = 0.5), the South can still enjoy profit gains deriving from the industrial sector. However, in equilibrium, South consumers enjoy a lower level of utility since their real income is lower due to higher prices ($P^* > P$).

But as trade becomes freer, the positive effect of production shifting on the price index diminishes to the extent that the price effect is not large enough to compensate for the negative effect of tougher competition. Hence, when trade is free enough ($\phi < \phi_S(\alpha, \sigma, \delta)$), northern profits decrease following production shifting to the North, southern firms are motivated to move back to the North and symmetric equilibrium once again becomes stable. According to the different values of the parameters α, σ and δ three outcomes are possible:

- $\phi_S > 1$ so that condition (5.40) always holds and the symmetric equilibrium is *unstable* for any value of ϕ.
- $\phi_S < 0$ so that condition (5.40) never holds and the symmetric equilibrium is *stable* for any value of ϕ.
- $0 \leq \phi_S \leq 1$ so that the stability properties of the symmetric equilibrium depend on ϕ.

We can summarize the case when capital is mobile as follows. Allowing for the elasticity of substitution to be larger than 1 ($1/(1 - \alpha) \geq 1$) and assigning a zero value to the 'love for variety' parameter ($v = 0$), the dynamic properties of the symmetric equilibrium change substantially with respect to the case when $1/(1 - \alpha) = 1$ and $v = 1/(\sigma - 1)$. In particular, when ϕ is low enough ($\phi < \phi_S$), catastrophic agglomeration may occur even with perfect capital immobility. Even if the South maintains the ownership of their firms relocated to the North, southern consumers enjoy a lower level of steady state utility since they have to afford higher prices due to the presence of transport costs. In this case, agglomeration leads to a static loss for consumers, which might or might not be compensated for by the dynamic gain due to the presence of localized spillovers.

When capital is immobile, things are much clearer: the presence of a further agglomeration force (the price effect) guarantees that the symmetric equilibrium becomes unstable for even higher values of transport costs (that is, lower values of ϕ). This seems to be enough to claim that, with $\alpha \geq 0$, $v = 0$, and with capital immobility and ϕ sufficiently high, catastrophic agglomeration occurs with probability 1.

5.3.3   Growth, Integration and the Geographical Allocation of Industries

Another clear result of NEGG models is that, when knowledge spillovers are not localized, the growth rate of innovation is not influenced by the geographical allocation of firms. In other words, when the cost of innovation is the same across space, geography does not affect growth. We show that this is not the case when we allow for the elasticity of substitution to be larger than 1: in this case geography does matter for growth when spillovers are global. For simplicity's sake, we still limit the analysis to the case when $v = 0$. We will focus on the case when capital is immobile and spillovers are global and calculate and compare the rate of growth of innovation in the symmetric and CP equilibrium. In the symmetric equilibrium, Tobin's q is equal to 1 for both regions:

$$q = q^* = \frac{E^w \mu(\tfrac{1}{2}, \phi)}{\sigma(\rho + g)} = 1.$$

Solving for E^w and using (5.39) we finally find:

$$g_S = \frac{2L\mu(\tfrac{1}{2}, \phi) - \rho(\sigma - \mu(\tfrac{1}{2}, \phi))}{\sigma} \tag{5.41}$$

which looks very similar to (5.12): the only difference is that now μ the expenditure shares for the M-good, is not constant but it may differ across regions and it is a positive function of the freeness of trade by (5.30) and (5.31). This gives us.

$$\frac{\partial g_S}{\partial \phi} = \frac{\partial \mu}{\partial \phi} \frac{1}{\sigma}(2L + \rho) > 0$$

and enables us to conclude that when the elasticity of substitution is larger than 1 the rate of growth of innovation is positively influenced by the process of economic integration. Thus integration has a growth effect. Why is this so? A higher ϕ means a larger expenditure share for M-goods in both regions. This increase leads to higher profits, which means, ceteris paribus, that there is a larger incentive for manufacturing firms to invest in R&D. We should stress that this growth-effect of integration is not present in the typical NEGG model.

As for the CP equilibrium, we make use of the condition according to which $q^* = 0$ and $q = 1$. In particular:

$$q = \frac{\pi}{(\rho + g)\sigma} = [s_E\mu(1,\phi) + (1 - s_E)\mu^*(1,\phi)]\frac{E^w}{\sigma(\rho + g)} = 1.$$

Since $E^* = L$ when $s_K = s_n = 1$ we find:

$$E = \frac{\sigma(\rho + g) - L\mu^*(1,\phi)}{\mu(1,\phi)}.$$

Using (5.35) with $s_n = 1$, we also have:

$$E = \frac{(L - g)\sigma + L\mu^*(1,\phi)}{\sigma - \mu(1,\phi)}.$$

By equating these two expressions we finally get:

$$g_{cp} = \frac{L[\mu(1,\phi) + \mu^*(1,\phi)] - \rho(\sigma - \mu(1,\phi))}{\sigma} \neq g_S.$$

This expression confirms that integration is good for growth ($\partial g_{cp}/\partial\phi > 0$) and sheds light on the fact that geography matters for growth even when spillovers are global. Indeed we can observe that:

$$g_{cp} > (<) g_S : L\left[\mu(1,\phi) + \mu^*(1,\phi) - 2\mu\left(\frac{1}{2},\phi\right)\right] > (<) \rho\left(\mu\left(\frac{1}{2},\phi\right) - \mu(1,\phi)\right)$$

with the right-hand term undoubtedly negative, since $\mu(\frac{1}{2},\phi) < \mu(1,\phi)$. So that a sufficient (but not necessary) condition for agglomeration to be growth-enhancing is that the sum of the expenditures shares for the M-goods in the two regions is larger in the CP than in the symmetric equilibrium:

$$\mu(1,\phi) + \mu^*(1,\phi) > 2\mu\left(\frac{1}{2},\phi\right).$$

This condition may or may not hold according to the values of the parameters δ, α and σ but, in any case, a change in the geographical allocation of industries will affect the rate of growth of innovation through its effect on the expenditure shares and hence on profits. In particular, there is surely a subset of parameter values such that agglomeration is *detrimental to growth* in both countries.

5.3.4   Full Specialization and Uneven Growth

In this section we will try to show why the conclusion that long-run real income growth rates are identical across regions is far from robust. The reason for the absence of long-run growth differentials in the typical NEGG model is to be found in the continual terms-of-trade gains. Thanks to technological progress in the industrial sector, the price index of manufactured goods decreases faster than that of the agricultural goods. This implies that the relative value of the commodity in which the periphery specializes – agricultural goods – increases overtime making the periphery's imports of manufacturing goods cheaper. This positive effect on the periphery's permanent income *perfectly offsets* the negative effect of slower productivity growth in the traditional sector. As already stated, this result strongly suggests policy rules that favour agglomeration of industrial activities since, in any case, the periphery would not suffer from any dynamic loss associated with the loss of the industrial sector. But is this always the case? What assumptions are needed in order to obtain this important result? And is the result robust to slight changes in this assumption?

One way to answer these questions can be found in a simple model of endogenous growth and trade contained in Lucas (1988). The economy considered by Lucas consists of two goods (a high-tech and a low-tech good, just like in NEGG models) and a continuum of trading countries. Consumers of each country choose how to allocate their income between the two goods according to a CES utility function. In a simple framework with zero transport costs, homogeneous goods and no capital accumulation (pure learning-by-doing growth), Lucas shows that: (1) countries specialize in the production of the good in which they have a (dynamic) comparative advantage; (2) long-run growth rate of real income differs across countries whenever the elasticity of substitution between high- and low-tech goods is non-unitary. In particular, when the elasticity of substitution is greater than 1 (which is considered by Lucas the most interesting case) countries producing (having a comparative advantage in) high-learning goods, will experience a higher-than-average real growth.

The mechanism behind this important result relies on the fact that, when goods are close substitutes, the terms of trade effect (the ever-increasing relative value of the low-tech good that makes the high-tech good relatively cheaper for the low-tech countries) is dominated by the direct effect of productivity. In other words, low-tech countries experience a lower growth because the relative value of low-tech goods does not increase as fast as would be necessary to compensate for their slower relative productivity rate of growth.

What happens to the long-run growth gap between countries in a typical NEGG model if we allow, as in Lucas (1988), the elasticity of substitution between traditional and manufacturing goods to be larger than 1? The relevance of this question appears to be very important for policy-makers because, if Lucas's results can be replicated in an NEGG model, then policies that favour agglomeration may give rise to ever-increasing regional inequalities.

We shall now analyse the problem posed by the introduction of such a generalization in an NEGG model and we will show that, with $\alpha > 0$ and love for variety ($v > 0$), the two countries do not generally grow at the same rate in real terms. It is worth stressing that this result does not depend on full specialization per se. This is shown by Bellone and Maupertuis (2003) who, allowing for complete specialization in a typical NEGG model, and therefore for unequal wages between countries (as in Grossman and Helpman, 1991), obtain the result that the 'industrial' country may enjoy a higher *level* of real income with respect to the 'agricultural' country but, since wages are constant in equilibrium, the two countries grow at the same rate in real terms. As the expenditure shares are constant because of CD preferences and thanks to 'love for variety', which constantly lowers the perceived index price for manufactures, the 'agricultural' country is still able to enjoy a constant increase in the relative price of the good it produces, which is exactly equal to the loss in the relative productivity given by the fact that only the industrial sector (and therefore the industrial country) benefits from technological progress.

5.3.4.1   Real growth and love for variety

Before analysing whether or not there is a case in which agglomeration generates ever-increasing inequalities, let us investigate the relationship between real growth (the rate of growth of real income and/or consumption) and love for variety (measured by the parameter v).

We first notice that the case we have considered so far, $v = 0$ and $\alpha \geq 0$ is associated with a situation of *real growth equal to zero in both countries* regardless of the geographical allocation of industries and the degree of economic integration. Let us see how this result is reached. First of all we notice that, in equilibrium, both expenditures and nominal income are constant in both regions. As for expenditure we simply refer to (5.35), which tells us that world expenditure is constant in steady state since it is a function of variables $(s_n, s_E, L$ and $g)$, which are all constant in steady state. And since S_E must be constant too, also E and E^* do not change along the balance growth path either. As for nominal income, we can note that:

$$Y = L + \left[\frac{s_E}{s_n + \phi(1 - s_n)} \mu(s_n, \phi) + \frac{\phi(1 - s_E)}{\phi s_n + (1 - s_n)} \mu^*(s_n, \phi) \right] \frac{E^w}{\sigma} \quad (5.42)$$

$$Y^* = L + \left[\frac{\phi s_E}{s_n + \phi(1 - s_n)} \mu(s_n, \phi) + \frac{(1 - s_E)}{\phi s_n + (1 - s_n)} \mu^*(s_n, \phi) \right] \frac{E^w}{\sigma}. \quad (5.43)$$

These expressions tell us, again, that Y and Y^* are also constant in steady state. But in order to calculate the real growth rate we need an expression for the perfect price index associated with the CES utility function (5.23). This is given[15] for the two regions, by:

$$P = \left(P_M^{\frac{\alpha}{\alpha-1}} \delta^{\frac{1}{1-\alpha}} n^{w\frac{1}{1-\sigma}(\frac{\alpha}{1-\alpha})} + (1 - \delta)^{\frac{1}{1-\alpha}} \right)^{\frac{\alpha-1}{\alpha}}$$

$$P^* = \left(P^*_M{}^{\frac{\alpha}{\alpha-1}} \delta^{\frac{1}{1-\alpha}} n^{w\frac{1}{1-\sigma}(\frac{\alpha}{1-\alpha})} + (1 - \delta)^{\frac{1}{1-\alpha}} \right)^{\frac{\alpha-1}{\alpha}}.$$

Since $(\dot{P}_M/P_M) = (\dot{P}^*_M/P^*_M) = -(g/(\sigma - 1))$ and $(\dot{n}^w/n^w) = g$ in steady state, we can easily conclude that, with $v = 0$:

$$\frac{\dot{P}}{P} = \frac{\dot{P}^*}{P^*} = 0$$

and, therefore:

$$\frac{\dot{Y}}{Y} - \frac{\dot{P}}{P} = \frac{\dot{Y}^*}{Y^*} - \frac{\dot{P}^*}{P^*} = 0.$$

If we maintain the assumption of $v = 0$ (indifference to variety), it is worth noting that this result also holds when we use a CD second-stage utility function, which is a particular case of the CES utility function we have used so far in this section.[16] A certain degree of love for variety is then a necessary condition in order to have *real growth*. However, as we have seen before, a positive degree of love for variety $(v > 0)$ associated to CES utility with $\alpha > 0$ leads to a situation in which the expenditure shares for manufactures are a positive function of the world stock of capital. We shall look now at the consequences and the analytical difficulties associated with this feature.

5.3.4.2 Agglomeration and uneven growth

For the sake of simplicity, we focus on a framework in which capital is immobile (we are interested in 'catastrophic' agglomeration) and spillovers are global. With CES utility and strictly positive v, the assumption stating that a single country's labour endowment will always be insufficient to meet global demand cannot be maintained. When preferences are represented by (5.23) this assumption requires that:

$$L < ([1 - \mu(s_n, \phi, n^w)]s_E + [1 - \mu^*(s_n, \phi, n^w)](1 - s_E)) E^w(n^w, s_n, s_E) \quad (5.44)$$

where:

$$E^w(s_E, s_n, n^w, \phi) = \frac{(2L - L_I - L_I^*)\sigma}{s_E(\sigma - \mu(n^w, s_n, \phi)) + (1 - s_E)(\sigma - \mu^*(n^w, s_n, \phi))}. \quad (5.45)$$

It is not easy to say what happens to the right-hand part of (5.44) in the long run as K^w and therefore even n^w grows. It is not our aim to provide a full analysis of the transitional dynamics of the model, but we try to present the intuition as follows. Suppose we start from a symmetric equilibrium where $w = w^* = 1$ and $s_n = 0.5$ and (5.44) holds. For low enough values of transport costs, this equilibrium also becomes unstable (even more so) in the CES case with $\alpha > 0$; that is, any positive shock on s_n brings about a cumulative advantage to the North, reinforcing the innovation profitability. In the meantime, μ will surely grow because both s_n and n^w are growing. As for μ^*, we have a positive effect given by the growth in n^w but also a negative effect given by the growth of s_n, which makes M-goods more expensive for the South. Moreover, as is clear from (5.45), world expenditure increases with n^w, so that the dynamic behaviour of the global demand for traditional products becomes very complex. A necessary condition for the traditional good to be produced in only one country is that global demand for traditional goods is never higher than L, which represents the production capacity of a single country. Since E^w is upper-bounded,[17] the right side of (5.44) will surely reach the value L in a finite time. So there certainly comes a time in which, thanks to the continuously decreasing price of the M-goods, the global demand for the traditional goods becomes so small that a single country's labour endowment is sufficient to completely satisfy it.

Then, when $\alpha > 0$ and $v > 0$, the traditional good will sooner or later be produced by a single country.

But since agglomeration ($s_n = 1$) occurs only asymptotically, the production of the T-goods will be located in only one region *before* the agglomeration process has ended. The theory of comparative advantage suggest to us that, at that time, the country that will produce the traditional good will be the one having a comparative advantage in it, that is, the one that is gradually losing its industrial sector and thus has a comparative disadvantage in the production of the M-good (say the South). What is the effect of such an event in the ongoing agglomeration process? Since wages will rise in the North, the agglomeration process will not be reversed if and only if investment in the R&D and M-sector remains unprofitable for the South despite its wage-cost advantage.[18]

It is then clear that CES preferences open the door to a number of very interesting and complex dynamics, which were precluded in the CD case. At this time, we just aim to point out that, if an equilibrium of complete specialization exists and can be reached (that is, it is stable, as in Lucas, 1988), *then it is characterized by a positive real growth gap between the North and the South and therefore leads to increasing inequalities between them.*

The most important consequence of full specialization is that, as in Bellone and Maupertuis (2003), when the traditional sector disappears in the North, northern wages are no longer linked to the price of the traditional good. We then have to take into account the variable w, that is, northern wage.[19] This implies, by (5.8), that each variety's price is now equal to w. Hence, when $s_K = s_n = 1$, the price index for the M-goods becomes:

$$P_M = \left[\int_{i=0}^{K+K^*} p_i^{1-\sigma} di \right]^{\frac{1}{1-\sigma}} = w n^{w \frac{1}{1-\sigma}} \qquad (5.46)$$

$$P_M^* = \left[\int_{i=0}^{K+K^*} p_i^{*1-\sigma} di \right]^{\frac{1}{1-\sigma}} = w(\phi n^w)^{\frac{1}{1-\sigma}}. \qquad (5.47)$$

As a consequence, even North and South expenditures shares for manufactures depend now on w:

$$\mu(n^w, 1, \phi, w) = \frac{1}{1 + (n^w)^{-\frac{\alpha v}{1-\alpha}} w^{\frac{\alpha}{1-\alpha}} (\frac{1-\delta}{\delta})^{\frac{1}{1-\alpha}}} \qquad (5.48)$$

$$\mu^*(n^w, 1, \phi, w) = \frac{1}{1 + (n^w)^{-\frac{\alpha v}{1-\alpha}} w^{\frac{\alpha}{1-\alpha}} \phi^{\frac{\alpha}{(1-\alpha)(1-\sigma)}} (\frac{1-\delta}{\delta})^{\frac{1}{1-\alpha}}} \qquad (5.49)$$

which means that their growth rate is the following:

$$\frac{\dot{\mu}}{\mu} = \frac{\alpha}{1-\alpha}\left(v\frac{\dot{n}^w}{n^w} - \frac{\dot{w}}{w}\right)(1-\mu) \tag{5.50}$$

$$\frac{\dot{\mu}^*}{\mu^*} = \frac{\alpha}{1-\alpha}\left(v\frac{\dot{n}^w}{n^w} - \frac{\dot{w}}{w}\right)(1-\mu^*). \tag{5.51}$$

Hence expenditure shares are constant if and only if $\dot{w}/w = v(\dot{n}^w/n^w)$. We can show that this is impossible when $\dot{n}^w/n^w$ is a positive constant. Let us start by taking into account three relevant market-clearing conditions.

First, the world labour market has to clear all of the time. In general, we must have that $2L = (L_T + L_T^*) + (L_M + L_M^*) + (L_I + L_I^*)$. But, with full specialization:

$$L_T^* = L$$

$$L_T = L_M^* = L_I^* = 0$$

$$L_I = \frac{\dot{n}^w}{n^w}$$

so that:

$$L = L_M + \frac{\dot{n}^w}{n^w}. \tag{5.52}$$

Second, as the M-goods market has to clear, the value of total production (which when $s_K = 1$ corresponds to the value of North production) must be equal to total expenditure. Since with complete agglomeration we have $E^* = L$, then:

$$wL_M\frac{\sigma}{\sigma-1} = E\mu + L\mu^*. \tag{5.53}$$

Finally, the traditional goods market has to clear too and therefore the value of total production (which in full specialization corresponds to the South's production) must be equal to total expenditures for the T-goods:

$$E(1-\mu) + L(1-\mu^*) = L. \tag{5.54}$$

Notice that this last condition is very similar to the no-full-specialization condition (5.7). Once we have introduced the new variable w, this condition can (and has to!) hold with equality: South production of T-good *must be equal* to global demand for T-goods. Using (5.52), (5.53) and (5.54) we find that:

$$E = \frac{\sigma w(L - \frac{\dot{n}^w}{n^w})}{\sigma - 1}. \tag{5.55}$$

This expression tells us that, in complete specialization, northern expenditure E and northern wage rate w must grow at the same rate in order to constantly clear the market.

By (5.54) we obtain:

$$E\frac{1 - \mu}{\mu^*} = L$$

so that, differentiating with respect to time, we have:

$$\frac{\dot{E}}{E} - \frac{\dot{\mu}}{1 - \mu} - \frac{\dot{\mu}^*}{\mu^*} = 0. \tag{5.56}$$

Substituting for (5.50) and (5.51) and since ($\dot{E}/E = \dot{w}/w$):

$$\frac{\dot{w}}{w} = \frac{\alpha + \alpha(\mu - \mu^*)}{1 + \alpha(\mu - \mu^*)} v\frac{\dot{n}^w}{n^w} < v\frac{\dot{n}^w}{n^w}.$$

In other words, northern wages have to grow in order to constantly maintain the market-clearing conditions but their growth cannot be large enough to offset the positive effect on prices of the growth of n^w. Hence both μ and μ^* increase and approach the unit value for $t \rightarrow \infty$. This is a considerable problem because it means that the balanced growth path can only be reached asymptotically. But even without formalizing the transitional dynamics, we can conclude that during this transition the two countries do not share the same real growth rate. First, we know that prices will decrease faster in the North. Indeed, we have:

$$\frac{\dot{P}}{P} = \frac{w^{\frac{\alpha}{\alpha-1}}\delta^{\frac{1}{1-\alpha}}n^{w^{\frac{m}{1-\alpha}}}}{w^{\frac{\alpha}{\alpha-1}}\delta^{\frac{1}{1-\alpha}}n^{w^{\frac{m}{1-\alpha}}} + (1-\delta)^{\frac{1}{1-\alpha}}}\left(\frac{\dot{w}}{w} - v\frac{\dot{n}^w}{n^w}\right)$$

$$\frac{\dot{P}^*}{P^*} = \frac{w^{\frac{\alpha}{\alpha-1}}\phi^{\frac{1}{1-\sigma}\frac{\alpha}{\alpha-1}}\delta^{\frac{1}{1-\alpha}}n^{w^{\frac{m}{1-\alpha}}}}{w^{\frac{\alpha}{\alpha-1}}\phi^{\frac{1}{1-\sigma}\frac{\alpha}{\alpha-1}}\delta^{\frac{1}{1-\alpha}}n^{w^{\frac{m}{1-\alpha}}} + (1-\delta)^{\frac{1}{1-\alpha}}}\left(\frac{\dot{w}}{w} - v\frac{\dot{n}^w}{n^w}\right)$$

so that $(\dot{p}/p) < (\dot{p}^*/p^*)$. Second, we know that southern expenditure remains fixed at level L, which corresponds to the value of production of the traditional good. Third, since both μ and μ^* increase over time, by (5.56) we also see that northern expenditure E increases. We can therefore conclude that:

$$\frac{\dot{E}}{E} - \frac{\dot{P}}{P} > \frac{\dot{E}^*}{E^*} - \frac{\dot{P}^*}{P^*} = -\frac{\dot{P}^*}{P^*}$$

so that, unlike in the CD case, real consumption growth is higher in the core than in the periphery. In a similar way, we can show that there is a positive gap between North and South real income growth.

Summing up, we have argued that the result indicating that real growth rates will be the same in both countries regardless of the geographical allocation of industries is a *very* particular case and it's not robust to slight changes in the assumption of the model. In particular, when the elasticity of substitution between the two kinds of goods may assume any value between 1 and ∞ it might well be that the core grows faster than the periphery in real terms. This result seems to have important consequences for policy-makers since, in this case, policies that favour agglomeration may generate ever-increasing regional inequalities. This more pessimistic viewpoint on the effects of agglomeration on core-periphery patterns is indirectly supported by the empirical evidence showing that the expenditure share in the agricultural good is decreasing as real income increases – a phenomenon compatible with an elasticity of substitution greater than one.

5.4 CONCLUSIONS

In this chapter we have dealt with the issue of the relationship between the agglomeration of economic activities and economic growth. In the first part we have surveyed the main results of a typical 'new economic geography and growth' (NEGG) model and we have seen how these results might be helpful in drawing up regional policy rules that favour the concentration of activities in only one region. In the second part of the chapter we challenged this optimistic vision of the consequences of agglomeration and we showed how these results are crucially based on very restrictive values of some parameters of the model and how they are sensitive to slight changes in these values. In particular, we have provided some analytical examples in which, according to different values of the degree of love for variety and of the elasticity of substitution between traditional and manufacturing goods, it is evident that (1) when trade is costly enough the symmetric equilibrium might not be stable even when capital is perfectly mobile; (2) the rate of growth might depend on the geographical allocation of industries even when spillovers are global; and (3) when industrial firms are concentrated in only one region, countries might not grow at the same rate in real terms. The main message of our analysis is that policy-makers should be aware of the fact that implementing regional policy rules suggested by NEGG models might actually harm the periphery. In other words, the effect of agglomeration might be different (and indeed more dangerous) than what has been commonly thought so far.

This message is all the more relevant if we consider that we have only focused on some particular aspects of NEGG models while there are other issues that deserve closer scrutiny. For example, what happens if we allow for intersectoral spillovers between the traditional and the manufacturing sector? This appears to be an important shortfall of NEGG models since our common sense suggests that knowledge might flow not only across space but even across different sectors. If we introduce some kind of intersectoral spillovers by allowing for technological progress even in the traditional sector, which benefits from the proximity of the domestic R&D and/or the manufacturing sector only, then agglomeration might be even more dangerous for the periphery since it would remove an important engine of growth. This result would be compatible with some empirical evidence according to which the traditional sector is more productive in 'industrial' countries. On the other hand, whenever we allow for technology to flow across regions with different specializations (in accordance with the evidence reported by Di Liberto, Mura and Pigliaru, 2004), then the negative growth impact of agglomeration discussed in Section 5.3.4 might well be mitigated. An intuition for that is provided by Murat and Pigliaru (1998), which generalize Lucas (1988) by introducing intersectoral *and* international spillovers: in such an analytical context, uneven growth is always ruled out and the only kind of damage for the periphery (that is, the 'agricultural' country) is a static one. But detailed analysis of the impact of intersectoral spillovers in NEGG models (which appears to be strongly needed) is left for future research.

NOTES

1. We would like to thank Bernard Fingleton, Gianmarco Ottaviano, Frederic Andrès and Frederic Robert-Nicoud for useful insights and suggestions. We are also grateful to seminar participants at the University of Cambridge, Sassari and Cagliari for helpful comments. All remaining errors are our own.
2. The interest UE (urban economics) poses for the NEG literature is well known. A large number of the working papers published by the European Investment Bank (the EU financing institution whose declared task is to contribute towards the integration,

balanced development and economic and social cohesion of the Member Countries) are written by leading exponents of the NEG theory.

3. Fujita and Thisse (2002) and Yamamoto (2002) belong to the class of NEGG models as well, but they adopt a framework that is slightly different from the one we would like to focus on in this work.

4. See, for example, Fujita and Thisse (2002) and Baldwin and Forslid (2000a) who adopt a framework allowing for workers' mobility.

5. See Baldwin (1999) and Baldwin et al. (2003) for similar analysis with depreciation.

6. The dynamics of the share of manufacturing firms allocated in the North is:

$$\dot{s}_n = s_n(1 - s_n)\left(\frac{\dot{K}}{K} - \frac{\dot{K}^*}{K^*}\right)$$

so that only two kinds of steady state are possible: (1) one in which the rate of growth of capital is equalized across countries; (2) one in which the manufacturing industries are allocated and grow in only one region.

7. Actually, this is true for each possible initial allocation of firms.

8. Martin and Ottaviano (2001) generate a feedback between growth and agglomeration by assuming vertical linkages rather than local spillovers in innovation. Because the innovation sector uses manufacturing goods as an input, the location of manufacturing affects the cost of innovation through trade costs. Yamamoto (2002) presents a similar model with circular causation between growth and agglomeration coming from the vertical linkages between the intermediate goods sector and the innovation sector.

9. For an empirical and theoretical support of this assumption see, respectively Moreno, Paci and Usai (2003) and Duranton and Puga (2004).

10. This point is clarified by Benassy (1996). In general, assume that the instantaneous utility function is $U[C_T, C_M]$ with $C_M = V_n(c_1, \ldots, c_n)$ homogeneous of degree one. We can define a function $\gamma(n)$ that represents the taste for variety and that depicts the utility gain derived from spreading a certain amount of production between n differentiated products instead of concentrating it on a single variety:

$$\gamma(n) = \frac{V_n(c_1, \ldots, c_n)}{V_1(nq)} = \frac{V_n(1, \ldots, 1)}{n}.$$

Our love for variety parameter is simply the elasticity of γ:

$$v(n) = \frac{n\gamma'(n)}{\gamma(n)}.$$

It's easy to verify that when $C_M = \left(\int c_i^{\frac{\sigma-1}{\sigma}} di\right)^{\frac{\sigma}{\sigma-1}}$ we have $\gamma(n) = \frac{1}{\sigma-1}$.

11. Murata (2004) is an exception in this respect.

12. For simplicity's sake we omit the arguments of the functions μ and μ^*.

13. Murata (2004) uses this utility function to show the relation between agglomeration and structural change. This assumption can also be found in the new Keynesian economics literature (see Blanchard and Kiyotaki, 1987, p. 649, for example), which is another strand of literature based on the model of monopolistic competition by Dixit and Stiglitz (1977).

14. The analysis can also be developed for any $\alpha \in (-1, 0)$ but, for simplicity's sake, we focus on the case where goods are good substitutes, which, as suggested by Lucas (1988), appears to be the most interesting one.

15. This expression is obtained by solving the static problem of minimizing nominal expenditures given a certain level of utility.

16. With CD utility function and $v = 0$, the perfect price index becomes:

$$P = P_M^\mu n^{w \frac{\mu}{1-\sigma}}$$

so that $\dot{P} = \dot{P}* = 0$.

17. When capital grows overtime at the constant rate g:

$$\lim_{t \to \infty} E^w(s_E, s_n, n^w, \phi) = \frac{(2L - g)\sigma}{\sigma - 1}.$$

18. Obviously, this requirement is more easily satisfied when spillovers are localized. See Bellone and Maupertuis (2003).

19. Notice that $w_I = w_M = w$ since workers are mobile across sectors within the same regions.

REFERENCES

Baldwin, R. (1999), 'Agglomeration and endogenous capital', *European Economic Review*, **43**: 253–80.

Baldwin, R. and R. Forslid (1999), 'Incremental trade policy and endogenous growth: a *q*-theory approach', *Journal of Economic Dynamics and Control*, **23**: 797–822.

Baldwin, R. and R. Forslid (2000a), 'The core-periphery model and endogenous growth: stabilizing and de-stabilizing integration', *Economica*, **67**: 307–24.

Baldwin, R. and R. Forslid (2000b), 'Trade liberalization and endogenous growth, a *q*-theory approach', *Journal of International Economics*, **50**: 497–517.

Baldwin, R. and P. Martin (2003), 'Agglomeration and regional growth', *Discussion Paper 3960*, Centre for Economic Policy Research, London.

Baldwin, R., P. Martin and G.M. Ottaviano (2001), 'Global income divergence, trade and industrialization: the geography of growth take-offs', *Journal of Economic Growth*, **6**: 5–37

Baldwin, R., R. Forslid, P. Martin, G. Ottaviano and F. Robert-Nicoud (2003), *Economic Geography and Public Policy*, Princeton: Princeton University Press.

Bellone, F. and M.A. Maupertuis (2003), 'Economic integration and regional income inequalities: competing dynamics of regional wages and innovative capabilities', *Review of International Economics*, **11**: 512–26.

Benassy, J.P. (1996), 'Taste for variety and optimum production patterns in monopolistic competition', *Economic Letters*, **52**: 41–7.

Blanchard, O.J. and N. Kiyotak (1987), 'Monopolistic competition and aggregate demand', *American Economic Review*, **77**: 647–66.

Di Liberto, A., R. Mura and F. Pigliaru (2004), 'How to measure the unobservable: a panel technique for the analysis of TFP convergence', *CRENoS Working Paper 04/05*.

Dixit, A.K. and J.E. Stiglitz (1975), 'Monopolistic competition and optimum product diversity', *Economic Research Paper No. 64*, University of Warwick.

Dixit, A.K. and J.E. Stiglitz (1977), 'Monopolistic competition and optimum product diversity', *American Economic Review*, **67**: 297–308.

Duranton, G. and D. Puga (2004), 'Micro-foundations of urban agglomeration economies', in J.V. Henderson and J.F. Thisse (eds), *Handbook of Regional and Urban Economies*, Vol. I, Elsevier, pp. 2063–117.

Fujita, M. and J.F. Thisse (2002), *Economics of Agglomeration: Cities, Industrial Location and Regional Growth*, Cambridge: Cambridge University Press.

Grossman, G. and E. Helpman (1991), *Innovation and Growth in the World Economy*, Cambridge, MA: MIT Press.

Lucas, R.E. (1988) 'On the mechanics of economic development', *Journal of Monetary Economics*, **22**: 3–42.

Krugman, P. (1991), 'Increasing returns and economic geography', *Journal of Political Economy*, **99**: 483–99.

Krugman, P.R. and A.J. Venables (1995), 'Globalization and the inequality of nations', *Quarterly Journal of Economics*, **60**: 857–80.

Kaldor, N. (1970), 'The case for regional policies', *Scottish Journal of Political Economy*, **80**: 337–48.

Martin, P. (1999), 'Public policies, regional inequalities and growth', *Journal of Public Economics*, **73**: 85–105.

Martin, P. and G. Ottaviano (1999), 'Growing locations: industry location in a model of endogenous growth', *European Economic Review*, **43**: 281–302.

Martin, P. and G. Ottaviano (2001), 'Growth and agglomeration', *International Economic Review*, **42**: 947–68.

Moreno, R., R. Paci and S. Usai (2003), 'Spatial spillovers and innovation activity in European regions', *CRENoS Working Paper 03/10*, forthcoming in *Environment and Planning*.

Murat, M. and F. Pigliaru (1998), 'International trade and uneven growth: a model with intersector spillovers of knowledge', *Journal of International Trade and Economic Development*, **7**: 221–36.

Murata, Y. (2004) 'Structural change and agglomeration', paper presented at the CEPR workshop on Economic Geography, Paris, 16–18 June, 2004.

Romer, P. (1990), 'Endogenous technological change', *Journal of Political Economy*, **98.5**: S71–S102.

Smulders, S. and T. van de Klundert (2003), 'Monopolistic competition and economic growth', in S. Brakman and B.J. Heijdra (eds), *The Monopolistic Competition Revolution in Retrospect*, Cambridge: Cambridge University Press.

Yamamoto, K. (2002), 'Agglomeration and growth with innovation in the intermediate goods sector', *Regional Science and Urban Economics*, **33**: 335–60.

6. Sinking the iceberg? On the treatment of transport costs in new economic geography

Bernard Fingleton and Philip McCann

6.1 INTRODUCTION

Recent developments in new economic geography have incorporated all issues related to transportation and transport costs by using Krugman's adaptation of Samuelson's original iceberg function. The proponents of these models argue that this allows them to develop models of spatial allocation and growth without any need to model transport costs or transport-related issues, the actual details of which they regard as being unimportant in determining the spatial allocation of resources of growth. In these new economic geography models, geography and space is introduced into new economic geography models in the form of an iceberg transport-costs function, in which part of the goods to be delivered are consumed by the very act of transporting.

In new international trade models (Helpman and Krugman, 1985; Krugman, 1990) and in the earliest forms of new economic geography models (Krugman, 1991a, 1991b) trade costs and transport costs were synomymous and aspatial, in that distance was not explicitly modelled. Rather, all such costs were incorporated within Samuelson's iceberg model. Greater distances simply imply larger values for the inverse iceberg formula. The major reason for the use of this formulation is that it allows for a direct mathematical manipulation of trade-costs functions in a manner that is consistent with the modelling techniques allowed for by Dixit-Stiglitz (1977) functions of monopolistic competition. This is because the iceberg function yields log-linear transport costs, and when this is added to the log-linear demand functions yielded by CES preferences, only the levels, and not the elasticities of, the demand functions are changed (Neary, 2001). The advantages of these properties were then extended to the case of models in which transport and distance costs were modelled explicitly.

In the mid-1990s, the nature and form of the Samuelson iceberg formula was fundamentally altered (Fujita and Krugman, 1995; Krugman, 1995).

In this new adapted iceberg model, the iceberg parameter refers to the amount of 'melting away' that takes place with geographical distance. Although this explicitly spatial iceberg formulation itself can be shown to be rather implausible (Fujita, Krugman and Venables, 1999; Fujita and Thisse, 2002; Neary, 2001), the adoption of it is made entirely on the basis of analytical tractability rather than on the basis of any observed reality (Krugman, 1998). Therefore, as long as it is accepted that the iceberg functions are employed for reasons only of analytical tractability, then the issue is not really problematic. On the other hand, where commentators begin to use these models in order to provide real-world insights then the issue becomes much more complicated. This is because the properties of the explicitly spatial iceberg model are not only implausible, but are also largely counter to all observed evidence from transport economics. The fact that the theoretical results of explicitly spatial new economic geography models are so dependent (Neary, 2001) on the implausible properties of the iceberg function, therefore means that fundamental problems of interpretation and application start to arise where empirical justifications (Fujita, Krugman and Venables, 1999, p. 98; Brakman, Garretsen and van Marrewijk, 2001, pp. 81–3) or analytical justifications (Krugman, 1998; Fujita, Krugman and Venables, 1999, pp. 49 and 59) for the Krugman iceberg assumption are provided. As such, any empirical inferences made on the basis of the models must necessarily be treated in a rather circumspect manner. Moreover, the current defences of the iceberg assumption adopted by new economic geographers can also be shown to be very much open to question, both on empirical grounds as well as on methodological grounds.

At this point it is important to be clear that the argument in this chapter refers only to the explicitly spatial versions of new economy models in which geographical distance is an explicit variable in the model (Krugman, 1995; Fujita and Krugman, 1995; Fujita and Mori, 1996, 1997; Fujita, Krugman and Venables, 1999; Fujita, Krugman and Mori, 1999). The argument here does not relate to the non-spatial versions of new economic geography (Krugman and Venables, 1995, 1997; Venables, 1996 or Ottaviano and Thisse, 2001, 2003) in which distance is not an explicit variable.

The aim of this chapter is to highlight and examine the highly implausible properties of the explicitly spatial iceberg transport-costs function. This is being done in order to explain why the iceberg assumption employed in the explicitly spatial versions of new economic geography models is actually a much weaker and more problematic assumption than has previously been generally noted. Although the implausibility of properties of this formulation may be well-understood by the proponents of these models, it would be reasonable to suggest that most other observers are probably unaware of these subtle issues. Moreover, it would also be fair to say that many of the proponents of new economic geography are themselves rather uncomfortable with the idea that the weaknesses of these assumptions might be highlighted, preferring to defend the strength of the overall research field. The extent to which this position may be justified depends on how important these assumptions are for not only the theoretical predictions of the models, but also the empirical testing of the models. Ironically, we will argue that the implausible properties of the iceberg transport-costs function themselves imply that the weakest aspect of the explicitly spatial new economic geography models may be the particular way in which geography itself is incorporated into the models. This is because geography enters these models specifically and only via the Krugman adaptation of the Samuelson (1952) iceberg model, the properties of which are implausible and counter to most observed evidence. On the other hand, as transport economists and regional economists have always accepted, there are very strong grounds for believing that the specification of the properties of the transport-costs functions is indeed essential in understanding the spatial allocation of activities.

At this point, it is essential for us to acknowledge that models of new economic geography have gone very much further than any other previous analytical system in developing a theoretical framework in which the spatial allocation of resources can be analysed within a general equilibrium framework. This is clearly understood by the field in general, and it is not our intention here to build upon, improve or replace such models with an alternative system. Rather, our aim is simply to point out that after considering the insights of transport economics, it becomes clear that one of the central assumptions of these new economic geography models is much more problematic than most people realize.

In order to develop the argument and to clarify the various theoretical, empirical and interpretative issues associated with iceberg costs, we first begin in the next section by explaining the traditional logic of the Samuelsonian iceberg transport-costs function. In Section 6.3 we explain how the traditional iceberg concept has been adapted within the new economic geography models, and reveal certain fundamental properties of this iceberg adaptation that have been largely ignored. Section 6.4 explains the structure of transport costs with respect to haulage distance and weight, which are typically observed empirically, and are also typically employed analytically in both transport economics and traditional regional economics. The reason for doing this is so that the properties of the iceberg model can be clearly contrasted with observed reality. In Section 6.5 we consider an alternative to the iceberg model that more closely reflects observed transport-costs structures. We conclude that the iceberg assumption is probably the weakest link in the new economic geography framework, which is problematic given that this is the only explicitly geographical variable is the schema.

6.2 THE SAMUELSON ICEBERG TRANSPORT-COSTS FUNCTION

The iceberg formulation of transportation costs was first employed by Samuelson (1952). The assumption of the iceberg function amounts to assuming that the technology used to produce a good is identical to that used in order to transport the good. As such, this must be a special case (Neary, 2001, p. 551). However, at the time it was first introduced as an analytical device; the attractiveness of employing this particular description of transportation costs was that it circumvented the problems associated with defining transport costs explicitly in geographical terms, as was being attempted by others at the time (Isard, 1956). In classical and neo-classical international trade models of the 1950s, which were essentially aspatial, this analytical device greatly simplified trade analysis by treating distance and transportation costs in exactly the same way as tariff costs. The logic of the Samuelsonian iceberg formulation can be explained in the following manner.

Suppose we have two markets, a home market H and a foreign market F. If a good x is produced in the home market H with a value of V_{XH}, and some of the good is consumed by the act of shipment, the value of the good that actually arrives in the foreign market is denoted as $\tau_x V_{XH}$, where $1 - \tau_x$ is the proportion of the good x consumed by the process of transportation from H to F. In order to determine the relative prices of the goods in the home market P_{XH} and in the foreign market P_{XF}, we must remember that the value of the good in the home market V_{XH} is the product of the domestic price per ton of the good P_{XH} multiplied by the tonnage of good x being shipped from the home market M_{XH}. Now, in the act of international shipment, although the price per ton of x paid by the foreign consumer to the domestic producer is P_{XH}, for each ton purchased at H, the total weight of good M_{XF} actually arriving in the foreign market F is only $\tau_x M_{XH}$ tons. In other words, the foreign price per ton P_{XF} actually paid by the foreign consumer is given as:

$$P_{XF} = P_{XH}(M_{XH}/M_{XF}) = P_{XH}/\tau_x \qquad (6.1)$$

where P_{XF} represents the cost to the foreign consumer of acquiring a ton of good x in the foreign market F. Similarly, for a foreign-produced good y of

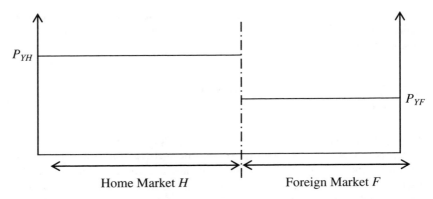

Figure 6.1   Iceberg prices of goods in different international markets

mill price P_{YF} per ton in the foreign market, the home market price of good y is denoted as:

$$P_{YH} = P_{YF}/\tau_y \qquad (6.2)$$

where τ_y represents the proportion of the good y not consumed in the process of transportation from F to H. Diagrammatically, these two situations can be represented by Figure 6.1.

As we see in Figure 6.1, the iceberg formulation depicts transportation costs as a stepwise discontinuity between the home and foreign prices of the respective goods, in which the extent of the discontinuity varies in proportion to the value of τ. Within any part of an individual country the prices of each of the goods are invariant. In other words there is no spatial pricing that is distance-related. As such, there is no economic geography within the individual country, which is essentially spaceless. On the other hand, moving across an international trade border results in a stepwise price increase for each good. Once again, however, there is no explicitly geographical aspect to this discontinuity. We can assign larger or smaller stepwise functions as we desire. For example, if the home and foreign countries are adjacent to each other, we may assume that τ is rather small, such that the stepwise discontinuity is small. On the other hand, if the two countries are far apart, we may assume that τ is rather large, such that the stepwise discontinuity is large. These assumptions, however, are essentially arbitrary, in that what we explicitly do not undertake is the formulation of any specific continuous relationship between the level of τ and the distance between the two countries. As such, transportation costs can be characterized and analysed in exactly the same way as a one-off trade tariff. Moreover, avoiding the specification of any specific relationship between transportation costs and distance means that transportation costs and trade tariffs can now be combined into a single parameter for ease of analysis. Geography is assumed away, as is traditional in models of international trade.

A second feature of the simple Samuelson iceberg model is that the transport cost per ton is invariant with respect to the tonnage of material delivered.

In the more recent 'new international trade' models most closely associated with the work of Helpman and Krugman (1985) and Krugman (1990), the Samuelsonian iceberg device is also adopted in conjunction with Dixit-Stiglitz (1977) descriptions of monopolistic competition and economies of scale. As with traditional classical and neo-classical trade models, these 'new international trade' models are still essentially aspatial, in that no specific continuous relationship between iceberg transportation costs and distance is specified. Economic geography as such still does not exist in these models.

6.3   ICEBERG TRANSPORT-COSTS FUNCTIONS IN NEW ECONOMIC GEOGRAPHY MODELS

A major intellectual shift occurred in the mid-1990s (Fujita and Krugman, 1995; Krugman, 1995), which adapted the functional forms employed in 'new international trade' models to the case of geographical space. The Dixit-Stiglitz (1977) functions are still employed, as are increasing returns to scale functions. However, the single most important technical innovation, which allowed a shift from 'new international trade' models and aspatial new economic geography models (Krugman, 1991a, 1991b) to explicitly spatial 'new economic geography' models (Fujita and Krugman, 1995; Krugman, 1995), was the specification of iceberg transport cost functions as continuous distance functions. Krugman (1995) redefined the aspatial Samuelsonian iceberg function into an explicitly geographical distance-related function, although a slightly different form has been employed (Fujita and Ogawa, 1995). Following the arguments in McCann (2005), the Krugman (1995) definition of iceberg transport costs is:

$$V_d = V_o e^{-\tau D} \tag{6.3}$$

whereby V_o is the value of the good at the origin location, τ is the iceberg decay parameter, D is the haulage distance, and V_d is the quantity of good actually delivered at the delivery location d. In this formula, τ represents the proportion of the remaining quantity of the good that 'melts' away each kilometre. Note that there is a subtle change here from the Samuelsonian version of the iceberg whereby $(1 - \tau)$ represents the proportion that melts away, and τ represents the remaining proportion of the good. If we set $W = V_d/V_o$ then we can re-write equation (6.3) as:

$$W = e^{-\tau D} \qquad (6.4)$$

Taking logs of both sides of equation (6.4) and differentiating both sides with respect to D gives:

$$\frac{1}{W}\frac{\partial W}{\partial D} = -\tau. \qquad (6.5)$$

In other words, as the haulage distance increases, the (negative) rate of growth of the value of good V_d actually delivered, divided by the original source value V_o of good produced, remains constant. τ represents the constant rate of (iceberg) distance-decay. We can represent this diagrammatically in Figure 6.2.

As we see, the absolute quantity of distance-decay per kilometre, as represented by the slope of the function, falls as haulage D increases. The vertical distance between the perforated line at level V_o and the iceberg function represented by the continuous strictly convex curve represents the absolute quantity of goods that 'melt' away over any given haulage distance. The convexity of this function suggests that, prima facie, the marginal costs of transportation, as represented by the quantity of good that melts away, falls with increasing distance.

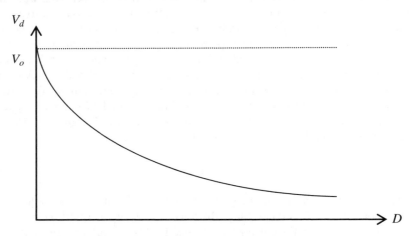

Figure 6.2   Iceberg distance-decay

The Krugman iceberg approach is also assumed (Fujita, Krugman and Venables, 1999, pp. 49 and 59) to be justified on the basis of a supposed Von Thunen (1826) pedigree, because in the original Von Thunen example of horse and cart technology, the haulage shipment of grain included the grain for horse-feed (Von Thunen, 1826, p. 13). However, as a justification for the iceberg model, there are major problems with this analogy. See Appendix for details.

The formulation described by equation (6.3) and Figure 6.1 is often assumed by commentators to be broadly consistent with empirical observations of transportation economies of distance, in which the delivered prices of goods are generally concave functions of distance. This, however, is not the case, because V_d does not represent the delivered price of the good. To see this, it is necessary to convert the Krugman (1995) iceberg formulation into a delivered-price function.

In order to convert an iceberg transport costs function into a delivered-price function, we must ask how much it costs a consumer at a given distance D from a production location to consume a given quantity of a good, and how this consumption cost varies with D. Here we must remember that the origin value of a good being shipped, denoted above as V_o, is defined as the product of the origin mill price P_o per ton of the good, multiplied by the tonnage of good M_o leaving the production location. On the other hand, the destination value of the good defined in terms of the origin value, denoted above as V_d, is given as the product of the origin mill price P_o per ton of the good, multiplied by the tonnage of good M_d actually arriving at the consumption destination. In order to determine the delivered price of the good allowing for the distance-decay, as with the Samuelsonian iceberg function, we can write the cost of purchasing one ton of a good of mill price P_o per ton shipped at a distance D as:

$$P_d = P_o(M_o/M_d) \tag{6.6}$$

where P_d represents the price per ton of the delivered good. If we recall from equations (6.1) and (6.3) that (M_o/M_d) can be rewritten as $(V_o/V_o e^{-\tau D})$, then we have:

$$P_d = P_o(V_o/V_o e^{-\tau D}) = P_o/e^{-\tau D} = P_o e^{-\tau D} \tag{6.7}$$

Taking the first and second order derivatives of equation (6.7) with respect to distance gives:

$$\frac{\partial P_d}{\partial D} = \tau P_o e^{\tau D} \tag{6.8}$$

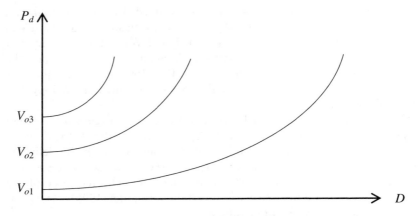

Figure 6.3   The relationship between the iceberg distance-costs formulation and the delivered price per ton

and:

$$\frac{\partial^2 P_d}{\partial D^2} = \tau^2 P_o e^{\tau D}. \tag{6.9}$$

From equations (6.8) and (6.9) we see that the relationship between the delivered price of the good and the haulage distance, described by equation (6.7), is therefore represented diagrammatically as in Figure 6.3.

As we see in Figure 6.3, in the Krugman iceberg formula, the relationship between the delivered price of the good and the haulage distance has two very specific characteristics. First, *all iceberg transport-costs functions are strictly convex with the haulage distance* D.

The second property of the iceberg model can be seen by taking the cross-partials of equations (6.8) and (6.9) with respect to the origin price of the good thus:

$$\frac{\partial\left(\dfrac{\partial P_d}{\partial D}\right)}{\partial P_o} = \tau e^{\tau D} \tag{6.10}$$

and:

$$\frac{\partial\left(\dfrac{\partial^2 P_d}{\partial D^2}\right)}{\partial P_o} = \tau^2 e^{\tau D}. \tag{6.11}$$

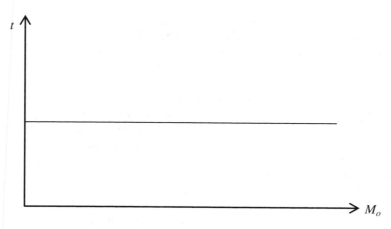

*Figure 6.4   The relationship between the iceberg distance-costs
formulation and the transport costs per ton-kilometre*

As we see in equations (6.10) and (6.11), in the Krugman iceberg model the
level of distance-delivered price convexity increases with the value of the
good being shipped, for any given value of τ. This property is depicted in
Figure 6.3, where by comparing the delivered prices for three goods of
origin prices V_{o1}, V_{o2} and V_{o3}, where $V_{o3} > V_{o2} > V_{o1}$, we can see that the
delivered price of the good rises with distance at a greater rate for goods
with higher origin prices than for goods with lower origin prices.[1]

A third feature of the Krugman iceberg model, is that for any given
haulage distance and for any given mill price per ton, the transport cost per
ton-kilometre t is *invariant* with respect to the weight of material M_o initially
hauled from the origin. This is depicted in Figure 6.4. Although in absolute
terms the total weight of material that is consumed in the act of transportation is directly related to the weight of material initially hauled from the
origin, this level of consumption is exactly in proportion to the origin weight.
The outcome of this is that the transport cost between any two locations is
always a constant fraction of the f.o.b. (free on board) price irrespective of
the quantity shipped between the two locations, thereby preserving the constant elasticity of demand (Krugman, 1998, p. 165). The invariance of the
transport rate per ton-kilometre in Krugman's explicitly spatial version of
the iceberg model is therefore directly parallel to the behaviour of the simple
Samuelsonian aspatial iceberg formula, in which the transport-costs per ton
are also invariant with respect to the total tonnage shipped.

All explicitly spatial models of new economic geography are based on
Krugman's explicitly spatial formulation of the iceberg function, rather

than on the aspatial Samuelsonian iceberg definition employed in new international trade models. The importance of the iceberg transport-costs assumption lies in the fact that predictions about the tendency for firms to agglomerate or diversify over space can be made on the basis of direct comparisons between the values of the (iceberg) transport costs, the elasticity of substitution and the share of manufacturing income, and these relationships are mapped in terms of bifurcation diagrams (Fujita, Krugman and Venables, 1999; Neary, 2001). But as we have seen, such explicitly spatial iceberg functions also have very specific properties. In particular, transport costs per ton-kilometre are always convex with respect to both the haulage distance, and independent of the quantity shipped over any given distance. In other words, all explicitly spatial models of 'new economic geography' are based on spatial price functions that are convex with respect to the haulage distance, and independent of the quantity shipped over any given distance.

The 'seemingly innocuous' (Neary, 2001) iceberg assumption may actually have much more profound implications for the outcomes and interpretations of new economic geography models than has previously been assumed. The reason for this is that, once we have introduced the assumption of the iceberg structure in new economic geography models, transport costs are then simply discussed in terms of being 'high' or 'low'. What is almost never discussed, however, is whether the *properties* of the iceberg assumption with respect to either haulage distance or quantity may affect any of the analytical results (Brakman et al., 2001; Fujita, Krugman and Venables, 1999). Even very 'low' values of τ lead to enormous destination-origin price ratios over relatively short distances.

The only critical comment on the issue so far is from Neary (2001, p. 550) who points out that the detailed results of the new economic geography research programme do rely on the iceberg assumption. This is important, because for location or spatial price theorists, the properties of transport functions are always at least as important to the analytical outcome of a spatial model as is the level of the transport costs (d'Aspremont, Gabszewicz and Thisse, 1979). The reason for this is that analytical solutions generated by optimization techniques are usually seen to depend crucially on the marginality conditions. Therefore, if we change the behaviour of the transportation costs function, the analytical outcomes may be completely changed. Moreover, this observation is generally true both analytically and empirically for any type of economic model involving transactions costs (Haurin, Hendershott and Kim, 1994; Muellbauer and Murphy, 1997).

At this point we present an excursus regarding not only the observed structure of transport costs, but also the theoretical rationale for such observations. This is necessary in order to clarify exactly the observed empirical and analytical conditions against which the assumptions of the iceberg model must be compared.

6.4   THE OBSERVED STRUCTURE OF TRANSPORT COSTS

Prior to the advent of new economic geography models, very few, if any, location or spatial pricing theorists would have ever employed convex transportation-costs functions in their models, of a type inherent in the iceberg function. The main reason for this is that almost all empirical evidence points to the contrary. The vast majority of empirical work in transportation economics points to the widespread existence of economies of scale in distance transportation. Transportation costs per ton-kilometre t are almost universally found to exhibit economies of distance, as represented in Figure 6.5a. The result of this is that ton-kilometre td transportation-costs and pricing structures are found to be strictly concave with distance, both within countries and between countries (Bayliss and Edwards, 1970; Bruce Allen, 1977; Jansson and Shneerson, 1987; Tyler and Kitson, 1987), as represented in Figure 6.5b.

Figure 6.5a demonstrates that the transport rate per ton-kilometre t falls as the distance increases. However, the rate of fall of the value of t itself falls as the haulage distance increases. Plotting how the value of t varies with the haulage distance produces the well-known and frequently observed convex shape depicted in Figure 6.5a.

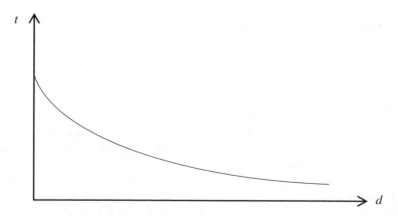

Figure 6.5a   Economies of distance in transportation

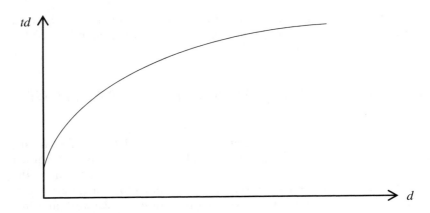

Figure 6.5b   Economies of distance in transportation

An alternative commonly used means of quoting transport costs and prices is that of quoting transport costs per ton, for any given shipment distance. Given that t represents the value of the transport rate per ton-kilometre, then the transport rate per ton is given by td. Once again, plotting how the transport rate per ton varies with the haulage distance gives us the familiar concave shape depicted in Figure 6.5b.

These transport-costs shapes are ubiquitous within the world of transportation and logistics. This is because such concave transportation-costs functions are actually the natural (envelope) outcome of the inventory-shipment-frequency optimization problems faced by all hauliers (McCann, 2001), and can be shown to hold irrespective of whether a single mode or multiple modes of transportation are used, or whether transportation vehicular technology exhibits constant or increasing returns to scale (McCann, 2001). The important point here, however, is simply that transport costs are almost always concave with distance, and that there are fundamental cost-optimization analytical reasons why this is so,[2] whereas there are hardly ever any cost-optimization arguments that imply convex transport costs.

As well as exhibiting economies of distance, transportation costs simultaneously also generally exhibit economies of scale, for any given distance (Bayliss and Edwards, 1970; Jansson and Shneerson, 1987). In other words, as the quantity q to be shipped over any given distance increases, the average transportation cost per ton-kilometre t falls. This situation is depicted in Figure 6.6. The unit transport cost–quantity relationship generally exhibits a convex form, and the reason for this, once again, is that it is the natural (envelope) outcome of the inventory-shipment-frequency

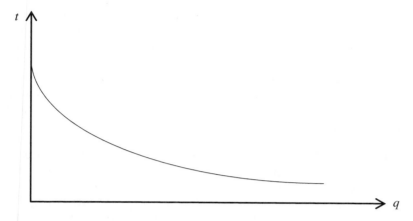

Figure 6.6   Economies of scale in transportation

optimization problems faced by all hauliers (McCann, 2001).[3] As with economies of distance, these results and costs structures can be shown to hold irrespective of whether a single mode or multiple modes of transportation are used, or whether transportation vehicular technology exhibits constant or increasing returns to scale (McCann, 2001).

Importantly, the transport price–cost features depicted in Figures 6.5a and 6.5b and Figure 6.6 generally operate simultaneously with respect to both the haulage distance and quantity, because they are derived from the same optimization arguments. As we see, these empirically observed properties are completely different form those exhibited by the iceberg functions.[4] Having explained in detail what observed transport rate structures look like, we are now in a position to reconsider the justifications for the assumptions implicit in the Krugman iceberg model.

6.4.1   Theoretical Justifications for the Iceberg Assumption

As we saw in the previous sections, the behaviour of the Krugman iceberg assumption with respect to both the haulage distance and the haulage weight is very specific, and in each case, is quite different from actual observed transport-costs behaviour. Where iceberg costs are defined in an aspatial setting, as in both traditional and new trade theories, as well as in the types of new economic geography models discussed by Venables (1996) or Ottaviano and Thisse (2001), there would appear to be no major problem with the iceberg assumption, because geography still does not actually enter the picture. On the other hand, however, where iceberg transport costs are defined explicitly with respect to space, the Krugman iceberg assumption becomes largely invalid both observationally and empirically. Krugman simply remarks that '*It is too bad*[5] that transport costs look nothing like that' (Krugman, 1998, p. 165), because the major justification for the iceberg assumption is not observational or empirical but analytical, in that it is a 'technical trick' employed for reasons of 'modeling convenience', thereby avoiding 'the need to model an additional industry' (Krugman, 1998, p. 165).[6] The actual real-world behaviour of transport-transactions costs is assumed in no way to either undermine or invalidate any of the new economic geography conclusions.

However, it is possible to argue that this justification for the iceberg assumption is not as straightforward as it first appears, in that the detailed results (Neary, 2001) of those new economic geography models that are set explicitly in geographical space may be very sensitive to this assumption. There are two theoretical reasons for this and two empirical reasons for this:

6.4.1.1 Tractability

In a discipline such as economics in which it is always necessary to make simplifying assumptions, Krugman's tractability justification for the iceberg assumption will be appealing to many. However, it is possible to argue that in this particular case, we must treat this justification with caution. The reason for this is that, as we have seen, the one original feature of the new economic geography research programme over new international trade theory is specifically the fact that it includes space-geography in its models via the use of the Krugman adaptation of the Samuelson iceberg model. Yet, it does so in a manner that is empirically wrong, and this may have very strong implications from an analytical point of view. This is because without the Krugman iceberg assumption, the results of new economic geography models as they are currently specified, could quickly become explosive. In order to see this, we have to understand that as these models currently stand, the convex iceberg transport costs embedded within the models act as a natural break and counterbalance to any localized economies of scale, thereby imposing spatial market limits on production, even without the presence of localized congestion costs. As such, spatial market areas can be delineated around the hinterland of each urban location. On the other hand, concave distance-transport cost structures allow for markets to be completely dominated above a certain price ceiling. Therefore, unless there are countervailing localized congestion costs, the combination of agglomeration economies in local production allied with both economies of scale and economies of distance in transportation, could easily cause any marginal migration of either labour or firms to lead to explosive localized growth, thereby forcing all activity to a single location rather than across a distribution of cities and city-sizes.

With such explosive localized growth no spatial urban system will emerge. It would therefore appear that concave transport costs would make the new economic geography models much more unstable over a greater range of transport rates and product variety indices than is implied by current analyses, because only localized congestion costs could act as a possible brake on explosive growth. In terms of the new economic geography modelling framework, this would imply that the parameter space for which the 'no-black-hole' condition[7] holds (Fujita, Krugman and Venables, 1999; Neary, 2001) will become greatly reduced.

It could therefore be argued that a principal methodological justification for the iceberg assumption is not simply that it is analytically tractable, but also that it generates the types of analytical simulation results that we would like to see.

6.4.1.2   A broad definition of spatial transactions costs
An alternative (and recently popular) theoretical way of justifying the use of the iceberg assumption of a strictly convex delivered price–distance relationship within new economic geography models is to say that the iceberg model incorporates all forms of distance-transactions and trade costs, including information costs, institutional barriers, cultural and linguistic differences (Ottaviano, 1999, p. 3; Ottaviano and Thisse, 1999, p. 3)[8] as well as transport costs (Fujita, Krugman and Venables, 1999, pp. 97–8). In other words, this justification assumes that if we were to take such a broad view of distance-transactions costs, the behaviour with respect to distance of these broadly–defined (information + transport) costs would be something akin to a strictly convex delivered price–distance relationship. Yet, empirical observation of these issues generally points to opposite conclusions. As such, it is necessary to treat this justification with real caution, and there are three reasons for this.

First, as we have seen in Section 6.4, the empirical observations of transport costs point to quite different spatial transactions costs structures. Therefore, in order for a broad definition of (information + transport) spatial transactions costs to be convex with distance, information transfer costs must generally be extremely convex with distance in order to counter the observed concavity of transport costs.

On this point, the growing empirical literature on the geography of patent citations and innovations (Acs, 2002) suggests that some types of information may be very localized for certain types of information-dependent activities, and this may provide a rationale for the development of cities.[9] Moreover, the fact that the density of information technology usage tends to be highly correlated with proximity (Gaspar and Glaeser, 1998) suggests that the quantity, variety (and possibly also quality) of information transmitted over space may actually increase with proximity. Information technology may therefore be both a complement to as well as a substitute for face to face contact. However, while it may be true that one of the reasons for the development of cities is to facilitate the information transfer associated with the production[10] or consumption process (Glaeser, Kolko and Saiz, 2001), the exact nature of the relationship between distance and the spatial transactions costs associated with information transfer is unknown. However, from general observations of the outcomes of information transfer over space, it may be possible to make certain inferences as to the nature of the relationship between distance and information-transfer costs. The extreme localization of some information-related activities, would tend to suggest that the spatial distance costs associated with information transfer within these sectors are likely to be at the very least, non-concave with distance.[11] On the other hand, for many information-related industries the costs of information transfer across space appear to exhibit very significant economies of distance. For example, observation of telephone charges, internet user charges and postal rates, suggests that many types of information-transmission costs are actually concave with distance, in a manner even more striking than in the case of transport costs. This appears to be particularly so for many international banking and business services (Cohen, 1998; Leyshon and Thrift, 1997). Therefore, these combined observations suggest that for many information-dependent sectors, the costs of spatial information transfer with respect to distance may be non-concave for information production inputs and concave for market outputs. This particular arrangement would tend to encourage explosive localized growth in information-related sectors.[12] However, the combination of non-concave input and concave output distance-information transfer costs suggested by the limited available evidence, is a very different set of transport cost structures than are assumed by the Krugman iceberg model. As such, empirical observations of either telecommunication costs or patent citation distributions do not necessarily support the argument that distance-transportation costs for both information inputs and outputs are appropriately characterized as being strictly convex with respect to distance, as is suggested by Krugman iceberg costs formula. Rather, the evidence points to possible differences in distance-cost structures between many inputs and outputs, in which economies of distance and economies of scale play a major role for many types of activities involving the transfer of goods or information over space. As we see here, therefore, there is almost no empirical evidence in favour of such a convex relationship between information costs and distance. On the contrary, there is much empirical evidence that suggests that many aspects of information-transmission costs are actually themselves concave with distance.[13]

Second, if such broadly defined transport costs were indeed convex with distance, then there would always be a market opportunity for fragmenting all non-trivial distance transactions into an infinite number of tiny sequential spatial transactions, the effect of which will be to make total spatial distance costs not only approximately linear with distance, but also approximately zero. The fact that we do not observe this in reality itself points to the fact that broadly-defined distance costs cannot be convex with distance.

Third, a convex distance-delivered price relationship could be generated if individual cross-border tariffs increased as the haulage distance increases, in a situation where transport costs were approximately linear with distance. However, there is no theoretical reason why individual cross-border tariffs should become progressively higher as the distance shipped increases. Moreover, even if by chance this were the case as a good is shipped from A to B, then the reverse journey from B to A would be characterized by tariffs that together generate a concave distance delivered-price relationship.

Commenting on this argument that the iceberg assumption reflects a broad definition of distance-trade costs, Neary (2001, p. 551) observes that in a field such as new economic geography, which emphasizes the role of increasing returns to scale 'of all industries it [transportation] seems to be characterized by high ratios of fixed to variable costs . . . This is particularly important if transport costs are interpreted broadly to include the communications and other costs associated with trade, which are likely to exhibit network externalities'. As such, the theoretical defence of the convex-with-distance iceberg model, associated with a broader definition of trade costs than simply transportation costs, seems to be very weak indeed. We now turn to the empirical defences.

6.4.2 Empirical Justifications for the Iceberg Assumption

Because there is no direct empirical evidence in favour of the convex distance-costs behaviour of the Krugman iceberg assumption, new economic geographers therefore tend to use two rather indirect empirical methods to justify their approach. The first method observes the volumes of trade flows with respect to distance, the second method uses international trade data and observes the relationship between the delivered prices of the goods and their origin prices over a range of geographical distances, while the third method uses composite estimates.

6.4.2.1 Trade volumes and gravity models

Although many of these distance-related costs are not observable directly, as we have already seen, for new economic geographers employing the iceberg model, the implicit justification for their approach is that when all of these various distance-costs issues are grouped together, the resulting distance-costs function will be convex with distance. While there is no evidence for this assumption, this unsubstantiated assumption allows a move from a Samuelsonian iceberg delivered-price relationship (discussed in Section 6.2) to something akin to a gravity model specification, which can then be tested and interpreted with respect to a new economic geography model. This is because it can be shown that the incorporation of the iceberg assumption within a CES framework leads to a trade specification that is structurally consistent with a gravity model specification (Brocker, 2002; Anderson and van Wincoop, 2003, 2004). However, there are strong empirical and theoretical grounds for arguing that using a gravity model to test a new economic geography framework is itself problematic.

From an empirical perspective, the first indirect empirical approach used by new economic geographers to justify the adoption of the iceberg transport-costs assumption is to consider the available evidence from gravity model estimates of international trade volumes with respect to distance. These suggest that the volume of international trade flows is generally observed to fall with increasing distance (Leamer and Levinsohn, 1996), and the elasticity of trade with respect to distance is typically found to be of the order of -0.9 to -1.5 (Overman, Redding and Venables, 2001).[14] However, although gravity models tell us that geographical distance does matter in terms of determining the volume of trade, gravity models themselves do not reveal whether the impact of geography on trade flows is primarily via the impact of geography on trade costs or on the impact of trade costs on trade volumes (Overman et al., 2001). Therefore, in terms of the issue being discussed in this chapter concerning the validity of the convex distance-price structure of the Krugman iceberg assumption, these gravity model estimations cannot be regarded as an independent empirical test either way. This is because, as we see from equations (6.4) and (6.5), the specification of the Krugman iceberg function does not reflect the elasticity of trade with respect to distance, and such estimations can only be instructive for our purposes if we also know the average distance shipped. In order to convert the iceberg function into a gravity model trade-distance elasticity, we must multiply the Krugman iceberg value τ by the average haulage distance D. Conversely, in order to convert gravity model estimates into Krugman iceberg τ values, we need to divide the gravity model estimates by the average distance shipped. Given the gravity model trade volume-distance elasticities that we typically observe, and assuming that the average distances of international trade shipments are of the order of hundreds of kilometres, then the values of τ that are consistent with the Krugman iceberg convex distance-costs structure will be defined in terms of tiny fractions of 1 per cent. As such, they will be incredibly small in comparison with the simulation values employed in the new economic geography literature. In fact, the values will be so small as to largely rule out the role of transport costs, distance and therefore geography itself. The raw empirical data therefore does not really provide any support for the adoption of the Krugman iceberg assumption.

The gravity model logic embedded in the Krugman iceberg function is an explicit assumption. In new economic geography models, the consumption patterns at any location L are determined by the costs of goods production at L and also the delivered prices of goods produced at any alternative location M within the location space set S, where L, $M \in S$. The assumption of the convex-with-distance iceberg delivered prices generates a gravity model-type structure. Therefore, the gravity model cannot be an independent test of the iceberg assumption. Moreover, although gravity models tell us that geographical distance does matter in terms of determining the volume of trade, gravity models themselves do not reveal whether the impact of geography on trade flows is primarily via the impact of geography on trade costs or on the impact of trade costs on trade volumes (Overman et al., 2001). Therefore, while the gravity model can be regarded as being consistent with the Krugman iceberg transport costs function, it is not in any way a justification or validation of it.[15] As Neary (2001, p. 54) points out, the various empirical work based on gravity flows do not provide an independent test of the new economic geography and iceberg transport costs models as against any plausible alternatives. The gravity and entropy-based framework (Wilson, 1970, 1974) is consistent with a whole range of different types of distance-costs functions and theoretical models (Sen and Smith, 1995) both before and subsequent to the advent of new economic geography. This is because spatial interaction models are inherently probabilistic in nature, and are not dependent on particular assumptions about spatial pricing.

6.4.2.2 Trade price data
The second possible indirect empirical approach to justifying the adoption of the Krugman iceberg assumption is simply to consider the relationship between origin (f.o.b.) and destination cost, insurance, freight (c.i.f) pricing/costing evidence available from international trade literature. Brakman et al. (2001, pp. 81–3) present various cross-country (c.i.f)/(f.o.b.) price ratio percentage estimates.[16] Looking at all such transport costs unweighted by trade volumes, Overman et al. (2001) suggest that the median (c.i.f.)/(f.o.b.) across all pairs of countries for which data is available is 1.28,[17] implying that an average of 28 per cent of the total delivered price is accounted for by transport and insurance costs.[18] Meanwhile, estimates from Hummels (1999b) and Limao and Venables (2001) suggest

that the elasticity of transport costs with respect to distance is typically of the order of 0.2 to 0.3. We can use these various empirical estimates in order to get a rough idea of the meaningful values of τ and the spatial units of distance D implied by the Krugman iceberg formulation.

If we denote distance D in terms of kilometres or miles, then adopting the Krugman (1998, p. 165) example where the value of τ is 0.01 (that is 1 per cent per kilometre or per mile), then we see that the delivered price is over 2.7 times greater than the mill price at a distance of 100 kilometres, over seven times greater at a distance of 200 kilometres, over 20 times greater than the mill price at a distance of 300 kilometres, and over 54 times greater than the mill price at a distance of 400 kilometres. On the other hand, if we set the value of τ at 0.1, which is the numerical value employed in the simulations of Fujita, Krugman and Venables (1999, p. 122), this implies that the delivered price at a distance of ten kilometres is 2.72 times greater than the mill price, after 30 kilometres is 20.08 times greater than the mill price, and after 100 kilometres is 22026 times greater than the mill price! Even two-dimensional simulations using actual geographical shapes and distances (Stelder, 2002) employ values of τ between 0.3 and 0.45, which imply that after ten kilometres the delivered prices are between 20 and 90 times the mill price, and after 100 miles, are trillions of times higher. While we may be able to argue that by simply increasing the unit definition of D these figures will be reduced to meaningful numbers, or alternatively converting D values by, for example, taking square roots or natural logs,[19] the individual spatial units of D that we must employ in order to make the delivered price–mill-price ratio meaningful is so large as to be simply too big for any reasonable level of geographical analysis for urban and regional distributions.

We can demonstrate this by example. Within the Krugman iceberg structure, from equation (6.7) we know that the (unweighted by trade volume) ratio of the delivered price P_d over the origin P_o price is given as:

$$\frac{P_d}{P_o} = \frac{P_o e^{\tau D}}{P_o} = e^{\tau D} \qquad (6.12)$$

Given that the (c.i.f)/(f.o.b.) percentage price ratio is given as (c.i.f./f.o.b.) -1×100, then we can use the observed (c.i.f)/(f.o.b.) percentage ratios to get a rough idea of meaningful spatial units of τ and D implied by the Krugman formula, by using the formula $(e^{\tau D} - 1) \times 100$ to represent the (c.i.f)/(f.o.b.) percentage price ratio and then solving for D for any given empirically observed value of the (c.i.f)/(f.o.b.) percentage price ratio.

Brakman et al. (2001, pp. 81–3) present various (Radelet and Sachs, 1998) cross-country (c.i.f)/(f.o.b.) price ratio percentage estimates. For some of the most geographically isolated countries in the world, such as New Zealand, this ratio is of the order of 10–11 per cent. Therefore, assuming that the average international shipment distances for New Zealand must be at least 2500 kilometres, as this is the distance to its nearest neighbour, then this would imply that the (non-trade weighted) value of τ is close to 0.000044, which is less than one two-thousandth of the values employed in the Fujita, Krugman and Venables (1999) simulations. In other words, individual units of D within the Fujita, Krugman and Venables (1999, p. 162–3) simulations would be of the order of 2200 kilometre units. With plausible values for the other parameters, this would imply that the calculated critical distance for an additional urban settlement of 1.1 units is over 2200 kilometres. These distance values for D are far too high for any meaningful level of geographical analysis, and the parameter values of τ are simply so low as to be indistinguishable from zero. This empirical evidence is not at all supportive of the application of the Krugman iceberg formula, because it implies that the iceberg costs are effectively zero. Geography as such will disappear.

As we see from this example, these empirical estimates imply that the Krugman iceberg τ values must be a tiny fraction of 1 per cent, in order to be consistent with observation. Therefore, as with the trade volume data in 6.4.2.1 above, the empirical estimates of the (c.i.f)/(f.o.b.) price ratios also imply that the values of τ will be so tiny as to rule out any role for distance, transportation costs, or even geography itself, in the spatial allocation of resources.

6.4.2.3 Composite estimates
As was mentioned above, gravity models themselves do not reveal whether the impact of geography on trade flows is primarily via the impact of geography on trade costs or on the impact of trade costs on trade volumes (Overman et al., 2001). Therefore, one way of trying to make this separation is to take the ratio of the distance elasticity of trade with respect to the distance elasticity of transport costs (Hummels, 1999a; Limao and Venables, 2001). An alternative approach is to use the predicted values of transport costs derived from an estimated transport costs equation as an independent variable in a gravity model (Overman et al., 2001).[20] However, these approaches still do not themselves throw any light on the issue as to the implied values of τ that are necessary for the Krugman iceberg model to be reconciled with observed trade data.

While it is possible to argue that all these various empirical techniques 6.4.2.1–6.4.2.3 probably do underestimate the true distance-deterrence (Gordon, 1978) effect of geography, the major point here is that when we apply the Krugman iceberg logic to empirical trade data, the tiny implied values of τ that would be necessary in order to make the Krugman iceberg structure consistent with the observed empirical values, suggest that any hypothetical iceberg structure would be barely convex at all with distance. Over most inter-regional scales, the iceberg transport-costs coefficient τ would therefore be interpreted as being so incredibly small that spatial transactions costs would always be approximately zero. As such, *total* transport costs per ton would be considered to be largely invariant with respect to distance, thereby obviating any role at all for geography in economics.

6.5   AN ALTERNATIVE TO ICEBERGS

A principal characteristic of the iceberg transport-costs function is the constant rate of 'melting', which is equal to τ. In other words, the iceberg loses a constant proportion of its total mass per unit of distance, and we have observed that one problem with this is that there are no economies of distance (or scale) as are apparent in the real world. We can, however, introduce economies of distance via alternative functions, and one that has been recently proposed by Fingleton (2005) is the power function, given as:

$$T_{od} = 1 + (\phi D)^{\Psi} \tag{6.13}$$

where T_{od} represents the transport costs incurred in shipping a good from origin o to destination d over a haulage distance D, and ψ is the parameter comparable to τ ($\phi > 0$ is an arbitrary scaling parameter). If the origin price is P_o and the delivered price is given as P_d, then the destination-origin price ratio is given as:

$$\frac{P_d}{P_o} = 1 + (\phi D)^{\Psi} \tag{6.14}$$

and the first and second cross-partial derivatives with respect to distance are:

$$\frac{\partial \left(\dfrac{P_d}{P_o} \right)}{\partial D} = \Psi D^{\Psi - 1} \phi^{\Psi} \tag{6.15}$$

and:

$$\frac{\partial^2 \left(\dfrac{P_d}{P_o} \right)}{\partial D^2} = \Psi (\Psi - 1) D^{\Psi - 2} \phi^{\Psi}. \tag{6.16}$$

If the value of Ψ lies between zero and one, then the first derivative is positive and the second derivative is negative. From both analytical work (McCann, 2001) and empirical work (Bayliss and Edwards, 1970; Bruce Allen, 1977; Jansson and Shneerson, 1987; Tyler and Kitson, 1987), the value of Ψ is most appropriately given as 0.5.

It is apparent that the power function entails increasing returns to distance, as additional units of distance produce smaller price increments. This means that transport costs per unit of distance diminish as distance increases, as is also evident were one to plot $(1 + (\phi D)^{\psi})/D$ against D. On the other hand, with the exponential function we find that $e^{\tau D}/D$ increases in D. However, the cost of replacing the usual iceberg function with the power function is a loss of simplicity. For the iceberg function, the elasticity of $W = V_d/V_o$, is given by $-\tau D$, so that the proportionate change in W per unit of distance is $-\tau$. As the iceberg drift from north to south (in the Northern Hemisphere), each extra kilometre sees a constant proportion of the mass melting. For the power function, the elasticity is:

$$\frac{- \psi D^{\psi}}{1 + D^{\psi}}.$$

And the proportionate change per unit of distance is:

$$\frac{- \psi D^{\psi}}{D(1 + D^{\psi})}$$

so that the further the distance the smaller the proportion. Using the iceberg analogy, an iceberg behaving like this in the Northern Hemisphere would be travelling north, losing its mass at a diminishing rate until freezing caused the proportion of mass lost to approach zero.

The iceberg cost function maintains the constant elasticity of demand assumption that is behind the basic NEG model, as was shown in Chapter 1. To recap, we assume that the demand function with iceberg transport costs is:

$$m(i) = \theta Y_i (p_j^M e^{\tau_M D_{ij}})^{-\sigma} G_i^{\sigma - 1}$$

in which $m(i)$ is the demand at i for a variety produced at j, in which θ is the expenditure share of M (monopolistic competition) varieties, Y_i is the income level at i, $p_j^M e^{\tau_M D_{ij}}$ is the price taking into account transport costs, τ_M is τ specific to M varieties, G is the price index and σ is the elasticity of substitution of M varieties. If we take naturals logs, the demand function becomes:

$$\ln m(i) = \ln\theta + \ln Y_i - \sigma\ln p_j^M - \sigma\tau_M D_{ij} + (\sigma - 1)\ln G_i$$

with a constant elasticity σ identical to the elasticity of substitution, which is unaffected by the presence of transport costs D_{ij}, although there will be a decrease in the level of demand as distance increases.

With the power transport-cost function for M activities, the log-linear demand function becomes:

$$\ln m(i) = \ln\theta + \ln Y_i - \sigma\ln p_j^M - \sigma\ln(1 + (\phi D_{ij})^\Psi) + (\sigma - 1)\ln G_i$$

with constant price elasticity equal to σ. As with the exponential function, using the power function the price p_j^M increases by, in this case, the factor $1 + (\phi D)^\psi$, and this is the same regardless of the actual level of demand. Analogous to iceberg transport costs, this factor is a constant proportion of the overall price, as would be apparent from a graph of the overall price (that is, including transport costs), and transport costs per se against distance, which would show that the same share is taken by transport regardless of distance.

Therefore, it seems that we can, with a small adjustment, introduce economies of distance into the NEG model, perhaps in the form of a power function, and indeed this has been shown to work better than the normal iceberg function for UK data (Fingleton, 2005). However, caution is due and the implications of alternatives need to be explored more fully than is possible here. For example, among the more interesting aspects of NEG are the multiple equilibria arising from its complex dynamic non-linear system, but it is unclear as yet precisely what alternative transport-costs functions would imply for the dynamics. We know from studying the iceberg model that there are circumstances in which lowering transport costs increases agglomeration since the periphery can be more easily served from the core. It appears that introducing a power function, with its increasing returns to transportation could increase the tendency for agglomeration, in other words, extend the range of the parameter space over which the black-hole condition, with symmetry under threat, holds.

Economies of scale are another issue, and coming from the direction of transportation research these are seen to matter greatly also, but these are not present under either the exponential or the power functions. Under the standard NEG model, the overall level of production of a variety at j, q_j^M, is:

$$q_j^M = \sum_i^R m(i) e^{\tau_D D_{ij}} = \theta \sum_i^R Y_i (p_j^M)^{-\sigma} (e^{\tau_D D_{ij}})^{1-\sigma} G_i^{\sigma-1}$$

and from this we see that the same τ would apply were production at j at a higher level, perhaps due to a higher level of income Y_i. Therefore there is no relationship between the transportation rate and the amount of shipping from j to i as production levels vary. Research on location production models suggests that stable locational equilibrium conditions are impossible with transport costs exhibiting economies of scale (McCann, 1998). As we have already seen, in general, economies of scale and economies of distance go hand in hand, because they are generated by exactly the same distance-shipment optimization principles (McCann, 2001).

6.6   DISCUSSION AND CONCLUSIONS

All of the available empirical evidence from transport economics and regional economics points to three major features of broadly-defined distance-transactions costs; namely economies of distance, economies of scale and also possible differences in the distance-cost structures between information inputs and outputs. Yet, the iceberg transport-costs formulas that underpin explicitly spatial versions of new economic geography models do not allow for any economies of distance and scale in the transportation of either goods or information to take place. Nor do they allow for possible variations in distance-cost structures between inputs and outputs, and particularly those associated with information-transactions costs. In a manner analogous to new trade theory, many new economic geography models simply describe distance-transport costs as being variously 'high' or 'low' (Fujita, Krugman and Venables, 1999; Ottaviano and Thisse, 2001). However, the argument presented here is that where explicitly spatial versions of new economic geography models are concerned, in which distance is an explicit model variable,[21] this analytical approach is simply not sufficient to allow for any direct empirical inferences or predictions regarding spatial outcomes to be made. The reason is that the structure of the distance costs embedded in the Krugman iceberg assumption is counter to any empirical reality.

There have also been several other theoretical attempts among new economic geographers to develop models with alternative transport structures.[22] However, none of these attempts have yet been able to resolve the basic iceberg-convexity problem outlined in this chapter. Moreover, the problem with the lack of real-world relevance of the iceberg assumption, however, is that it is this iceberg assumption, *and this assumption alone*, that has so far allowed for a movement from new trade theory to explicitly spatial versions of new economic geography, at least as they currently stand. The whole edifice in many ways appears to be supported by the weakest pillar, at least to the extent that we are interested in the geography of such models.[23]

In terms of the future developments of economic geography modelling and analysis, Isard (1999, pp. 383–4) argues that the 'first advance would involve dropping the iceberg assumption regarding transport costs' because actual transport rates contrast sharply with the iceberg formula. Therefore, it would be necessary 'to discard this notion (essentially a trick from mathematics) in . . . an effort at evolving models for applied research. There are major indivisibilities and both increasing and decreasing returns in transportation activity in reality, which then affect the nature of increasing and decreasing returns in other activity. Ignoring these indivisibilities is ignoring a basic aspect of space as it realistically impinges upon activity'. A power function approach (Fingleton, 2005) that allows for economies of distance may therefore be the way forward. However, as long as the theoretical and empirical problems associated with implausibility of the iceberg transport costs formula are largely ignored by proponents of the field, the domain of the explicitly spatial versions of new economic geography models will remain almost entirely within the realm of theoretical modelling. New economic geography will provide very few new insights for transport economists, and transport economists will provide few insights relevant for new economic geography. The very assumption that defines geography and transport costs within the explicitly spatial versions of the new economic geography schema will remain its Achilles' heel.

APPENDIX: THE RELATIONSHIP BETWEEN THE ICEBERG LOGIC AND THE VON THUNEN MODEL

Proponents of new economic geography attempt to justify their theoretical approach by claiming that the iceberg formula has a longstanding pedigree in spatial economic analysis, in that Von Thunen (1826, p. 13) is supposed to have used a similar technique. Yet, given the quantity of work in this area, it may appear rather surprising that the apparent equivalence (Fujita, Krugman and Venables, 1999) between orthodox iceberg costs and the transport functions employed in traditional location model approaches, such as the Von Thunen model and its descendants, have gone largely unnoticed. Yet, there is a perfectly good reason for this previous lack of awareness: they are not really equivalent at all.

Following the arguments of Fujita, Krugman and Venables (1999, pp. 49 and 59), it may appear prima facie that the iceberg transport-cost formulation and orthodox spatial price functions of the type used to analyse models such as Von Thunen, are largely consistent with each other. From the perspective of microeconomic theory, however, in many cases they may be considered to be quite different from each other. In order to understand both the similarities and the essential differences between the different types of functions, as with the Samuelson iceberg logic, we must convert the Von Thunen and Krugman iceberg transport-cost functions into spatial price functions, in which the cost of purchasing and transporting a unit quantity of a good over distance is related to the distance of shipment.

We may recall that in the Von Thunen (1826) description of transport costs, whereby farmers lead their horses and carts to the market location C to sell their produce, part of the agricultural cargo may be consumed by the carthorse en route to the market. Let the weight of the cart be defined as k tons, and the weight of goods leaving the production location as M_o. Assuming the horse consumes the cargo during the haulage process, only a fraction of the initial shipment value V_o actually arrives at the market C, with the value of the good actually delivered being V_c. Adopting the previous notation we can specify this relationship as:

$$V_c = P_o(M_o - mD_{oc}) \qquad (A6.1)$$

where m is the quantity of good consumed by the horse(s) per kilometre hauled, M_o is the origin weight of cargo being carried, and P_o is the origin mill price per ton of the good, and D_{oc} is the distance between the origin and the market location C.

Assuming the rate of consumption of the cargo by the horse is a function of the initial total shipment weight,[24] then m is defined as:

$$m = f_m(k + M_o). \qquad (A6.2)$$

The specification in equation (A6.2) allows for constant returns to scale in terms of (horse cargo-consumption) transportation costs.[25] In other words, m varies only with respect to $(k + M_o)$, and not with respect to D_{oc}.

Adapting the iceberg logic to this specific Von Thunen transport-cost function, implies that at the market, the delivered price per ton of the good P_c must be:

$$P_c = P_o(M_o/(M_o - mD_{oc})). \qquad (A6.3)$$

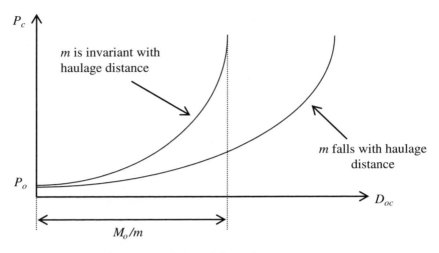

Figure A6.1   Iceberg-Von Thunen delivered prices

If *m* is invariant with respect to the weight of $(k + M_o)$ up to the capacity of the cart, diagrammatically this will produce a convex distance cost–price function as described by Figure A6.1, in which the delivered price per ton P_c will apparently be infinite at a market that is of distance M_o/m kilometres from the origin. If, however, *m* is a function of the total outstanding haulage weight, then *m* will fall as the haulage distance increases, because of the decreased total consumption by the horse(s). As we also see in Figure A6.1, this will produce a function in which the degree of convexity of the delivered-price distance function is reduced. Importantly, however, the underlying convex price–distance relationship is unchanged. Applying the iceberg logic even to the Von Thunen model still implies that all distance-price functions are convex.

There appears to be something of a problem, however, in that the convex Von Thunen delivered price–distance descriptions of Figure A6.1, which are generated here by employing the iceberg analogy, are largely at odds with most descriptions of a Von Thunen model (Mills, 1972) described by Figure A6.2. In these more usual descriptions, if the market price per ton of the agricultural good is P_{c1}, and the transportation costs per kilometre *m* are invariant with respect to the distance hauled, the negative-sloping Von Thunen distance-rent gradient would be linear in D_{oc}, with the gradient of the slope equal to $-m$. Alternatively, if *m* exhibits economies of distance, such as where horses consume less cargo as the remaining weight hauled falls, then the rent gradient will be convex in D_{oc}. Therefore, how are we to reconcile the orthodox characterization of Von Thunen depicted in

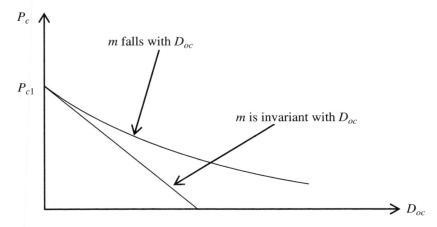

Figure A6.2 Orthodox Von Thunen distance–price relationships

Figure A6.2 with the iceberg-type descriptions of Von Thunen described in Figure A6.1?

Part of the problem is that in the iceberg model in general, irrespective of whether it is of the Samuelson or Krugman type, the delivered prices are calculated with respect to the initial mill price, whereas in the Von Thunen model, the mill prices are calculated with respect to the delivered market price. Unfortunately, these two different approaches are not symmetrical. Fundamentally, this reflects the problem that all iceberg types of models define delivered prices in relative multiplicative terms, where orthodox spatial pricing models define delivered prices in additive terms.

If the iceberg logic is applied to the Von Thunen model it would interpret the ratio of the delivered market price P_d divided by the surplus value at the production location as being the appropriate price index. However, this iceberg-type of interpretation is not strictly the delivered price of the good, but rather the opportunity costs of the good. In the Von Thunen model described by Figure A6.2, the value per ton of the good is set at the destination market point C, and the distance-cost function does not represent the relationship between delivered-price of the good and the distance hauled, but rather the relationship between the distance hauled and the residual *surplus* made by the farmer (McCann, 2001), comprising all of the factor rewards. At a critical distance between the market and the farmer's production location,[26] the surplus value of production to the farmer is zero. In other words, the opportunity costs of production to the farmer at any distance greater than or equal to this critical distance are infinite. This notion, however, is largely at odds with most orthodox interpretations of

Von Thunen. Therefore, the argument that Von Thunen (1826) provides an intellectual pedigree for iceberg models cannot really be substantiated.

NOTES

1. Ottaviano and Thisse (2003, p. 19) argue that the iceberg assumption implying that a rise in the price of a good leads to a proportional rise in its transport costs is unrealistic. However, if we adopt a logistics-costs definition of transport costs (McCann, 1993, 1998), which also includes the inventory-holding costs as well as the movement costs involved in transportation, then transport costs are always seen to vary with the square root of the price of the good. This price-varying assumption can actually therefore be argued to be somewhat realistic.
2. The traditional explanation for such concave transportation costs functions rested on the static distinction between fixed terminal costs and variable movement costs (Thorburn, 1960; Alonso, 1964). More recently, however, it has become clear that such concave transportation-costs functions are actually the natural (envelope) outcome of the inventory-shipment-frequency optimization problems faced by all hauliers (McCann, 2001).
3. There are some limited cases relating to zoning and service quality where the value of t is invariant with respect to q, but in the vast majority of cases this relationship is convex (McCann, 2001).
4. There is one other third and final way in which the iceberg functions are very different from the observed transport-rate functions, and this is in the way that the mill price of the good is assumed to affect the distance-transport costs. As we see, the iceberg transport costs imply that distance costs are a function of the origin value of the good. Although simple transport rate structures do not incorporate such a relationship, as was mentioned in Note 2 broader definitions of distance-transactions costs such as the logistics costs, which also include all of the inventory costs associated with transportation as well as the basic transport costs, can be shown to be direct functions of (the square root of) the mill price (McCann, 1993, 1998, 2001).
5. These are our italics, not Krugman's.
6. 'In location theory, transportation costs are of the essence; yet any attempt to develop a general-equilibrium model of economic geography would be substantially complicated by the need to model the transportation as well as the goods-producing sectors. Worse yet, transportation costs can undermine the constant demand elasticity that is one of the crucial simplifying assumptions of the Dixit-Stiglitz model' (Krugman, 1998, pp. 164–5).
7. Moreover, as Neary (2001, p. 542) points out, the 'no-black-hole' condition is only an assumption, and is not a property of the model (Fujita, Krugman and Venables, 1999, pp. 58–9).
8. Ottaviano (1999, p. 3) define transport costs as encompassing any impediment to trade. Such costs will include costs 'due to the sheer existence of distance (e.g. transport costs), others arise from institutional barriers (e.g. tariffs or quality and safety standards) or even from linguistic and cultural differences (e.g. business practices)'.
9. However, whether the spatial limits of this information-localization phenomenon are at the level of the individual city or at a much larger regional level is still an open question empirically (Arita and McCann, 2000; Cantwell and Iammarino, 2000), and depends both on the nature of the firms and of the industry in question.
10. Following Marshall's (1920, p. 271) often-quoted comment that the 'mysteries of the trade become no mysteries; but are as it were in the air'. These mysteries of the trade are viewed in more modern terms as representing localized information externalities. Interestingly, Marshall was not the first observer of these phenomena. A detailed discussion of these issues in the context of a 'manufacturing district' was provided in *British Parliament Papers* half a century before Marshall's comments of 1890.

11. However, exactly how the costs of information transfer vary with respect to distance within the urban setting, as against outside of the urban setting, is unknown. Such costs may be genuinely strictly convex with distance, such that the spatial boundary of the city is where the delivered-price gradient of information inputs tends towards being infinite. On the other hand, such information-transfer costs may be largely invariant with respect to distance within the urban setting but reach a natural limit, beyond which they are infinite outside of the urban setting.

12. As such, information input and output transmission costs, which are non-concave and concave with distance, respectively, may provide a rationale for the rise of both the financial services 'global city' phenomenon (Gordon, 2002) and also for the type of high-technology cluster phenomenon such as Silicon Valley, which has a global market for its outputs. Indeed, these are the very types of industrial clusters that attract so much attention from researchers in (new) economic geography. However, these information-related opportunity cost issues are very different from pecuniary externality explanations (Ottaviano and Thisse, 2001) or transactions-coordination cost issues (Gordon and McCann, 2000) associated with manufacturing complexes.

13. Moreover, it can be shown analytically that if information opportunity costs are integrated with commuting costs and the time spent in face to face contact, the optimization results generate an (envelope) spatial information-transmission function that is also concave with distance (McCann, 1995).

14. Fujita, Krugman and Venables (1999, p. 98) suggest figures of between -0.6 and -1.0.

15. To adopt a full Wilsonian spatial interaction perspective within a regional system would actually require that, as well as the flows of goods and services, the labour migration adjustment mechanism in the model would also exhibit a gravity-type relationship (Fotheringham, 1991). This is not done in NEG models, and in this sense the gravity-type interactions are somewhat selective.

16. These are calculated as (c.i.f./f.o.b.) -1×100.

17. These values rise as the level of infrastructure of the country deteriorates. For example, the predicted value of this ratio for a pair of countries with infrastructure quality at the 75th percentile rises to 1.40 (Overman et al., 2001).

18. Looking at commodities, an unweighted average of freight rates is typically two to three times higher than the trade weighted average (Overman et al., 2001).

19. This introduces same added complexity, since this function becomes degenerative at small distances with negative values below one tending to minus infinity towards zero distance, and it no longer preserves the simplifying assumption of a constant proportionate rate of decay per unit of distance.

20. This former approach typically gives ratios of between -2 to -5 whereas the latter approach typically gives a value of around -3 (Overman et al., 2001). As Overman et al. (2001, p. 10) demonstrate, this elasticity is on the transport cost factor, so that doubling transport costs from 20 per cent to 40 per cent reduces trade volumes to $(1.4/1.2)^{-3}$ $= 0.63$ of their initial level. This estimate is more or less the same order of magnitude as the results generated by a simple rule of thumb method that would calculate the elasticity of trade with respect to transport costs by the former method of dividing the observed values for the distance elasticity of trade -0.9 to -1.5 (Overman et al., 2001) or -0.6 to -1.0 (Fujita, Krugman and Venables, 1999) by the observed values for the distance elasticity of transport costs (1.28). These figures give a range of -0.46 to -1.17.

21. The argument here applies to all of the explicitly spatial NEG models that are currently of a one-dimensional nature, plus the two-dimensional spatial simulation versions (Stelder, 2002).

22. Ottaviano, Tabuchi and Thisse (2002) employ a quadratic-linear modelling framework, and show that Krugman's main findings carry over to a setup where there are linear demands and per unit transport costs, although they gave up the income effect. Behrens et al. (2003) show that multiplicative and additive cost structures do not change the main findings in a two-region setup, but that things are very different when there are more than two countries and two regions. Behrens and Murata (2005) propose an even more general class of monopolistic models associated with non-iceberg transport costs.

23. Neary (2001, pp. 548–50) argues that the treatment of firm dynamics in new economic geography is also very problematic. In particular, there is no price discrimination in these models. However, Ottaviano and Thisse (2003, p. 30) argue that this is a reasonable approximation of what could be obtained in a general equilibrium model with strategic interactions.
24. The Von Thunen model assumes a fixed absolute decay-consumption rate per unit distance per horse, rather than a proportionate rate as in the Krugman iceberg assumption.
25. For example, if the initial weight of cart plus cargo leaving the farm is x tons, where x is the limit of the pulling capacity of a single horse, then one horse will be required to pull the cart, whereas if the initial weight of cart plus cargo is $2x$ tons, two horses will be required to pull it.
26. Where the consumption of the carthorse in equations (A6.2, A6.3) implies that $M_o = mD$.

REFERENCES

Acs, Z.J. (2002), *Innovation and the Growth of Cities*, Cheltenham, UK and Northampton, MA, USA : Edward Elgar.

Alonso, W. (1964), 'Location theory', in J. Friedmann and W. Alonso (eds), *Regional Development and Planning: A Reader*, Cambridge, MA: MIT Press.

Anderson, J.E. and E. van Wincoop (2003), 'Gravity with gravitas', *American Economic Review*, **93**: 170–92.

Anderson, J.E. and E. van Wincoop (2004), 'Trade costs', *Journal of Economic Literature*, **42**: 1–52.

Arita, T. and P. McCann (2000), 'Industrial alliances and firm location behaviour: some evidence from the US semiconductor industry', *Applied Economics*, **32**: 1391–403.

Bayliss, B.T. and S.L. Edwards (1970), *Industrial Demand for Transport*, Ministry of Transport, HMSO, London.

Behrens, K. and Y. Murata (2005), 'General equilibrium models of monopolistic competition', mimeograph, CORE, Université Catholique de Louvain.

Behrens, K., C. Gaigné, G.I.P. Ottaviano and J.F. Thisse (2003), 'Interregional and iternational tade: sventy yars after Ohlin', *Discussion Paper 4056*, Centre for Economic Policy Research, London.

Brakman, S., H. Garretsen and C. van Marrewijk (2001), *An Introduction to Geographical Economics*, Cambridge: Cambridge University Press.

Brocker, J. (2002), 'Modeling interregional and international trade', Working Paper, University of Kiel, Faculty of Economics.

Bruce Allen, W. (1977), 'The demand for freight transportation: a micro approach', *Transportation Research*, **11**: 9–14.

Cantwell, J. and S. Iammarino (2000), 'Multinational corporations and the location of technological innovation in the UK regions', *Regional Studies*, **34**: 317–22.

Cohen, B.J. (1998), *The Geography of Money*, Ithaca, NY: Cornell University Press.

d'Aspremont, C., J.J. Gabszewicz and J.-F. Thisse (1979), 'On Hotelling's stability in competition', *Econometrica*, **47**: 1145–50.

Dixit, A. and J. Stiglitz (1977), 'Monopolistic competition and optimal product diversity', *American Economic Review*, **67**: 297–308.

Fingleton, B. (2005), 'Towards applied geographical economics: modelling relative wage rates, incomes and prices for the regions of Great Britain', *Applied Economics*, **37**: 2417–28.

Fotheringham, A.S. (1991), 'Migratian and spatial structure: the development of the competing destinations model', in J. Stillwell and P. Congdon (eds), *Migration Models: Macro and Micro Approaches*, London: Bellhaven.

Fujita, M. and P. Krugman (1995), 'When is the economy monocentric? Von Thunen and Chamberlin unified', *Regional Science and Urban Economics*, **25**: 505–28.

Fujita, M. and T. Mori (1996), 'The role of ports in the making of major cities: self-agglomeration and hub effect', *Journal of Development Economics*, **49**: 93–120.

Fujita, M. and T. Mori (1997), 'On the dynamics of frontier economies: endogenous growth or the self-organization of a dissipative system?', *Annals of Regional Science*, **32**: 39–62.

Fujita, M. and H. Ogawa (1982), 'Multiple equilibria and structural transition of non-monocentric urban configurations', *Regional Science and Urban Economics*, **12**: 161–96.

Fujita, M. and J.-F. Thisse (2002), *Economics of Agglomeration*, Cambridge: Cambridge University Press.

Fujita, M., P. Krugman and T. Mori (1999a), 'On the evolution of hierarchical urban systems', *European Economic Review*, **43**: 209–51.

Fujita, M., P. Krugman and A.J. Venables (1999b), *The Spatial Economy: Cities, Regions and International Trade*, Cambridge, MA: MIT Press.

Gaspar, J. and E.L. Glaeser (1998), 'Information-technology and the future of cities', *Journal of Urban Economics*, **43**: 136–56.

Glaeser, E.L., J. Kolko and A. Saiz (2001), 'Consumer city', *Journal of Economic Geography*, **1**: 27–50.

Gordon, I.R. (1978), 'Distance deterrence and commodity values', *Environment and Planning A*, **10**: 889–900.

Gordon, I.R. (2002), 'Global cities, internationalization and urban systems', in P. McCann (ed.), *Industrial Location Economics*, Cheltenham, UK and Northampton, MA, USA: Edward Elgar.

Gordon, I.R. and P. McCann (2000), 'Industrial clusters: complexes, agglomeration and/or social networks', *Urban Studies*, **37**: 513–32.

Haurin, D.R., P.H. Hendershott and D. Kim (1994), 'Housing decisions of American youth', *Journal of Urban Economics*, **35**: 28–45.

Helpman, E. and P.R. Krugman (1985), *Market Structure and Foreign Trade*, Cambridge, MA: MIT Press.

Hummels, D. (1999a), 'Towards a geography of trade costs', mimeo, Graduate School of Business, University of Chicago.

Hummels, D. (1999b), 'Have international transportation costs declined?', mimeo, Graduate School of Business, University of Chicago.

Isard, W. (1956), *Location and Space-Economy*, New York: Technology Press, Wiley.

Isard, W. (1999), 'Further thoughts on future directions for regional science: a response to Fujita's remarks on the general theory of location and space-economy', *Annals of Regional Science*, **33**: 383–8.

Jansson, J.O. and D. Shneerson (1987), *Liner Shipping Economics*, New York: Chapman and Hall.

Krugman, P.R. (1990), *Rethinking International Trade*, Cambridge, MA: MIT Press.

Krugman, P. (1991a), 'Increasing returns and economic geography', *Journal of Political Economy*, **99**: 483–99.

Krugman, P. (1991b), *Geography and Trade*, Cambridge, MA: MIT Press.

Krugman, P.R. (1995), *Development, Geography and Economic Theory*, Cambridge, MA: MIT Press.

Krugman, P.R. (1998), 'Space: the final frontier', *Journal of Economic Perspectives*, **12**: 161–74.

Krugman, P. and A.J. Venables (1995), 'Globalization and the inequality of nations', *Quarterly Journal of Economics*, **110**: 857–80.

Krugman. P. and A.J. Venables (1997), 'Integration, Specialization and adjustment', *European Economic Review*, **40**: 959–68.

Leamer, E. and J. Levinsohn (1996), 'International trade theory: the evidence', in G. Grossman and K. Rogoff (eds), *Handbook of International Economics 3*, Amsterdam: Elsevier.

Leyshon, A. and N. Thrift (eds) (1997), *Money Space*, London: Routledge.

Limao, N. and A.J. Venables (2001), 'Infrastructure, geographical disadvantage, transport costs, and trade', *The World Bank Economic Review*, **15**: 451–80.

McCann, P. (1993), 'The logistics-costs location-production problem', *Journal of Regional Science*, **33**: 503–16.

McCann, P. (1995). 'Journey and transactions frequency: an alternative explanation of rent-gradient convexity', *Urban Studies*, **32**: 1549–57.

McCann, P. (1998), *The Economics of Industrial Location: A Logistics-costs Approach*, Berlin: Springer-Verlag.

McCann, P. (2001), 'A proof of the relationship between optimal vehicle size, haulage length and the structure of distance-transport costs', *Transportation Research*, **35A**: 671–93.

McCann, P. (2005), 'Transport costs and new economic geography', *Journal of Economic Geography*, **5**: 305–18.

Marshall, A. (1920), *Principles of Economics* (8th edn.), London: Macmillan.

Mills, E.S (1972), *Studies in the Structure of the Urban Economy*, Baltimore: John Hopkins University Press.

Muellbauer, J. and A. Murphy (1997), 'Booms and busts in the UK housing market', *Economic Journal*, **107**: 1701–27.

Neary, J.P. (2001), 'Of hype and hyperbolas: introducing the new economic geography', *Journal of Economic Perspectives*, **39**: 536–61.

Ottaviano, G.I.P. (1999), 'Ad usum delphini: a primer in new economic geography', *European University Institute Working Paper*, ECO No. 99/28, Florence.

Ottaviano, G.I.P. and J.-F. Thisse (1999), 'Integration, agglomeration and the political economics of factor mobility', *European University Institute Working Paper* ECO No. 99/27, Florence.

Ottaviano, G.I.P. and J.-F. Thisse (2001), 'On economic geography in economic theory: increasing returns and pecuniary externalities', *Journal of Economic Geography*, **1**: 153–79.

Ottaviano, G.I.P. and J.-F. Thisse (2003), 'Agglomeration and economic geography', in J.V. Henderson and J.-F. Thisse (eds), *Handbook of Urban and Regional Economics IV*, Amsterdam: North-Holland.

Ottaviano, G.I.P., T. Tabuchi and J.-F. Thisse (2002), 'Agglomeration and trade revisited', *International Economic Review*, **43**: 409–36.

Overman, H.G., S. Redding and A.J. Venables (2001), 'The economic geography of trade production and income: a survey of empirics', *Discussion Paper 2978*, Centre for Economic Policy Research, London.

Radelet, S. and J. Sachs (1998), 'Shipping costs, manufactured exports, and economic growth', mimeo, Harvard University.

Samuelson, P. (1952), 'The transfer problem and transport costs: the terms of trade when impediments are absent', *Economic Journal*, **62**: 278–304.

Sen, A. and T.E. Smith (1995), *Gravity Models of Spatial Interaction Behavior*, New York: Springer.

Stelder, D. (2002), 'Geographical grids in "new economic geography" models', in P. McCann (ed.), *Industrial Location Economics*, Cheltenham, UK and Northampton, MA, USA: Edward Elgar.

Thorburn, T. (1960), *Supply and Demand of Water Transport*, Stockholm: EFI.

Tyler, P. and M. Kitson (1987), 'Geographical variations in transport costs of manufacturing firms in Great Britain', *Urban Studies*, **24**: 61–73.

Venables, A.J. (1996), 'Equilibrium locations of vertically linked industries', *International Economic Review*, **37**: 341–59.

Von Thunen, J.H. (1826), *Der Isolierte Staat*, translated by C.M. Wartenberg 1966, *Von Thunen's Isolated State*, Oxford: Pergamon Press.

Wilson, A.G. (1970), *Entropy in Urban and Regional Modelling*, London: Pian.

Wilson, A.G. (1974), *Urban and Regional Models in Geography and Planning*, New York: John Wiley.

7. Specialization and regional size

John Dewhurst and Philip McCann

7.1 INTRODUCTION

In this chapter we investigate the relationship between the size of an area and the extent of its industrial specialization. Much recent literature in regional economics and new economic geography suggests that certain patterns of industrial specialization, and by implication, regional trade, will be empirically evident within the spatial economy. In particular, renewed theoretical interest on the role played by agglomeration economies in determining the patterns of regional specialization, has also led to the development of new empirical efforts aimed at identifying such agglomeration effects. However, a fundamental point that has been largely overlooked in the literature on agglomeration is the fact that the outcomes of these empirical exercises may themselves also be affected by our chosen spatial units of analysis. As such, it is necessary to be rather cautious where empirical evidence is used to support theoretical arguments of agglomeration externalities. In order to discuss the relationship between the size of a region and its level of specialization we analyse UK sectoral employment data at a variety of different levels of spatial aggregation. This allows us to distinguish the effect of regional size on measures of industrial specialization from those related to agglomeration economies.

In the following sections we outline how this issue is generally understood by researchers. In Section 7.2 we explain the general understanding in the literature regarding the relationship between employment specialization, density and agglomeration effects. In Section 7.3 we focus on the problematic issues that the size of a region and the size of the spatial units of analysis raise for empirical measures of agglomeration. In Section 7.4, we present details of the methodology and the data employed, and Section 7.5 provides the results plus a commentary of the results. We conclude in Section 7.6 with an overview of the findings and the implications of these findings for research in general.

The overall findings of the analysis do confirm that regional specialization is indeed generally inversely related to the size of a region, as well as to the position of the area within the urban hierarchy. However, it is also necessary to be aware of the fact that this relationship is not only non-monotonic, but also that this relationship may be subject to the issues raised by the modifiable unit area problem (Openshaw and Taylor, 1979). These results therefore require us to be very careful and cautious when interpreting empirical results of sectoral specialization and diversity as evidence of various types of agglomeration economies.

7.2 EMPLOYMENT SPECIALIZATION, DENSITY AND AGGLOMERATION EFFECTS

The spatial concentration and dispersion of industry is a commonly observed phenomenon, and the degree to which different regions and countries specialize in the production of different goods and services is a key issue within economics. In particular, geographical variations in the patterns and distribution of activity cause, and are caused by, the development of international and inter-regional trading activities. In traditional trade theory (Pomfret, 1991) the heterogeneous nature of the spatial economy was primarily perceived to be due to spatial variations in factor endowments. Most trade theory, however, has been fundamentally aspatial in nature. Location theory, on the other hand, which is explicitly spatial in nature, has attempted to explain such factor endowment variations in terms of the relationship between transport costs, production theory (Isard, 1951; Moses, 1958) and observations of agglomeration behaviour (Hoover, 1937; Chinitz, 1961, 1964; Vernon, 1966). This tradition, dating back to Weber (1909) and Marshall (1920), discussed the conditions under which firms within the same sector will cluster together geographically.

While this issue has been for many years a central research focus for regional and urban economics, over recent years it has received much more attention from a range of economists as various authors have attempted to provide both theoretical refinements to, and also empirical tests for, new economic geography models. One of the central tenets of these new economic geography models is that spatial variations in economic activity are related to the effects of localized agglomeration economies (Krugman, 1991a, 1998; Venables, 1996). While the spatial concentration of production factors and activities may arise from firm-specific internal economies of scale (Hoover, 1937, 1948), it has long been recognized that firms in an industry may also benefit from locating close to each other (Marshall, 1920) due to agglomeration economies, namely locally-specific positive externalities that are external to any particular firm. Where firms cluster together in space, these locally-specific positive externalities are required in order to offset the negative effects of the appreciation in local land and labour costs, itself caused by the spatial clustering of activities. However, the effects of any such agglomeration economies can be ambiguous. In some cases, positive local externality effects may operate across a variety of industries and as such, will have little observable effect on regional specialization as the variety of firms attracted to an area will be high.

Since Hoover (1937, 1948) these effects have generally been denoted as urbanization economies, the hypothesized operation of which has been most widely articulated by Jacobs (1961, 1969, 1984). The central feature of such urbanization externalities is that they are deemed to operate across all co-located activities irrespective of the sector. But equally, there may be types of agglomeration externalities that are industry-specific, originally denoted by Hoover (1937, 1948) as localization economies, and originally articulated, among others, by Marshall (1920), Hoover (1937) and Isard and Kuenne (1953). These types of externalities may act so as to foster increases in local industrial specialization, because the central assumption here is that any such externalities are deemed as being industry-specific. In other words, such locally-specific positive externalities are also assumed to be industry-specific as well as location-specific externalities.

A second, well-developed, theme in the traditional literature relating to specialization is that of central place theory (Christaller, 1966). This literature is concerned with the question of the heterogeneous distribution of urban centres. Within this explicitly spatial framework, the observed hierarchical structuring of the urban system was argued by central place theorists (Beavon, 1977; Christaller, 1966) to be primarily a result of the spatial market areas required to support the provision of higher-order goods and services. According to this theory larger settlements higher up the urban hierarchy are likely to provide a wider range of functions than smaller settlements. If this were the predominant factor in explaining industrial location one would expect larger settlements to be more industrially diverse than smaller ones (Parr, 2002).

Some aspects of the central place literature have acknowledged the presence of agglomeration effects (Lösch, 1954). However, more modern approaches to analysing the spatial economy have emphasized the central role played by agglomeration economies in fostering continued localized growth (Fujita and Mori, 1997; Krugman, 1991b) and attempted to fuse models of agglomeration with central place theory. These approaches have cast new light on the process of development in the spatial economy (Fujita and Krugman, 1995), by integrating the role played by localized agglomeration effects with factor mobility and spatial competition between locations. These models work on the assumption that consumption and production is based on a Dixit-Stiglitz (1977) preference for variety argument, and the actual balance between centrifugal and centripetal forces provides a description of the growth over time of the urban hierarchy (Fujita and Mori, 1997), which is characterized by a different range of goods and services provided at each location (Fujita, Krugman and Venables, 1999; Huriot and Thisse, 2000; Fujita and Thisse, 2002). The results of these general equilibrium models imply that the higher the rank-ordering (Mills, 1980) of the urban area, the greater will be the variety of goods and services produced and provided for locally. Conversely, locations lower down the urban hierarchy will tend to be characterized by the production of a lower variety of locally produced goods. The outcome of these patterns is that locations lower down the urban hierarchy will generally tend to be more specialized in their exports and more diverse in their imports than higher-order urban areas (Parr, Denike and Mulligan, 1975).

To the extent that agglomeration economies do exist, in higher-order locations the external benefits associated with spatial industrial clustering will be spread across a diverse range of sectors, whereas in lower-order sectors, the external benefits of clustering will tend to be contained within a small number of industrial sectors. In Hoover's (1948) classification terminology the outcome of these models is therefore that higher-order urban areas will generally exhibit greater economies of urbanization, whereas lower-order urban areas will generally exhibit greater economies of localization. However, in new economic geography models, the inter-relationships between the levels and variety of production output, labour inputs and industrial categories are all explicitly assumed ex ante within the schema, so that analytically there is a direct correspondence between the variety of production, the variety of employment and the variety of trade relationships. From the point of view of local employment patterns, therefore, these theoretical arguments concerning preferences for variety, and the resulting differences in the spatial distribution of the range of activities provided for at each location, imply that in general, higher-order urban areas will exhibit a relatively diverse range of local employment activities, whereas lower-order areas will tend to exhibit a highly skewed sectoral employment distribution. In other words, in comparison with the national sectoral distribution of employment activities, higher-order centres will tend to be relatively less skewed and specialized than lower-order areas. Conversely, in comparison with the national sectoral distribution of employment activities, lower-order centres will tend to be relatively more skewed and more specialized than lower-order areas.

From orthodox urban economic theory (Fujita, 1989; Mills, 1980), we also know that in general, higher-order urban areas will typically exhibit greater local population densities per square kilometre than lower-order urban areas. Combining this insight with the rank-ordering arguments discussed above from new economic geography models, therefore suggests that areas with a greater distribution of local industrial sectors will also tend to be areas with a higher population density. Conversely, areas with a lower population density will tend to be areas exhibiting a lower range of local production sectors, and consequently a more skewed and more specialized sectoral employment distribution. In terms of regional specialization and patterns of sectoral employment distribution, these are the basic predictions of modern urban-systems theory.

The theoretical arguments underpinning the spatial heterogeneity of production are thus well developed. However, the empirical identification of the agglomeration economies that contribute to industrial clustering and dispersion is notoriously difficult. The result of this is that problems start to arise as we move from theoretical predictions to empirical evaluations. This is because the actual effect of agglomeration externalities on each industrial sector, or range of sectors, is a priori not identifiable, and therefore ex post indirect measures are generally adopted to try to identify the effects of such externalities (Gordon and McCann, 2000, 2005).

On the basis of the new economic geography arguments above, which imply a direct correspondence between the variety of production, the variety of employment, and the nature and extent of agglomeration externalities, observations of sectoral employment distributions in particular localities have therefore become the most commonly used method of identifying the operation of either urbanization or localization economies. However, this approach is not as straightforward as might be supposed. The standard technique in applied regional economic modelling is to relate local employment patterns to trade patterns (McCann and Dewhurst, 1998), and this is done by treating data on the former as a proxy for the latter. Yet, this is a very indirect approach, the weakness of which is that it is based on the assumption of universal Leontief production and consumption technologies. In a similar vein, using measures of local employment variety as evidence of either localization or urbanization economies is also problematic, because such an approach is based on strong theoretical assumptions relating to the direct correspondence between the variety of local production, the variety of local employment and the variety of regional trade relationships.

There are four major problems associated with using local labour or employment data in the assessment of agglomeration externalities. First, using employment data to distinguish between localization economies (Marshall, 1920) and urbanization economies (Hoover, 1937, 1948; Jacobs, 1960) is problematic from an empirical perspective, because the results of these models appear to be very sensitive to the level of sectoral aggregation used. These problems are themselves partly a result of the classification frameworks employed in SIC (Standard Industrial Classification) systems.

For example, if we consider comparisons across sectors, at broad two-digit levels of sectoral aggregation, the classification of manufacturing industries tends to be much more varied and detailed than for many service activities. The result of this is that in analyses that concentrate on individual cities, at two-digit aggregation levels certain large cities that have relatively large finance and business services sectors, may appear to be very specialized in comparison to smaller cities with a range of manufacturing and other non-service activities, and this might therefore lead us to conclude that service sector localization economies are the dominant aspect of the city. On the other hand, at three-digit and four-digit levels of disaggregation, the same cities may appear to be relatively very highly diversified, as the complexity and variety of many service industries increases. At this lower level of dis-aggregation, this might lead us to conclude that economies of urbanization are dominant. Yet, in this situation, our conclusions are largely dependent on the sectoral definitions at different levels of disaggregation.

Similar problems arise for analyses of agglomeration within individual sectors but across locations. For example, the pioneering analysis of US manufacturing agglomeration effects by Glaeser et al. (1992) employed a two-digit level of sectoral disaggregation, while that of Henderson, Kuncoro and Turner (1995) employed a three-digit level of sectoral dis-aggregation. The results of these two analyses for the same broad industry category of manufacturing appear very different, with the former finding evidence for urbanization effects, while the latter found evidence of local-ization effects. The result of these findings suggests that the testing of agglomeration economies and new economic geography models appears to be somewhat dependent on both the quality and also level of disaggrega-tion of the data. Unfortunately, there is no theoretical guidance as to what is the most appropriate level of sectoral disaggregation.

Second, distinguishing whether industrial clustering is indeed actually due primarily to the existence of localized externalities, or rather is simply the outcome of similar location optimization behaviour by similar firms (McCann, 1995) is also empirically very difficult, and really requires add-itional microeconomic data on transactions and buyer–supplier relation-ships (Gordon and McCann, 2000, 2005). Third, the various measures and indices of industrial specialization that are available to us themselves often produce quite conflicting results, with the relative rankings of different places being rather unstable, depending on which index is employed (Dewhurst and McCann, 2002). Fourth, the results of these types of analy-ses are very sensitive to the size of the geographical areas employed for the data aggregation.

The first three of these issues have been discussed at length in the respec-tive papers listed above, and will not be discussed any further here. The last point, however, has been hardly discussed at all, and yet in many ways, it is this last point that is most specifically related to the types of geographical empirical issues we are interested in here.

7.3   EFFECT OF REGIONAL SIZE ON MEASURES OF SPECIALIZATION AND AGGLOMERATION

The extent of specialization in a region will have an effect on both the volume of regional trade and the pattern of that trade. There appears to be a consensus among regional modellers, and especially those concerned with constructing regional input–output tables partially on the basis of regional employment data (Flegg, Webber and Eliot, 1995), that smaller regions engage in relatively greater amounts of trade and are more open, because they are more specialized. It can be demonstrated analytically that the hypothesized inverse relationship between the relative openness of a region and its size does not necessarily hold in all circumstances (McCann and Dewhurst, 1998), because the relationship is non-monotonic. The reason for this non-monotonicity is that the region's pattern of trade and employment specialization for each individual sector, depends on the actual geographical boundaries of a region, and the relationship between the location of these boundaries and the locations and sectoral characteristics of individual firms and industries (McCann and Dewhurst, 1998) on either side of these boundaries.[1]

As a general principle, however, there is some tentative evidence that supports the assumption regarding the inverse relationship between the level of specialization of a region and its size. For the 11 standard regions of the United Kingdom, Twomey and Tompkins (1996) found that the differences between the regional sectoral employment patterns and that of the national sectoral employment pattern appeared to be higher for the regions with smaller populations. If the Twomey and Tompkins (1996) observation is typical, it would suggest that the most common regional specialization measure for an individual sector, namely that of the location quotient LQ, will tend to diverge increasingly from a value of one, as a region gets smaller. This is somewhat problematic because a perceived advantage of the location quotient index is that is allows for direct comparisons across industries and regions of levels of local specialization. However, this finding suggests that LQ comparisons across areas of different size may not be as informative as a prima facie analysis would suggest, and may actually be rather misleading in some cases. An example here is that of the cluster identification exercises that are now commonplace in many countries (DTI, 2001), and that are largely based on local area LQ measures. These cluster identification exercises use LQ measures of individual regional-industrial sectors as indirect evidence of clustering and agglomeration economies of localization. However, if the areas of analysis vary across space, then these spatial variations will themselves also lead to variations in LQ measures, without there necessarily being any localization externalities evident. The reason for this is that, even in the absence of any agglomeration effects, the distribution of activities across space is not even, but rather it is random (Ellison and Glaeser, 1997). The variance in spatial distributions across spatial units will therefore tend to increase for smaller spatial units. Either the non-standardization of spatial units, or alternatively a systematic focus on very small spatial units, may therefore lead to spurious inferences regarding the relative importance of localization economies.

In the above case, spurious indirect evidence in favour of localization economies may be generated simply due to problems of spatial disaggregation, in situations where no agglomeration effects actually take place. At the same time, variations on the scale and disaggregation of spatial units may also hide the effects of localization economies, in situations where agglomeration effects are actually operating. In much of the applied urban and regional literature, a central problem of discussing agglomeration economies is that of identifying the spatial extent over which such agglomeration effects may take place. Indeed, empirical evidence suggests that the critical spatial extent to which agglomeration effects are localized can vary enormously between locations, between industries and between firm types, with some effects being evident only at the suburban level (Feloy et al., 1997; Grabher, 2001), some at the urban level, some at the regional or even at the super-regional level (Arita and McCann, 2000; Gordon and McCann, 2005) and others even at the inter-regional or international level (Leyshon and Thrift, 1997; Cohen, 1998; Cantwell and Iammarino, 2000).

The theoretical models discussed in Section 7.2 above do not explicitly consider the question of the critical spatial extent over which the agglomeration spillovers take place. Rather, in new economic geography models, and also in most orthodox urban economics models, localization economies are assumed to operate at a particular point in space. However, there are several well-founded reasons for these spatial variations in the extent of agglomeration economies, each of which relate to Marshall's (1920) characterization of the sources of agglomeration economies. The first reason is that the spatial extent over which informal knowledge is shared between actors can vary between industries and organizations, depending on the firm's technological profile and the nature of its required knowledge and information inputs (Cantwell and Iammarino, 2000). Second, the spatial area over which specialist suppliers can operate may differ significantly between industries and locations, depending on the products or services being provided and the transport and communications technologies employed. Third, the search and job-matching processes within local labour markets may also operate over different spatial areas, depending on the extent of local employment commuting (Simpson, 1992) and infrastructure availability. A general observation is that larger and more technologically advanced firms typically have critical relationships with both customer, suppliers and local inputs, which extend over much larger geographical scales than do smaller firms or firms that are less technologically advanced (Arita and McCann, 2000; Gordon and McCann, 2000, 2005).

The size of the chosen unit area of analysis itself may therefore affect the empirical results of exercises aimed at identifying agglomeration externalities. This is equally true for measures of either regional industrial specialization or measures of spatial industrial concentration.[2] This is because different spatial area definitions will include or exclude different types of knowledge or labour-supply spillover effects between firms in different locations, depending on the types of firms located within the geographical boundaries of the areas of analysis. In particular, empirical observations using very small spatial areas will tend not to pick up the effects of many localization economies between larger or more technologically advanced firms, and their resulting spatial interaction effects, because the industrial linkages implied by such effects will tend to take place across much larger spatial areas than simply the adjacent areas. On the other hand, empirical observations using very large regional spatial areas will reflect the aggregation and averaging of the effects of many different localization economies and resulting spatial interaction effects, which take place over a variety of different spatial areas contained within the large region. While the use of spatial econometrics can check for the presence of spatial interactions, the choice of the appropriate spatial units for spatial econometric analyses is still partly a matter of data availability and administrative definitions, neither of which are necessarily appropriate for capturing the particular agglomeration dynamics operating. Attempts at modelling local regional specialization with respect to national employment data are therefore subject to the spatial areas chosen for analysis, even without the existence of agglomeration effects, the presence of which makes these problems even more complex.

The empirical results of discussions concerning the existence of agglomeration effects are thus very sensitive to the spatial areas chosen for analysis (Cheshire and Carbonaro, 1995). The outcome of this is that direct comparisons between countries or between regions of levels of industrial specialization, as indirect proxy evidence of local agglomeration economies, cannot be taken on face value, unless the spatial units have been carefully chosen. Neither can proxy indicators of agglomeration based on measures of regional spatial concentration be directly compared across individual countries unless, once again, the spatial units of analysis have been carefully chosen. Therefore, in the light of the issues discussed in Sections 7.2 and 7.3, in order to identify the extent to which a clear relationship exists in general between regional size and regional specialization, a more systematic analysis is required that allows both for the spatial heterogeneity associated with the hierarchical urban system, and the existence of agglomeration economies. In the next section we will discuss various measures of regional specialization, and two of these measures will then be employed in an econometric assessment of the relationship between regional size and specialization.

7.4 METHODOLOGY AND DATA

A number of measures of regional industrial specialization have been adopted in the literature (Dewhurst and McCann, 2002). In most, if not all cases, these are based on some transformation of the set of location quotients for the region in question. As the empirical work of the chapter is based upon a set of employment data, the exposition below in based on location quotients measured in employment terms, but it should be remembered that such quotients may be better derived from output data if that is available.

The location quotient LQ for an industry i in region r is given as:

$$LQ_{ir} = \frac{E_{ir}/E_{in}}{E_r/E_n} \tag{7.1}$$

where:

E_{ir} is the employment in industry i in region r;
E_{in} is the employment in industry i in nation n;
E_r is the total employment in region r;
E_n is the total employment in nation n.

The location quotient provides us with an index of relative regional specialization for a single industry in a single region. One may note that this is more often referred to as the Balassa Index in the international trade literature. However, in order to discuss the specialization of a region across industrial sectors we need to employ a measure of aggregate regional industrial specialization, which takes account of local variations in specialization between and across sectors.

In this chapter we concentrate on the example of two measures of aggregate regional specialization. These measures are both based on the location quotient LQ index, as are almost all such indices (Dewhurst and McCann, 2002) that are specifically designed to take account of aggregate specialization across a range of m possible industrial and commercial sectors.

The first measure of aggregate regional specialization we employ here is taken from Blair (1995, p. 113) who, for m possible industrial sectors, defines an Index of Specialization, BIS, as:

$$\text{BIS} = \sum_{i=1}^{m} \delta_i \left[\left(\frac{E_{in}}{E_n} \right) - \left(\frac{E_{ir}}{E_r} \right) \right] \qquad (7.2)$$

where:

$\delta_i = 1$ if $LQ_{ir} < 1$
$\quad = 0$ otherwise.

This may be written as:

$$\text{BIS} = \sum_{i=1}^{m} \delta_i \left[(1 - LQ_{ir}) \left(\frac{E_{in}}{E_n} \right) \right]. \qquad (7.3)$$

This index is the sum of the positive differences in the proportions of employment in industry i in nation n and in region r, calculated across m possible industrial sectors As Blair points out, equivalently one could sum the absolute value of the negative differences, and indeed some measures of concentration adopt such an approach (Dewhurst and McCann, 2002).

The second measure of aggregate regional specialization we employ here is that adopted by Amiti (1998) in a study of specialization within the European Union, in which she uses a Gini coefficient. For each region one ranks the location quotients in descending order. One may then plot the cumulative sum of the numerator against the cumulative sum of the denominator and calculate the Gini coefficient of regional specialization as twice the area between the plotted line and the 45° degree line.

In order to provide an empirical analysis of the relationship between regional specialization and regional size we analyse employment data from the NOMIS[3] database, which gives Census of Employment information broken down by sector and location for the whole of Great Britain. The data analysed here is taken from the 1995 census. This data is available at varying degrees of spatial disaggregation. For the empirical analysis in this chapter we have used information at three levels of spatial disaggregation. The most disaggregated level is that of Local Authority districts. There are 459 of these. We also make use of data at the county and regional levels. There are 64 counties – the Shetlands, Orkneys and Western Isles being treated as one unit, distinct from the Highlands. There are 11 regions, with the data for Greater London being given separately from those for The Rest of the South-East. When all the sub-national areas are combined there are 533 observations, as Greater London occurs in the data set both as a county and as a region.

In order to construct the two measures of specialization it is necessary to utilize the data for Great Britain as a whole. We use an industrial disaggregation at the four-digit level (called 'classes' in the data set). There are 504 of these. However, the last two are not relevant, being 'Private Households with Employed Servants' and 'Extra-territorial Organizations and Bodies', and one class, 'Mining of Uranium and Thorium Ores' was reported as having no employees. A more substantive problem, however, exists in agriculture. The figures for the agriculture sector reported in the data set are, in the main, taken from data provided by the Ministry of Agriculture and Fisheries (MAFF). Due to more stringent disclosure rules adopted by MAFF, data on employment in the agricultural sector is not available at the Local Authority district level. Thus the agriculture sector has to be omitted from all the calculations. As a result in the analysis below we use a disaggregation into 489 industries. Therefore, in what follows, we refer to the total non-agricultural employment in an area as the size of the regional economy. In the empirical work of the following section use is also made of population densities for the areas, which are taken from *Regional Trends*, 33 (1998) London, Office for National Statistics.

From Table 7.1 we see that as the size of the area of analysis increases the average location quotient value varies only slightly. However, both the average standard deviation and the average coefficient of variation of the location quotient values fall sharply as the size of the area of analysis increases. On the basis of our arguments in Section 7.2, this suggests that as the size of the area of analysis falls, a greater number of sectors will cease to exhibit any significant presence in the area, thereby increasing the number of sectoral location quotient values that approach or equal zero. The result of this will be that, on average, the area will tend to become more specialized in aggregate terms as a smaller number of sectors will be represented within each area of analysis. As we see from Table 7.2, this is confirmed by both of our measures of aggregate regional industrial specialization, and Table 7.3 shows the correlations between the two measures of aggregate regional industrial specialization at the various levels of spatial disaggregation available.

Table 7.1   Average values of the mean location quotients, standard deviations and coefficients of variation across regions, counties and Local Authority districts

Spatial level	Average location quotient	Average standard deviation	Average coefficient of variation
Regions	1.0318	1.0802	104.15
Counties	1.0549	2.7142	240.89
Local Authority districts	1.0754	5.1064	429.51

Table 7.2   Average values of size and specialization measures at various spatial levels

Spatial level	Average employment	Average Index of specialization	Average Gini coefficient
Regions	1924799	0.15177	0.22733
Counties	330825	0.24823	0.36846
LA districts	46128	0.38990	0.55283

Table 7.3   Correlation between the Index of Specialization and the Gini coefficient

Spatial level	No. of areas	Correlation coefficient
Regions	12	0.9946
Counties	64	0.9957
LA districts	459	0.9901
All areas *	533	0.9938

Note: * Greater London is included in both the Regions and Counties figures but only once in the All areas figures.

Figures 7.1 and 7.2 show scatter diagrams for the Index of Specialization and the Gini coefficient respectively against the value of the logarithm of total employment using all the sub-national data. Two features of Figures 7.1 and 7.2 are worthy of comment. First there is a marked and apparently linear relationship between the measures of specialization and the logarithm of total employment. Second there are three noticeable outliers. The first is at [log(size) = 12.426, Index = 0.705, Gini = 0.839], the second at [log(size) = 13.068, Index = 0.474, Gini = 0.616] and the third at [log(size) = 14.976,

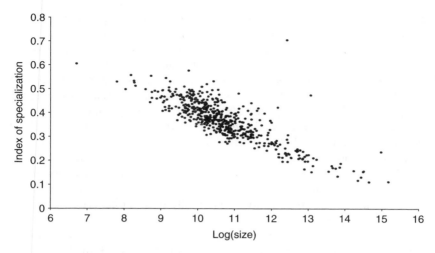

Figure 7.1   Index of Specialization and log(size): all sub-national units

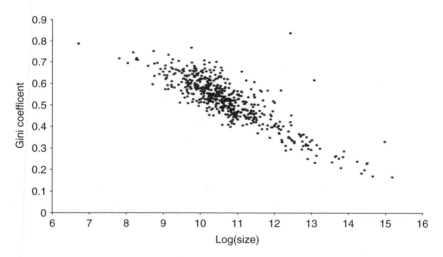

Figure 7.2   Gini coefficient and log(size): all sub-national units

Index = 0.237, Gini = 0.331]. In all case the values of the Index of Specialization and the Gini coefficient seem too high compared with the rest of the data. In fact these data points refer to the City of London, the City of Westminster and Greater London respectively. In each case the degree of specialization is greater than one would expect, given the rest of the data, for regional economies of their respective sizes. Given the peculiar nature of the economies this is perhaps not too surprising.

Notwithstanding the apparent linearity exhibited in Figures 7.1 and 7.2, there are compelling reasons for choosing to adopt a non-linear specification when modelling the relationship between specialization and the logarithm of size. First, whereas the actual values of the dependent variable, whether the Index of Specialization or the Gini coefficient, are, by construction, constrained to lie between zero and one, the fitted values from any unconstrained linear regression would not be so constrained. Second, as the size of the regional economy becomes close to zero both measures of specialization must also become close to zero and as the size of the regional economy approaches that of the nation, the values of both measures tend to one. Finally, and more pragmatically, linear specifications, in virtually all of the cases examined, fail the Ramsey RESET test for adequacy of functional form.

A common way to model variables that are constrained to lie between zero and one is to use a logistic curve (Ramanathan, 1998, pp. 281–2) and that is the procedure adopted here. The logistic model may be written as:

$$Y = \frac{1}{1 + \exp[-(\alpha + \beta X)]} \tag{7.4}$$

with $\beta > 0$.

As X tends to $-\infty$, Y tends to zero and as X tends to $+\infty$, Y tends to one. This model may be estimated by transforming Y according to:

$$Z = \ln\left[\frac{Y}{1 - Y}\right] \tag{7.5}$$

and using the regression model $Z = \alpha + \beta X$.

Because both the Index of Specialization and the Gini coefficient have the opposite limits to Y in the description above, the transformation used in this here is:

$$Z = \ln\left[\frac{1 - M}{M}\right] \tag{7.6}$$

where M is the measure of aggregate specialization. As such, in the model below, rather than measuring industrial specialization we are measuring the inverse of specialization, which is industrial diversity.

On the basis of the arguments regarding localization economies in Section 7.2 one might expect greater specialization in regions where there is a denser spatial concentration of industry, due to the presence of industry-specific localization economies. Conversely, one might expect rather less specialization and more diversity in regions of the same size, where the activities are less densely concentrated. Therefore, as well as controlling for the employment size of a region E_r, in order to capture this effect we have followed Ciccone and Hall (1996) and included the density of employment in the area, ED_r, defined as the number of employees per square kilometre, as an explanatory variable in the model. As we have seen in Section 7.2, central place theory and new economic geography also suggests that larger settlements, higher up the urban rank-ordering, would tend to be less specialized than smaller settlements, because of the greater range of functions they might be expected to supply over larger hinterland areas. This suggests that two regions with the same size, in terms of total employment, might be expected to differ in specialization and diversity if one was a city region and one was a rural region. In order to capture this possible effect we have included in the regression model the density of population in the region, PD_r, as an additional explanatory variable, arguing that the density of population might be regarded as a reasonable proxy for the place of the region in the settlement hierarchy.

Allowing for the possibility that we will still have to treat the City of London, the City of Westminster and Greater London, denoted as CL, CW and GL respectively, as special cases, the general form of the model estimated is therefore:

$$Z_r = \alpha + \beta \ln E_r + \gamma \ln ED_r + \delta \ln PD_r + \theta_1 CL + \theta_2 CW + \theta_3 GL + \varepsilon_r \quad (7.7)$$

where ε_r is a random error term. A priori, from our previous arguments we expect $\beta > 0$, $\partial Z / \partial ED_r < 0$ and $\partial Z / \partial PD_r > 0$. Table 7.4 shows the regression results.

7.5   RESULTS AND COMMENTARY

The results of equation (7.7) are given in Table 7.4. The equations seem reasonably well specified, have considerable explanatory power and the signs of the statistically significant coefficient estimates accord with our a priori expectations. In particular, in Great Britain, regional specialization is seen to increase and regional diversity is seen to decrease with the employment density of the region. At the same time, regional specialization is seen to decrease and regional diversity is seen to increase with the population density of the region. These results support our two initial hypotheses from new economic geography and central place theory. In terms of the central

Table 7.4 Regression results (number of observations = 533)

		Index of Specialization	Gini Coefficient
α	Coefficient (t-ratio)	−3.2952	−4.6384
		(−32.27)	(−38.23)
β	Coefficient (t-ratio)	0.3491	0.4044
		(44.21)	(43.10)
γ_1	Coefficient (t-ratio)	−0.00004115	−0.00003781
		(−5.464)	(−4.226)
γ_2	Coefficient (t-ratio)	−0.1960	−0.2551
		(−5.8106)	(−6.364)
δ	Coefficient (t-ratio)	0.1835	0.2467
		(5.417)	(6.131)
θ_1	Coefficient (t-ratio)	2.3373	2.1289
		(3.991)	(3.060)
θ_3	Coefficient (t-ratio)	−0.7272	−0.7663
		(−5.464)	(−3.788)
R-squared		0.8245	0.8173
F-statistic[a]		411.75	392.14
RESET[b]		3.499	0.540
Het[c]		2.836	0.917
Exclusion[d]		2.481	2.256

Notes:
a. $F_{6,526}\ (0.05) \leq 2.160$.
b. Ramsey's RESET test based on squared fitted values for adequacy of functional form: $F_{1,525}(0.05) \geq 3.841$.
c. Test for homoskedastic errors based on regression of squared residuals on squared fitted values: $F_{1,531}(0.05) \geq 3.841$.
d. F-test for exclusion of *CW* and *PD*: $F_{2,524}(0.05) \geq 2.996$.

focus of this chapter, however, after controlling for variations in employment density and population density, regional specialization is seen to increase and regional diversity is seen to decrease, as the size of the region falls. Conversely, as the size of the region increases, regional specialization falls and regional diversity increases, after controlling for variations in employment density and population density. This finding supports our initial speculation that suggested that the observed measures or regional specialization will also depend in part on the size of the area chosen as a region of analysis.

Our general results suggest that caution is therefore required when interpreting empirical measurements of industrial specialization or industrial diversity as proxy indicators of localization economies or of urbanization economies. The reason for this, as we have seen, is that the empirical results themselves may not be independent of the chosen level of spatial disaggregation. Given that agglomeration effects cannot be directly observed, approaches to the identification of agglomeration economies at an aggregate spatial level, which proceed by splitting up a spatial area into a series of sub-areas (Ellison and Glaeser, 1997),[4] must be interpreted carefully. Similarly, approaches that compare levels of specialization between different spatial areas, such as between different countries (Amiti, 1998), must also be treated very cautiously. The problem is that the sensitivity of the results to the spatial units employed means that it is strictly not possible to compare directly these various measures between different regions or countries. Only direct comparison between different industries in the same area are strictly possible. The same argument also holds for any inferences made concerning the impact of localized agglomeration effects on regional trade patterns.

The empirical exercise here demonstrates that discussions of agglomeration that are made on the basis of inter-regional or international comparisons of local specialization, can only be interpreted in any meaningful manner if the comparison areas are both of a similar scale and also a similar position within the urban hierarchy. Therefore, measures that also control for both the employment and population density, as well as for the actual (logged) size of the individual aerial units, may allow for more appropriate comparisons between regions or countries. Otherwise, we are likely to be finding spurious evidence of agglomeration in situations where none actually exists, or alternatively ruling out agglomeration effects, in situations where they may actually exist.

One interesting point to note here is that given their sizes, employment densities and population densities, the City of London, the City of Westminster and Greater London are all rather more specialized than might be expected from either central place theory or from models of new economic geography. This finding is important for scholars working on the structure and behaviour of the London economies (Gordon, 2002; Buck et al., 2005; CoL, 2004), and also accords with the New York findings of Glaeser (2005). As such, in the case of the United Kingdom and the United States, the very largest cities are actually among the most specialized cities, even allowing for the effects of population size and density on measures of specialization. This outcome is rather contrary to the predictions of the theoretical models outlined earlier, and is also rather different from the experience of the other large, but smaller, cities of the same economies (Glaeser, 2005) all of which appear to be rather more diversified than either London or New York. However, from the available evidence it appears that this is a relatively recent observation. During the 1950s (Lichtenberg, 1960) and

1960s (Chinitz, 1961a), New York was not only the largest US city but was also relatively much more diverse than other smaller US cities. The situation was the same for London (CoL, 2004). However, this situation appears to have completely reversed, with both New York and London now being highly specialized in financial and business services. The reasons for these changes appear to be related primarily to the particular specialized roles that have emerged since the 1960s for London and New York within the global financial services system (Casson and McCann, 1999; Gordon, 2002).

Although the results appear convincing and are, we believe, robust, there are some caveats about the empirical exercise that should be aired. The first concerns the sample of observations used. In the empirical work we combined Local Authority districts, counties and regions. Primarily this was done to enable us to consider a wider range of regional sizes than would otherwise have been the case. Nonetheless, this procedure introduces a complication that we have not sought to address as yet. Several districts make up a county and in turn several counties make up a region. This suggests that the measures of specialization for individual counties and regions cannot be independent of the measures observed at the spatial levels of disaggregation within the counties and regions. Given the nature of the measures of specialization the degree of dependence is hard, if not impossible, to assess. Nevertheless it may be that explicitly recognizing that interdependence might qualify our results. The rather more general question of whether the results are robust with respect to the level of regional disaggregation will also be addressed in future work. As data for the agriculture sector is available at higher levels of regional disaggregation than the district level, such work may enable the effects of omitting the agricultural sector in this work to be assessed.

Second, we make no allowance for any form of spatial autocorrelation. Although there does not appear to be any strong grounds for believing that the residuals should be spatially autocorrelated or that specialization spills over from one area to contiguous areas in some manner, we recognize that the data might support such contentions, particularly at the smaller area level of analysis. In future work we hope to extend the analysis by considering an even finer spatial dissagregation, namely that of ward-level data. In that case it would seem more likely that spillover effects might occur and thus the need for examining spatial correlation patterns would become more necessary.

Third, for some small district areas, the accuracy of the population density measure as a proxy for the ranking of the area within the urban hierarchy will inevitably suffer from the problem of employment commuting. From urban economic theory (Fujita, 1989), the reason for this is that different areas within and around a single settlement will exhibit population density differences, dependent on their distance from the city centre. This means that central areas in some lower order cities may exhibit higher population densities than outlying areas in higher-order cities, although the former are part of a lower-order travel-to-work area. Although this may affect some of the relative area rankings, over a large number of urban centres and a large number of areas, this should not adversely affect our results.

Fourth, the results use only one level of industrial disaggregation and pertain to one year only. Testing the effect of different levels of industrial disaggregation (Karaska, 1968) on the results is the next stage in the research agenda. As the industrial disaggregation used here is the finest that the data allow, this work will have the added benefit of illuminating, to some degree, the effects on the analysis of having to omit the agricultural sector. Extending the analysis to cover a period of time, perhaps by considering two years reasonably well apart in time, will also enrich the results. A test of whether the parameter values of the estimated models, and indeed the models themselves, remain constant over time would be of considerable interest. Evidence of changes in the parameters over time might, for example, allow one to shed light on the degree of convergence and/or divergence of regional economies in the United Kingdom from a perspective that has not been adopted before.

Finally, it has been necessary for us to estimate the model using the particular areal divisions and levels of disaggregation available to us. Any estimates based on the sub-division of a given spatial area into different sized spatial units will to some extent suffer from the modifiable areal unit problem (Openshaw and Taylor, 1979). However, we do not believe that our overall results are fundamentally affected by this problem, in that the signs on the estimated coefficients, which are produced by estimating the model across the range of nested areal unit sizes, are entirely consistent with the a priori predictions of urban systems theory.

7.6   CONCLUSIONS

Our results provide strong evidence of a negative relationship between regional specialization and regional size. Allowing for the variations in regional specialization predicted by new economic geography and central place theory, it is clear that measures of regional specialization will also in part be affected by the chosen size definition of the region. Our results provide a word of caution for analyses that seek for indirect evidence of agglomeration effects on the basis of proxy indices of industrial specialization and diversity. Moreover, this argument applies equally to efforts at identifying agglomeration effects at an aggregate spatial level by splitting up a spatial area into a series of sub-areas, and also to attempts at cross-area comparisons of specialization and agglomeration. The reason is that empirical results themselves may not be independent of the chosen level of spatial disaggregation. Any inferences concerning the impact of localized agglomeration effects on regional trade patterns, which are made on the basis of inter-regional or international comparisons of local specialization, can only be interpreted in any meaningful manner if the comparison areas are of both a similar scale, and also a similar position within the urban hierarchy. Our analysis also has implications for regional input–output modelling. Regional trade estimates based on a location quotient comparison of national and regional employment structures may become progressively more unreliable as the size of the area of analysis falls. Similarly, our argument would all but rule out the application of minimum requirements techniques (Ullman and Dacey, 1960) at all but the very large regional area level. Finally, our analysis suggest that, even allowing for the effects of both scale and density, specialization among the very largest urban centres may be rather different than theoretical models imply.

APPENDIX: MEASURES OF AGGREGATE SPATIAL CONCENTRATION

A common measure of spatial concentration is the Hirschmann-Herfindahl index of spatial concentration developed by Ellison and Glaeser (1997). This index measures the extent to which an individual industry is spatially concentrated within a country, and is defined as:

$$HHI = \sum_{r=1}^{k} (s_{ir} - x_r)^2 \qquad (A7.1)$$

where s_{ir} is the share of industry i's national employment in region r and x_r is region r's share of total national employment. Following Black and Henderson (1999), equation (A7.1) can be rewritten as:

$$HHI = \sum_{r=1}^{k} \left(\frac{E_{ir}}{E_{in}} - \frac{E_r}{E_n} \right)^2 . \qquad (A7.2)$$

As we see from equation (A7.2) the Hirschmann-Herfindahl index of spatial concentration is the sum of the squared differences between the numerator and the denominator terms of the LQ. For an industry that is evenly distributed across all regions, that is, for an industry whose LQs are equal to unity in all regions, the value of *HHI* is always zero. However, for an industry that is spatially concentrated, the value of *HHI* is sensitive to both the size and also the actual spatial boundaries of the spatial units chosen.

In order to see this, we can consider several examples. If we take a country that is divided into two regions, regions 1 and 2, each of which has an equal total employment population, and industry *i* is entirely concentrated in region 1, then the value of *HHI* is calculated as $HHI = (1 - 0.5)^2 + (0 - 0.5)^2$ $= 0.5$. If the administrative definitions of same country were then changed, so that the country was now divided into four regions of equal total employment size, by splitting region 1 into two equal parts and splitting region 2 into two equal parts, if the industry was still concentrated entirely into one region, then the value of *HHI* would now be calculated as $HHI = (1 - 0.25)^2$ $+ 3(0 - 0.25)^2 = 0.625$. If the country was broken up into 100 equal-sized regions, and the industry was still concentrated entirely within one region, then the value of *HHI* would now be calculated as $HHI = (1 - 0.01)^2 +$ $99(0 - 0.01)^2 = 0.99$. Even though there has been no change in the location of firms, the industry will appear to have become more spatially concentrated as the spatial units of analysis become smaller. The upper bound of this process as the spatial units become smaller is a value of 1.

Similarly, if we begin with the two-region case of two equal-sized regions 1 and 2, and then change administrative definition of the country so that it is now comprised of two regions, one of which contains 99 per cent of total national employment and the other region contains only 1 per cent of total national employment, if the industry was entirely located in the smaller region, then the value of *HHI* would now be calculated as $HHI = (1 - 0.01)^2 + (0 - 0.99)^2 = 1.96$. Even though there has been no change in the location of firms, the industry will appear to have become more spatially concentrated as the spatial units of analysis become more skewed and unequal. The upper bound of this process as the spatial units become more unequal in size is a value of 2. Given that the deviations are squared, the Hirschmann-Herfindahl index of spatial concentration tends to be dominated by the two or three largest cities (Black and Henderson, 1999).

These examples indicate that measures of industrial spatial concentration, which are constructed on the basis of *LQ* values in a manner similar to measures of regional aggregate specialization, are therefore also subject to the similar problems associated with the measurement of specialization outlined in this chapter. In particular, as with measures of specialization and diversity, because of the sensitivity of the results to the spatial units chosen, it is not possible to directly compare measures of spatial concentration between different national areas. Only comparisons between different industries in the same areas are strictly possible.

NOTES

1. In the absence of regional trade data, the standard approaches to developing regional sectoral trade estimates are based on location quotient employment ratios (Harris and Liu, 1998; Mayer and Pleeter, 1975), which are related to the national employment distribution. However, the arguments here concerning local specialization and the heterogeneity of the spatial economy imply that these measures will become progressively less accurate as the size of the area of analysis falls (Flegg et al., 1995; McCann and Dewhurst, 1998). This is because the smaller is the chosen region of analysis, the more it will deviate from the national employment distribution, and to the extent that agglomeration and spatial interaction effects do take place at the local level, the less appropriate will be the national employment pattern as a benchmark.
2. The Appendix provides a discussion of the problem in the case of the Ellison and Glaeser (1997) use of the Hirschmann-Herfindahl index.
3. National Online Manpower Information Service.
4. See Appendix.

REFERENCES

Amiti, M. (1998), 'New trade theories and industrial location in the EU: a survey of evidence', *Oxford Review of Economic Policy*, **14**: 45–53.

Arita, T. and P. McCann (2000), 'Industrial alliances and firm behaviour; some evidence from the US semiconductor industry', *Applied Economics*, **32**: 1391–403.

Beavon, K.S.O. (1977), *Central Place Theory: A Reinterpretation*, London: Longman.

Black, D. and V. Henderson (1999), 'Spatial evolution of population and industry in the United States', *American Economic Review: Papers and Proceedings*, **89**: 321–7.

Blair, J.P. (1995), *Local Economic Development: Analysis and Practice*, Thousand Oaks, California: Sage.

Buck, N., I.R. Gordon, A. Harding and I. Turok (eds) (2005), *Changing Cities*, London: Routledge.

Cantwell, J.A. and S. Iammarino (2000), 'Multination corporations and the location of technological innovation in the UK regions', *Regional Studies*, **34**: 317–32.

Casson, M.C. and P. McCann (1999), 'Globalization, competition, and the corporation: the UK experience', in M. Whitman (ed.), *The Evolving Corporation; Global Imperatives and National Responses*, Washington DC: Group of Thirty.

Cheshire, P. and G. Carbonaro (1995), 'Convergence-divergence in regional growth rates', in H.W. Armstrong and R.W. Vickerman (eds), *Convergence and Divergence Among European Regions*, London: Pion.

Chinitz, B. (1961), 'Contrasts in agglomeration: New York and Pittsburgh', *American Economic Review*, **51**: 279–89.

Chinitz, B. (1964), 'City and suburb', in B. Chinitz (ed.), *City and Suburb: The Economics of Metropolitan Growth*, Englewood-Cliffs, New Jersey: Prentice-Hall.

Christaller, W. (1966), *Central Places in Southern Germany*, translated by C.W. Baskin, Englewood-Cliffs, New Jersey: Prentice-Hall.

Ciccone, A. and R.E. Hall (1996), 'Productivity and the density of economic activity', *American Economic Review*, **86**: 54–74.

Cohen, B.J. (1998), *The Geography of Money*, Ithaca and London: Cornell University Press.

CoL (2004), *London's Place in the UK Economy*, London: Corporation of London.

Dewhurst, J.H.Ll. and P. McCann (2002), 'A comparison of measures of industrial specialization for travel-to-work areas in Great Britain, 1981–1997', *Regional Studies*, **36**: 541–51.

Dixit, A.K. and J.E. Stiglitz (1977), 'Monopolistic competition and optimum product variety', *American Economic Review*, **67**: 297–308.

DTI (2001), *Business Clusters in the UK: A First Assessment Vols. 1–3*, London: Department for Trade and Industry.

Ellison, G. and E.L. Glaeser (1997), 'Geographic concentration in US manufacturing industries: a dartboard approach', *Journal of Political Economy*, **105**: 889–927.

Feloy, M., I.R. Gordon, P.E. Lloyd, and P. Roe (1997), *London Employer Survey 1996–1997*, London: London Training and Enterprise Councils.

Flegg, A.T., C.D. Webber and M.V. Eliot (1995), 'On the appropriate use of location quotients in generating regional input–output tables', *Regional Studies*, **29**: 547–62.

Fujita, M. (1989), *Urban Economic Theory*, Cambridge: Cambridge University Press.

Fujita, M. and P. Krugman (1995), 'When is the economy monocentric? Von Thunen and Chamberlin unified', *Regional Science and Urban Economics*, **25**: 505–28.

Fujita, M. and T. Mori (1997), 'Structural stability and evolution of urban systems', *Regional Science and Urban Economics*, **27**: 399–442.

Fujita, M. and J.-F. Thisse (2002), *Economics of Agglomeration*, Cambridge, MA: MIT Press.

Fujita, M., P. Krugman and A.J. Venables (1999), *The Spatial Economies: Cities, Regions and International Trade*, Cambridge, MA: MIT Press.

Glaeser, E.L. (2005), 'Urban colossus: why is New York America's largest city', *Economic Policy Review*, **11**: 7–24, Federal Reserve Bank of New York, New York.

Glaeser, E., H.D. Kallal, J.A. Schinkmann and A. Shleifer (1992), 'Growth in cities', *Journal of Political Economy*, **100**: 1126–52.

Gordon, I.R. (2002), 'Global cities, internationalization and urban systems', in P. McCann (ed.), *Industrial Location Economics*, Cheltenham, UK and Northampton, MA, USA: Edward Elgar.

Gordon, I.R. and P. McCann (2000), 'Industrial clusters: complexes, agglomeration and/or social networks?', *Urban Studies*, **37**: 513–32.

Gordon, I.R. and P. McCann (2005), 'Innovation, agglomeration and regional development', *Journal of Economic Geography*, **5**: 523–43.

Grabher, G. (2001), 'Ecologies of creativity: the village, the group and the heterarchic organisation of the British Advertising Industry', *Environment and Planning A*, **33**: 351–74.

Harris R.I.D. and A. Liu (1998), 'Input–output modelling of the regional economy and external trade', *Regional Studies*, **32**: 851–62.

Henderson, J.V., A. Kuncoro and M. Turner (1995), 'Industrial development in cities', *Journal of Political Economy*, **103**: 1067–85.

Hoover, E.M. (1937), *Location Theory and the Shoe and Leather Industries*, Harvard: Harvard University Press.

Hoover, E.M. (1948), *The Location of Economic Activity*, New York: McGraw-Hill.

Huriot, J.-M. and J.F. Thisse (2000), *Economics of Cities*, Cambridge: Cambridge University Press.

Isard, W. (1951), 'Distance inputs and the space economy. Part II: the locational equilibrium of the firm', *Quarterly Journal of Economics*, **65**: 373–99.

Isard, W. and R.E. Kuenne (1953), 'The impact of steel upon the Greater New York-Philadelphia Region, *Review of Economics and Statistics*, **35**: 289–301.

Jacobs, J. (1961), *The Death and Life of Great American Cities*, New York: Vintage Books, Random House.

Jacobs, J. (1960), *The Economy of Cities*, New York: Vintage Books, Random House.

Jacobs, J. (1984), *Cities and the Wealth of Nations*, New York: Vintage Books, Random House.

Karaska, G.J. (1968), 'Variation of input–output coefficients for different levels of aggregation', *Journal of Regional Science*, **8**: 215–27.

Krugman, P. (1991a), *Geography and Trade*, Cambridge, MA: MIT Press.

Krugman, P. (1991b), 'Increasing returns and economic geography', *Journal of Political Economy*, **99**: 183–99.

Krugman, P. (1998), 'What's new about the new economic geography', *Oxford Review of Economic Policy*, **14**: 7–17.

Leyshon, A. and N. Thrift (1998), *Money/Space*, London: Routledge.

Lichtenberg, R.M. (1960), *One Tenth of a Nation*, Cambridge, MA: Harvard University Press.

Losch, A. (1954), *The Economics of Location*, New Haven, CT: Yale University Press.

Marshall, A. (1920), *Principles of Economics*, London: Macmillan.

Mayer, W. and S. Pleeter (1975), 'A theoretical justification for the use of location quotients', *Regional Science and Urban Economics*, **5**: 343–55.

McCann, P. (1995), 'Rethinking the economics of location and agglomeration', *Urban Studies*, **32**: 563–77.

McCann, P. and J.H.Ll. Dewhurst (1998), 'Regional size, industrial location and input–output expenditure coefficients', *Regional Studies*, **32**: 435–44.

Mills, E.S. (1980), *Urban Economics*, Glenview, IL: Scott, Foresman and Co.

Moses, L. (1958), 'Location and the theory of production', *Quarterly Journal of Economics*, **78**: 259–72.

Openshaw, S. and P.J. Taylor (1979), 'A million or so correlation coefficients: three experiments on the modifiable areal unit problem', in N. Wrigley (ed.), *Statistical Applications in the Spatial Sciences*, London: Pion.

Parr, J.B. (2002), 'The location of economic activity: central place theory and the wider urban system', in P. McCann (ed.), *Industrial Location Economics*, Cheltenham, UK and Northampton, MA, USA: Edward Elgar.

Parr, J.B., K.G. Denike and G.E. Mulligan (1975), 'City size models and the economic base: a recent controversy', *Journal of Regional Science*, **15**: 1–15.

Pomfret, R. (1991), *International Trade*, Oxford: Blackwell.

Ramanathan, R. (1998), *Introductory Econometrics with Applications*, The Dryden Press.

Simpson, W. (1992), *Urban Structure and the Labour Market*, Fort Worth: Oxford University Press.

Twomey, J. and J.M. Tompkins (1996), 'Supply potential in the regions of Great Britain', *Regional Studies*, **30**: 783–90.

Ullman, E. and M. Dacey (1960), 'The minimum requirements approach to the urban economic base', *Papers and Proceedings of the Regional Science Association*, **6**: 174–94.

Venables, A.J. (1996), 'Equilibrium locations of vertically linked industries', *International Economic Review*, **37**: 341–59.

Vernon, R. (1966), 'International investment and international trade in the product cycle', *Quarterly Journal of Economics*, **80**: 190–207.

Weber, A. (1909), *Theory of the Location of Industries*, translated by C.J. Friedrich, 1929, Chicago: University of Chicago Press.

8. A non-parametric analysis of productivity, efficiency and technical change in EU regional manufacturing, 1986–2002

Mark Roberts, John S.L. McCombie and Alvaro Angeriz

8.1 INTRODUCTION

Studies of cross-regional productivity differences and their evolution over time have, with the twin emergence of better data sets and a rising tide of interest amongst economists in spatial issues, become increasingly popular over the last decade and a half.[1] This is especially true for the European Union, where further impetus has, of course, been provided by the advent of Economic and Monetary Union (EMU). Despite this, however, relatively little, if anything, is known about whether cross-regional differences in productivity growth in the EU are attributable to spatial differences in the efficiency with which factors are employed or spatial disparities in the rate of technical change. Indeed, the theoretical framework typically used as the backdrop for empirical research in this area assumes that all regions are technically efficient and that technology is a pure public good. That is to say, the framework typically used is an 'old' neoclassical growth framework that implicitly assumes that all regions are not only operating on their production functions, but that they share the *same* production function. This being the case, spatial differences in productivity are purely attributable to spatial differences in labour productivity emanating from differences in the capital intensity of production. Likewise, spatial differences in rates of productivity growth take the form of spatial differences in labour productivity growth attributable to different regions being in different degrees of (steady-state) disequilibrium.[2]

It is against the above backdrop that this chapter aims to make a contribution. Thus, complementing the work of Angeriz, McCombie and Roberts (2006), the chapter presents results obtained from a study of EU regional productivity differences, where, for each region, productivity change is calculated using the Malmqüist index of total factor productivity (TFP) change and is then decomposed into indices of efficiency change and technical change. The calculation of the Malmqüist index and its subsequent decomposition is achieved through the application of data envelopment analysis (DEA) techniques. These (non-parametric) techniques have been extensively used in a wide range of microeconomic studies into, for example, the efficiency of train operating companies (see, inter alia, Angeriz and Pollitt, 2005; Cantos, Pastor and Serrano, 1999 and Cowie, 1999). They have also been used in a much smaller range of macroeconomic studies into cross-country productivity and efficiency differences (see, for example, Arestis, Chortareas and Desli, 2005 and Färe et al., 1994), but, so far as the authors are aware, there is only one previous example (Karadǎg, Onder and Deliktas, 2005) of their application at the regional level. The study covers the time period 1986–2002, thereby incorporating the crucial period of deepening EU integration dating from the signing of the Single European Act in 1986 to the introduction of euro notes and coins in the EMU area on 1 January 2002, and concentrates on the manufacturing sector. Although manufacturing is now only a relatively small sector for most EU regional economies, the focus upon it is easily justified. Thus, manufacturing goods continue to account for a large proportion of regional exports and the competitiveness of a region's exports is seen, by many, as being crucial in determining its overall prosperity (see McCombie and Thirlwall, 1994, Chp 8 and Rowthorn, 2000). Finally, to help uncover spatial patterns in the results obtained, the study makes use of spatial data analysis techniques. These techniques originated in geography, but are becoming increasingly popular tools for spatial economists.

The structure of the rest of this chapter is as follows. In the next section, Section 8.2, an intuitive, primarily non-technical, introduction into the Malmqüist index of TFP change, its calculation and decomposition using DEA techniques, is provided. Section 8.3 then describes in more detail the EU regional data set to which the study applies these techniques. Following this, Section 8.4 describes the results, with Section 8.5 providing spatial data analysis of the results. Finally, Section 8.6 draws matters to a close with a few concluding observations.

8.2 THE MALMQÜIST TFP CHANGE INDEX, ITS CALCULATION AND DECOMPOSITION USING DEA TECHNIQUES[3]

The most familiar and widely used index of TFP change is the so-called Törnqvist index. This is the index that Solow calculated for the United

States in his seminal 1957 paper and that forms the basis of the traditional growth accounting literature, regional applications of which include, inter alia, Hulten and Schweb (1984). However, Solow attributed all changes in TFP to technical progress[4] and, certainly, the assumption frequently made in the interpretation of this index is that of efficiency in the use of inputs (Angeriz et al., 2006, p. 503).

By contrast, the Malmqüist index explicitly introduces the notion of technical inefficiency, which is assessed by means of distance functions. These distance functions can be either input- or output-oriented. An *input-oriented* distance function measures the maximal proportional contraction of inputs that can be achieved whilst holding output constant, whereas an *output-oriented* distance function measures the maximal proportional expansion of output that can be achieved whilst holding the mix of inputs constant. In this study, the preference is for output-oriented distance functions because, intuitively, these seem to make more sense in the regional context of interest. These output-oriented distance functions are measured *relative* to a benchmark frontier, which, using DEA, is constructed as the 'best practice' frontier for the sample. Thus, a frontier that *envelopes* the regional combinations of manufacturing output and inputs is constructed using linear programming techniques and a region is classified as being technically inefficient if it lies *inside* this frontier. In such a case, the distance function takes on the value of a positive fraction. This is illustrated intuitively for the one-output–one-input case using Figure 8.1. In this figure, the best practice frontier that envelopes the data in period t is shown as $y_t = f(x_t)$. The region (region A) with the output-input combination in period t $(y_{A,t}, x_{A,t})$ lies inside this frontier because, given its input, it could, potentially, produce twice as much output. This being the case, its distance function will be equal to 0.5 because to project the region onto the best practice frontier it is necessary to deflate its output by 0.5. Worth noting is that these distance functions are themselves interesting because they provide for technical efficiency (TE) scores, corresponding to the Debreu (1951) and Farrell (1957) measures of technical efficiency.[5]

Besides their inherent interest, distance functions provide the basis for calculating the Malmqüist index of TFP (MTFP) change. In particular, distance functions can be calculated not only relative to the current period frontier but also to the frontiers of subsequent periods. MTFP change is then measured as the *change* in the distance function between two periods with respect to a common frontier. To illustrate intuitively again, Figure 8.1 shows that by period $t+1$ the output-input combination of region A has changed to $(y_{A,t+1}, x_{A,t+1})$. To deflate on to the best practice frontier in period t it is now necessary to divide output by a figure *greater than*

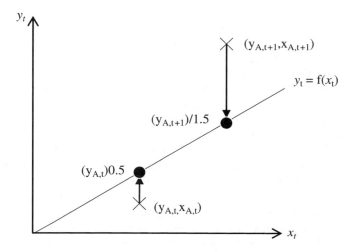

Figure 8.1   The calculation of output-oriented distance functions

unity. Say that this figure is 1.5 so that, defined *relative to the period t frontier*, the value of the distance function has increased from 0.5 to 1.5. This being the case, MTFP change between periods t and $t + 1$ is given as 1.5/0.5 = 3 (= 200 per cent). Of course, had the distance functions instead been calculated relative to the period $t + 1$ frontier rather than the period t frontier, then a different answer for MTFP change would have been obtained. For this reason, following the influential work of Färe et al. (1989, 1994), it is standard practice to define MTFP change as the geometric average of productivity change calculated relative to the frontiers of *both* periods. That is to say, as:

$$MTFP\Delta = \left[\frac{D^t(x_{t+1}, y_{t+1})}{D^t(x_t, y_t)} \cdot \frac{D^{t+1}(x_{t+1}, y_{t+1})}{D^{t+1}(x_t, y_t)} \right]^{0.5} \qquad (8.1)$$

where $D^t(.)$ denotes the value of the distance function calculated relative to the period t frontier and $D^{t+1}(.)$ denotes the value of the distance function calculated relative to the period $t + 1$ frontier.

Of course, in the example given in Figure 8.1, it is unclear to what extent the positive MTFP change is attributable to region A catching up with the best practice frontier through improvements in technical efficiency and to what extent it is attributable to technical change in the form of movement of that frontier itself. Thus, although the output-input combination

$(y_{A,t+1}, x_{A,t+1})$ places region A above the best practice frontier as defined in period t, it is not clear whether this is closer to the best practice frontier in period $t+1$ than was the combination $(y_{A,t}, x_{A,t})$ to the best practice frontier in period t. Therefore, even though MTFP change may have been strongly positive, it is theoretically possible that, *relatively* speaking, technical efficiency declined. It is this that provides the rationale for the decomposition of MTFP change into efficiency change and technical change. Efficiency change (if positive) is defined as moving closer to the (changing) best-practice frontier over time and may result from processes of technological diffusion, as well as processes of policy-induced structural change that improve the output that can be obtained from a given input mix. For example, from the traditional Heckscher-Ohlin model, it might be expected that, through the Rybczynski effect, deeper European integration might have promoted more efficient use of regional inputs, especially in peripheral areas, through encouraging increased specialization in the production of commodities that use intensively the factors with which a region is well endowed. If this is so, deeper European integration will have promoted catch-up with the best practice frontier. Also to be noted is that efficiency change may capture changes in capacity utilization within a region attributable to changes in aggregate demand. As for technical change, this is defined as the movement in the best practice frontier relative to a region's position. In particular, following Färe et al. (1989, 1994) again, MTFP change can be shown to be equal to the product of measures of efficiency and technical change as just defined. Thus:

$$MTFP\Delta = \frac{D^{t+1}(x_{t+1}, y_{t+1})}{D^t(x_t, y_t)} \left[\frac{D^t(x_{t+1}, y_{t+1})}{D^{t+1}(x_{t+1}, y_{t+1})} \cdot \frac{D^t(x_t, y_t)}{D^{t+1}(x_t, y_t)} \right]^{0.5} \quad (8.2)$$

where the first term on the right-hand side of equation (8.2) captures the rate of efficiency change and the second term captures the rate of technical change.

Before progressing to describe the data set used in the study, it is important to note the assumption of constant returns to scale implicit in Figure 8.1, which has been used to illustrate the intuition behind distance functions and their use to calculate the index of MTFP change. This assumption was made because it mirrors the assumption employed in the DEA exercise. It is possible to construct best practice frontiers, and, therefore, the MTFP change index, upon the alternative assumption of variable returns to scale. There are, however, both theoretical and practical problems with this and, as is discussed in more detail in Angeriz et al. (2006, pp. 505–6), it is strongly advised against in the DEA literature.

8.3 DESCRIPTION OF THE DATA

The data set to which DEA was applied comes from Cambridge Econometrics' European Regional Database, which itself extends Eurostat's REGIO database. Regions are defined at the NUTS1 level, which represent the lowest level of spatial disaggregation at which Eurostat provides regional data. These regions are roughly equivalent to, for example, the old standard regions of the United Kingdom or the German Länder, with each having a population of between three and seven million.[6] Overall, the NUTS1 regions number 63 in the sample and cover ten different EU countries, these being Austria, Belgium, France, Germany, Greece, Italy, Netherlands, Portugal, Spain and the United Kingdom. To provide further coverage the data was supplemented with national data for several EU countries – namely, Denmark, Finland, Ireland, Sweden and Switzerland. This enlarges the sample to 68 'regions'. Important to note, however, is that only the addition of Ireland makes any difference to the results for the other regions. This is because, as shown below, only Ireland helps to define the best practice frontier at some point during the sample period.

In conducting the DEA exercise, manufacturing output was measured as gross value-added (GVA) and two factor inputs – capital and labour – were used. As explained in Angeriz et al. (2006, pp. 506–7), data on gross investment between 1980 and 1985 was used to construct estimates of regional capital stocks in 1986 with capital stocks in subsequent years being calculated using a perpetual inventory method. Labour input, meanwhile, was measured as total hours worked. Both GVA and capital stocks were measured in 1995 constant prices at purchasing power parity exchange rates. As mentioned in Section 8.1, the overall sample period was 1986–2002, a period that incorporates the primary era of deepening European integration.

8.4 RESULTS

8.4.1 Temporal Evolution of the MTFP, Efficiency and Technical Change Indices

Figure 8.2 shows the overall average picture for the 68 regions in the sample as it evolved between 1986 and 2002. In particular, it plots the evolution of the weighted means of the MTFP, efficiency and technical change indices, where the weights used are the share of each region in overall manufacturing GVA. As can be seen, MTFP growth was on a positive upwards trend until 1988, after which there was a slowdown, which continued until 1993 with MTFP growth becoming negative in 1992. Following this, however, MTFP growth

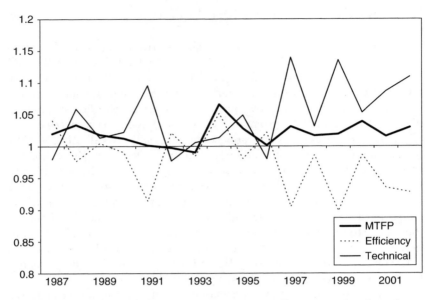

Figure 8.2   Weighted annual means of MTFP, efficiency and technical change, 1986–2002

recovered strongly to record its highest increase in 1994. MTFP change then settled down, fluctuating at around 1.02 or 2 per cent per annum for the remainder of the sample-period, with the overall average rate of growth over the entire sample period being 1.0186 or 1.86 per cent per annum.

Decomposing MTFP change into efficiency and technical change, it can be seen that efficiency and technical change followed symmetric patterns around the x-axis. Thus, technical change was generally positive throughout the entire sample period, whilst efficiency change was generally negative with year-to-year fluctuations between the two indices being negatively correlated. However, overall, the positive technical change (average rate of growth = 1.0428 or 4.28 per cent per annum) was stronger than the negative efficiency change (average rate of growth = 0.9768 or −2.32 per cent per annum). This negative correlation between technical change and efficiency change doubtless reflects the fact that, ceteris paribus, outwards movements of the best practice frontier leaves a region with the same input mix further from that frontier. In other words, it reflects the fact that efficiency is a relative concept in DEA. Nevertheless, the fact that, even in relative terms, the technical efficiency of the average European NUTS1 region declined between 1986 and 2002 is interesting in the light of the dramatic deepening of EU integration that has been highlighted as occurring during this time period. Contrary to what might be expected, therefore, deepening EU integration was accompanied not by the widespread adoption of best practice technologies and methods, but, rather, by a general falling (further) behind of the best practice frontier.

8.4.2 The Cross-sectional Pattern of MTFP, Efficiency and Technical Change .

Turning to the cross-sectional pattern of MTFP, efficiency and technical change over the entire sample period, Table 8.1 shows that the distribution showed a slight negative skew for all three indices, whilst rates of MTFP change were slightly more dispersed across the sample of regions than were either rates of efficiency or technical change. However, perhaps more interesting than this, are the regions identified as having the highest and lowest (average) rates of MTFP, efficiency and technical change. Thus (the Republic of) Ireland recorded both the fastest rate of MTFP and efficiency change over the sample-period. Indeed, as discussed in Angeriz et al. (2006, p. 504), Ireland was the only region to enjoy both strictly positive average MTFP and efficiency change over the sample period, this reflecting the fact that it is only Ireland that seems to have caught up with the European best practice frontier in manufacturing since the signing of the Single European Act. By contrast, it is the Ile de France region, which incorporates Paris, that has benefited most from technical change since 1986, its annual

Table 8.1   Descriptive statistics for MTFP, efficiency and technical change, 1986–2002

	Mean	Standard Deviation	Skew	Kurtosis	Maximum		Minimum	
MTFPΔ	1.0164	0.0190	−0.5738	4.4557	1.0690	Ireland	0.9570	Nisia Aigaiou, Kriti (GR)
EFFICΔ	0.9738	0.0140	−0.2086	5.0797	1.0190	Ireland	0.922	Nisia Aigaiou, Kriti (GR)
TECHΔ	1.0437	0.0151	−1.4574	4.8217	1.061	Ile de France (FR)	0.9950	Attiki (GR)

Notes:
Skew is measured as $(1/N)\Sigma_i(x_i-\mu)^3/(\sigma^2)^{3/2}$ where N is the number of observations (= 68), x_i is the value of the variable x for observation i, μ is the mean value of variable x, and σ is the standard deviation.
Kurtosis is measured as $(1/N)\Sigma_i(x_i-\mu)^4/(\sigma^2)^2$.

average rate of technical change being an impressive 1.061 or 6.1 per cent per annum. As for the slowest rates of MTFP, efficiency and technical change, these were all recorded by Greek regions. In particular, the Greek islands of Nisia Aigaiou and Kriti experienced both the lowest average rates of MTFP and efficiency change over the sample period, which may be a reflection of the fact that, being primarily dependent upon tourism, they constitute the region with the smallest manufacturing sector in the sample, the mean share of manufacturing in total output over the sample period being only 8.52 per cent. Meanwhile, Attiki, which includes the Greek capital, Athens, was the region to record the slowest rate of technical change in the sample. Indeed, as indicated in Table 8.2, along with the West Midlands in the United Kingdom, Attiki was the only region in the sample to experience a negative effect of technical change.

With one exception, Table 8.2 shows that the above cases all constituted outliers according to the 1.5 interquartile ratio rule. The exception is perhaps the biggest surprise – there was nothing 'unusual' about the fast rate of technical change that the Ile de France region benefited from. This is because the (unweighted) average rate of technical change across regions in the sample was 1.0437 or 4.37 per cent per annum (this is almost identical to the weighted

Table 8.2   Outlying observations for MTFP, efficiency and technical change, 1986–2002

	Q1	Median	Q3	IQ$_{range}$	High Outliers	Low Outliers
MTFPΔ	1.0100	1.0180	1.0290	0.0190	Ireland = 1.069	Nisia Aigaiou, Kriti (GR) = 0.957; Vareia Ellada (GR) = 0.977; West Midlands (UK) = 0.9707; N. Ireland (UK) = 0.978; Attiki (GR) = 0.981
EFFICΔ	0.9640	0.9740	0.9830	0.0190	Ireland = 1.019	Nisia Aigaiou, Kriti (GR) = 0.922
TECHΔ	1.0360	1.0500	1.0550	0.0190	–	Nisia Aigaiou, Kriti (GR) = 0.995; West Midlands (UK) = 0.998; Noord-Nederland (NL) = 1.005

average rate of technical change of 1.0428 or 4.28 per cent per annum reported earlier, indicating that regions with larger manufacturing sectors did not experience faster rates of technical change), which compares favourably with the 6.1 per cent per annum change experienced by Ile de France.

Regarding the remaining outliers, these do not show any real surprises. Noord-Nederland was an outlier with respect to its low rate of technical change, but, as shown below, it is the only region that was found to be on the best practice frontier of the sample in both 1986 and 2002.

8.4.3 The Cross-sectional Patterns of Technical Efficiency (TE) Scores and their Persistence over Time

Not only is it interesting to examine the cross-sectional patterns in the MTFP, efficiency and technical change indices, but also in the technical efficiency (TE) scores that enter into their calculation. Thus, Table 8.3 presents descriptive statistics for the technical efficiency scores in 1986 and 2002 respectively (remember, a region's TE score in year t corresponds to its output-oriented distance function measured using both its input mix and the best practice frontier in year t). For the former year, at the outset of the road to the single market, it can be seen that the average TE score was 0.7050. In other words, given the best practice frontier in 1986, the average region could have produced 30 per cent more manufacturing

Table 8.3 Descriptive statistics for 1986 and 2002 technical efficiency scores

	Mean	Standard Deviation	Skew	Kurtosis	Maximum		Minimum	
TE, 1986	0.7050	0.1474	0.1406	2.6133	1.0000	Noord-Nederland (NL), London, S. West (UK)	0.3470	Campania (IT)
TE, 2002	0.4667	0.1338	1.8435	8.7765	1.0000	Noord-Nederland (NL), Ireland	0.1650	Nisia Aigaiou, Kriti (GR)

Notes:
Skew is measured as $(1/N)\Sigma_i(x_i - \mu)^3/(\sigma^2)^{3/2}$ where N is the number of observations ($= 68$), x_i is the value of the variable x for observation i, μ is the mean value of variable x, and σ is the standard deviation.
Kurtosis is measured as $(1/N)\Sigma_i(x_i - \mu)^4/(\sigma^2)^2$.

output with the same input mix. In turn, as shown by the maximum TE scores, the best practice frontier in 1986 was defined by three regions – Noord-Nederland, London and the South West of the United Kingdom.[7] Compared with these regions, the worst performing region in 1986 was Campania in the south of Italy, which, according to its TE score, had the potential to increase output from its input mix by 65.3 per cent through the combination of higher utilization, favourable structural change and the adoption of best practice methods and technologies.

By 2002, at the start of the introduction of euro notes and coins into the EMU area, it can be seen that the picture has changed quite dramatically. Thus, the cumulated impact of negative efficiency change over the sample period is given stark resonance by the decline in the average TE score to 0.4667, indicating a near 24 per cent decline in efficiency for the average region compared with the (improving) best practice frontier. Just as in 1986, Noord-Nederland helps to define this frontier. However, London and the South West of the UK no longer appear as best practice regions, their place on Europe's efficiency frontier having been taken by Ireland. This reflects the earlier reported result that Ireland was the only region in the sample to record strictly positive efficiency change between 1986 and 2002, which, in turn, reflects its spectacular growth of manufacturing GVA over the period (see Angeriz et al., 2006, p. 508). Furthermore, by 2002, the identity of the 'worst practice' region had changed from Campania in Italy to Nisia Aigaiou and Kriti in Greece, this reflecting the latter's highly negative rate of efficiency change over the sample period. Indeed, it can be seen that this negative efficiency change was such that by 2002, Nisia Aigaiou and Kriti were, given their input mix, only able to produce 16.5 per cent of the manufacturing output potentially available from the best practice frontier. Finally, we can see that, between 1986 and 2002, not only was there a mean shift in the level of technical efficiency, but there was also a dramatic change in the shape of the distribution of TE scores. Hence, whereas in 1986 the distribution of TE scores was approximately normal,[8] by 2002 it had become much less symmetric, exhibiting a noticeable positive skew and a much higher kurtosis, which reflects a flattening, and spreading out, of the distribution. Thus it seems that a small number of regions continued to benefit from higher levels of technical efficiency, but, relatively speaking, the great mass of regions fell substantially behind.[9]

In light of the above, it is interesting to ask to what extent did regions persist in their positions in the distribution of TE scores between 1986 and 2002? To answer this question, a simple univariate OLS regression was estimated. In this regression, a region's TE score in 2002 was taken as the dependent variable and its TE score in 1986 as the independent variable. This yielded the following results:

$$TE_{i, 2002} = \underset{(0.0688)}{0.1321} + \underset{(0.0952)}{0.4746.TE_{i, 1986}} + \varepsilon_{i, 1986, 2002}$$

t-ratio   1.9260   4.9838
$$[p = 0.0584] \quad [p = 0.0000]$$

$$N = 68, R^2 = 0.2736, R^2(adjusted) = 0.2624$$

which indicates a positive correlation between a region's TE score in 1986 and its TE score in 2002 that is significant at the 1 per cent level in a two-tailed test. However, the variation in TE scores in 1986 accounts for less than 30 per cent of the variation in TE scores in 2002. Therefore, whilst it can be concluded that there was a significant amount of persistence in the spatial pattern of TE scores over the sample period, there was also, clearly, a noticeable amount of 'churning' within the distribution. To some extent, this has been seen in the results already reported. Thus, for example, it has been seen that whilst Noord-Nederland persisted in its position as a best practice region over the sample period, London and the South West of the United Kingdom did not.[10]

8.5   SPATIAL DATA ANALYSIS

Using a simple contiguity matrix, Angeriz et al. (2006, pp. 511–15) go on to conduct spatial data analysis on the full set of DEA results reported above. In doing so, they report evidence of significant global spatial auto-correlation for the MTFP change index and both the 1986 and 2002 TE scores. In particular, for all three indices, they find that Moran's I is significantly greater than its expected value and Geary's C is significantly less than its expected value. This indicates that the spatial autocorrelation found is positive, indicating that, on average, *like* values of each index tended to cluster.[11] In other words, there was a tendency for fast (slow) MTFP change regions to cluster together in geographic space and, similarly, high (low) efficiency regions to cluster together geographically. Having detected global spatial autocorrelation, Angeriz et al. (2006) then went on to investigate the localized nature of this spatial autocorrelation through the use of local Moran statistics. A local Moran statistic is referred to by Anselin (1995b, see also 1995a, p. 42) as a local indicator of spatial association (LISA) because it decomposes a global measure of spatial autocorrelation (in this case, Moran's I) into an observation-specific measure of significant spatial clustering of like values. However, whilst local Moran statistics hold the advantage of being a LISA, they do not, by themselves, enable distinction between high value clusters of a variable and low value clusters.[12] To overcome this problem, this chapter instead makes use of Getis-Ord G_i^* statistics to investigate the precise geography of clustering in the MTFP change and TE score indices.[13] For each observation i, the Getis-Ord G_i^* statistic is defined as follows:

$$G_i^* = \left(\sum_{j=1}^{N} w_{ij}x_j \right) \Big/ \left(\sum_{j=1}^{N} x_j \right) \qquad (8.3)$$

where w_{ij} are the elements of the (non-row-standardized) contiguity matrix ($w_{ij} = 1$) if regions i and j share a common administrative border, $w_{ij} = 0$ if not), and x_j is the value of the variable under investigation for region j.[14]

The results obtained from this exercise are reported in the maps in Figures 8.3, 8.4 and 8.5. In particular, these maps plot significant values of the Getis-Ord G_i^* statistic where significance has been assessed against a standard normal distribution through the computation of standardized z-values (computed by subtracting the theoretical mean from the calculated value of the G_i^* statistic and dividing through by the theoretical standard deviation) (see Anselin, 1992, p. 141). Figure 8.3, for MTFP change, shows the existence of five distinct, statistically significant, clusters of local spatial autocorrelation. Out of these, two represent (relatively) fast-growth clusters, whilst three represent slow-growth clusters. The first fast-growth cluster cuts across national boundaries and is provided by Sweden combined with Finland. Meanwhile, the second is contained within France and comprises Ile de France and the surrounding region of Bassin Parisien. As for the slow-growth clusters, two of these exist in peripheral EU countries and represent no surprise. In particular, the four Greek NUTS 1 regions together form a slow MTFP change cluster that is significant at the 10 per cent level, whilst there is also a slow-growth cluster centred on the Spanish region of Sur. However, the remaining (statistically significant) slow-growth cluster is more puzzling, being centred as it is on the South East region of the United Kingdom.

A possible explanation for this 'puzzle' is provided by Figure 8.4, which plots statistically significant values of the G_i^* statistic for the 1986 TE scores. From this, it can clearly be seen that the South East region of the United Kingdom formed the statistical heart of a high efficiency cluster at the outset of the sample-period. Consequently, the South East, together with the majority of the remaining NUTS 1 regions in England and Wales, were operating either on or close to the best practice frontier in 1986,[15] thereby limiting their scope for fast MTFP growth through any possible catch up process.

Apart from the UK cluster, it can be seen from Figure 8.4 that there was one other statistically significant cluster of high TE scores in 1986. This

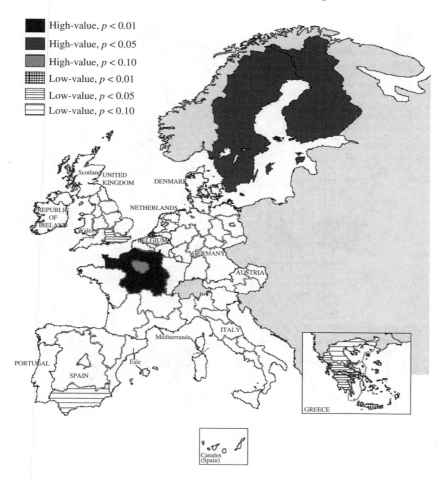

Figure 8.3   Significant values of Getis-Ord G_i^* statistics for MTFP change, 1986–2002

cluster centres on the Belgian region of Vlaams Gewest and spills over national boundaries into the Dutch regions of West-Nederland, Zuid-Nederland and Oost-Nederland.[16, 17] As with the fast MTFP growth cluster of Sweden and Finland discussed above, this calls into question the relevance of national boundaries in terms of defining meaningful areas of economic activity, suggesting that such boundaries need not provide spatial limits to the scope of externalities. Meanwhile, besides the UK and Belgian-Dutch high-efficiency cluster, it can be seen that there also existed three

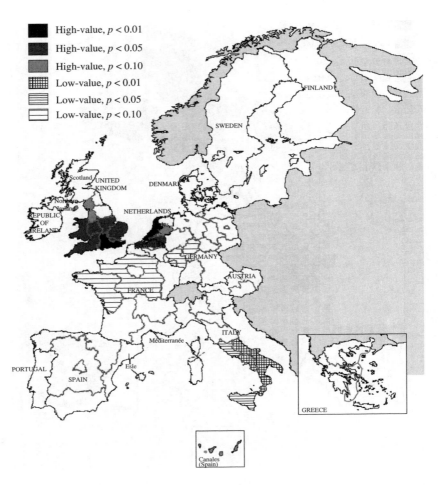

Figure 8.4   Significant values of Getis-Ord G_i^* statistics for 1986 technical efficiency scores

low-efficiency clusters in 1986. The most (statistically) significant of these is provided by the southern regions of Italy and suggests a possible explanation for the notorious north–south divide in that country. As for the other two low-efficiency clusters, these exist at the 10 per cent level and are provided by, first, the neighbouring French regions of Ouest and Bassin Parisien, and, second, by the German regions of Saarland, Rhineland-Pfalz and Hessen.

Finally, Figure 8.5 shows how, by 2002, both the UK and Belgian-Dutch high-efficiency clusters, although still present, had become fragmented, as

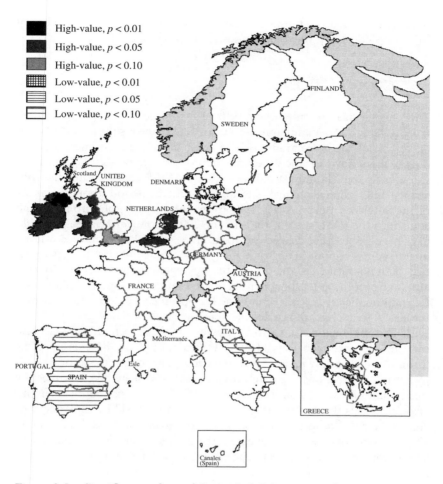

Figure 8.5   Significant values of Getis-Ord G_i^* statistics for 2002 technical efficiency scores

was the case with the low-efficiency cluster in southern Italy. Also evident is the emergence of a new high-efficiency cluster involving Ireland and a new low-efficiency cluster involving the Sur and Centro regions of Spain, the former doubtless reflecting (the Republic of) Ireland's impressive catch up to the European best practice frontier in manufacturing. It can also be noticed that, by 2002, the German low-efficiency cluster was no longer statistically significant. Overall, this process of fragmentation of existing (statistically significant) clusters and the emergence and disappearance of other clusters reflects the noticeable distribution 'churning' in technical efficiency scores that was found, and reported upon, earlier.

8.6   CONCLUSION

This chapter has presented the results of a study of EU regional productivity differences in manufacturing. In particular, the results of a study that makes use of the non-parametric technique of data envelopment analysis (DEA) that allows for the decomposition of productivity change, as measured using the Malmqüist index of TFP (MTFP) change, into efficiency change and technical change. The study covers the period from the signing of the Single European Act in 1986 to the introduction of euro notes and coins into the EMU area at the start of 2002. However, whereas it might have been hoped that deeper European integration has promoted a levelling up across regions in terms of their ability to operate on the 'best practice' manufacturing frontier, quite the opposite has been found. Indeed, although recording reasonable MTFP growth, the average EU region has fallen dramatically further behind the European best practice frontier over the last 20 years, recording a decline in relative technical efficiency of 24 per cent. The only regions found to have escaped this pattern of falling technical efficiency are (the Republic of) Ireland and Noord-Nederland, the former being the only region for which deeper European integration seems to have brought a positive catch-up process. Obviously, the key question that remains is what accounts for this result? The analysis conducted in this chapter reveals the important spatial dimensions of MTFP and efficiency change over the sample period, but does not directly address this question. Thus, it does not reveal to what extent the changes in efficiency experienced are attributable to changes in capacity utilization resulting from developments on the demand-side and to what extent they are attributable to adverse supply-side developments. This signals an important area of future research.

NOTES

1.   This rising tide of interest has been partly stimulated by the development of better analytical and econometric techniques for modelling the space economy. Thus, with respect to the development of better analytical techniques, the last decade and a half has witnessed the emergence of the so-called new economic geography or geographical economics literature on the back of advances in the modelling of imperfect competition (see, for example, Fujita, Krugman and Venables, 1999). Meanwhile, with respect to the development of better econometric techniques, there has been a simultaneous development and acceptance of spatial econometric techniques, partly aided by the release of

such packages as *SpaceStat* and *GeoDa*. Also to be noted is that rising interest in issues pertaining to the space economy has not been confined to cross-regional productivity differences. Thus, for example, there has been increased interest amongst prominent economists in spatial disparities in unemployment rates (see, most notably, Blanchard and Katz, 1992).

2. Most notable in this context is Barro and Sala-i-Martin's (1991, 1992, 2004) work on convergence. This has spawned a mini-industry of research into cross-regional productivity differences predicated on a Solow-Swan-type framework.

3. For a more technical description of the use of DEA techniques to both calculate and decompose the Malmqüist TFP change index see Angeriz et al. (2006, pp. 503, 506–7). This more technical description also contains precise details of the linear programs used in this study.

4. This is a simplification. At the start of his article, Solow explicitly states that he is 'using the phrase "technical change" for any kind of shift in the production function. Thus slowdowns, speed-ups, improvements in the education of the labor force, and all sorts of things will appear as "technical change" ' (Solow, 1957, p. 2). However, by the end of the article, Solow has slipped into, what seems to be, an exclusive association of technical progress with innovation. Furthermore, there is no explicit attempt to separate technical inefficiency from technical progress, as with the Malmqüist index of TFP change.

5. These TE scores are amongst the output described and analysed in Sections 8.4 and 8.5 of the chapter.

6. For a slightly more detailed overview of Eurostat's NUTS classification see http://europa.eu.int/comm/eurostat/ramon/nuts/basicnuts_regions_en.html.

7. This finding that the South West was a best practice frontier in 1986 is probably attributable to the existence of high-tech manufacturing centred on the region's primary city of Bristol. The authors are grateful to Tony Thirlwall for pointing this out.

8. Strictly speaking, the distribution could not have been normal because the TE score is bounded from below by 0 and from above by 1. Nevertheless, a Wald test indicates that the hypothesis of normality of the distribution cannot be rejected for 1986.

9. Partly reflecting this is that, whereas in 1986, there were, according to the 1.5 interquartile ratio rule, no outliers in the distribution of TE scores, by 2002 this was not the case. In particular, by 2002, Noord-Nederland, Ireland and West-Nederland were all outliers because of their high TE scores. The Nisia Aigaiou and Kriti region was also an outlier in 2002 because of its low TE score.

10. Ignoring the error term, the estimated regression equation can be rearranged to give $\Delta TE_{i, 1986-2002} = 0.1321 - 0.5254.TE_{i, 1986}$. This implies that, on average, regions with a TE score in 1986 greater than 0.2514 experienced a decline in technical efficiency over the subsequent 16-year period. All regions within the sample fulfilled this condition and, as reported, only Ireland and Noord-Nederland escaped declines in their TE scores.

11. The opposite case, where unlike values tend to cluster, is referred to as negative spatial autocorrelation.

12. For this reason, Angeriz et al. (2006, pp. 511–15) combine their use of local Moran statistics with Moran scatterplot maps.

13. The geography of clustering was also investigated for the efficiency and technical change indices, despite the absence of significant spatial autocorrelation at the global level. These results are available from the authors upon request.

14. In the calculation of Getis-Ord G_i^* statistics, $j = i$ is included in the sum in the numerator of equation (8.3). This is in contrast to Getis-Ord G_i statistics, in which $j = i$ is not included. It seemed more sensible to use G_i^* rather than G_i statistics to investigate the localized nature of clustering because the former provide a measure of spatial clustering that includes the region under consideration, whilst the latter do not (see Anselin, 1992, p. 141).

15. Thus, not only were London and the South West regions of the United Kingdom helping to define the best practice frontier in 1986, but all other regions in England and Wales bar the East Midlands had 1986 TE scores in excess of 0.8 (see Angeriz et al., 2006, Table A2, pp. 522–3).

16. Given its status as a best practice region, it might seem surprising that the G_i^* statistic for Noord-Nederland was not also statistically significant for 1986. The explanation for this seems to be that Noord-Nederland is bordered on the east by the German region of Niedersachsen, which only had a 1986 TE score of 0.561, which was below the mean TE score shown in Table 8.3.
17. It could plausibly be argued that, in fact, the UK and Dutch-Belgian clusters should be viewed as a single cluster.

REFERENCES

Angeriz, A. and M. Pollitt (2005), 'Measuring the performance of Britain's privatised train operating companies', mimeo, Judge Business School, University of Cambridge.

Angeriz, A., J.S.L. McCombie and M. Roberts (2006), 'Productivity, efficiency and technological change in European Union regional manufacturing: a data envelopment analysis approach', *The Manchester School*, **74**: 500–525.

Anselin, L. (1992), *SpaceStat Tutorial: A Workbook for Using SpaceStat in the Analysis of Spatial Data*, University of Illinois.

Anselin, L. (1995a), *SpaceStat Version 1.80: User's Guide*, University of Illinois.

Anselin, L. (1995b), 'Local Indicators of Spatial Association – LISA', *Geographical Analysis*, **27**: 93–115.

Arestis, P., G. Chortareas and E. Desli (2005), 'Technical efficiency and financial deepening in the non-OECD economies', *International Review of Applied Economics*, **20**: 353–73.

Barro, R.J. and X. Sala-i-Martin (1991), 'Convergence across states and regions', *Brookings Papers on Economic Activity*, **1**: 107–82.

Barro, R.J. and X. Sala-i-Martin (1992), 'Convergence', *Journal of Political Economy*, **100**: 223–51.

Barro, R.J. and X. Sala-i-Martin (2004), *Economic Growth* (2nd edn), Cambridge, MA: MIT Press.

Blanchard, O. and L. Katz (1992), 'Regional evolutions', *Brookings Papers in Economic Activity*, **1**: 1–75.

Cantos, P., J.M. Pastor and L. Serrano (1999), 'Productivity, efficiency and technical change in the European railways: a non-parametric approach', *Transportation*, **26**: 337–57.

Cowie, J. (1999), 'The technical efficiency of public and private ownership in the rail industry. The case of Swiss private railways', *Journal of Transport Economics*, **33**: 241–52.

Debreu, G. (1951), 'The coefficient of resource utilization', *Econometrica*, **19**: 273–92.

Färe, R., S. Grosskopf, B. Lindgren and P. Roos (1989), 'Productivity developments in Swedish hospitals: a Malmqüist output index approach', *Discussion Paper 89-3*. Department of Economics Southern Illinois University, Carbondale.

Färe, R., S. Grosskopf, M. Morris and Z. Zhang (1994), 'Productivity growth, technical progress and efficiency in industrialized countries', *American Economic Review*, **84**: 66–82.

Farrell, M.J. (1957), 'The measurement of productive efficiency', *Journal of the Royal Statistical Society, Series A*, **CXX**: 253–90.

Fujita, M., P.R. Krugman and A.J. Venables (1999), *The Spatial Economy: Cities, Regions, and International Trade*, Cambridge, MA: MIT Press.

Hulten, C.R. and R.M. Schwab (1984), 'Regional productivity growth in US manufacturing: 1951–78', *American Economic Review*, **74**: 152–62.

Karadăg. M, A.O. Onder and E. Deliktas (2005), 'Growth of factor productivity in the Turkish manufacturing industry at provincial level', *Regional Studies*, **39**: 213–33.

McCombie, J.S.L. and A.P. Thirlwall (1994), *Economic Growth and the Balance-of-Payment Constraint*, London: Macmillan.

Rowthorn, R. (2000), 'Kalecki centenary lecture: the political economy of full employment in modern Britain', *Oxford Bulletin of Economics and Statistics*, **62**: 139–73.

Solow, R.M. (1957), 'Technical change and the aggregate production function', *Review of Economics and Statistics*, **39**: 312–20.

9. A methodology for evaluating regional political economy

Paul Plummer and Eric Sheppard

9.1 INTRODUCTION

> Econometricians conceptualize (the economic) system as a complex, non-linear, interdependent, multivariate, disequilibrium dynamical process dependent on agents' expectations and their adjustments, subject to random shocks, and involving many phenomena that are unobservable; relevant time-series data are inaccurate and exist for only short periods and for a few major variables; economic theories are highly simplified abstractions usually of a comparative statics form invoking many explicit ceteris paribus clauses (with yet others implicitly required), most of which are invalid in empirical applications – little wonder that our macroeconomic representations are less than perfect. David Hendry, (1980, p. 399) *Econometrics – Alchemy or Science*

Compared with the situation faced by economic geographers, econometricians get off lightly. We would add to the above list: problems of spatial interdependencies and spatial heterogeneity; theories that range across many more disciplines than economics and that cannot be reduced to agents' behaviour; the additional challenges of constructing spatio-temporal data sets; and a lack of disciplinary consensus on ontology, epistemology and methodology. In this chapter, we take up this challenge by investigating what it means to carry out spatial modelling in contemporary economic geography. Specifically, we focus on the challenges posed by the complexity of spatio-temporal dynamics for our understanding of the evolving economic landscape. We highlight the ways in which competing conceptions of the capitalist space economy handle this complexity in terms of both bridging the gap between theory and model (*analytical adequacy*) and in terms of bringing observation to bear on the explanation claims contained in those theories and models (*epistemological adequacy*).

Our starting point here is a commitment to a socio-spatial ontology that takes seriously the possibility that the geographical world constitutes a complex, non-linear system. Paradigmatically, complex systems are characterized by non-linear interdependencies between system elements that can result in persistent out-of-equilibrium dynamics. While the existence and local stability properties of equilibria are always an important component of spatio-temporal analysis, the possibility that a complex dynamical system spends much of its time out of equilibrium cannot be dismissed. While we recognize that the geographical world could be otherwise, we seek to explore what it means to do quantitative economic geography in a context where we cannot a priori dismiss the proposition that the geographical world is complex. Put otherwise, we are interested in exploring the potential of complexity-based modelling for representing the geographical world.

In this chapter, we propose mathematical and statistical tools to analyse complex spatial dynamic socioeconomic systems. This is lightly-trodden ground, in part because of the dualism that supposedly constitutes research at the intersection of geography and economics. Conventional wisdom divides this research into two separate fields, one grounded in the methodological prescriptions and theoretical suppositions of neoclassically-oriented new economic geography (NEG) and the other in the qualitative methodologies and social/cultural constructs of mainstream economic geography. Elsewhere, we have argued that this dualism, while shared by proponents on both sides, can be called into question (Plummer and Sheppard, 2001, 2005). Here, we suggest how rigorous quantitative analysis (usually associated with the former) can be utilized to analyse a conflict-ridden dynamic capitalist space economy, whose spatiality is an emergent feature of that economy – a socio-spatial dialectic.[1]

In the subsequent sections of the chapter we will argue that recognizing the presence of complexity and non-linearity poses major challenges for the pursuit of mathematical and statistical modelling in economic geography, laying out the principal challenges, as we see them (Section 9.2). Briefly, they stem from limitations in both spatial analytic methods, where quantitative empirical research is dominated by analyses of location patterns and flows and spatio-temporal analysis is restricted to examining deviations around putative spatial equilibria (cf. Bennett, 1979; Haining, 1990; Elhorst, 2001), and in quantitative economic geography, which has come to be dominated by a 'new' economic geography with a similar predilection for equilibrium analysis. In Section 9.3, we propose a strategy for determining the analytical adequacy of theories of political economy, illustrated with an example from our own research in regional political economy (the Plummer-Goodwin model), suggesting that this approach has more general applicability to theories of complex spatial dynamics.

As yet, our methodological tools for evaluating the empirical adequacy of theories postulating such spatial dynamics are underdeveloped, but progress is possible. In Section 9.4 we sketch out a broad framework that seems to us a possible way to move forward, albeit at the expense of rethinking our preconceptions about what constitutes spatial analysis. We propose a methodology that extends recent advances in 'qualitative' and time-series econometrics, applying mathematical theories of symbolic and coding dynamics to the spatio-temporal context (Brock, 2001; Day and Pavlov, 2001; Brida and Punzo, 2003). Whilst there has been some exploration of the complex dynamical behaviour of non-linear out-of-equilibrium spatial economies (Plummer, 1996; Plummer, 1999; Jackson and Sonis, 2001), to date none of this has sought to exploit the potential of the coded dynamics approach for offering insight into the general structure of spatial economic dynamics. In the concluding section we conjecture about the possibilities and limitations of our chosen methodology for understanding the evolution of the capitalist space economy. In the spirit of seeking to transcend the gulf currently separating geographical economics from economic geography, we discuss the philosophical implications of this rethinking. In particular, we focus on the potential of both Bayesian and computation modelling strategies for engagement with issues of both analytical and empirical adequacy in understanding the dynamics of the capitalist space economy.

9.2 CONTRASTING ONTOLOGIES: THE CHALLENGE OF COMPLEXITY

Competing visions of the capitalist space economy inevitably deploy different socio-spatial ontologies, which inform what aspects of geographical reality call for explanation and what counts as an adequate account of that reality. The ontological commitment associated with a particular vision in turn entails practical methodological questions regarding the sets of norms and suppositions that determine both *analytical adequacy* and *epistemological adequacy*, within that ontology. We compare and contrast two such visions here – visions that share a predilection for mathematical and statistical reasoning but in other ways are quite different. The 'new' economic geography, grounded in Dixit-Stiglitz models of Chamberlinian monopolistic competition, currently dominates mathematical and statistical modelling at the intersection of geography and economics. Yet this is certainly not the only way in which mathematical and statistical reasoning can be employed to construct explanations of the evolving economic landscape. We contrast it with what we have elsewhere dubbed regional political economy (Sheppard, Plummer and Haining, 1998; Sheppard, 2000; Plummer, 2003).

The 'new' economic geography departs significantly from traditional neo-classical models in the assumptions that it makes regarding the ways in which capitalist economies should be understood. Conventional assumptions regarding the nature of competitive markets, exhibiting constant returns to scale, are replaced with assumptions specifying increasing returns and Chamberlinian competition. Space is taken seriously, generally characterized, in the tradition of classical location theory, as an undifferentiated (homogeneous) space within which a set of discrete entities are equally spaced on a line, circle, infinite plane or torus. This abstracts from differences in relative location. Spatial separation is modelled as an exogenous 'distance friction' parameter, usually in the tradition of Samuelson's 'iceberg' formulation (but see Ottaviano, Tabuchi and Thisse, 2002; Behrens et al., 2003).

Notwithstanding such differences in specification, principles of analytical adequacy align with those of neoclassical economics. Analytical adequacy requires that spatial patterns must be derivable from the actions of fully informed, rational individual or representative agents maximizing their economic self-interest, given spatial structures, production technologies and Dixit-Stiglitz preferences (microfoundations). These patterns must also constitute a general economic equilibrium, in which markets clear, free entry drives profits to zero (net of fixed costs), intended consequences are realized, and no agent has an incentive to destabilize the equilibrium (Nash equilibrium). Finally, general analytical solutions must be derivable – a requirement motivating what are otherwise conceded to be highly unrealistic simplifying assumptions. Given these principles of analytical adequacy, NEG models generate results that challenge some conventional neoclassical principles. In particular, it is concluded that multiple, at least locally stable, spatial equilibria are possible; that the nature and multiplicity of these equilibrium landscapes depend on key parameters; and that there is 'path dependence' in the limited sense that the equilibrium selected depends on past history and exogenous shocks.[2] The simplified treatment of space and the methodological individualism of a 'microfoundations' approach reduce the number of equilibria. Finally, conventional welfare analysis reveals that derived general equilibrium solutions are not optimal in the sense that they maximize social welfare (Ottaviano and Thisse, 2004), raising questions about the social benefits of unrestrained spatial competition (a debate initiated by Lösch, 1954 [1940]).

Within this paradigm, epistemological adequacy reduces to testing predicted equilibrium patterns against observations. The 'new' economic geography has focused largely on theoretical frameworks whose highly simplified geographies and microfoundations make them difficult to directly test empirically (Neary, 2001). As a consequence, as elsewhere in mainstream economics, epistemological adequacy has fallen back on assessing the abilities of these models to account for a set of stylized facts about spatial configurations of specialization and trade, agglomeration and regional economic growth. (In geography, by contrast, aware since the 1970s of the 'pattern-process problem' – that many processes can generate the same spatial pattern – there is much scepticism about the reliability and discriminatory power of such stylized facts as the rank-size rule.) With respect to regional economic growth, economic geography has undertaken a series of econometric studies, seeking to account for observed trajectories and persistent inequalities in terms of macroeconomic theoretical models that are consistent with the economic geography worldview (Barro and Sala-i-Martin, 1992; Fingleton, 2003; Martin and Sunley, 1998; Rice and Venables, 2003). Such models are augmented by conditioning variables describing regional characteristics, and more recently by including a measure describing the productivity gap relative to the most productive region, and inter-regional spillover effects (Plummer and Taylor, 2001a, 2001b; Fingleton, 2003). Spillover effects are a vital addition to avoid the common but highly problematic assumption that regional economies are independent of one another. The principal focus remains on movement with respect to equilibrium, however: an equilibrium trajectory defining a fixed pattern of spatial differentiation.[3]

Regional political economy shares a quite different socio-spatial ontology, with the ecumenical family of political economy approaches popular among economic geographers (cf. Clark, Gertler and Feldman, 2000; Sheppard and Barnes, 2000). Here, economic landscapes do not derive solely from individual behaviour. Different classes of economic actors have conflicting interests (workers' wages; capitalists' profits and landholders' rents). These are not resolved into harmonious stable equilibria through competition, because some classes have more power to realize their goals, at the expense of others. As a consequence, individual actions are guided by both (emergent) socioeconomic structures and individual agency. Prices are not determined by marginal utility and productivity, as they depend in part on the ability of different collectivities of actors to control a share of the economic surplus (Sraffa, 1960; Roemer, 1981). Equilibria exist, but are likely to be unstable because representatives of any class can improve their share of the net surplus, at the expense of others, through collective action. Capitalism, then, is neither self-regulating nor harmonious, and cannot maximize social welfare.

Space is incorporated into this framework through the ontology of a socio-spatial dialectic (Soja, 1980; Sheppard, 2006). In this view, space – the relationships defining how well places are connected to one another – is an emergent feature of society, which has its own distinct impacts on trajectories of socioeconomic change. On the one hand, space is produced: the distance between places is not given exogenously, by Euclidean distances and exogenous freight rates, but co-evolves with the economic system. Transportation and communications technologies and infrastructures change as a result of the profit-maximizing efforts of the industries producing accessibility (as well as the actions of its workers and state institutions), thereby altering space. Space, then, is conceptualized as an emergent Einsteinian and Leibnitzian relational space, rather than an exogenous, Newtonian grid. The spatial configurations that do emerge, in turn shape capitalism's spatio-temporal trajectories. It has been shown that the socio-spatial dialectic profoundly complicates capitalism, as it becomes even harder for agents to foresee the longer-term and collective consequences of their individual actions. Unintended consequences, whereby actions set in train a sequence of events with the opposite net effect to that intended (for example, actions taken to increase individual profits eventually result in lower average profit rates), become the norm rather than the exception (Harvey, 1982; Sheppard, 1990).

Faced with these complexities, the vast majority of scholarship in economic geography has turned to non-mathematical (dialectical or qualitative case study) strategies of theory and empirical analysis, finding mathematical and statistical tools too limiting for analysing such situations. Influential here has been critical realism, which argues that the multiplicity of outcomes generated by a general process in distinct spatial contexts requires 'intensive' case study analysis rather than 'extensive' statistical analysis (Sayer, 1984). Recent developments under the general rubric of complexity suggest otherwise, however (Sheppard, 1996). Indeed, it can be argued that mathematical complexity theory and dialectical analysis are closely related. Rosser (2000) and King (2001) have noted connections between complexity modelling and dialectics, but David Harvey's description of dialectics provides a more comprehensive starting point.

Harvey (1996, Ch. 3) notes that relational dialectics emphasizes the understanding of relations over the analysis of things; analyses things as heterogeneous and internally contradictory; conceptualizes space and time as contingent and contained within processes; emphasizes transformative behaviour (qualitative change); and entails the interdigitation of parts and wholes and the interchangeability of subject and object, cause and effect. Complexity theory has all these characteristics (Prigogine, 1996), opening up the possibility that mathematical and statistical tools can be applied that are consistent with a dialectical socio-spatial ontology. To do so, however, requires adopting different principles of analytical and epistemological adequacy to those of economic geography, including computation-intensive simulations and post-positivist empirical analysis.[4] It is also desirable to develop principles of epistemological adequacy that make possible comparative assessment of theoretical models from geographical economics and regional political economy, if conversations are to occur across the divide constructed as separating these approaches. The next two sections explore these challenges, in turn.

9.3   MODELLING THE CAPITALIST SPACE ECONOMY

Early research in regional political economy confirmed the intuition of Marxist theories of uneven development, that the social and spatial con- tradictions of a capitalist space economy create a perpetual disequilibrium dynamic (Harvey, 1982). While it has been possible to model the processes underlying this instability (Sheppard and Barnes, 1990; Webber and Rigby, 1999), empirical application of these theories has been plagued by a lack of detailed spatio-temporal data. In some cases, this has been tempered by detailed case study analysis and use of confidential census data (Scott, 1996; Rigby and Essletzbichler, 2003), but evaluating a key proposition of regional political economy, that regional economic dynamics are shaped by evolving inter-regional multi-sectoral input-output relationships, has foundered on the lack of fine resolution temporal and spatial input-output data. We therefore consider an aggregate theory of regional economic dynamics with modest data requirements; the multi-regional extension of Richard Goodwin's (1967) theoretical model of economic cycles developed in Plummer (1999) – henceforth the Plummer-Goodwin model. This model is one way of coping with inter-regional economic dynamics within the regional political economy approach, with the merit of relative simplicity obtained at the cost of suppressing the complexity of more disaggregate inter-sectoral and inter-firm competitive accumulation dynamics (cf. Sheppard, 1983; Sheppard, 1990; Sheppard, Haining and Plummer, 1992; Plummer, 1996a; Plummer, 1996b).

There are sound theoretical and methodological considerations for choosing this model as representative of a regional political economy approach, because it conforms to a socio-spatial ontology that conceptualizes the economy as a structurally complex evolving dynamical system. Indeed, Punzo and Velupillai (1996) and Velupillai (1998a) identify the Goodwin model as the core of the Goodwin code; a mathematical modelling methodology characterized by three norms. First, models should be formulated using the mathematics of non-linear systems and, subsequently, analysed in terms of their global behaviour. Paradigmatically, Goodwin formulated models that utilized the mathematical theory of non-linear oscillators. Typically, such oscillators are locally unstable but globally stable, endogenously generating irregular propagating macroeconomic growth and fluctuations. Second, economic structures should be conceptualized in terms of the interactions between the components constituting such systems, a key insight that is consistent with regional political economy. For a given structure of sectoral interdependencies, it is possible to define either (cross-) dual price-quantity or wage-employment out-of-equilibrium adjustment mechanisms, whose analytical properties have been extensively studied by classical and post-Keynesian political economists, for non-spatial systems (Dumenil and Levy, 1987; Goodwin and Punzo, 1987; Flaschel and Semmler, 1988). Third, the integrating concept between the global behaviour of non-linear dynamic systems and multisectoral economic structures are the assumptions made about the behaviour of either individual economic agents or whole economic systems. In contrast with the rationality assumption underpinning the 'new' economic geography, decision-making in a Goodwin-type model is conceptualized in terms of out-of-equilibrium problem-solving. Typically, this is modelled as a computational algorithm representing a disequilibrium adjustment process 'groping' towards an equilibrium (Velupillai, 1998b).

9.3.1   The Plummer-Goodwin Model

The original Goodwin model examines the long-term accumulation dynamics of a capitalist economy, in the spirit of Marx, by tracing the logic of the cyclical dynamics of employment and income distribution and the long-run growth trend. Its essential feature is that endogenously generated fluctuations are driven by conflict between workers and capitalists over the distribution of the economic surplus generated in production. Plummer (1999) extends the logic of this model to incorporate a classical/Marxian investment hypothesis, in which inter-regional movements of capital occur in response to profit rate differentials and imperfectly grounded expectations that constrain the ability of capitalists to implement their investment plans. He also supplements Goodwin's 'reserve army' competitive wage bargain hypothesis with a non-competitive 'Fordist' wage bargaining hypothesis. A characteristic feature of the Plummer-Goodwin model is that individual regions are geographically embedded, in the sense that the outcome in any one region depends on the nature and degree of competition between all regions. This occurs directly, through inter-regional investment flows, and indirectly, via the wage bargaining hypothesis in each region and its impact on the distribution of income in that region.

Formally, the Plummer-Goodwin model is a system consisting of the complex interdependencies between regional capital accumulation (*regional accumulation dynamics*), the functional distribution of income (*regional distributional dynamics*), and regional labour market dynamics (*regional employment dynamics*). Defining U_{it} as labour's share of region i's economic surplus $U = [U_1, \ldots, U_i, \ldots, U_n]$, e_{it} as the regional employment rate, $e = [e_1, \ldots, e_i, \ldots, e_n]$, and q_{it} as the share of total capital in each region, $q = [q_1, \ldots, q_i, \ldots, q_n]$, the laws of motion for N interdependent regional economies can be represented by three sets of interrelated reduced-form non-linear equations (for derivation of these equations see Plummer, 1999):

Regional accumulation dynamics:

$$\frac{\dot{q}_{it}}{q_{it}} = \beta_1 \left(\sum_{j=1}^{N} q_{jt} U_{jt} - U_{it} \right). \tag{9.1}$$

Regional distributional dynamics:

$$\frac{\dot{U}_{it}}{U_{it}} = \beta_{2i}(e_{it} - e^*) + \beta_{3i}(U^* - U_{it}). \tag{9.2}$$

Regional employment dynamics:

$$\frac{\dot{e}_{it}}{e_{it}} = (U^* - U_{it}) + \beta_1 \left(\sum_{j=1}^{N} q_{jt} U_{jt} - U_{it} \right). \tag{9.3}$$

By hypothesis, regional accumulation dynamics are characterized by capitalist investment behaviour, whereby regions of above-average profitability will attract additional investment, as capitalists move to disinvest from regions with below-average profitability. Here, regional profitability is assumed to be inversely proportional to labour's share of each region's economic surplus (U). Formally, changes in the proportion of total capital stock invested in region i, time t (q_{it}) depend on differences between the profitability in that region, and average economywide profitability. Capitalists' responsiveness to profit rate differentials depends on a measure of the information available to them about investment opportunities in each region (β_1), which translates into a speed of adjustment parameter in the equation of regional employment dynamics.

Regional distributional dynamics describe how labour's share of a region's economic surplus, U_{it}, depends on the mix of wage bargaining hypotheses in that region. First, competitive wage bargaining is modelled through the impact of the regional employment rate (e_{it}) on the distribution of income, whereby tighter labour markets increase labour's power in the wage bargaining process. If the current employment rate in a region (e_{it})

is higher (lower) than the equilibrium employment rate in that region (e_i^*), then regional labour share rises (falls). The equilibrium employment rate is determined exogenously, by the rate of technological change and the rate of growth of the regional labour supply, and β_{2i} (> 0) is a parameter representing the responsiveness of labour share to employment differentials. Second, under Fordist non-competitive wage bargaining, a compromise between capital and labour allows labour to retain some productivity gains generated in production (U_{it}). If the current regional labour share (U_{it}) is greater (less) than the equilibrium labour share (U_i^*) then regional labour share falls, where equilibrium labour share is given by the regional rate of growth in productivity and the rate of growth in the regional supply of labour. The rate of adjustment of regional labour share towards equilibrium, β_{3i}, (> 0) depends on the nature and degree of compromise between labour and capital over the distribution of the net surplus generated in production.

Finally, regional employment dynamics depend on the difference between the regional supply of and demand for labour. In the reduced form, labour supply is modelled simply as an exogenous growth trend in each region. Labour demand depends on output growth and labour productivity; regional output growth depends on regional capital accumulation, and hence on relative regional profitability. Regions of above-average profitability will attract additional investment, as capitalists move to disinvest from regions with below-average profitability, where β_1 (> 0) is the responsiveness of investment to profit rate differentials.

These equations of motion describe the out-of-equilibrium adjustment mechanisms that produce a set of expected space-time trajectories in the Plummer-Goodwin model. Mathematically, the global behaviour of the interacting parts of such an equation system corresponds to the iterative steps of an algorithmic procedure that computes a solution to the system of interdependent equations. Assuming that such a dynamic system converges to a fixed point, this solution describes the properties of the expected spatial configuration of employment, income distribution and capital accumulation, and the flow of investment between regional economies. The analytical relevance of such an equilibrium solution depends on the likelihood that the system will be found at such a fixed point, or equivalently whether the algorithmic procedure can reach an equilibrium solution from an out-of-equilibrium position.

For the Plummer-Goodwin model, it was only possible to establish analytical conditions, on the existence and stability of a dynamic equilibrium growth path, for essentially independent regional economies. This is equivalent to the original Goodwin cycle model, with the significant caveat that the model is structurally unstable in the sense that the qualitative behaviour out-of equilibrium depends on how wage bargaining relationship is modelled. Competitive wage bargaining produces Goodwin cycles whilst non-competitive wage bargaining produces dampened oscillations driving the system towards a spatial equilibrium configuration of employment, income distribution and capital accumulation. In the more general case of regionally interdependent economics, little can be said about the analytical properties of these laws of motion, beyond the observation that adding inter-regional interdependence to Goodwin significantly complicates the possible dynamic scenarios (that is, space matters). Preliminary exploration using numerical experimentation for simple regionally interdependent systems suggested the possibility of complex and persistent out-of-equilibrium dynamics that transcend the structurally unstable oscillations characteristic of the simple Goodwin model. Figure 9.1 (Plummer, 1999, Fig. 4) illustrates this for two representative regions of a multi-region economy. In this relatively simple case, region 1 is characterized by non-competitive wage bargaining with competitive wage bargaining elsewhere. In this instance, the presence of a region with non-competitive wage bargaining is sufficient to ensure that the dynamics of employment and distribution in some of the regions do not converge to either a steady-state equilibrium growth path or a Goodwin cycle. Rather, the multiple region model appears to display the types of non-repeatable dynamics that are characteristic of complex and chaotic dynamic systems.

9.4   TOWARD EMPIRICAL ADEQUACY

The potential path-dependent nature of complex dynamical systems, and the considerable sensitivity of their spatio-temporal trajectories to parameter values and external shocks create significant problems for analysis and validation. An observed sequence of maps of output, employment and labour share may be the result of any one of many possible dynamic scenarios, generated by some unknown model with unknown parameter values. We don't know which theory generated the observed outcome, what the parameters of the theory are, or which of the possibly infinite number of scenarios consistent with a proposed theory and set of parameter values we are observing. (Even a known non-linear dynamic model, such as the Plummer-Goodwin model, with known parameters, can generate a large variety of potential spatial dynamic trajectories, or map sequences.) It is thus virtually impossible to infer from observations to theory under these circumstances, a corollary of the 'pattern-process problem' in spatial analysis, even if we are willing to ignore the problem of theory-laden data.

Region 1

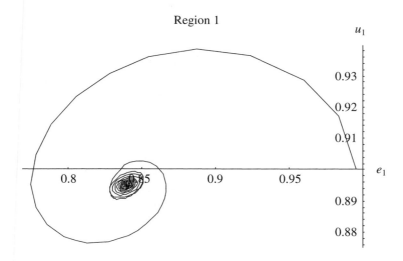

Region 2

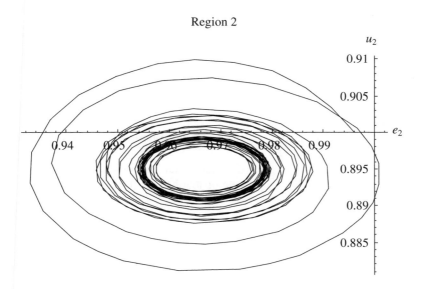

Notes:
u_1, u_2 = Regional labour share in net income.
e_1, e_2 = Regional employment rate.

Figure 9.1   Inter-regional dynamics

Analysis must begin, therefore, with a prior belief or worldview – a theory that we have some prior belief in. We distinguish the following:

1. Theory: Our prior belief/worldview about how the world works.
2. A theoretical model (T): A mathematical representation of the system of interest, constructed in light of (1). This is an abstract object that is capable of conceptual manipulation, such as theorem-proof and computational experiments.
3. Expected model outcomes: A set, E, containing the (potentially infinite number of) expected outcomes, each of which can be represented as a time-series of maps generated by the theoretical model, under particular parameters (including initial conditions).
4. Observed outcome (O): a time-series of maps derived from observations of the world.

We adopt a Bayesian strategy for examining the relationship between these four elements, to incorporate the subjective starting point of our prior belief in, say, the Plummer-Goodwin model. Neglecting the set of expected outcomes, Bayes's rule states:

$$P(T_i|O) = \frac{P(O|T_i)P(T_i)}{P(O)} \qquad (9.4)$$

where:

$P(T_i|O)$ = the posterior probability that the theory i is true, given the observed outcome;
$P(O|T_i)$ = the likelihood of the observed outcome, given the truth of the theory;
$P(T_i)$ = our prior degree of belief in our theoretical model;
$P(O)$ = $\Sigma_j P(O|T_j)P(T_j)$ is the probability of the observed outcome.

T_i is theory i from the set of all possible theories. If E is the set of expected outcomes generated by T_i, then:

$$P(O|T_i) = \sum_{k \in E} P(O|E_k)P(E_k|T_i) \qquad (9.5)$$

where:

$P(O|E_k)$ = the likelihood of the observed trajectory, given expected trajectory k;
$P(E_k|T_i)$ = the likelihood of expected trajectory k, given theory i.

9.4.1 Computing a Manageable Set of Expected Outcomes

For complex dynamical theoretical models, the enormous variety of particular expected trajectories precludes calculation of (9.5) unless the set E can be simplified. Recent work by Lionello Punzo and associates, drawing on Richard Day (1995), suggests a strategy for greatly reducing E, drawing on the mathematics of symbolic dynamics (cf. Brida, Anyul and Punzo, 2003). Day notes that the evolution of any dynamical model can be represented as a trajectory in its phase space (the space containing all possible values of the variables of the theoretical model). Figure 9.2 illustrates this

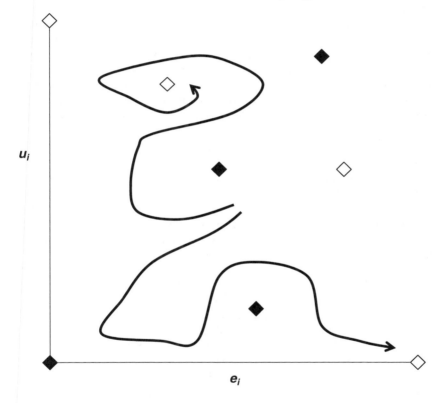

Notes:
U_i = Labour share in region i.
e_i = Employment rate in region i.
→ = Trajectory in U_i, e_i state space.
◊ = Stable equilibrium.
◆ = Unstable equilibrium.

Figure 9.2   Complex phase space dynamics

idea, for a theoretical model that has been simplified to a single region with two variables, each bounded between one and zero. For a given set of initial conditions and set of parameter values, the laws of motion modelling these variables describe the complex dynamics occurring within that state space. The phase space is complex as the system evolves with respect to many stable and unstable equilibria. The figure illustrates how complex dynamics can generate very different trajectories from a similar starting point.

Under quite general conditions, this phase space can be subdivided into a series of subspaces, or regimes, 'within each of which dynamical behavior is distinct, for example, monotonic growth, monotonic decline, cycles, or erratic behavior' (Day, 1995, p. 26). If the dynamic model is linear and univariate, then the entire phase space consists of a single regime oriented around the sole equilibrium point (which is why a Taylor's expansion is sufficient to determine global behaviour in this case [Gandolfo, 1995]). Of course, if the equilibrium is unstable the dynamical system may leave the phase space altogether, as the variable becomes negative and thus meaningless (in Day's terminology the system enters the null regime and collapses). While multivariate linear models may have more than one dynamical regime, transitions from one to another are impossible in the absence of exogenous changes in parameter values and/or initial conditions (Table 9.1).

Non-linear dynamic models generally possess a variety of dynamical regimes, or 'local models', however, and furthermore it is possible for the trajectory of the dynamical model to move between regimes even in the absence of external disruptions. The state space, X, of the Plummer-Goodwin model (a $3N$-dimensional space containing all possible values of the vector of variables defined by the laws of motion in equations

Table 9.1   Regime dynamics for different kinds of dynamical systems (adapted from Brida and Punzo, 2003)

Model	How Many Regimes Can Exist Within the Phase Space?[5]	Do Regime(s) Depend on Initial Conditions?	Do Regimes Depend on System Parameters?	Is Transition Between Regimes Possible?
Linear, univariate	One	No[6]	Yes[7]	N/A
Linear multivariate	Many	Yes[8]	Yes	No
Piecewise linear[9]	Many	Yes	Yes	Yes[10]
Fully non-linear[11]	Many	Yes	Yes	Yes

[9.1]–[9.3]), can thus be partitioned in principle into a series of subspaces, each of which exhibits a distinctive dynamic trajectory. An intuitive sub-division, is to partition the state space into its various domains of attrac-tion, within which dynamical trajectories move with respect to some equilibrium, null regime (such as negative investment), or limit cycle.

The dynamical regime characterizing a subspace of X is defined as the pair (φ_k, X_k), $k = 1, \ldots, K$, where φ_k is the dynamical law for this subspace and X_k is the partition of X within which this law applies. Figure 9.3 visu-alizes a possible partition into three dynamical regimes, for the dynamical trajectories depicted in Figure 9.2.

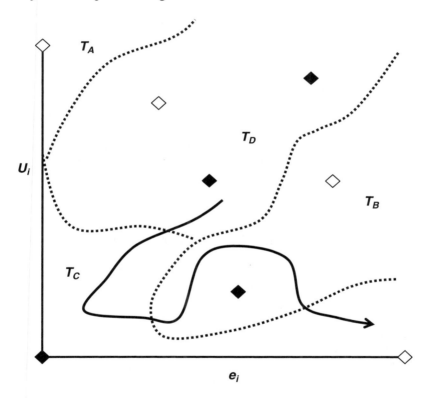

Notes:
U_i = Labour share in region i.
e_i = Employment rate in region i.
→ = Trajectory in U_i, e_i state space.
◊ = Stable equilibrium.
◆ = Unstable equilibrium.

Figure 9.3   Coding and symbolic dynamics

The dynamic trajectories of complex geographical systems can be characterized, therefore, at two levels of aggregation, the intra- and inter-regime scales. Within each subspace given by (φ_k, X_k), a particular dynamical regime or 'local model' operates, describing the short-term behaviour of the system within this part of its state space. In the longer term, however, transitions from one local dynamical regime to another are possible. The dynamics of the system can be described at either level of aggregation. For example, cycles or oscillations may characterize the dynamics of a local model, but may also characterize a system's inter-regime dynamics, if it shifts from dynamical regime A to regime B and back again.

Brida et al. (2003) show that a univariate piecewise linear business cycle model of the Hicks type (Table 9.1, row 4) is partitioned into three dynamical regimes, A, B and C, and derive the possible transitions between regimes. Transitions can be represented as a binary transition matrix where zeros represent mathematically impossible transitions. For example, if there are three dynamical regimes, A, B and C, and the transition matrix is the identity matrix, then transition between regimes is impossible (for example, the system is multivariate linear; Table 9.1, row 2): a system stays in its initial state. If inter-regime dynamics are coded as a temporal lexicographic sequence of dynamical regimes characterizing the evolution of the system, the only possibilities are AAAA . . . , BBBB . . . or CCC . . . . If the transition matrix is like Figure 9.4a, however, its inter-regime dynamics will follow a regular cycle described by the following sequence: ABCAB-CABC . . . . If the matrix is all ones (Figure 9.4b), every possible sequential permutation of the three letters, A, B, C is possible.

Such a transition matrix describes the possible sequences of dynamical regimes that the non-linear system may move between, termed coded dynamics. Brida et al. (2003) note three difficulties with this approach, and Day adds a fourth. First, defining regimes is far from straightforward. Mathematical schemes based on symbolic dynamics may not match well with a partitioning that is consistent with the theoretical model used by an analyst. In addition, the number and location of local models in the state space, and the nature of the dynamical laws governing each one, will depend on, and be altered by perturbations in, external conditions (parameter values and initial conditions). Second, deriving the transition matrix

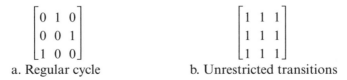

$$\begin{bmatrix} 0 & 1 & 0 \\ 0 & 0 & 1 \\ 1 & 0 & 0 \end{bmatrix} \qquad \begin{bmatrix} 1 & 1 & 1 \\ 1 & 1 & 1 \\ 1 & 1 & 1 \end{bmatrix}$$

a. Regular cycle   b. Unrestricted transitions

Figure 9.4   Transition matrices for a three-regime coded dynamic system

can be difficult even for low-dimensional dynamical systems. They note that the full potential of this approach will come in analysing high-dimensional non-linear systems, in which intra-regime dynamics are also non-linear, but such systems have not yet been examined to determine whether this speculation is correct. Third, it may not be possible to infer which theoretical model underlies an observed or simulated coded sequence of dynamic regimes: one coding sequence may be consistent with many models. Fourth, Day points out that even when an off-diagonal element in the transition matrix, say t_{AB}, is non-zero, it does not follow that B can be reached from anywhere in A. He notes that there may well be subspaces of regime A from which this transition is impossible. Thus a 'one' in the transition matrix describes only a possibility, of unknown likelihood. Day argues that determining whether an actual transition would occur requires a complex recursive analysis, as it depends not only on the current state but the preceding sequence (Day, 1995, Section 3.3).

9.4.2   Computing a Log-odds Measure of Empirical Adequacy

Use of symbolic dynamics to reduce E to a much smaller number of permissible lexicographic sequences of dynamical regimes for theoretical model i, simplifies (9.5) to:

$$P(O|T_i) = \sum_{k=1}^{K} P(O|E_k)P(E_k|T_i) \qquad (9.6)$$

where K is much smaller than E.

Substituting equation (9.6) into equation (9.4), empirical support for a theoretical model depends on the likelihood of the observed outcome, given the set of expected outcomes that are generated by the theoretical model:

$$P(T_i|O) = \frac{\sum_{k=1}^{K} P(O|E_{ik})P(E_{ik}|T_i)P(T_i)}{\sum_{j}\sum_{k_j=1}^{K_j} P(O|E_{jk_j})P(E_{jk_j}|T_j)P(T_j)} \qquad (9.7)$$

where the set K may differ for each theory j. Complete calculation of the posterior probability depends on prior knowledge of the set, J, of all possible theories. This cannot be not known, however, so a pragmatic strategy is to compare two theories we do know. For two theories, i and j, the denominator of (9.7) would be identical. It is thus possible to calculate the relative plausibility of two competing theories by taking the ratio of (9.7) as computed for each theory – comparing their relative likelihoods conditional on our prior belief in each. Theory i is then preferred to theory j if:

$$\frac{P(O|T_i)}{P(O|T_j)} = \frac{\sum_{k=1}^{K} P(O|E_{ik})P(E_{ik}|T_i)P(T_i)}{\sum_{k=1}^{K_j} P(O|E_{jk_j})P(E_{jk_j}|T_j)P(T_j)} > 1 \qquad (9.8)$$

Re-expressing and re-arranging, our preference for theory i over theory j (C_{ij}) depends on the log-likelihood ratio between the two theories and the prior belief in theory i, relative to theory j. Theory i is then preferred to theory j if:

$$C_{ij} = \ln\left(\frac{\sum_{k=1}^{K} P(O|E_k)P(E_k|T_i)}{\sum_{k=1}^{K_j} P(O|E_{k_j})P(E_{kj}|T_j)}\right) > \ln\left(\frac{P(T_j)}{P(T_i)}\right) \qquad (9.9)$$

where the left-hand side of (9.9) is the relative log-likelihood and the right-hand side is the relative belief in each theory. We prefer theory i over theory j ($C_{ij} > 1$) if the evidence in favour of theory i relative to theory j is greater than prior belief in theory j relative to theory i.

Summarizing, a Bayesian perspective allows us to incorporate the influence of subjectively held prior beliefs into determining empirical adequacy, releasing spatial analysis from an empiricist dependence on (theory-laden) observations. Pragmatism then suggests a strategy of comparing two known theories (for example, from geographical economics and regional political economy, respectively) because empirical adequacy cannot be determined for one theory in isolation.

9.4.3   Operationalization: Determining the Posterior Probability

In order to use this coding scheme to calculate the relative likelihood of two theoretical models (equation [9.9]), it is necessary to characterize the set of regimes, K, the possible transitions between regimes, t_{AB}, the likelihood of each transition and the likelihood of the observed sequence, O, given T and E. Empirical estimates will not generally exist for all system parameters, and dynamical trajectories may be highly sensitive to small errors in these estimates. In addition, the structure and transition possibilities for the state space may also depend on system parameters. This means that the steps involved in coding the dynamics of a state space for each theoretical model must be repeated for a range of plausible values of each system parameter. Based upon the tools of coding dynamics, we propose the following algorithm to compare the expected spatio-temporal trajectories, generated through numerical experimentation on each theoretical model, with an observed trajectory (for example, for the UK regional economy).

9.4.3.1   Stage one: calculating a grid of possible system parameters

Begin with S^m, a vector of the system parameters of the theoretical model under investigation, in which the j-th parameter takes on a value in the range: $(s_{min,j}, s_{min,j} + \delta_j, s_{min,j} + 2\delta_j \ldots < s_j < \ldots s_{max,j})$. Here s_j is the best empirical estimate of parameter j, for example, for the United Kingdom, $s_{min,j}$ and $s_{max,j}$ are plausible upper and lower bounds (narrower for estimated than for unknown parameters), and δ_j is the search grid increment. For the Plummer-Goodwin model, the vector of system parameters consists of adjustment parameters reflecting the responsiveness of capital accumulation to profit differentials and labour market responsiveness, and exogenous regional growth trends in labour supply and labour productivity.

9.4.3.2   Stage two: partitioning the state space into regimes

For S^m, determine the partitioning of the state space into local regimes (φ_k^m, X_k^m). Two approaches are possible:

1. Analytical derivation: Determine the location of all equilibria and limit cycles, and the boundaries of their domains of attraction and repulsion. Analytical derivation is possible using both topological tools generalized from conventional stability and bifurcation in non-linear systems and a new set of measure theoretic tools including Lyapunov exponents, fractal dimensions and entropies (Lorenz, 1989; Medio, 2001).
2. Computation: Overlay a fine grid of points spanning the state space. Initiate system dynamics from each grid point. The set of trajectories thus generated can be aggregated to compute a mapping of non-overlapping zones characterized by identical laws governing local dynamic behaviour.

9.4.3.3   Stage three: calculating the transition matrix

For S^m, determine the transition matrix, T^m, defining which transitions between local regimes are possible. Again, analytical and computational approaches are possible. It would be best to determine not only whether a transition is possible, but also its likelihood. This would result in a non-binary matrix T^m, for which entry $t_{A,B}^m$ is the probability of a transition from regime A to regime B. For example, the smaller the measure of A in the state space, the larger the boundary between A and B, and the larger the sub-region of A from which a transition to B is possible (dubbed by Day the unstable set in regime A), increasing the probability that $t_{A,B}^m \cdot T^m$ is a probabilistic transition matrix, whose rows sum to one. If the probability of a transition is independent of its history, then T^m is a static Markov transition matrix, but Day's difficulty, noted above, suggests that $t_{A,B}^m$ may depend on the previous trajectory and thus vary over time. For example, if it is the case that entering A from regime C brings the system into a subset of A from which B cannot be reached, whereas entering A from B brings the system into the pertinent unstable subset of A, then:

$$\Pr(A \to B|t) = t_{A,B,t}^m = \begin{array}{l} 0:B \to A_t \\ t_{A,B}^m:C \to A_t \end{array} \tag{9.10}$$

where the notation $B \to A_t$ means that the system reached regime A at time t via regime B.

A computational approach to estimating T^m would involve:

1. estimating the location of any unstable sets within each unstable regime, as a part of computationally simulating the regime structure under step two above;
2. computing system dynamics from a spatially stratified random sample of starting points in the state space, including all regimes and their subsets, to estimate the probability of transitions between regimes/subsets, and their conditional dependence on the system's previous history;
3. aggregating the results for regime subsets into regimes, to estimate $t_{A,B,t}^m$.

9.4.3.4   Stage four: computing the probability of observing *O*

For S^m, calculate the probability that O will occur, given T^m. This involves comparing the observed trajectory between dynamic regimes to the set of expected trajectories that begin at or near the initial condition given by the initial state of the observed trajectory, with the same duration as the observed trajectory (τ time periods).

Because dynamic trajectories are potentially very sensitive to small changes in initial conditions, it is not sufficient to consider only the precise starting point described by the data. Thus the following steps are necessary:

1. Beginning with the observed initial state and the transition matrix T^m, compute:
   a. the set of possible lexicographic sequences of regimes over τ time periods and their relative likelihoods;
   b. the set of possible regimes that the system may be in after $1, 2, \ldots \tau - 1$ time periods, and their relative likelihood;

2. repeat for a grid of initial conditions centered on those given by the initial empirical state;
3. compute a probability distribution of possible lexicographic sequences and regimes after $1, 2, \ldots \tau - 1$ time periods, as an average of the likelihoods computed under steps 1 and 2;
4. determine the likelihood of the observed lexicographic sequence, and that of the observed regimes after $1, 2, \ldots \tau - 1$ time periods, with respect to the expected outcomes, by locating the observed dynamics within the probability distribution of expected outcomes (for example, are they in the tail of the distribution of expected outcomes?) to enable calculation of $\Sigma_{k=1}^{K} P(O|E_k, S^m) P(E_k|T_i, S^m)$, for T_i, S^m.

9.4.3.5   Stage five: accounting for uncertainty about system parameters

Since system dynamics are potentially highly sensitive to system parameters, which we can never know with complete precision, steps two to four should be repeated for each vector of system parameters calculated in step one. Under the assumption that all combinations of parameter values within S are equally likely (in the absence of prior information to suggest otherwise): $P(O|T_i) = \Sigma_k P(O|T_i, S^k)$.

9.4.3.6   Stage six: comparing the two theoretical models

On the basis of completing steps one to five for each theoretical model, and prior beliefs in each theory, compute the degree to which one theory may be preferred over the other (equation 9.8). This is our best estimate of the relative merits of the two contrasting theories for explaining observed trajectories of, say, regional employment, income distribution and capital accumulation.

9.5   METHODOLOGICAL AND PHILOSOPHICAL IMPLICATIONS

In the world of geographical economics, spatial economic analysis seems relatively straightforward. Patterns of spatial equilibrium can be predicted, data collected, and statistical analysis used to determine goodness of fit of prediction to observation. Of course, many problems persist, of the kind referred to by Hendry in the opening quote, compounded by difficulties in implementing spatial statistical methods, but a well-recognized procedure can be followed. This procedure can also be philosophically justified by appeal to a positivist, logical empiricist epistemology, which still has considerable currency in the natural and quantitative social sciences (despite its unpopularity among philosophers of science, who have identified many difficulties of principle and application).

These procedures are not adequate for the socio-spatial ontology of regional political economy, because the pervasiveness of conflict, and the likelihood of unintended and unwanted consequences (compounded in a spatially extensive economy), mean that the capitalist space economy is characterized by the out-of-equilibrium dynamics of non-linear models with high levels of complexity. The reason for this difficulty has little to do with whether the theory can be represented as a mathematical model. As we have indicated in Section 9.3 and elsewhere (Sheppard and Barnes, 1990; Sheppard, Haining and Plummer, 1992; Plummer, 1996), it is possible (if unpopular) to construct mathematical models consistent with this socio-spatial ontology, favoured by geographers.

Unless we have a priori reason or evidence to accept the proposition that space and time are Newtonian, or that the system is in spatial equilibrium, we conclude that economic geographers should undertake spatio-temporal analysis rather than spatial analysis, because the observed system may well be far from equilibrium. Space-time trajectories are highly sensitive to parameter values and starting points, and may experience disruptions in their dynamics when they transition from one dynamic regime to another, meaning that any one theory may be associated with a variety of possible trajectories. Theoretical analysis of such systems is plagued by an inability to derive general mathematical theorems, forcing analysts (in disciplines ranging from physics to the social sciences) to resort to computation and simulation. Empirical analysis is further plagued by the fact that there is one observed trajectory, to be compared with a potentially huge number of possible theoretical trajectories even for a single theoretical model. Pragmatism dictates the necessity of comparing two theories with one another, rather than one theory with one set of observations. Since such judgements are inevitably shaped by analysts' prior belief in a theory (a point made long ago by Karl Popper (1959) in his critique of logical positivism), it is important to take this subjectivity into account in calculating the impact of empirical evidence on our confidence in one theory by comparison to another. We thus advocate applying Bayes's theorem to account for how investigators' prior belief in their preferred ontology and theoretical model influences their ex post confidence in its performance (Salmon, 1990).

In short, quantitative economic geography following the socio-spatial ontology of regional political economy, while mathematically rigorous, requires application of principles of analytical adequacy associated with twenty-first century complexity theory rather than what Mirowski (1984) calls the nineteenth-century mathematics of the calculus. It also entails post-positivist principles of epistemological adequacy, rather than the implied logical empiricism of geographical economics. Post-positivist epistemologies are popular in the more qualitative traditions of economic geography, raising questions about whether the principal philosophical divide falls between quantitative and qualitative approaches, or between the two socio-spatial ontologies popular, respectively, in economics and geography.

NOTES

1. We acknowledge and value the importance of qualitative methodologies, such as ethnographies and discourse analysis, in geographic research, and would even seek to extend the dialogue to include such approaches and the epistemologies that underlie them. Yet discussion of these is beyond the domain of this chapter.
2. It is worth noting that some work in mainstream economics is beginning to challenge the focus on equilibrium solutions (cf. Markose, 2005), but there has been little attention as yet in economic geography to modelling, let alone empirically evaluating, out-of-equilibrium dynamics (Krugman, 1996; Fujita, Krugman and Venables, 1999; Brakman, Garretsen and von Marrewijk, 2001; Rice and Venables, 2003).
3. In economics some attention is being given to stylized facts that are not grounded in 'overly-restrictive and detailed parametric assumptions on the theoretical models', see Durlauf and Quah (1999). This is also being taken up in regional science , see Quah (1996).
4. Logical empiricism is often characterized in terms of a symmetry between prediction and explanation. This symmetry is inapplicable to models exhibiting complexity, where deterministic causal models may have effectively unpredictable outcomes, see Kellert (1993) and Albin (1998).
5. If 'many', then the regime varies with location in phase space, but the topology of the phase space (that is, the location and dynamics of the regimes) depends on initial conditions and/or model parameters.
6. The intuition here is that if there is only one regime, you are in it no matter where you start from.
7. For example, location and/or stability of a regime may depend on model parameters.
8. For example, the regime you are initially in depends on initial conditions.
9. That is, a non-linear model between regimes, but one where intra-regime dynamics are linear.
10. That is, transition matrix for regimes has non-zero off a diagonal elements.
11. That is, intra-regime dynamics are non-linear.

REFERENCES

Albin, P.S. (1998), *Barriers and Bounds to Rationality: Essays on Economic Complexity and Dynamics in Interacting Systems*, Princeton: Princeton University Press.
Barro, R.J. and X. Sala-i-Martin (1992), 'Convergence', *Journal of Political Economy*, **100**: 223–51.
Behrens, K., C. Gaigné, G.I.P. Ottaviano and J.-F. Thisse (2003), 'Interregional and international trade: seventy years after Ohlin', *Discussion Paper 4065*, Centre for Economic Policy Research, London.

Bennett, R.J. (1979), *Spatial Time Series*, London: Pion.

Brakman, S., H. Garretsen and C. von Marrewijk (2001), *An Introduction to Geographical Economics*, Cambridge, UK: Cambridge University Press.

Brida, J.G. and L. Punzo (2003), 'Symbolic time series analysis and dynamic regimes', *Structural Change and Economic Dynamics*, **14**: 159–83.

Brida, J.G., M.P. Anyul and L. Punzo (2003), 'Coding economic dynamics to represent regime dynamics. A teach-yourself exercise', *Structural Change and Economic Dynamics*, **14**: 133–57.

Brock, W.A. (2001), 'Complexity-based methods in cycles and growth: any potential value added?', in L.F. Punzo (ed.), *Cycles, Growth and Structural Change: Theories and Empirical Evidence*, London: Routledge.

Clark, G.L., M. Gertler and M. Feldman (eds) (2000), *The Oxford Handbook of Economic Geography*, Oxford: Oxford University Press.

Day, R.H. (1995), 'Multiple-phase economic dynamics', in T. Maruyama and W. Takahishi (eds), *Lecture Notes in Economics and Mathematical Systems*, Berlin: Springer.

Day, R.H. and O.V. Pavlov (2001), 'Qualitative dynamics and macroeconomic evolution in the very long run', in L.F. Punzo (ed.), *Cycles, Growth and Structural Change: Theories and Empirical Evidence*, London: Routledge.

Dumenil, P. and D. Levy (1987), 'The dynamics of competition: a restoration of the classical view', *Cambridge Journal of Economics*, **11**: 133–64.

Durlauf, S.N. and D.T. Quah (1999), 'The new empirics of economic growth', in J.P. Taylor and M. Woodford (eds), *Handbook of Macroeconomics*, Amsterdam: North-Holland, pp. 235–308.

Elhorst, J.P. (2001), 'Dynamic models in space and time', *Geographical Analysis*, **33**: 119–40.

Fingleton, B. (ed.) (2003), *European Regional Growth*, New York: Springer Verlag.

Flaschel, P. and W. Semmler (1988), 'The integration of dual and cross-dual adjustment processes in Leontief systems', *Ricerche Economiche*, **42**: 403–32.

Fujita, M., P. Krugman and A. Venables (1999), *The Spatial Economy: Cities, Regions and International Trade*, Cambridge, MA: MIT Press.

Gandolfo, G. (1995), *Economic Dynamics*, New York: Springer.

Goodwin, R.M. (1967), 'A growth cycle', in C.H. Feinstein (ed.), *Socialism, Capitalism and Economic Growth*, Cambridge, UK: Cambridge University Press.

Goodwin, R.M. and L. Punzo (1987), *The Dynamics of a Capitalist Economy*, Boulder, Colorado: Westview Press.

Haining, R.P. (1990), *Spatial Data Analysis in the Social and Environmental Sciences*, Cambridge: Cambridge University Press.

Harvey, D. (1996), *Justice, Nature and the Geography of Difference*, Oxford: Blackwell.

Harvey, D. (1982), *The Limits to Capital*, Oxford: Basil Blackwell.

Jackson, R.W. and M. Sonis (2001), 'On the spatial decomposition of forecasts', *Geographical Analysis*, **33**: 57–75.

Kellert, S.M. (1993), *In the Wake of Change*, Chicago: University of Chicago Press.

King, I.T. (2001), *Dialectical Social Science in the Age of Complexity*, Lewiston, NY: Edwin Mellen Press.

Krugman, P. (1996), *The Self-organizing Economy*, Oxford, UK: Blackwell.

Lorenz, H.-W. (1993), *Nonlinear Dynamic Economics and Chaotic Motion*, Berlin: Springer-Verlag.

Lösch, A. (1954 [1940]), *The Economics of Location*, New Haven: Yale University Press.

Martin, R. and P. Sunley (1998), 'Slow convergence? The new endogenous growth theory and regional development', *Economic Geography*, **74**: 201–27.

Medio, A. and M. Lines (2001), *Nonlinear Dynamics: A Primer*, Cambridge: Cambridge University Press.

Mirowski, P. (1984), 'Physics and the marginalist revolution', *Cambridge Journal of Economics*, **8**: 361–79.

Neary, J.P. (2001), 'Of hype and hyperbolas: introducing the new economic geography', *The Journal of Economic Literature*, **XXXIX**: 536–61.

Ottaviano, G. and J.-F. Thisse. (2004), 'Agglomeration and economic geography', in J.V. Henderson and J.-F. Thisse (eds), *Handbook of Urban and Regional Economics*, Amsterdam: Elsevier, pp. 2564–608.

Ottaviano, G., T. Tabuchi and J.-F. Thisse (2002), 'Agglomeration and trade revisited', *International Economic Review*, **43**: 409–36.

Plummer, P. (1996a), 'Competitive dynamics in hierarchically organized markets: spatial duopoly and demand asymmetries', *Environment and Planning A*, **28**: 2021–40.

Plummer, P. (1996b), 'Spatial competition amongst hierarchically organised corporations: prices, profits, and shipment patterns', *Environment & Planning A*, **28**: 199–222.

Plummer, P. (1999), 'Capital accumulation, economic restructuring, and non-equilibrium regional growth dynamics', *Geographical Analysis*, **31**: 267–87.

Plummer, P. (2003), 'Modelling economic landscapes: a geographical perspective', *Regional Studies*, **37**: 687–99.

Plummer, P. and E. Sheppard (2001), 'Must emancipatory economic geography be qualitative? A response to Amin and Thrift', *Antipode*, **30**: 758–63.

Plummer, P. and E. Sheppard (2005), 'Geography matters: agency, structures, and dynamics', mimeo.

Plummer P. and M. Taylor (2001a), 'Theories of local economic growth: concepts, models and measurement', *Environment & Planning A*, **33**: 385–99.

Plummer P. and M. Taylor (2001b) 'Theories of local economic growth: model specification and empirical validation', *Environment & Planning A*, **33**: 219–36.

Popper, K. (1959), *The Logic of Scientific Discovery*, New York: Basic Books.

Prigogine, I. (1996), *The End of Certainty: Time, Chaos and the New Laws of Nature*, New York: The Free Press.

Punzo, L.F. and K.V. Velupillai (1996), 'The economy as a structurally complex evolving dynamical system. Goodwin contours', *Economic Notes*, **25**: 179–206.

Quah, D. (1996), 'Empirics for economic growth and convergence', *European Economic Review*, **40**: 1353–75.

Rice, P. and A.J. Venables (2003), 'Equilibrium regional disparities: theory and British evidence', *Regional Studies*, **37**: 675–87.

Rigby, D. and J. Essletzbichler (2003), 'Agglomeration economies and productivity differences in US cities', *Journal of Economic Geography*, **2**: 407–32.

Roemer, J. (1981), *Analytical Foundations of Marxian Economic Theory*, Cambridge: Cambridge University Press.

Rosser Jr, J.B. (2000), 'Aspects of dialectics and non-linear dynamics', *Cambridge Journal of Economics*, **24**: 311–24.

Salmon, W.C. (1990), 'Rationality and objectivity in science, or Tom Kuhn meets Tom Bayes', in C.W. Savage (ed.), *Scientific Theories*, Minnesota Studies in the Philosophy of Science, Minneapolis, MN: University of Minnesota Press.

Sayer, A. (1984), *Method in Social Science: A Realist Approach*, London: Hutchinson.

Scott, A.J. (1996), 'The craft, fashion, and cultural-products industries of Los Angeles: competitive dynamics and policy dilemmas in a multisectoral image-producing complex', *Annals of the Association of American Geographers*, **86**: 306–23.

Sheppard, E. (1983), 'Commodity trade, corporate ownership and urban growth', *Papers of the Regional Science Association*, **52**: 175–86.

Sheppard, E. (1990), 'Modeling the capitalist space economy: bringing society and space back', *Economic Geography*, **66**: 201–28.

Sheppard, E. (1996), 'Site, situation and social theory', *Environment and Planning A*, **28**: 1339–42.

Sheppard, E. (2000), 'Geography or economics? Contrasting theories of location, spatial pricing, trade and growth', in G. Clark, M. Gertler and M. Feldman (eds), *Handbook of Economic Geography*, Oxford, UK: Oxford University Press.

Sheppard, E. (2006), 'Dialectical space-time', in N. Castree and D. Gregory (eds), *David Harvey: A Critical Reader*, Oxford, UK: Blackwell.

Sheppard, E. and T.J. Barnes (1990), *The Capitalist Space Economy: Geographical Analysis after Ricardo, Marx and Sraffa*, London: Unwin Hyman.

Sheppard, E. and T.J. Barnes (2000), *A Companion to Economic Geography*, Oxford: Blackwell.

Sheppard, E., R.P. Haining and P. Plummer (1992), 'Spatial pricing in interdependent markets', *Journal of Regional Science*, **32**: 55–75.

Sheppard, E., P. Plummer and R. Haining (1998), 'Profit rate maximization in interdependent markets', *Journal of Regional Science*, **38**: 659–67.

Soja, E. (1980), 'The socio-spatial dialectic', *Annals of the Association of American Geographers*, **70**: 207–25.

Sraffa, P. (1960), *The Production of Commodities by Means of Commodities*, Cambridge: Cambridge University Press.

Velupillai, K.V. (1998a), 'The vintage economist', *Journal of Economic Behavior and Organization*, **37**: 1–31.

Velupillai, K.V. (1998b), *Computable Economics*, Oxford: Oxford University Press.

Webber, M.J. and D. Rigby (1999), 'Accumulation and the rate of profit: regulating the macroeconomy', *Environment and Planning A*, **31**: 141–64.

10. FDI: a difficult connection between theory and empirics

Anna Soci

10.1 INTRODUCTION

A good rule of scientific research should be to define the subject precisely and then to examine its relevance. In the case of foreign direct investment (FDI) these two tasks are the only straightforward aspect of this complex phenomenon.

What is FDI? FDI is a balance of payments concept involving cross-border transfer of funds. Firm k in country i sets up a productive facility in country j by implanting a new firm (green-field investment) or acquiring an existing firm l or some part of it. The result must be the:

> obtaining [of] a lasting interest by a resident entity in one country ('direct investor') in an entity resident in an economy other than that of the investor ('direct investment enterprise'). The lasting interest implies the existence of a long-term relationship between the direct investor and the enterprise and a significant degree of influence on the management of the enterprise.[1]

The idea of 'control', which was present in earlier definitions, has been abandoned in favour of a broader though no less vague concept. What 'lasting interest' means is 'a stake of 10% or more of the ordinary shares or voting power of an incorporated enterprise or the equivalent of an unincorporated enterprise' (OECD, 1996, p. 8). This is the threshold in the United States, whereas the legislation in the European Union is not yet completely uniform. The immediate consequence of an FDI is that a national firm acting as above becomes, by definition, a multinational enterprise (MNE, or MNC, or TNC): firm k in country i is the parent firm in the *source* country, and firm l in country j is the foreign affiliate in the *host* country. Once such a relationship is established, any capital transactions between the two are FDI: purchases of equity, reinvested earnings and increases in the net creditor position of the parent vis-à-vis the affiliate. The merger of firm k with firm l is also an FDI of a type not giving rise to a transnational firm but to a new national firm in the country elected as the home country. Thus, M&As (mergers and acquisitions) are not synonymous with MNEs' activity. They are not even synonymous with FDI since they can relate as well to the union between foreign affiliates and firms located in the same host economy, not to mention the accounting differences between the two (UN, 2001, p. 289). And, a fortiori, MNEs' activity is not synonymous with FDI: for instance, the parent firm can decide to raise funds for its foreign affiliate directly on the foreign local market or can decide that its affiliate allocates funds on the same local market, without any cross-border transfer involvement.

Why should we care about FDI? Here too the answer is straightforward. First, FDI had an unforeseen and dramatic upsurge in the 1980s and it has been growing since then faster than trade or worldwide nominal income. Second, its nature changed. Since statistics were kept and until the 1970s FDI used to flow from rich countries to poor countries, thereby creating considerable concern about political issues such as the exploitation of underdeveloped but rich nations and the collusive links between multinationals and local political regimes. In the last 15 to 20 years FDI has been flowing from rich countries to rich countries, with the noticeable exception of the countries in transition to a market economy. Some relevant features of these countries such as the high level of human capital tend, however, to situate them in a more advanced stage of development even though they are officially classified as developing countries. Moreover, notwithstanding the remarkable yearly rate of increase of private capital flows to these countries, especially to the CEECs, at the end of the 1990s the whole region was still attracting roughly the same amount of FDI (as a percentage of GDP) as South, East and South-East Asia, less than Latin America and the Caribbean, and slightly more than Africa, averaging about 2.6 per cent as a share of world FDI inflows and about 8 per cent as a share of developing countries' FDI inflows. In other words, FDI is nowadays a true feature of the industrialized world: MNEs number several tens of thousands, and their affiliates several hundred thousands; developed countries account for more than three-fourths of total inflows, and within the developed countries group, the European Union, United States and Japan account still for around three-fourths. The third, good and less trivial, reason to be interested in FDI is that it is potentially able to modify the productive structure of a country and the context of its industrial relations, thus posing severe challenges to policies.

Does FDI possess a theoretical explanation and – if, hopefully, it does – what progress has been made in its empirical testing? Here serious troubles start to appear since there is no consolidated theory and consequently there exists an impressive number of empirical studies often so contradictory as to induce some scholars to switch to so-called 'meta-analysis' (for instance,

Görg and Strobl, 2001 and Djankov and Murrell, 2002) or to sensitivity-analysis (like Chakrabarti, 2001) in order to provide some meaningful evaluation. The existing surveys themselves cannot cope with covering the entire subject, with the notable exceptions of an 'old' study by the UN Centre on Transnational Corporations (1992), which covers the 1980s, a period when the studies of FDI were relatively fewer, and of Caves (in its updated edition 1996), which unfortunately stops early. Markusen's 1995 article – often referred to as a survey – looks only at the empirical evidence on MNEs' specific features; the more recent Lipsey's (2002) paper surveys the effects of FDI on both home (trade and factor demand) and host countries (wages, productivity and growth) but he has a clearly greater stress on the latter, which basically means that he focuses on spillovers. Blomström and Kokko (1998 and 2003); Görg and Strobl (2001); Görg and Greenaway (2002, 2004); Saggi (2002), treat only spillovers; Markusen and Maskus (2001) concentrate on what they call the general-equilibrium model of MNEs; Blonigen (2005), reviews what *he* considers the most important and novel papers in the empirical literature on both the partial and general equilibrium sides; Gattai (2005), relates exclusively to the internalization issue. All these contributions share a certain degree of disquiet about the wide multiplicity of results. Does the topic need a unifying theory, or do the scholars need to stop using the general label of FDI and to start to inquire separately into its many aspects as if they were not reconcilable and to recognize that different explanations are needed for different kinds of FDI (as some prestigious scholars of FDI, like Dunning and Lipsey, seem to suggest)?

Since the main topic of this book is new directions in economic geography, we will concentrate here on those aspects of FDI that are more closely related to spatial aspects and that either support or oppose the prescriptions of NEG theory. Thus, we will avoid organizing the discussion around the home-host country effects of FDI, which would force us to take into consideration elements that are beyond the scope here, such as the effects on employment in the source country or those on growth in the destination countries. This last topic, which is highly controversial, has been surveyed many times, as we recalled earlier.

We will look very briefly at the internalization issue – which has traditionally been part of business economics – since the new trade theory is starting to incorporate it. Some more attention will be devoted to a widely discussed topic – the relationship between FDI and trade – since it gives interesting insights on the more recent theory of FDI coming out of the NEG approach. Studies inquiring about 'location' will be considered for the same reasons. Furthermore, the studies on transition-economies will be more extensively reviewed since they might represent a 'laboratory' test of the NEG insofar as FDI is occurring in a *vacuum*: no trade, high NT barriers, adverse institutions and no tradition of FDI at all. Last but not least, we will not enter into the technical aspects of empirical evaluation, since the methods used – tools, data, sample, time span and others – vary so widely that it is almost impossible to make a meaningful comparison.

10.2   THE MISSING LINK

Even though this chapter is devoted to the empirics of FDI, it is worth recalling the main steps in the evolution of the theory. In fact, we are convinced that the unsatisfactory state of the empirics of FDI arises from the lack of a link with the theory: the new trade theory (NTT) – even in its latest version of the knowledge-capital model – encompasses MNEs and FDI without appropriate coverage of space, which is one of the main issues for FDI, while the new economic geography puts great emphasis on the concept of space but it has very little room for FDI. Very recent efforts in the direction of bridging FDI and the NEG effectively, such as Ekholm and Forslid (2001) and Egger et al. (2005), have not yet had proper empirical follow up.

10.2.1   The Evolution of the Theory

After the over-quoted pioneering work by Hymer (1976), and an isolated and rarely quoted theoretical study by Hirsch (1976), the conceptual framework used until very recently was the one proposed by Dunning (1977), which is generally referred to as the 'OLI paradigm', the acronym for Ownership, Location, Internalization. Three conditions have to be fulfilled in order for a firm to become a multinational: there must be an ownership (O) advantage such as to make it profitable for the firm to relocate its own production (or at least part of it) abroad; there must be some localization (L) advantage, typically linked to the host country's specific characteristics; it must be more convenient for the firm to manage its advantages internally (I) rather than trade them through the market. The ownership advantages are mainly nested in the so-called proprietary 'intangible' assets or knowledge-capital assets (such as firm-specific technical knowledge or human capital, particular properties like trademarks and other characteristics able to differentiate the product, brand reputation included, or simply the firm's ability to innovate frequently), which 'take on the quality of public goods, that is their marginal usage cost is zero or minimal . . . and, although their *origin* may be partly determined by the industry or country characteristics of enterprises, they can be used anywhere' (Dunning, 1977,

p. 401, italics in original). In other words, they can be spread over more than one plant, thus generating the so-called firm-economies of scale (or economies of multi-plant production, or multi-plant economies of scale). The ownership advantage must exist in order to offset the transaction costs incurred by the firm in expanding abroad, typically those related to learning 'how to do things' in foreign countries, that is, the foreign culture and legal system, often a foreign language. The location advantage can originate from barriers to trade or from greater proximity to final markets, and they can also be country-specific, such as those related to the availability of inputs at cheaper prices. Thirdly, there must be an incentive to keep under the same 'head' (the internalization advantage) the control of the geographically dispersed production instead of resorting to trade arrangements like licensing, franchising and others.

In order to give rise to MNEs, ownership, location and internalization advantages must obviously be such as to render foreign production more profitable than trade. Notwithstanding many criticisms (for all, see Graham, 1996, pp. 186–91) of the 'OLI paradigm' for not being a theory, it appeared to be a very useful framework for gathering together different features of firms' opportunities to become multinationals, and it has helped in the empirical assessment of the phenomenon.

On a parallel route, trade theory was looking for a theoretical assessment of the existence of multinationals. 'For a long time FDI has been a subject area where anything goes: the typical trade textbook or trade course is rigorous and model oriented until it reaches multinationals, then suddenly becomes a mixture of anecdote and loose, if valuable, insights' (Krugman, 1983, p. 72). It was not an easy task, since traditional theory was certainly not the right place to deal with firms facing such a complex decision-making problem. As Helpman and Krugman (1985, p. 3) point out:

> In the perfectly competitive, constant return world of traditional theory there are no visible firms and thus no way to discuss issues hinging on the scope of activities carried out within firms. Again, in reality much international trade consists of intrafirms' transactions rather than arms' length dealings between unrelated parties, and multinational firms are a prominent part of the international landscape.[2]

The evidence of trade between industrial countries – fairly similar in their relative factor endowment – and of a substantial amount of intra-industry trade – that is, two-way trade in the differentiated goods of the same industry, which are very likely to have similar factor intensity – barely (if ever) conformed to the conventional theory, which explained trade *entirely* by differences among countries. The new trade theory of the 1980s allowed for (static) internal economies of scale due to increasing returns, and consequent imperfect competition as a market structure (mainly Cournot oligopoly and monopolistic competition).[3] The seminal paper was Helpman (1984), with upstream activities (headquarter services or intermediate goods) highly specific to downstream activity, all being subject to economies of scale. In this kind of situation it is likely that an integrated firm will arise in order to avoid bilateral monopolies considered to be a source of various inefficiencies. The firm is either a single-product one, in the case where its highly specialized inputs such as management and product-specific R&D are in a location that is geographically separate from the serviced plants, or it has production facilities in more than one country in the case of the intermediates, becoming vertically integrated. A sort of implicit two-step decision-making process is at work: increasing returns give firms incentives to integrate – thus becoming multinationals – and cost considerations suggest to them where to locate. Put differently, the true novelty is given by the explicit modelling of increasing returns, whilst location follows the traditional theories. In this setting, which still in harmony with the Heckscher/Ohlin context insofar as different factor costs given by differences in endowment across countries are concerned, *intra*-industry trade can take place, but there is no room for trade between similar, equally developed, countries (where factor-prices should be equal).

In the same year – 1984 – another seminal contribution appeared by Markusen, similar to and yet different from the Helpman one insofar as it relies more on Dunning's original insight and the related industrial organization literature. Markusen's model pushes further the implications of the presence of intangibles, building on the concept of multi-plant economies of scale, that is to say advantages possessed by a single owner of two or more production facilities over independent owners of the same production facilities. Management or R&D – the same services invoked by Helpman's model – work here as a joint input giving a single two-plant firm a cost-efficiency over two single-plant firms. The paper avoids any kind of Heckscher/Ohlin effect since the countries under consideration are *equal* in every respect, above all in their factor endowment. Because of multi-plant economies of scale alone, the multinational enterprise sets up production facilities in both countries, so becoming a *horizontally* integrated firm: plants in different locations (countries) produce the same product. No wonder that since then the Markusen paper – and the author himself – became the father of the 'horizontal' model, whereas Helpman's paper is referred to as the prototype of the 'vertical' models.

A third important step was the contribution of Horstmann and Markusen (1987a), where transport costs started to have an effective role. In traditional trade theory they did nothing except reduce slightly the gains from trade, since in a world of unequal countries (that is to say, with different endowments) factor costs were doing the job: trade. In a world of equal countries with no theoretical difference in factor costs (and prices), what can do the job are transport (export) costs. More precisely, a horizontal MNE would arise in equilibrium 'if firm specific and export costs are large relative to plant-scale economies' (Horstmann and Markusen, 1987a, p. 110). In fact, firm-specific activities – such as research, for instance – are a sunk cost that gives rise to multi-plant scale economies insofar as they give MNEs a cost advantage over potential domestic producers. These activities and transport (export) costs offset the plant-level scale economies, which would lead to centralized production and serving the market through exports.

Alongside the proper NTT and by the hand of one of its fathers, Paul Krugman, another strand of research came into the picture in the very early 1990s (Krugman, 1991a, 1991b, 1995, 1998), and has been evolving into the now well-known NEG.[4] In this broad and highly fertile approach, which through time has been able to fertilize mainstream economics (Fujita et al., 1999; Fujita and Thisse, 2002; Baldwin et al., 2003), the main focus is on industry-localization. Revisiting the Marshallian tradition of external economies, Hirschman's idea of backward and forward linkages, Myrdal's (and Kaldor's) suggestion of circular (and cumulative) causation, and letting these pieces of theories interact in models of monopolistic competition of the Dixit-Stiglitz type with increasing returns, location choices become an endogenous variable. Multiple equilibria are generally present, since the outcomes depend on the specific assumptions of the models and on the values of the parameters as well. The mobility of production factors (both labour and capital, that is to say, firms) in response to a changing context contributes to endogenizing the pattern of location, which can mutate through time. Complete polarization of industry in an (industrial)-core/(agricultural)-periphery-shaped world, multiple clusters (that is to say, agglomerations of geographically scattered firms in narrowly defined sectors of activity), and dispersion of firms, can occur as well. As a corollary, important for the international trade flows, *intra*-industry trade and *inter*-industry trade are expected when there is, respectively, industry-dispersion or industry-concentration at sector level. Transport costs are an essential element for both the dispersion and the concentration of industries insofar as they exhibit a non-monotonic relationship with the decisions of firms about location. Thus so far the main body of the literature.

As far as multinationals are concerned, unfortunately the NEG was not a theory of the firm. Notwithstanding the new perspective of the choice of location as a strategic variable, which makes space a priority, and notwithstanding the existence of the proper environment – imperfect competition and market power – the multinationals are absent. The firm is still synonymous with a plant, where increasing returns are nested: that is to say, the firm is still an organization that produces one good in one location. Quite rightly Markusen (1995, p. 169 and 1998, p. 11) calls this approach à la Krugman the 'national-firm-model' to indicate that this unique production facility represents a theoretical setting not so suitable for studying the emergence of a multinational, which is by definition a multi-plant firm.

However, the emphasis on the strong linkages between industrial location and the geographical characteristics of the market (both size and closeness) – which are main features in the NEG approach, together with the prominent role of transport costs – helped in forming a 'new' way of looking at that MNEs' activity of making FDI instead of relying on trade. At the beginning of the 1990s some key elements – common to the most cited papers throughout: Horstmann and Markusen (1992); Brainard (1997); Markusen and Venables (1998); Markusen and Venables (2000) – consolidated the theoretical background in an eclectic model. These key elements are: some activity with the 'jointness'[5] feature constituting the firm-level economies of scale, plant-level economies of scale, transport (or tariff, or export) costs. The type of product, whether differentiated or homogeneous, does not seem to have any dramatic importance: 'the rich results obtained below demonstrate that product differentiation is not required to produce such results' (Markusen and Venables, 1996, p. 188, fn. 3). The interplay of these elements determines the plant-location decision of firms, and the eventual market structure. In this theoretical setting both horizontal and vertical multinationals can exist, even though the main theoretical interest – led by the need to be in tune with the empirical evidence – tends towards the horizontal type. Noticeably, an increase in transport costs induces horizontal integration but works against vertical integration, in a ceteris paribus situation.

Thus, in this generation of models, horizontal MNEs arise when – broadly speaking – the cost structure is larger than plant-level scale economies, and when the countries are similar, in size and relative factor endowment, thus matching the main elements of the empirical evidence. In some of them the NEG flavour is more evident both in the structure of the model and in the role of distance. For instance, in Brainard (1997), countries are similar in size and factor endowment, and firms' decision whether to export or to produce in the foreign countries is based upon a trade-off between the advantages of local concentration versus proximity to final markets, in what has become famous as the 'proximity-concentration' hypothesis. Firms must balance the benefits of exploiting plant-economies of scale with the costs of transport and trade. Roughly speaking, the higher the latter and firm-economies of scale are relative to plant-economies of scale, the more FDI will take place serving horizontal MNEs. No difference in factor endowment among countries is present, and two-way trade in the same industry can occur. After the important 'diversion' represented by Markusen and Venables (1998), where their attention is on the size of the countries in what since has been called the 'convergence' hypothesis, eventually the theory reached a 'unified treatment' in Markusen et al. (1996). Here the three models present in the literature – all having in common increasing returns to scale and imperfect competition – arise from a unique root, as special cases for some set of parameter values. The three models are: (1) a 'new trade theory' based one (a single-plant, national firm); (2) one with a horizontal multinational, which chooses between serving a foreign market by exports or by building a branch plant; and (3) one with a vertical multinational. In this contribution, and in Markusen (1998), as well, the theory gives an answer (sometimes more, sometimes less convincing) as to how and when horizontal multinationals vertical multinationals and national firms prevail over each other, due to the interplay of transport costs, size of countries, firms' (and countries') factor intensity, firm-level and plant-level economies of scale (for all, see Markusen, 1998, pp. 19–24).

Once again, transport costs turn out to be a crucial variable: more specifically, given firm and plant scale economies, the same transport costs regime has opposite effects depending on the difference or the similarity between countries. High transport costs support horizontal MNEs between countries that are similar in size and factor endowment, whereas they favour concentration the larger one country is compared with the other, for a given factor intensity. In fact, national firms with headquarters in the larger country do not have any incentive to become MNEs and to make a fixed-cost investment to serve a small market, while export costs would be tolerable even with high transport costs because there is not much output to be shipped to the small country. Nor is there any reason why vertical MNEs should arise, given the similarity in factor endowment and the high transport costs regime. On the other side, low transport costs mean that the country size ceases to be an advantage and depresses MNEs' activity, both horizontal and (with similar country-endowment) vertical.

After Markusen (2002), there is little doubt that the 'knowledge-capital model', as he first called it, should be *the* model capable of accounting for the presence of multinationals in trade theory. Its main prediction is that horizontal multinationals are present in countries similar in both size and relative factor endowments (provided that trade costs are not too low).

This generation of eclectic models copes with the first two elements of the OLI paradigm: ownership and localization. In fact, the 'firm-specific' asset with the 'jointness' characteristic, which gives rise to multi-plant economies of scale, can be many things: inter alia, superior technological knowledge, organizational and managerial skills pertaining to the human capital of the firm, patents, trademarks or particular design that can make the firm's product unique. All these constitute the so-called 'intangibles', which are the essence of the ownership advantage. The technical component of the production facilities (the plant-economies of scale), together with the physical characteristics of both home and host countries (factor endowment) plus their geographical features (size and proximity) and some element of policy (transport costs) make it possible to debate the issue of location. Nevertheless, additional important characteristics like the presence of ports or other natural elements that can affect the economic organization are not touched on by this literature, whereas they are studied by trade specialists like Krugman in the contiguous field of urban economics. Also, the existence of policies capable of improving the mobility of production, such as the presence and quality of infrastructures, is not taken into consideration in the main literature. Besides that, what these models do not address is the issue of internalization: why should a firm behave as a self-sufficient unit instead of collaborating with foreign firms through commercial agreements?

10.3　THE TRIAD: TRADE, FDI AND COMMERCIAL AGREEMENTS

An important preliminary issue in the FDI story is that it belongs to a triad of decisions where the two missing elements are trade and commercial agreements. Thus, to inquire about the causes of FDI means inevitably raising the question about the feasibility of its alternatives: exports and licensing, the latter being the most common choice in an array that includes franchising, subcontracting, joint ventures and other strategic options. Firms can well serve foreign markets through exports without becoming multinationals, as they used to do before the phenomenon of transnationality became such a widespread one. Analogously, firms can avoid the costs and inconvenience of setting up production facilities abroad by giving some other firm the legal right to exploit its products commercially. Let us look briefly at the latter, that is to say the internalization issue, or the letter I of the 'OLI paradigm'.

'Internalization is the only one of the three key elements not already incorporated into trade theory. . . . Internalization is one of our critical "black boxes" always appealed to but never explained' (Ethier, 1986, pp. 805–6). Thus, internalization is taken as a matter of course. In the NTT of the 1980s only two papers make a serious exception to the rule: Ethier (1986) and Horstmann and Markusen (1987b). The former includes in the model firm-specific assets such as research effort and product quality, while the second includes the firm's reputation for quality. Both papers basically found that direct investment prevails over licence when there is imperfect information in the product market. The numerous and varied kinds of information-asymmetries are concisely reviewed by Markusen (1995, pp. 181–5), and more extensively by Caves (1996, Ch. 7). Notwithstanding the growing literature on business organization in the 1990s, very few papers came from the side of trade theory to deal with the problem of internalization. Ethier and Markusen (1996), treated the specific point of the possible dissipation of intellectual property: in order to prevent this, firms choose to transfer the knowledge-capital internally. The theoretical setting combines elements typical of the new trade theory with features of the industrial organization theory, specifically considering the firm's inability to enforce contracts. Moreover, it allows a complex interplay of location and internalization aspects insofar as foreigners learn faster how to produce the goods when they are produced in their country rather than when they are imported. Although the results depend heavily on the parameters, the main suggestion is 'that similarities in relative factor endowment may promote direct investment when account is taken of the desire to protect knowledge-based capital' (Ethier and Markusen, 1996, p. 24).

Horstmann and Markusen (1996), investigated the costs of gathering information about new markets, setting up a model that predicts 'that a contractual arrangement is more likely when markets are on average small and investment mistakes are very costly . . . and conversion from a contractual arrangement to owned sales operation can be achieved quickly' (Horstmann and Markusen, 1996, p. 3). These findings seem to be confirmed by empirical evidence from studies on survey data relating to Australian firms in East Asia and Japanese firms in Australia, which the authors quote.

Brainard (1997), includes advertising and R&D intensity in her equations as proxies of proprietary advantages, concluding that 'brand advantages associated with high advertising intensity require a local presence, while those associated with R&D are compatible with either mode of selling abroad'.

While Barba-Navaretti and Venables (2004), overview recent works applying the theory of the firm to the rise of multinationals, a set of extremely interesting theoretical contributions from trade theory – surveyed with great efficacy by Gattai (2005) – appeared very recently, which treat the decision on outsourcing in the two dimensions of ownership and location. Unfortunately, no empirical evidence has yet followed from these studies. Moreover, they relate to vertical FDI, which is now considered by scholars less relevant (at least quantitatively) than the horizontal one.[6]

Unlike the international trade literature, business and industrial organization economics are richer in studies on this specific aspect of multinational activity (Caves, 1996, especially Ch. 7). It appears evident that this approach is more fruitful for studying the problem of internalization, which is undoubtedly highly dependent on the way a firm is structured and organized. Nevertheless, the results are not clear-cut, given the many facets of the topic, even though they seem to agree on some basic facts: in general, licensing is preferred to direct investment when the size of the market does not allow entry at a sufficient scale, when firms lack experience of foreign markets, when the industry's technology is changing rapidly so that the rents to the intangible asset are short-lived. By contrast, direct investment is the chosen option when licensing is very costly to arrange because of the difficulty of defining the capability to be transferred or of enforcing the agreement, for instance in the new technologies sector. Buckley and Casson (1998), confirm these basic results in a setting where all the major entry strategies – licensing, franchising, subcontracts and joint ventures – are present.

The relation between FDI and trade is no less complex. 'Yet we have a poor understanding of the ways in which direct foreign investment is just a simple substitute for trade, and the ways in which it is something quite different' (Markusen and Venables, 1999, p. 336). After a predominance of the substitutability effect between factor movement and trade – mainly coming from the often-quoted Mundell contribution (1957) – the theory of trade was leaning towards its opposite. Markusen (1983), for instance, develops a model that in a sense goes behind the Heckscher-Ohlin world insofar as it reaches the different factor endowment situation – which is the starting point there – as a result of trade in factors. Thus, beginning with equally endowed countries, factors move (because of differences in production technology, and various types of distortions), and this 'factor mobility creates a factor proportions basis to reinforce the other basis for trade' (Markusen, 1983, p. 355).

Notwithstanding the theoretical peculiarity of this model, one of its predictions – the complementary linkage between FDI and trade – soon proved to be supported by data (as reviewed in Caves, 1996, pp. 30–34). In fact, MNEs started to become an object of interest, and if the Mundell tariff-jump argument is always valid and provides a basis for FDI being a substitute for trade, the presence of MNEs well explains their complementary nature due, for instance, to increased trade in differentiated production. Thus, trade and FDI turn out to be probably both substitutes and complements, as they already appeared to be in Krugman (1983), which contains in a nutshell the main elements subsequently present in the literature, and where it is clearly stated and theoretically demonstrated that the relationship depends on the kind of integration (horizontal or vertical). With a product differentiation model, a substitution-type relationship arises:

> countries want to trade because they have acquired different technologies, taking the form of the knowledge of how to produce different products. They can trade this knowledge either directly, through technology transfer within multinational firms (or by licensing, except that we have ruled this out); or they can trade it indirectly, through trade in commodities embodying their special technological advantages. The choice of method depends on the costs: transport costs encourage direct technology transfer, costs of multinational operation promote trade. The product differentiation model suggests then an interpretation of multinational enterprises as vehicles for trade in information. Trade and multinational enterprise are substitutes just as trade and factor mobility are substitutes in the Heckscher-Ohlin model. (Krugman, 1983, p. 64)

With a model of vertical integration, 'trade and multinational enterprise will be complements rather than substitutes' (ibid.). In fact, once intermediate goods and different stages of production are explicitly taken into account, the negative relationship easily turns into a positive one. Vertical FDI will lead to increased exports if the foreign affiliates are solely engaged in assembly or sale of goods produced by their parent firms. The same outcome would still be expected when the foreign affiliates' activity is mainly marketing-oriented or is concentrated in the retail sector just in order to increase their parents' exports. Moreover, some vertical integration is often present also in the horizontal FDI, insofar as foreign affiliates process semi-final goods imported from the home country in order to make them suitable for the foreign market.

The models in the NTT showed much less concern with the effects of FDI on trade, both because they aimed at investigating a wider set of different issues, and because the evidence of *intra*-industry trade between similar countries leads in itself to fewer worries about pure trade-balance considerations. Nevertheless, the connections between FDI and trade are still at issue, coming out mainly as a by-product of the equilibrium solutions of theoretical models. For instance, Markusen and Venables (1998), predict a non-monotonic relationship: a convergence in country characteristics at first leads to an increase and then to a reduction in the volume of trade as MNEs begin to displace national firms. Markusen and Venables (1996), reach the conclusion of a negative relationship between the two, showing that the prominent role of MNEs in converging areas would crowd out trade. In general, the main prediction of the 'knowledge capital model' is that the relationship between FDI and trade should be negative, since the 'philosophy' itself of the model points to a choice between being a national firm, a vertical or a horizontal multinational. That is to say, in general, to export or not to export. If it is true that the presence of horizontal multinationals constitutes the necessary condition in order to have two-way trade, it is not automatic that trade should increase since the earlier exports can just be transformed into some exports and some imports of the production located abroad. Two-way trade was the puzzling phenomenon to be explained, and these models did it successfully. On the other hand, these are not models that can cope with the effects on the host countries, which could be the other traditional channel to create trade.[7]

Since everybody agrees that the relationship between FDI and trade is an empirical question, given the contradictory prescriptions of the theory, what is the state of the empirics? Contradictory as well.

The structural lack of coherent data on multinational activity for the majority of countries mostly resulted in studies concerning some selected areas, particularly the United States and Sweden, and to some extent Japan. Since Caves (1996), accurately reviews the main contributions before that date, and Lipsey (2002), considers some additional ones, let us here just recall some studies not covered by either and address the state of the art. Hufbauer et al. (1994), find country-dependent results: in Japan and Sweden FDI tends to promote imports more than exports, while in the United States it seems to increase exports more than imports. After ten years the result for Japan is shown to be still valid by Farrell et al. (2004), who add the new finding that the relationship between FDI and trade depends on industry as well. This consideration is shared also by Head and Ries (2001), who specifically address the point of what happens to a firm's exports through time once it has made FDI. Their sample exhibits net complementarity even though the large automobile firms substitute between the two.

In his 1994 contribution Hufbauer surveys ten major studies that have examined the relationship between outward FDI flows and home country exports, finding that these studies agree – with some exceptions – about the existence of a positive relationship and thus support the thesis of complementarity. Noticeable exceptions are Svensson (1996), who uses firm-level data for Swedish MNEs, and Braunerhjelm (1998), still on Sweden. But the Hufbauer complementarity thesis also has support from a small analogous and only marginally overlapping survey reported by Falzoni (1993), and a more up-to-date one provided by Mori and Rolli (1998). Blomström and Kokko (1994) for Sweden, and more recently Morikawa (1998), for Japan, Wilamoski and Tinkler (1999), for the United States versus Mexico, all confirmed the positive relationship between FDI and exports (and FDI and current-account balance as well, which is quite another topic).

Graham (1994), reports similar results for overall US foreign activity, and for a big sample of the world's largest industrial MNEs, concluding that 'the international evidence thus largely supports the conclusion that direct investment abroad and exports are complementary rather than substitutes' (Graham 1994, p. 142). His firm conviction, however, turns into a more doubting position in Graham (1996). By contrast, Blomström et al. (1988), repeat their previous result for Sweden (and the United States): the relationship between FDI and exports either is non-existent or it is positive. A doubtful judgement again is the one by Barrell and Pain (1997b), where the United Kingdom, Germany, France and Sweden are investigated, while the result of substitutability comes out more firmly in a later contribution of theirs (Barrell and Pain, 1999a). With new panel data, there is 'evidence of a statistically significant negative relationship between net outward investment and export performance for many European countries and the US . . . In contrast, there was evidence of a positive long-term relationship between outward investment and exports for Japan' (ibid., p. 38).

As a possible explanation for the sharp difference in results with many earlier studies, like those quoted above, the authors suggest that the effects of FDI on trade depend also on the maturity and accumulation of investments over time. The presence of a statistically significant negative relationship between outward investment and home country export performance comes out also in Pain and Wakelin (1998), even though they also find significant country heterogeneity. On the contrary, Fontagné and Pajot (1997), validate the thesis of complementarity between trade and FDI for France, and to a lesser extent for the entire pool of countries considered, which includes the United States, Sweden, the EU12, Japan, Italy and the Netherlands. More recently, Di Mauro (2000), found that at an aggregate level (her set includes France, Germany, Italy, United Kingdom, Japan, South Korea, United States and Canada) the relationship between FDI and trade is one to one. To sum up, in Lipsey's words: 'While there are examples of negative associations, they are not frequent, and positive associations are more common' (Lipsey, 2002, p. 13).

As Head and Ries (2001) rightly point out, what emerges clearly from the tate of the literature is the impossibility of a general appraisal of the phenomenon: the sign of the correlation closely depends at least on the type of the specific industrial sector and on the nature of the investment as well, not to mention considering trade related only to goods or also to services. Resource-seeking and trade-facilitating investments tend to complement trade and to increase it; while the latter does so by its very nature, the former acts in a more complex way, generating imports in the short run, and exports only in the long run after having hopefully improved the competitiveness of the country. The market-oriented investments can have a mixed role, and the final outcome is difficult to forecast: they can displace exports, thus tending to be a substitute for trade, but they can also create trade through new exports from the parent or other national firms to the affiliates or to other foreign firms in goods complementary to those supplied by the affiliates. Last but not least, the so-called 'strategic' investment (made in order to modify rival oligopolistic relations) can have ambiguous effects as well, depending on whether or not the affiliates assume an autonomous role in the horizontal integration process. If they become differentiated production units, exports to the home country will be created (as well as imports from other affiliates in other countries). Again in Lipsey's words:

> The effect may depend on whether the foreign operations' relation to home operations is 'horizontal' or 'vertical' . . . It may also depend on whether the foreign operations are in goods industries or in service industries, are in developed or developing countries, or are in industries with plant level or firm level economies of scale. (2002, p. 3)

Estimation techniques, too, are considered to be responsible for these wide differences in results: cross-sections, panels and time series – with better relative performance depending on the data they have to analyse – do not necessarily converge in their outcomes. Amiti and Wakelin (2003), brilliantly survey the further problem of finding contradictory results even *within* the same techniques. The multitude of data issues concerning the measure of multinational activity must also be mentioned. The uncomfortable result is that all this 'leaves the motivated reader rather perplexed, at the end, as to the confidence that should be placed in the findings of any particular study' (Chakrabarti, 2001, p. 90).

In fact, almost none of the existing studies really share the theoretical model provided by trade theory, very often giving the impression of being examples of 'measurement without theory'. Either they precede its consolidation or they just cite it as a theoretical source for including this or that variable. Notable exceptions are, of course, the main actors of the NTT/NEG approach. However, they are mainly interested in the (uneasy) task of ascertaining empirically the validity of their own theories. Thus, Carr et al. (2001), specifically address the point of the estimate of the 'knowledge capital model' – finding a strong support for it[8] – and Markusen and Maskus (2002), estimate an unrestricted model that nests the three models: the vertical, the horizontal and the knowledge capital (and here the strong support is for the horizontal model). Carr et al. (2001), find also that a convergence in country sizes increases affiliate sales in both directions. The Markusen-Venables' hypothesis of convergence already found some empirical support in Ekholm (1998), too, and very recently also in Barrios et al. (2001), who specifically aimed to verify it. Brainard (1997), finds *qualified* empirical support for the proximity-concentration trade-off, and Brainard (1993), adds further proof, rejecting a pure factor proportions explanation of multinational activity, whilst Ekholm (1998), finds just *some* empirical support for the proximity-concentration trade-off hypothesis.[9]

As for the specific issue of FDI–trade – which is not trivial, since it is related to one of the main prescriptions of the theory – Brainard (1997) found mixed evidence for the relationship (which in her case was between affiliate-sales and exports) depending on the inherent characteristics of the products, and Markusen (1997) seems to point to complementarity. Carr et al. (2001), find that trade and investment are mostly complements, even though the presence of some substitutability when the countries are similar is not completely ruled out, and Markusen and Maskus (2002), again find the same results. The outcome that to a great extent there is a negative correlation when trade flows are finished products, and a positive one when they are intermediate inputs comes out too from several studies reviewed by Blonigen (2005). Markusen and Maskus (2001), have an ambiguous result insofar as joint market size has a larger positive impact on local sales than exports: is the fact that they are both increasing, even though at a different rate, evidence of substantial complementarity or substantial substitutability? In any case, in the authors' words, 'evidence is slowly emerging that affiliate production complements increased trade in intermediates but in general substitutes for trade in final goods' (Markusen and Maskus, 2001, p. 39).

The recent contribution by Amiti and Wakelin (2003), seems to give a great deal of clarity to the issue by estimating the effects of investment liberalization on trade flows, which depend on the type of FDI that will be generated. They take from the theory the background and the predictions and rigorously make the two propositions to be empirically verified: 'when countries are similar in size and factor endowments, and trade costs are moderate to high, lower investment costs reduce exports' (Amiti and Wakelin, 2003, p. 7) – since it will generate horizontal FDI – and 'when countries differ in relative factor endowments and in size, and trade costs are low, then lower investment costs stimulate exports' (ibid.), since it will generate vertical FDI. The authors provide the estimates, which support the hypothesized propositions, and suggest that previous studies on the effects of FDI on trade might give conflicting results probably because they were constraining the relationship to be the same across all countries, which is in contrast with the theory.

In the meantime, trade theorists are adding a new piece of theory that will probably open new horizons. Looking exclusively at the horizontal FDI, Helpman et al. (2003), introduce intra-industry firm heterogeneity into the proximity-concentration trade-off literature, which predicts that foreign markets are served more by exports than by FDI when plant-economies of scale become more relevant and transport (export) costs lower. Productivity differences among the firms divide them into those that serve only the domestic market and those that engage in both exports and FDI. Productivity will still decide which will prefer the former mode, and which the latter. The foreign affiliate production type is geared to the host market, but the model could also be extended to incorporate the case of a third market: the so-called export-platform case, which is now attracting some interest in the literature on trade (Ekholm et al., 2003) as a new and more complicated pattern of FDI. The predictions of the proximity-concentration trade-off, with the addition of a strong effect for the new theoretical feature of heterogeneity within the sector, are confirmed in the US case for the manufacturing sector. Girma et al. (2004), provide another piece of empirical evidence for Ireland, finding that MNEs are in fact the most productive firms, although they cannot reject the hypothesis that domestic and export-oriented firms have the same productivity. Similar in spirit is Mody et al. (2002) and (2003): their model suggests an additional incentive to make FDI insofar as the more specialized the firms are in the source country, the more they can cream-skim in the host country. The role of this 'information advantage', a practical case of 'intangible capital', is supported by their empirical estimate.

10.4   FDI AND SPACE

FDI is intrinsically interwoven with the concept of space since it represents the activity of firms in non-national physical territories. It *implies* a choice about space, especially for the decision about new plant locations. Thus, FDI could be explained as a pure NEG outcome, insofar as it reacts to both its typical backward-linkage mechanism and to transport costs. It could be explained as well by other direct forces of agglomeration: externalities such as those in the labour market à la Marshall, or those resulting from technological spillovers. As Mayer and Mucchielli (1999), suggest, the choice can be thought of as a spatial hierarchical process where the effect of the variables depends on the decision level. On the contrary, very few empirical studies specifically address the influence of space on FDI.[10] Studying empirically the determinants of foreign affiliates' location choice often means simply building some specification related to the local and more distant demand in the effort to capture the 'market potential' effect.[11] Along the same lines, a 'distance' variable – usually within a gravity equation – is meant to represent the role of transport costs (and very often it also becomes the representative of the cultural gap that exists among distant locations). Data problems certainly limit the empirical methodology: for instance, the relationship between space and FDI should be investigated at the level of very small areas (external economies vanish in large areas) and should be related to green-field plants only (in other types of FDI space is already determined). However, this ad hoc treatment might also be due to the lack of a robust bridge between the NEG and FDI theory.

Research on the movements of firms – the industrial concentration issue – has been flourishing recently, especially with the prospect of the European integration. However, the studies on concentration and specialization do not inquire into the MNEs' decisions. They treat 'industries' and not the proprietary nature of the firms. They tell us that firms move, but they do not tell us where they move from because the perspective is mainly regional and national instead of international, and the focus is on the industrial structure. Some inferences could be drawn from the characteristics of the industries where these movements take place. MNEs are more present where intangible assets are relatively more important than plant-economies of scale (Markusen, 1995), and their presence is associated with a high ratio of R&D relative to sales, a large number of white-collars, and product differentiation (Markusen, 1998). An effort in this direction is represented by Guerrieri and Manzocchi (1996), who, in researching whether the process of integration has favoured the convergence or the polarization of the industrial structures across European countries, also ask whether FDI contributed to the observed trend. The answer is (indirectly) positive, since there is no clear evidence of structural convergence, and since FDI is concentrated in sectors characterized by factors that strengthen the national features of specialization rather than triggering a process of structural convergence (like supply- and demand-side linkages, and the presence of skilled labour and knowledge spillovers).

The topic of integration is a crucial one, since it is expected to shape the industrial outlook of countries (regions and areas), with important consequences for labour re-allocation, and for patterns of employment and unemployment. If the spread of industries towards foreign countries is a reaction to trade and export barriers, the obvious prediction is an investment diversion effect following a process of economic integration: a reduction of *intra-regional* (for instance, *intra*-EU) FDI – and MNEs' activity in general – is expected when trade costs and other impediments to free trade between the components of the region become less and less relevant. We know from the NEG, however, that the relationship is likely to be U-shaped: from dispersion – to overcome the problem of high transport costs – to concentration – following their decrease during the integration processes – to dispersion again when further reductions in transport costs make the disadvantages of agglomeration outweigh its advantages. Moreover, if FDI is something other than a tariff-jump phenomenon – as the discussion of the previous sections should have suggested – the effects arising from the integration process could be more complex and not so easily detectable.

The process of European integration has undoubtedly influenced the location decision of firms: new markets, new legislation, new customers, foster the re-adjustment and re-organization of economic activity. The single currency and the reduced transaction costs should help firms in exploiting with greater efficiency some of the more intrinsic characteristics of industrial location, such as geography strictu sensu (for instance, closeness to transportation hubs) or a better availability of endowment (for instance, proximity to research labs). At the same time, integration should accelerate the process of industrial agglomeration *if* some profitability accrues to the firm through being close to other firms, as happens, for instance, when knowledge-intensive production processes are involved. Market expansion, creation of scale economies, production efficiency and other characteristics of a customs union should promote greater innovative activity and reinforce the ownership advantages, thus stimulating additional direct investment (Markusen, 1998). As a matter of fact, these kinds of agglomeration advantages (dynamic agglomeration economies) are reputed to be more and more important, while easy access to inputs and to final markets are of diminishing importance.

Yannopoulos (1992), gives an overview of the literature on the relationship between European integration and FDI up to the beginning of the 1990s. The empirical debate in the late 1960s and early 1970s showed that the location pattern of total US investment abroad changed significantly after the formation of the EC, and that the latter definitely had a strong influence on the former. The intra-EC investment too appeared to experience a change: some empirical studies – reviewed in the article – revealed that the formation of a European customs union coincided with a rise in the EC non-domestic production of European Community firms through an increase in the number of foreign subsidiaries of EC firms established in other countries of the Community. Subsequent studies (Barrell and Pain, 1997a, 1997b, 1999a, 1999b; Pain, 1997; Pain and Lansbury, 1997; Braunerhjelm et al., 2000; Girma, 2002) confirm that the formation of the European Union has stimulated the MNEs' activity.

The positive relationship between a process of economic integration and FDI implies the existence of a set of variables able to influence their location, which are magnified during the process. This is surely the case for the market potential, or for more favourable legislation, or for a greater degree of industrialization. However, variables like the presence and the quality of infrastructures, the attributes of the workforce, and previous links with the area are important locational factors fairly independent of the integration process, and not so much examined. On these specific variables representative of the agglomeration forces for the FDI case,[12] some studies exist focusing on a few host or source countries. Wheeler and Mody (1992), provide a robust result on agglomeration for US firms, and Billington (1999), replicates it insofar as he shows that the agglomeration variables emerge as important at a regional level (within the United Kingdom) instead of at country level (the choice of the United Kingdom from among seven different industrialized source countries).

Using the same Wheeler and Mody framework – a 'model' consisting of one equation whose right-hand side is the set of variables intended to capture the various effects – Kumar (2000), too gets the result that US and Japanese MNEs are sensitive to the agglomeration variables: the extent of urbanization, geographical proximity, the availability of better infrastructure. Head et al. (1995), show that the location of Japanese FDI is significantly influenced by the location of previous Japanese investment in the same industry, thus giving proof of a self-reinforcing mechanism in the agglomeration process (and Head et al., 1998 subsequently investigate the industry characteristics that are systematically related to agglomeration). The same result about Japanese firms in horizontal *keiretsu* is reached by Blonigen et al. (2005), who find that the horizontal *keiretsu* activity affects a firm's FDI location decision. The idea of the existence of agglomeration economies that motivate foreign-owned establishments to cluster among themselves is further explored from a different perspective by Shaver (1998), who wonders whether there exists a different locational pattern between foreign- and US-owned firms, finding that in 1987, the year of observation, the location distribution in the United States was indeed different. The reason is found both in a 'technological' difference between the establishments, which requires different inputs, and in the necessity for foreign-owned firms to counterbalance the disadvantage they have with respect to US-owned firms by choosing states where the labour market is more flexible. The existing clustering is likely to increase insofar as the entrants benefit from looking at the experiences of previous foreign entrants. This tendency of firms to emulate 'similar' firms' location decisions and to concentrate where the demand is highest – Harris's (1954) market potential argument – is further confirmed for the Japanese case by Head and Mayer (2004), who estimate the optimal location choice arising from a model of imperfect competition in a multi-location setting.

Braunerhjelm and Svensson (1996), find that in the case of Swedish MNEs the agglomeration effects show up as strongly positive and significant: firms are clearly attracted by the presence of others in the same industry, and the forces of agglomeration appear to attract FDI in high-technology industries. In a subsequent contribution they add that this pattern of agglomeration is limited to R&D-intensive production, in line with the results of the literature on spillovers (Braunerhjelm and Svensson, 1998). Becker et al. (2005) find that German MNEs are attracted by host countries with relatively abundant supplies of skilled labour, but they do not find any such evidence for Sweden, which is in contrast with the Braunerhjelm and Svensson result. Crozet et al. (2004), too, provide clear evidence of a strong relationship between agglomeration and spillovers for MNEs' location decision in France. They also show that there seems to be a 'learning' process insofar as foreign firms select initially the locations closer to their home market and subsequently prefer to privilege the location of the final demand. A similar explanation was found for Italy too by Mariotti and Piscitello (1995), who found that the acquisition decisions of foreign investors in the host country are mainly ruled by information costs. Still on France – this time on French MNEs' location abroad – Ferrer (1998) also finds that agglomeration effects play a significant role.

At a very local level, Guimarães et al. (2000), for Portugal and Basile (2004), for Italy represent an effort to isolate the purely spatial motivations of FDI. The former study provides evidence that agglomeration economies – especially in the form of service agglomeration – have a decisive impact on the location of foreign investment. The latter analyses data at a NUTS 3 degree of disaggregation for Italy, and finds the 'nationality' effect exists here too: for green-field facilities, foreign investors are influenced by past foreign investments more than by the presence of domestic competitors. Unfortunately, the two studies are not comparable, as very often happens, as far as the empirical methodology is concerned.

Finally, as far as the economies in transition are concerned, the choice of where to locate is likely to be less relevant since the majority of FDI in these countries are acquisitions enforced by the privatization process. Motivations for location such as the presence of other firms from the same sector, or from the same country, are probably absent since such factors did not exist until quite recently. However, the results of the wide research coordinated by Gradev are that 'territorial distribution of FDI, both regionally and nationally, reveals similar patterns of concentration in areas with the highest labour costs in the region/country, less problems with unemployment, and a good educational level and developed infrastructure' (Gradev, 2001, p. 13). In other words, FDI is more triggered by the quality of labour than by its pure cost. In the Polish case specifically, Altomonte and Resmini (2002) find no evidence for agglomeration patterns involving only multinational firms.

10.5 FDI AND THE ECONOMIES IN TRANSITION

The case of the economies in transition represents the apotheosis of the loss of connection between theory and empirics. If the two are not in step in the industrialized countries' case, no wonder that they are even further apart here. Statistics are still scarce and full of discontinuities, and language barriers and differences in economic and institutional structure compound the difficulties. Moreover, these countries are neither developed nor underdeveloped, since the amount of human capital they possess is as great as that of the industrialized countries. The theory developed to account for the two-way trade between similar advanced economies cannot be applied, and the approaches used in the theory of development are not exactly suitable either. Thus, the choice for the estimation equation is justified pragmatically rather than presented as the outcome of a structural derivation, and the variables that can supposedly influence the FDI towards the transition economies are added to or subtracted from an equation, sometimes of the 'gravity' type. Until the end of the 1990s, relatively few studies took a quantitative approach to the complex relationship between FDI and the economies of the EU newcomers. Most surveys and econometric studies belonging to this first wave are concisely reviewed by Holland et al. (2000), which allows us to concentrate here on the more recent ones.

It is certainly true that the study of transition-economies implies the need for a set of variables concerning the overall social and political situation in addition to the more commonly used control variables such as the size of the market (and/or potential demand) and some (mainly labour) cost differential. The first should capture the horizontal MNEs' activity *replicating* production in a market-seeking strategy, while the second one should give account of the vertical MNEs' activity *fragmenting* production in an efficiency-seeking vision. A measure of the gographical distance is often added, to capture either the transport costs or the cultural gap, or both. These countries have been experimenting during the 1990s with a radical change in the legal system and in the entire set of formal institutions. In the transition-countries' case, relative backwardness in their business operating conditions, including the ongoing process of liberalization and privatization, and some political risk concerning the quality of the institutional environment and of the legal framework must therefore be considered. Variables intended to capture these aspects are in general added to the main set without any specific theoretical underpinning, with the noticeable exception of Altomonte (2000), who quotes the option theory of investment where 'the expected uncertainty of investors is related to efficiency, transparency, and enforceability of the institutional framework of the host economy'.

Among the others, Bevan et al. (2004) are very accurate in the description of the effects of the institutional environment and in providing the testable hypotheses. Their contribution is by and large also the most complete, insofar as these aspects are concerned. In a broadly exhaustive list, the variables considered as representative of 'institutions' in a general sense are: the operation risk index (ORI) in Altomonte (2000) and Resmini (2001); political risk index (PRI) and legal framework index – all provided by BERI (Business Environment Risk Intelligence) – respectively in Singh and Jun (1996) and in Altomonte (2000); the credit rating index elaborated by Institutional Investment in Bevan and Estrin (2004); the World Bank institutional and legal quality indices in Garibaldi et al. (2001); the EBRD index for the degree of development of security markets and non-financial institutions in Garibaldi et al. (2001); an EBRD overall composite index in Deichmann (2001), in Javorcik (2002) and in Bevan et al. (2004); Transparency International's corruption-perception index in Javorcik (2002); the Euromoney market-perception index in Garibaldi et al. (2001) and in Frenkel et al. (2004); some indices elaborated by individual scholars such as the indicator of risk derived through the principal components analysis in Holland and Pain (1998); the 'liberalization index' calculated by de Melo et al. (1996) and utilized also by Kinoshita and Campos (2003) and by Garibaldi et al. (2001); an index of capital flows restrictions computed by Garibaldi et al. (2001); infrastructure condition indicators again elaborated by individual scholars, like in Deichmann (2001) and in Melloni and Soci (2005); and indicators of the privatization process and methods usually proxied by dummy variables. As recalled above, Bevan et al. (2004), cover all the aspects: besides the composite 'transition index' already mentioned, they consider small- and large-scale privatization, the private sector share in GDP, the method of privatization, the bank and non-bank reform, the price liberalization, the trade liberalization, the competition policy, the coverage and the effectiveness of the legal system.

Some broad 'regularities' in the results can be detected notwithstanding the fact that the empirical estimates range over different time spans, and sets of home and host countries, and technical procedures as well.

First, the institutional variables just mentioned are highly significant. As a matter of fact, surveys of foreign investors reported by Lankes and Venables (1996) reveal that the political and socioeconomic conditions are the key obstacles to investment. The same authors find that 'host-country transition progress, perceived political stability and low perceived risk levels are associated not only with the overall level of FDI inflow, but also with the character of the investment' (p. 346). That is to say, an investment that is more firmly maintained, and more integrated with the general policies of the parent firm.[13] A later large research study coordinated by Gradev

(2001) confirms that the strategic decision-set involves a large bundle of considerations concerning the political climate and the infrastructural conditions. A composite variable for investment climate is in fact extremely important also in Deichmann (2001) and the aggregate 'institutional' index is significant in Bevan et al. (2004). The perception of risk – proxied through various variables – and the state of economic liberalization and of reforms are highly significant in Garibaldi et al. (2001) and Javorcik (2002). The PRI and ORI variables are extremely significant in Singh and Jun (1996); the ORI variable has a strong effect in Altomonte (2000) and in Resmini (2001), where it has a particular impact in scale-intensive sectors; the risk index and the economic development index play a substantial role in Frenkel et al. (2004); the proxy for infrastructures and the indices for the external liberalization are the most robust variables in Kinoshita and Campos (2003). Only Lansbury et al. (1996) and Bevan and Estrin (2004), find no role for the 'country risk' variable. However, they both use nonconventional variables: the former adopts 'the principal component of . . . inflation, government debt stock, government deficit, and the inverse of the reserve cover ratio' (Lansbury et al., 1996, p. 113), and the latter uses the credit rating of the Institutional Investor, which is an indicator based upon the opinion of international banks. It is quite conceivable that institutional investors believe that the process of transition is too big to fail even though it necessarily has some costs, and that no such worries enter their decisional process of investing in this area.

As far as privatization is concerned, Djankov and Murrell (2002) – which is the most exhaustive study to our knowledge – assert that the aggregate effects of privatization on enterprise restructuring in the CEECs are positive and that different types of owners – that is to say, different methods of privatization – are of great economic importance since they have different effects on the business environment. Also, Kalotay and Hunya (2000), Holland and Pain (1998) and Melloni and Soci (2005) affirm that the methods matter, while Bevan et al. (2004) assess that they do not have meaningful implications for FDI. Nevertheless, they find that the privatization variables are highly significant, and Estrin et al. (2004) add the result that mass privatization enhances growth. Within the long list of variables tested by Bevan et al. (2004), only non-bank reform and price liberalization turn out not to be significant: foreign direct investors probably do not resort to local financial markets, and prefer protected markets to liberalized ones in order to gain market power.

Second, the size of the market and the potential demand – sometimes called 'gravity factors' – are consolidated variables. They were surveyed as fairly important in Holland et al. (2000) and they turn out to be extremely significant in Altomonte (2000), Javorcik (2002), Bevan et al. (2004) and

Bevan and Estrin (2004), the latter also showing a significant 'announcement' effect related to the EU accession of some CEECs and indicative of future demand and new markets. An effect of this kind has been found (Cieślik and Ryan, 2004) for Japanese firms that act in a relatively isolated economy and make FDI also because the host country has a potential for serving other markets. The stimulus to FDI from the expected accession has also been given theoretical support in Manzocchi and Ottaviano (2001).

Other 'traditional' variables seem to provide less consistent results. In any case, it should be recalled that transition is a *process* that has been evolving very rapidly, making it quite conceivable that some motivations are no longer in effect. Thus, results that are sometimes contradictory should not come as a surprise. An interesting case is that of the 'distance' variable, which is not significant in Altomonte (2000), while it was significant earlier (see Cieślik, 1996). Distance being a proxy for customary relations, it is quite conceivable that at the beginning of the transition process FDI tended to come from closer neighbours – mainly Germany and Austria – and that only subsequently would more remote partners – more 'culturally distant' partners – intervene. This is the 'proximity-matter' argument very often present in the literature on FDI.

Analogously, in the earlier studies the proxies for endowments (generally some difference between labour costs at home and in the host country) do not have the significance they acquire – if any[14] – later on and, at least at the beginning, they seem more important in choosing the location *among* the countries in transition (Holland and Pain, 1998; Lansbury et al., 1996). For instance, the labour-cost differentials are not significant in Cieślik (1996), while they do turn out to be significant in the later work by Altomonte (2000), Deichmann (2001) and Bevan and Estrin (2004). The explanation could easily be that at the beginning of the process the option was a first-mover market-seeking one, coming from those developed countries that were more able to disentangle what was going on in the transition-countries. In fact, the evidence is that the first wave of FDI was made by small or medium-sized enterprises from neighbouring countries, together with MNEs based in Germany, Austria, the Netherlands and also, but not mainly, in the United States (Cieślik and Ryan, 2004).

Lankes and Venables (1996), too, recall that the function of the projects (serving the local market or being export-supply-oriented) varies with the progress in transition. Again, no (or a limited) role for the cost variables is consistent with an early structure of large 'horizontal' MNEs – mainly interested in the replication of both production and distribution – that evolves towards a structure where 'vertical' MNEs are also present, interested in some form of fragmentation of their production, and enlarges eventually to a group with a conspicuous presence of smaller latecomers: labour-intensive SMEs more sensitive to costs. Resmini's (2001) sectoral results, for instance, provide evidence of such a structure. The role of incentives (fiscal, financial and others) seems limited from the beginning of the transition, as the early studies by Lansbury et al. (1996) and Economists Advisory Group Ltd. (1998), suggest. Sass (2003) and Halpern and Muraközy (2005) provide more recent confirmation.

In the case of transition, the longstanding relationship between FDI and trade is seen through the eyes of the host countries, probably because their concern about the process of transition focuses on the reaction of their economic structure to the new and shocking situation. The question now is: do FDI inflows contribute to developing the exports of the host countries? Evidence for their complementarity is provided by numerous studies. Besides those cited in Holland et al. (2000), it is worthwhile recalling Singh and Jun (1996); Hunya (1997); Brenton et al. (1999); Altzinger and Bellak (1999); Eltetö (2000); Kaminski (2001); Deichmann (2001); Javorcik (2002); Bevan and Estrin (2004); Bradshaw (2005), and Kaminski and Ng (2005). Nevertheless, the view that FDI contributes to exports insofar as it is connected with both exports and imports is both reductive and optimistic, and it can lead eventually to trade deficits rather than surpluses (Hunya, 1997; Kalotay and Hunya, 2000). It is better to say that FDI contributes to the openness of these economies, and to their further integration in a worldwide context.

Finally, let us consider the effects of FDI on the internal transformation of the economies, and on growth. As is well known, FDI is expected to be beneficial insofar as it provides a source of financial capital crucial for the transition process, since the domestic sources are necessarily scarce in these countries, and insofar as it spills over into the rest of the economy. It should be a means to transfer technology (both embodied in the real physical capital equipment and disembodied, such as production and management know-how). The presence of foreign companies should improve the overall efficiency and expose domestic companies to international standards. FDI would provide the state with income from the privatization process, and the taxes that ensue. Unfortunately, none of these effects emerge in transition as unequivocally robust outcomes, as the summary provided by Sass (2003, Table 5, p. 18) confirms.

We will here just add to that table. In the early years of transition there did not appear to be any contribution of FDI to overall growth (Holland et al., 2000), as it is quite conceivable that this effect requires a substantial amount of time to be registered. That is why the studies showing some effect are mainly about the Czech Republic, Hungary and Poland, which are the countries with the longest experience of transition. As far as the effects on growth are concerned, it seems largely agreed that FDI has contributed to growth, with robust evidence that foreign-owned firms outperformed domestic ones, giving rise to both macroeconomic and to microeconomic restructuring (see Hunya, 2000, p. 194 and also Bosco, 2001, specifically on Hungary). Holland and Pain (1998), find that the inward flows enhanced technical progress, but with all the problems of measurement connected with this issue. Whether or not overall growth was also augmented by spillovers from foreign-owned to domestic firms is less clear (Knell, 2000). Barrell and Holland (2000), provide results showing that FDI contributed to labour-augmenting technical progress in most manufacturing sectors in the Czech Republic, Hungary and Poland, due to the *intangibles* introduced by foreign firms.

Marin et al. (2003), find evidence of technology spillovers in the case of German firms to their affiliates in the CEECs. It should not be forgotten that they mostly belong to the high-technology sector, and the German firms protect themselves by choosing full ownership as the dominant entry mode. By contrast, Uminski and Stepniak (2004), show for Poland that it is just a 'second rank' category of technical progress that has very often been transferred. In the Czech case, Kinoshita (2001), finds that spillovers exist and are stronger where R&D is higher, which can be thought of as a confirmation of the presence of absorptive capacity (Kokko, 1994).

Again in the Czech Republic, even though the positive impact of FDI on total factor productivity of the recipient firms is confirmed also by Djankov and Hoekman (2000), these same authors find that foreign participation in an industry has a *statistically significant negative effect* on the performance of other firms not having foreign partnership, as though a competition effect was dominating the technological effect. Konings (2001) – for Bulgaria and Romania – and Holland et al. (2000) – for Poland, the Czech Republic and Hungary – confirm these results. It seems that foreign ownership limits the options for future company strategies and for R&D activity (Hunya, 1997), and that some crowding out of domestic firms has taken place (UNCTAD, 1999 and UNCTAD, 2003). However, notwithstanding the fact that sometimes the acquired firms are flattened to sub-units, and that the staff is reduced, all the surveys of the 1990s indicate that the new organizational discipline and the innovative role of being part of the MNE network led to an overall improvement in the industrial relations world (Kalotay and Hunya, 2000). Finally, Halpern and Muraközy (2005) – in a study concerned with distance and the spatial effects of spillovers – find strong spillovers operating at a small distance from the foreign-owned firms to the domestic ones.

At a first glance, the employment side suffers most, and the unemployment created by the enterprise restructuring has not been absorbed by FDI. At least for the Czech Republic and Slovakia, inward flows had minimum effects on employment, did not upgrade skills, produced marked wage differentials between areas with and without FDI and did not democratize industrial relations (Smith and Pavlinek, 2000). Approximately the same conclusions are drawn by Gradev (2001). In the Polish case, being privatized had a positive impact on employment but this is a short-run effect since it is concentrated within a range of three to six years after privatization (Mickiewicz et al., 2005). However, positive linkage effects on employment generated by foreign manufacturing firms are found for the Polish economy by Altomonte and Resmini (2002) – in a setting where upstream and downstream industries are present – and for the Czech economy on an 18-sector basis by Kippenberg (2005), showing that the linkages of 'FDI firms' to domestic firms depend to a great extent on *sectoral* characteristics.

10.6   CONCLUSIONS

The scope of FDI, the characteristics of the firms that produce it, the industrial structure of the markets to which it turns, the distinguishing features of the sector in which it occurs, and the typology of the host countries, all make FDI a puzzling phenomenon when considered in aggregate form. The array of empirical results reveals that FDI is an extremely relevant facet of reality but one that lacks a unified theoretical explanation, and it seems at this point very unlikely that such a unified theory will emerge. On the other hand, there is reason to believe that progress might be made when one considers some of the more narrowly defined aspects of FDI.

Within this perspective, NEG could help to throw some light on aspects of FDI that are of considerable interest. Space – both in its physical and economic sense – must play a decisive role in the decision of firms regarding where they should locate, or re-locate. Unfortunately, little effort has been made up until now to incorporate much more than the 'flavour' of space into the theoretical and empirical framework of FDI. The suggestion is, therefore, that future research should abandon the macro-view of FDI and rely more and more on detailed firm-studies and micro-data, with a greater emphasis on the spatial elements. With this perspective it is possible that there will be a more serious interplay between FDI analysis and the developing theories of NEG and of 'old' and 'new' trade theory, as these theories mature and become more strongly integrated with other branches of economics also.

NOTES

1. OECD (1996, pp. 7–8). This is the current definition of FDI, endorsed also by the IMF, and accepted by the UN.
2. However, Markusen (1995 and 1998), will raise this same critique to the 'new trade theory'.
3. See – as a summa of the new trade theory – Helpman and Krugman (1985), especially Ch. 2.
4. For a brilliant survey of the new economic geography of the 1990s, see Ottaviano and Puga (1998).
5. 'Jointness' happens when the same headquarters' asset is used in multiple production locations without reducing the services provided in any location.
6. The most up-to-date synthesis of the empirical literature states that, at least for the United States, 'it seems clear that vertical motivations are not prevalent in the general FDI patterns' (Blonigen, 2005, p. 26).
7. As mentioned in the introduction, the whole topic of the host-country effect goes beyond the scope here and will not be addressed.
8. Unfortunately, Blonigen et al. (2003), detected a serious misspecification in Carr et al. (2001), and showed that, once corrected for it, the estimates no longer reject the horizontal model in favour of the knowledge capital model. However, this should not have implications for the relationship with trade.
9. It should not be forgotten that Ekholm uses Swedish data while Brainard works on US data.
10. Dunning (1998), just lists the variables influencing the location by MNEs in the 1970s and 1990s.
11. Head and Mayer (2003), review the few studies based on the 'market potential'.
12. Several studies exist on the agglomerative motives for firms *without* both FDI and MNEs. LaFountain (2005) is the most recent example of an extensive study that intends to test the predominant influence on firms' location decision discriminating among natural advantage models (which emphasize proximity to specialized inputs), production externality models (which emphasize proximity to sources of positive externalities in production) and market access models (which emphasize proximity to customers).
13. It should not be forgotten that the geo-political risk turned out as a very relevant motivation for the firms also in a study not specifically focusing on the transition such as Wheeler and Mody (1992).
14. The 'wage' variable is not significant even in a fairly recent paper such as Garibaldi et al. (2001).

REFERENCES

Altomonte, C. (2000), 'Economic Determinants and Institutional Frameworks: FDI in Economies in Transition', *Transnational Corporations*, **9**: 75–106.
Altomonte, C. and L. Resmini (2002), 'Multinational Corporations as a Catalyst for Local Industrial Development. The Case of Poland', *Scienze Regionali*, **1**: 29–58.
Altzinger, W. and C. Bellak (1999), 'Direct Versus Indirect FDI: Impact on Domestic Exports and Employment', *Wirtschaftsuniversität Wien*, Working Paper No. 9.
Amiti, M. and K. Wakelin (2003), 'Investment Liberalization and International Trade', *Journal of International Economics*, **61**: 101–26.
Baldwin, Richard E. et al. (2003), *Economic Geography and Public Policy*, Princeton, US: Princeton University Press.

Barba Navaretti, Giorgio and Anthony J. Venables (2004), *Multinational Firms in the World Economy*, Princeton, US: Princeton University Press.

Barrell, R. and D. Holland (2000), 'FDI and Enterprise Restructuring in Central Europe', *Economics of Transition*, **8**: 477–504.

Barrell, R. and N. Pain (1997a), 'The Growth of FDI in Europe', *National Institute Economic Review*, **160**: 63–75.

Barrell, R. and N. Pain (1997b), 'Foreign Direct Investment, Technological Change and Economic Growth within Europe', *Economic Journal*, **107**: 1770–86.

Barrell, R. and N. Pain (1999a), 'The Growth of FDI in Europe', in R. Barrell and N. Pain (eds), *Innovation, Investment, and the Diffusion of Technology in Europe*, Cambridge, UK: Cambridge University Press.

Barrell, R. and N. Pain (1999b), 'Domestic Institutions, Agglomerations and Foreign Direct Investment in Europe', *European Economic Review*, **43**: 925–34.

Barrios, S. et al. (2001), 'Multinational Enterprises and New Trade Theory: Evidence for the Convergence Hypothesis', *Discussion Paper 2827*, Centre for Economic Policy Research, London.

Basile, R. (2004), 'Acquisition Versus Green-field Investment: the Location of Foreign Manufacturers in Italy', *Regional Science and Urban Economics*, **34**: 3–25.

Becker, S. et al. (2005), 'Location Choice and Employment Decisions: a Comparison of German and Swedish Multinationals', *Discussion Paper 4887*, Centre for Economic Policy Research, London.

Bevan, A. and S. Estrin (2004), 'The Determinants of Foreign Direct Investment into European Transition Economies', *Journal of Comparative Economics*, **32**: 775–87.

Bevan, A. et al. (2004), 'Foreign Investment Location and Institutional Development in Transition Economies', *International Business Review*, **13**: 43–64.

Billington, N. (1999), 'The Location of Foreign Direct Investment: an Empirical Analysis', *Applied Economics*, **31**: 65–76.

Blomström, M. and A. Kokko (1994), 'Home Country Effects of Foreign Direct Investment: Evidence from Sweden', in S. Globerman (ed.), *Canadian-based Multinationals*, Calgary, CA: Calgary University Press.

Blomström, M. and A. Kokko (1998), 'Multinational Corporation and Spillovers', *Journal of Economic Surveys*, **12**: 247–77.

Blomström, M. and A. Kokko (2003), 'Human Capital and Inward FDI', *Discussion Paper 3762*, Centre for Economic Policy Research, London.

Blomström, M. et al. (1988), 'U.S. and Swedish Direct Investment and Exports', in R.E. Baldwin (ed.), *Trade Policy Issues and Empirical Analysis*, Chicago, US: University of Chicago Press.

Blonigen, B.A. (2005), 'A Review of the Empirical Literature on FDI Determinants', *NBER Working Paper 11299*, National Bureau of Economic Research.

Blonigen, B.A. et al. (2003), 'Estimating the Knowledge Capital Model of the Multinational Enterprise: Comment', *American Economic Review*, **93**: 980–94.

Blonigen, B.A. et al. (2005), 'Industrial Groupings and FDI', *Journal of International Economics*, **65**: 75–91.

Bosco, M.G. (2001), 'Does FDI Contribute to Technological Spillovers and Growth? A Panel Data Analysis of Hungarian Firms', *Transnational Corporations*, **10**: 43–67.

Bradshaw, M.J. (2005), 'FDI and Economic Transformation in Central and Eastern Europe', in D. Turnock (ed.), *FDI and Regional Development in East Central Europe and the Former Soviet Union*, Aldershot: Ashgate.

Brainard, L.S. (1993), 'An Empirical Assessment of the Factor Proportions Explanation of Multinational Sales', *NBER Working Paper 4583*, National Bureau of Economic Research.

Brainard, L.S. (1997), 'An Empirical Assessment of the Proximity–Concentration Trade-off Between Multinational Sales and Trade', *American Economic Review*, **87**: 520–44.

Braunerhjelm, P. (1998), 'Organization of the Firm, Foreign Production and Trade', in P. Braunerhjelm and K. Ekholm (eds), *The Geography of Multinational Firms*, Boston: Kluwer.

Braunerhjelm, P. and R. Svensson (1996), 'Host Country Characteristics and Agglomeration in Foreign Direct Investment', *Applied Economics*, **28**: 833–40.

Braunerhjelm, P. and R. Svensson (1998), 'Agglomeration in the Geographical Location of Swedish MNEs', in P. Braunerhjelm and K. Ekholm (eds), *The Geography of Multinational Firms*, Boston, Kluwer, pp. 99–115.

Braunerhjelm, P. et al. (2000), 'Integration and the Regions of Europe: How the Right Policies Can Prevent Polarization', Centre for Economic Policy Research, Monitoring European Integration (10).

Brenton, P. et al. (1999), 'Economic Integration and FDI: an Empirical Analysis of Foreign Investment in the EU and in Central and Eastern Europe', *Empirica*, **26**: 95–121.

Buckley, P.J. and M. Casson (1998), 'Analysing Foreign Market Entry Strategies: Extending the Internalization Approach', *Journal of International Business Studies*, **29**: 539–62.

Carr, D.L. et al. (2001), 'Estimating the Knowledge-capital Model of the Multinational Enterprise', *American Economic Review*, **91**: 693–708.

Caves, R.E. (1996), *Multinational Enterprises and Economic Analysis*, Cambridge: Cambridge University Press.

Chakrabarti, A. (2001), 'The Determinants of FDI: Sensitivity Analyses of Cross-country Regressions', *Kyklos*, **54**: 89–114.

Cieślik, A. (1996), 'Foreign Direct Investment in Central Europe's Transition: Early Results', *Economic Discussion Papers No. 28*, Faculty of Economic Sciences, University of Warsaw.

Cieślik, A. and M. Ryan (2004), 'Explaining Japanese Direct Investment Flows into an Enlarged Europe: a Comparison of Gravity and Economic Potential Approaches', *Journal of the Japanese and International Economics*, **18**: 12–37.

Crozet, M. et al. (2004), 'How Do Firms Agglomerate? A Study of FDI in France', *Regional Science and Urban Economics*, **34**: 27–54.

Deichman, J.I. (2001), 'Distribution of FDI among Transition Economies in Central and Eastern Europe', *Post-Soviet Geography and Economics*, **42**: 142–52.

de Melo, M. et al. (1996), 'From Plan to the Market: Patterns of Transition', The World Bank, Policy Research Working Papers No. 1564.

Di Mauro, F. (2000), 'The Impact of Economic Integration on FDI and Exports: a Gravity Approach, Centre for European Policy Studies Working Document No. 156.

Djankov, S. and B. Hoekman (2000), 'Foreign Investment and Productivity Growth in Czech Enterprises', *The World Bank Economic Review*, **14**: 49–64.

Djankov, S. and P. Murrell (2002), 'Enterprise Restructuring in Transition: a Quantitative Survey', *Journal of Economic Literature*, **40**: 739–92.

Dunning, J.H. (1977), 'Trade, Location of Economic Activity and MNE: a Search for an Eclectic Approach', in B. Ohlin et al. (eds), *The International Allocation of Economic Activity*, London, UK: Macmillan.

Dunning, J.H. (1998), 'Location and the MNE: a Neglected Factor?', *Journal of International Business Studies*, **29**: 45–66.

Economists Advisory Group Ltd. (1998), 'Foreign Direct Investment', *The Single Market Review*, **1**: Impact on Trade and Investment.

Egger, P. et al. (2005), 'Knowledge-capital Meets New Economic Geography', Center for Economic Studies and Institute for Economic Research Working Paper No. 1432.

Ekholm, K. (1998), 'Proximity Advantages, Scale Economies, and the Location of Production', in P. Braunerhjelm and K. Ekholm (eds), *The Geography of Multinational Firms*, Boston, Kluwer.

Ekholm, K. and R. Forslid (2001), 'Trade and Location with Horizontal and Vertical Multi-region Firms', *Scandinavian Journal of Economics*, **104**: 101–18.

Ekholm, K. et al. (2003), 'Export-platform Foreign Direct Investment', NBER Working Paper 9517, National Bureau of Economic Research.

Éltetö, A. (2000), 'The Impact of FDI on the Foreign Trade of CECs', in G. Hunya (ed.), *Integration through FDI*, Cheltenham, UK and Northampton, MA, USA: Edward Elgar.

Estrin, S. et al. (2004), 'Privatization Methods and Economic Growth in Transition Economies', Fondazione ENI-Enrico Mattei Working Paper No. 105.04.

Ethier, W.J. (1986), 'The Multinational Firm', *Quarterly Journal of Economics*, **CI**: 805–33.

Ethier, W. and R.J. Markusen (1996), 'Multinational Firms, Technology Diffusion and Trade', *Journal of International Economics*, **41**: 1–28.

Falzoni, A.M. (1993), 'Investimenti diretti e commercio internazionale: complementi o sostituti?', CESPRI, Working Paper No. 65.

Farrell, R. et al. (2004), 'Determinants of Japan's FDI: an Industry and Country Panel Study, 1984–1998', *Journal of the Japanese and International Economics*, **18**: 161–82.

Ferrer, C. (1998), 'Pattern and Determinants of Location Decisions by French Multinationals in European Regions', in J.-L. Mucchielli (ed.), *Multinational Location Strategy*, London, JAI Press.

Fontagné, L. and M. Pajot (1997), 'How FDI Affects International Trade and Competitiveness: an Empirical Assessment', Centre d'Etudes Prospectives et d'Informations Internationales Document de Travail No. 07–17.

Frenkel, M. et al. (2004), 'A Panel Analysis of Bilateral FDI Flows to Emerging Economies', *Economic Systems*, **28**: 281–300.

Fujita, M. et al. (1999), *The Spatial Economy*, Cambridge, US: MIT Press.

Fujita, M. and J.-F. Thisse (2002), *Economics of Agglomeration, Cities, Industrial Location, and Regional Growth*, Cambridge: Cambridge University Press.

Garibaldi, P. et al. (2001), 'What Moves Capital to Transition Economies?', *International Monetary Fund, Staff Papers*, **48**: 109–45.

Gattai, V. (2005), 'From the Theory of the Firm to FDI and Internalization: a Survey', Fondazione ENI-Enrico Mattei, No. 51.2005.

Girma, S. (2002), 'The Process of European Integration and the Determinants of Entry by Non-EU Multinationals in UK Manufacturing', *The Manchester School*, **70**: 315–35.

Girma, S. et al. (2004), 'Exports, International Investment, and Plant Performance: Evidence from a Non-parametric Test', *Economic Letters*, **83**: 317–24.

Görg, H. and D. Greenaway (2002), 'Much Ado About Nothing? Do Domestic Firms Really Benefit from FDI?', CEPR DP No. 3485, August, also available in *World Bank Research Observer*, **19**(2): 171–97 (2004).

Görg, H. and D. Greenaway (2004), 'Much Ado About Nothing? Do Domestic Firms Really Benefit from FDI?', *World Bank Research Observer*, **19**: 171–97.

Görg, H. and E. Strobl (2001), 'Multinational Companies and Productivity Spillovers: a Meta-analysis', *Economic Journal*, **111**: F723–F739.

Gradev, G. (2001), 'EU Companies in Eastern Europe: Strategic Choices and Labour Effects', in G. Gradev (ed.), *CEE Countries in EU Companies' Strategies of Industrial Restructuring and Relocation*, Brussels: European Trade Union Institute.

Graham, E.M. (1994), 'Canadian Direct Investment Abroad and the Canadian Economy: Some Theoretical and Empirical Considerations', in S. Globerman (ed.), *Canadian-based Multinationals*, Calgary, CA: Calgary University Press.

Graham, E.M. (1996), 'The (Not Wholly Satisfactory) State of the Theory of Foreign Direct Investment and the Multinational Enterprise', *Journal of International and Comparative Economics*, **20**: 183–206.

Guerrieri, P. and S. Manzocchi (1996), 'Patterns of Trade and Foreign Direct Investment in European Manufacturing: "Convergence" or "Polarization"', *Rivista Italiana degli Economisti*, **1**: 213–31.

Guimarães, P. et al. (2000), 'Agglomeration and the Location of FDI in Portugal', *Journal of Urban Economics*, **47**: 115–35.

Halpern, L. and B. Muraközy (2005), 'Does Distance Matter in Spillover?', *Discussion Paper 4857*, Centre for Economic Policy Research, London.

Harris, C.D. (1954), 'The Market as a Factor in the Localization of Industry in the United States', *Annals of the Association of American Geographers*, **44**: 315–48.

Head, K. and T. Mayer (2003), 'The Empirics of Agglomeration and Trade', *Discussion Paper 3985*, Centre for Economic Policy Research, London.

Head, K. and T. Mayer (2004), 'Market Potential and the Location of Japanese Investment in the European Union', *Review of Economics and Statistics*, **86**: 959–72.

Head, K. and J. Ries (2001), 'Overseas Investment and Firm Exports', *Review of International Economics*, **9**: 108–22.

Head, K. et al. (1995), 'Agglomeration Benefits and Location Choice: Evidence from Japanese Manufacturing Investments in the United States', *Journal of International Economics*, **38**: 223–47.

Head, K. et al. (1998), 'Industry Agglomeration and the Location of Foreign Affiliates', in J.-L. Mucchielli (ed.), *Multinational Location Strategy*, London: JAI Press.

Helpman, E. (1984), 'Increasing Returns, Imperfect Markets, and Trade Theory', in R.W. Jones and P.B. Kenen (eds), *Handbook of International Economics*, Vol. I, Amsterdam: Elsevier Science.

Helpman, E. and P. Krugman (1985), *Market Structure and Foreign Trade*, Cambridge, MA and London: MIT Press.

Helpman, E. et al. (2003), 'Export versus FDI', *Discussion Paper 3741*, Centre for Economic Policy Research, London.

Hirsch, S. (1976), 'An International Trade and Investment Theory of the Firm', *Oxford Economic Papers*, **28**: 258–70.

Holland, D. and N. Pain (1998), 'The Diffusion of Innovation in Central and Eastern Europe: a Study of the Determinants and Impact of Foreign Direct Investment', National Institute of Economic and Social Research Working Paper No. 137.

Holland, D. et al. (2000), 'The Determinants and Impact of FDI in Central and Eastern Europe: A Comparison of Survey and Econometric Evidence', *Transnational Corporations*, **9**: 163–212.

Horstmann, I.J. and J.R. Markusen (1987a), 'Strategic Investment and the Development of Multinationals', *International Economic Review*, **28**: 109–21.

Horstmann, I.J. and J.R. Markusen (1987b), 'Licensing Versus Direct Investment: a Model of Internalization by the Multinational Enterprise', *Canadian Journal of Economics*, **20**: 464–81.

Horstmann, I.J. and J.R. Markusen (1992), 'Endogenous Market Structure in International Trade (Natura Facit Saltum)', *Journal of International Economics*, **32**: 109–29.

Horstmann, I.J. and J.R. Markusen (1996), 'Exploring New Markets: Direct Investment, Contractual Relations and the Multinational Enterprise', *International Economic Review*, **37**: 1–19.

Hufbauer, G. et al. (1994), 'Determinants of Direct Foreign Investment and its Connection to Trade', *UNCTAD Review*, 39–51.

Hunya, G. (1997), 'Large Privatization, Restructuring and Foreign Direct Investment', in S. Zecchini (ed.), *Lessons from the Economic Transition: Central and Eastern Europe in the 1990s*, Boston, Kluwer.

Hunya, G. (2000), 'Recent FDI Trends, Policies and Challenges in South-East European Countries', Wiener Institut für Internationale Wirtschftsvergleiche Research Report No. 273.

Hymer, S. (1976), 'The International Operations of Nationals Firms: a Study of FDI', PhD thesis, MIT [1960], Boston: MIT Press.

Javorcik, B.S. (2002), 'The Composition of FDI and Protection of Intellectual Property Rights: Evidence from Transition Economies', *World Bank Policy Research*, Working Paper No. 2786.

Kalotay, K. and G. Hunya (2000), 'Privatization and FDI in Central and Eastern Europe', *Transnational Corporations*, **9**: 39–66.

Kaminski, B. (2001), 'How Accession to the EU has Affected External Trade and FDI in CEE', *World Bank Policy Research*, Working Paper No. 2578.

Kaminski, B. and F. Ng (2005), 'Production Disintegration and Integration of Central Europe into Global Markets', *International Review of Economics & Finance*, **14**: 377–90.

Kinoshita, Y. (2001), 'R&D and Technology Spillovers through FDI: Innovation and Absorptive Capacity', *Discussion Paper 2775*, Centre for Economic Policy Research, London.

Kinoshita, Y. and N.F. Campos (2003), 'Why Does FDI Go Where it Goes? New Evidence from the Transition Economies', *Discussion Paper 3984*, Centre for Economic Policy Research, London.

Kippenberg, E. (2005), 'Sectoral Linkages of FDI Firms to the Czech Economy', *Research in International Business and Finance*, **19**: 251–65.

Knell, M. (2000), 'FIEs and Productivity Convergence in Central Europe', in G. Hunya (ed.), *Integration Through FDI*, Cheltenham, UK and Northampton, MA, USA: Edward Elgar.

Kokko, A. (1994), 'Technology, Market Characteristics, and Spillovers', *Journal of Development Economics*, **43**: 279–93.

Konings, J. (2001), 'The Effects of FDI on Domestic Firms: Evidence from Firm-level Panel Data in Emerging Economies', *Economics of Transition*, **9**: 619–33.

Krugman, P.R. (1983), 'The "New Theories" of International Trade and the Multinational Enterprise', in C.P. Kindleberger and D.B. Audretsch (eds), *The Multinational Corporations in the 1980s*, Boston: MIT Press.

Krugman, P.R. (1991a), *Geography and Trade*, Boston, MIT Press.

Krugman, P.R. (1991b), 'Increasing Returns and Economic Geography', *Journal of Political Economy*, **99**: 483–99.

Krugman, P.R. (1995), *Development, Geography and Economic Theory*, Boston, MIT Press.

Krugman, P.R. (1998), 'Space: the Final Frontier', *Journal of Economic Perspectives*, **12**: 161–74.

Kumar, N. (2000), 'Explaining the Geography and Depth of International Production: the Case of US and Japanese Multinational Enterprises', *Weltwirtschaftliches Archiv*, **136**: 442–77.

LaFountain, C. (2005), 'Where Do Firms Locate? Testing Competing Models of Agglomeration', *Journal of Urban Economics*, **58**: 338–66.

Lankes, H.P. and A.J. Venables (1996), 'FDI in Economic Transition: the Changing Pattern of Investment', *Economics of Transition*, **4**: 331–47.

Lansbury, M. et al. (1996), 'FDI in Central Europe since 1990: an Econometric Study', *National Institute Economic Review*, No. 156.

Lipsey, R.E. (2002), 'Home and Host Country Effects of FDI', *NBER Working Paper 9293*, National Bureau of Economic Research.

Manzocchi, S. and G.I.P. Ottaviano (2001), 'Outsiders in Economic Integration: the Case of a Transition Economy', *Economics of Transition*, **9**: 229–49.

Marin, D. et al. (2003), 'Ownership, Capital or Outsourcing: What Drives German Investment to Eastern Europe?', in H. Herrmann and R. Lipsey (eds), *Foreign Direct Investment in the Real and Financial Sector of Industrial Countries*, Heidelberg and New York: Springer.

Mariotti, S. and L. Piscitello (1995), 'Information Costs and Location of FDI within the Host Country: Empirical Evidence from Italy', *International Journal of Business Studies*, **26**: 815–41.

Markusen, J.R. (1983), 'Factor Movements and Commodity Trade as Complements', *Journal of International Economics*, **14**: 341–56.

Markusen, J.R. (1984), 'Multinationals, Multi-plant Economies, and the Gains from Trade', *Journal of International Economics*, **16**: 205–26.

Markusen, J.R. (1995), 'The Boundaries of Multinational Enterprises and the Theory of International Trade', *Journal of Economic Perspectives*, **9**: 169–89.

Markusen, J.R. (1997), 'Trade Versus Investment Liberalization', *NBER Working Paper 6231*, National Bureau of Economic Research.

Markusen, J.R. (1998), 'Multinational Enterprises and the Theories of Trade and Location', in P. Braunerhjelm and K. Ekholm (eds), *The Geography of Multinational Firms*, Boston: Kluwer.

Markusen, J.R. (2002), *Multinational Firms and the Theory of International Trade*, Cambridge, MA and London, MIT Press.

Markusen, J.R and K.E. Maskus (2001), 'General-equilibrium Approaches to the Multinational Firm: a Review of Theory and Evidence', National Bureau of Economic Research Working Paper No. 8334.

Markusen, J.R. and K.E. Maskus (2002), 'Discriminating Among Alternative Theories of the Multinational Enterprise', *Review of International Economics*, **10**: 694–707.

Markusen, J.R. and A.J. Venables (1996), 'The Increased Importance of Direct Investment in North Atlantic Economic Relationships: a Convergence Hypothesis', in M.B. Canzoneri et al. (eds), *The New Transatlantic Economy*, Cambridge: Cambridge University Press.

Markusen, J.R. and A.J. Venables (1998), 'Multinational Firms and the New Trade-theory', *Journal of International Economics*, **46**: 183–203.

Markusen, J.R. and A.J. Venables (1999), 'Foreign Direct Investment as a Catalyst for Industrial Development', *European Economic Review*, Special Issue on Trade and Geography, **43**: 335–56.

Markusen, J.R. and A.J. Venables (2000), 'The Theory of Endowments, Intra-industry and Multinational Trade', *Journal of International Economics*, **52**: 209–34.

Markusen, J.R. et al. (1996), 'A Unified Treatment of Horizontal Direct Investment, Vertical Direct Investment and the Pattern of Trade in Goods and Services', National Bureau of Economic Research Working Paper No. 5696.

Mayer, T. and J.-L. Mucchielli (1999), 'La Localisation a l'Etranger des Entreprises Multinationales', *Economie et Statistique*, **326–27**: 159–76.

Melloni, N. and A. Soci (2005), 'Institutional Change and FDI in Three Selected CEECs: the Czech Republic, Hungary and Poland', mimeo.

Mickiewicz, T. et al. (2005), 'Privatization, Corporate Control and Employment Growth: Evidence from a Panel of Polish Firms, 1996–2002', *Economic Systems*, **29**: 98–119.

Mody, A. et al. (2002), 'The Role of Information in Driving FDI: Theory and Evidence', *Discussion Paper 3619*, Centre for Economic Policy Research, London.

Mody, A. et al. (2003), 'The Role of Information in Driving FDI Flows: Host-country Transparency and Source-country Specialization', National Bureau of Economic Research Working Paper No. 9662.

Mori, A. and V. Rolli (1998), 'Investimenti Diretti all'estero e Commercio: Complementi o Sostituti?', *Banca d'Italia, Temi di discussione del Servizio Studi* No. 337, Ottobre.

Morikawa, K. (1988), 'Impact of Japanese FDI on Japanese Trade Surplus', *Journal of Policy Modeling*, **20**: 427–60.

Mundell, R.A. (1957), 'International Trade and Factor Mobility', *American Economic Review*, **47**: 321–35.

OECD (1996), 'Vertical Intra-industry Trade between China and OECD Countries', *Technical Papers* No.114.

Ottaviano, G.I.P. and D. Puga (1998), 'Agglomeration in the Global Economy: a Survey of the New Economic Geography', *World Economy*, **21**: 707–31.

Pain, N. (1997), 'Continental Drift: European Integration and the Location of UK FDI', *The Manchester School Supplement*, **65**: 94–117.

Pain, N. and M. Lansbury (1977), 'Regional Economic Integration and FDI: the Case of German Investment in Europe', *National Institute Economic Review*, **160**: 87–99.

Pain, N. and K. Wakelin (1998), 'Export Performance and the Role of Foreign Direct Investment', *The Manchester School Supplement*, **66**: 62–88.

Resmini, L. (2001), 'The Determinants of Foreign Direct Investment into the CEECs: New Evidence for Sectoral Patterns', *Economics of Transition*, **8**: 665–89.

Saggi, K. (2002), 'Trade, FDI, and International Technology Transfer: a Survey', *The World Bank Research Observer*, **17**: 191–235.

Sass, M. (2003), 'Competitiveness and Economic Policies Related to Foreign Direct Investment', mimeo, Ministry of Finance of Hungarian Government, WP No. 3.

Shaver, M.J. (1998), 'Do Foreign-owned and US-owned Establishments Exhibit the Same Location Pattern in US Manufacturing Industries?', *Journal of International Business Studies*, **29**: 469–92.

Singh, H. and K.W. Jun (1996), 'Some New Evidence on Determinants of Foreign Direct Investment in Developing Countries', *Transnational Corporations*, **5**: 67–105.

Smith, A. and P. Pavlínek (2000), 'Inward Investment, Cohesion and the "Wealth Of Regions" in East-Central Europe', in J. Bachtler et al. (eds), *Transition, Cohesion and Regional Policy in Central and Eastern Europe*, Aldershot: Ashgate.

Svensson, R. (1996), 'Effects of Overseas Production on Home Country Exports: Evidence Based on Swedish Multinationals', *Weltwirtschaftliches Archiv*, **122**: 304–29.

Uminski, S. and A. Stepniak (2004), 'Technology Transfer Through FDI to Poland. In Line with the Lisbon Process Objectives?', *Research Centre on European Integration*, University of Gdansk, mimeo.

United Nations Centre on Transnational Corporations (1992), *The Determinants of FDI*, New York: United Nations.

United Nations Conference on Trade and Development (UNCTAD) (1999), *World Investment Report: FDI and the Challenge of Development*, New York, United Nations.

United Nations Conference on Trade and Development (UNCTAD) (2001), *World Investment Report: Promoting Linkages*, New York, United Nations.

United Nations Conference on Trade and Development (UNCTAD) (2003), *World Investment Directory*, **8**: Central and Eastern Europe.

Wheeler, D. and A. Mody (1992), 'International Investment Location Decision: the Case of US Firms', *Journal of International Economics*, **33**: 57–76.

Wilamoski, P. and S. Tinkler (1999), 'The Trade Balance Effects of US FDI in Mexico', *Atlantic Economic Journal*, **27**: 24–37.

Yannopoulos, G.N. (1992), 'Multinational Corporations and the Single European Market', in J.C. Cantwell (ed.), *Multinational Investment in Modern Europe: Strategic Interaction in the Integrated Community*, Aldershot, UK and Brookfield, US: Edward Elgar.

11. Agglomeration and Internet exchange points: an exploration of the Internet morphology

Alessio D'Ignazio and Emanuele Giovannetti

11.1 INTRODUCTION

11.1.1 Internet Connectivity

Does geographical location play a role in sustaining cooperation among Internet companies? While there is a growing literature on how information and communication technology (ICT) affects inter-firm relations, less attention has been paid to their effects on Internet service providers (ISPs), the firms that provide the interface between final users and the Internet. In this chapter we investigate the possibility that geographical agglomeration of ISPs affects their propensity to peer[1] at Internet exchange points[2] (IXPs). In particular, we focus on the over 30 IXP members of the European Internet Exchange Points Association (Euro-IX), studying more in depth, three major IXPs among them: the London Internet Exchange (LINX), the Deutsche Commercial Internet Exchange (DE-CIX) and the Amsterdam Internet Exchange (AMS-IX). We explore how ICT exerts two opposite effects on agglomeration: a weakening of the centrifugal forces, due to the lessening of the isolation market power, and a redesigning of the barycentre of the centripetal forces, focusing agglomeration around virtual locations. Our empirical analysis of the bilateral peering decisions involving the ISPs connected with the LINX in London, the DE-CIX in Frankfurt and the AMS-IX in Amsterdam confirms that peering is significantly influenced by several elements: a major role seems to be played by the reputation effects and knowledge between each other, the possibility of routing traffic to the destination network relatively soon, as well as the level of traffic imbalances between ISPs. The difference in the dimension of the ISPs is in general significant and consistent, while we obtain contrasting results concerning the role of physical distance.

315

11.1.2   Agglomeration

Spatial asymmetries, geographical agglomeration, industrial districts and their morphological changes in time are commanding a growing empirical and theoretical interest amongst economists. In one of the earliest contributions of this renewed debate, Krugman (1991) identifies concentration as 'the most striking feature of the geography of economic activity'. More recently, Fujita and Thisse (2002) describe agglomeration as the interplay between two forces: localized positive externalities, which have a centripetal effect, and transport costs, which act as centrifugal force.

Since Marshall (1920), agglomeration has been attributed to three forces: a pooled labour market, greater provision of non-traded inputs and knowledge spillovers. Glaeser et al. (1992) stressed the importance of geographic proximity in defining the extent of knowledge spillovers within firms of a given industry to explain the agglomeration in cities. Proximity matters, since a basic input for firms' activities, tacit knowledge, is assumed to be only transferable through face-to-face interaction: 'the transfer of information through modern transmission devices requires its organization according to some pre-specified patterns, and only formal information can be codified in this way' (Fujita and Thisse, 2002, p. 172). Our study is motivated by the belief that this assumption has been, at least partially, undermined by many of the technological innovations brought out by the Internet: indeed, images and sounds stored in the Internet, while being transmitted through a codified information and transmission protocol usually not understood by the users, still convey tacit visual and musical messages to them and can be reacted upon in real time.

Following the widespread use of the Internet, geographical proximity may matter less than connectivity or language affinity. Hence, it should be considered as just one of the parameters affecting the degree of transmissibility of the knowledge, tacit and non-tacit, relevant to the specific activity under study. The relevance and impact of proximity on knowledge transfers will then differ across industries, according to their productive and organization features, and will reflect the evolution of the new technologies and their human-machine interface.

The chapter is organized as follows: Section 11.2 introduces the debate on the effects of ICT on the relevant notion of distance, either related to geographical or virtual dimensions, and discusses the role of trust and reputation in situations characterized by repeated incomplete contracts, as it happens in industrial districts. Section 11.3 provides a brief description of the main forms of interconnection in the Internet, with a special focus on the nature of peering agreements. Section 11.4 discusses the rationale for observing agglomeration in the peering decision, while Section 11.5

presents the econometric analysis of the peering decisions within three relevant Euro-IX members Internet exchange points: LINX (London), AMS-IX (Amsterdam) and DE-CIX (Frankfurt). Finally, Section 11.6 concludes.

11.2   DISTANCE AND THE INTERNET

One of the most relevant economic effects of the Internet can be traced in the dramatic reduction in transport costs. This is particularly true for digital goods, whose transport costs converged to zero, but the logistics and distribution of a much wider set of commodities was affected too. The reduction in transport costs induces a necessary reconsideration of both the notion and role played by geographical distance in the process of agglomeration of the production activities. A first immediate consequence of lower transport costs can be seen in the reduced profitability for local market power due to geographical isolation from competitors. This weakens the traditionally acknowledged incentives underlying centrifugal forces for firms' location decisions.[3] Quah (2000), has been one of the first researchers developing a model for a *spaceless* economy: in this framework he found that clustering in economic activity occurs across the time zones, while location along longitudes remains undetermined.

This chapter focuses on the analysis of the relevance of geography for the Internet industry itself. Forman, Goldfarb and Greenstein (2002) found that Internet usage and access in the United States vary across regions and industries. Although Internet use is widespread, not all industries adopt the Internet to enhance computing processes in order to have a competitive advantage (for example, electronic commerce). Furthermore, rural and smaller urban areas often lag somewhat behind.[4] Other case studies, as, for example, Isaksen (2004) and Power and Lundmark (2004), come to the conclusion that there is evidence for industry clusters in ICT-related sectors. To a certain degree, the location of such clusters may be explained by previously existing industrial agglomerations that have a high demand for ICT and related services. For example, financial services have a significant need for fast and secure network connections, hence the importance of network infrastructure. Otherwise, clustering is often explained by the role of face-to-face contact, which becomes more important as production processes become more fragmented and as firms have to rely on incomplete contracts, thus highlighting the importance of mutual trust (Spagnolo, 1999). For example, Learner and Storper (2001) stress the relevance of face-to-face relations for the establishment of trust.

Independently of the Internet-mediated human communication speed and cost, it has often been argued that direct human interaction characterizes the idea of place as different from space. Specifically a place provides identification for the individuals belonging to it, hence it is characterized by 'insiderness' (Relph, 1976). Insiderness reintroduces distance between places that might have near-zero Internet-mediated communication costs. However, this does not necessarily link a place to a specific geographical location: insiderness of an online community will in fact define borders, through identification, but these are not often drawn in geographic space, particularly so if the place considered lies in cyberspace.

The trade-off between centripetal and centrifugal forces, defining agglomeration and districts' boundaries, is therefore not only affected by the impact of new technologies on the costs-relevance of distance, but also depends on whether these facilitate the emergence of cyber-places characterized by local externalities only benefiting participating peers. Technology might, therefore, have two opposite effects on agglomeration processes: one weakening the centrifugal forces, due to lower transport costs, and the other facilitating agglomeration around virtual districts.

To become a sustainable alternative to geographically defined districts, the virtual ones will have to develop the ability to establish, maintain and verify reputation and trust. Hence the relevant issue in understanding the possible emergence of virtual districts becomes: do new technologies provide the means for the emergence of conventions necessary to facilitate trust in cyber-mediated exchanges? Online places have been historically characterized by behavioural codes, also called netiquette, the breaking of which often has disruptive consequences for the deviant's reputation within the community. If there is competition between geographical and virtual districts, their relative competitive advantage will depend on whether the monitoring of these codes is easier through geographical proximity or via online interaction, and on whether the ensuing necessity of a credible retaliation of a deviant's behaviour is more easily implemented within an online connected community or in a geographically clustered one. These elements taken together should drive the agglomeration/polarization dynamics in the specific industry under study, defining the shape and borders, if existing, of the geographical or virtual distribution of the industry.[5]

Understanding the role of face-to-face interaction, once it is agreed that this no longer has the monopoly over the possibility of transmission of tacit knowledge, becomes crucial for understanding its possible relevance in economic exchanges. A crucial feature of traditional geographically clustered industrial districts is their microstructure composed by small firms, characterized by vertically disintegrated production due to vertical specialization and a flexible system of vertical and horizontal subcontracting. In this framework, reputation forces are important for the cost-effective governance of small transactions and flexible informal subcontracting.

Agglomeration may or may not help in terms of better information flows since, as argued in previous sections, ICT may soon effectively substitute for face-to-face and community-managed information transmission. But geographical closeness may help the reputational governance of districts' subcontracting systems by allowing for community embeddedness – hence for social sanctioning power to enforce exchanges – and for better trust-building thanks to personal, face-to-face interaction. This force will be particularly important when crucial aspects of inter-firm transactions are not easily monitored or verifiable. As discussed below, in the peering decision between ISPs, there are substantial aspects of the transaction that are impossible to measure or monitor, so that the peering decision may require substantial trust and informal cooperation between peering partners. This may activate the centripetal force discussed above: face-to-face meetings and social connections may facilitate the governance of peering agreements, and the former may benefit from geographical proximity.

11.3　THE INTERNET

The Internet is composed of many independent networks of very different sizes, located around the globe, all directly or indirectly interconnected with each other. This last feature guarantees the Internet's most important property: universal exchange of traffic between all end users (universal connectivity). The industry is still rather unregulated, and networks are left completely free to decide where, how and with whom to interconnect. Lacking a really dominant network, competitive forces and positive network externalities have been sufficient until now to keep all the networks interconnected.

Small Internet service providers (ISPs) rely on interconnections both among themselves and to larger networks for the delivery of their customers' data packets to their destinations outside the range of the ISP's own subscribers. The largest networks are called backbones. These own or lease national or international high-speed fibre optic networks and deliver packets around the world to the many smaller networks connected to them.

11.3.1　INTERCONNECTION AGREEMENTS

Two simple types of interconnection agreements have emerged to regulate traffic at exchange points between networks: transit agreements and peering agreements. In a transit agreement, a large network – the transit provider – offers access to the entire Internet to a smaller customer network against the payment of a fee often related to the capacity of the connection link.

Under a peering agreement two networks exchange the traffic directed to each other's end users only. Monetary settlements between peering partners are excluded, although recently some networks have started charging for peering (Miller, 2002). Peering can be seen as a reciprocal, non-monetary exchange relationship that often implies various forms of cooperation. Peering, when taking place privately, implies establishing direct exchange points between the two networks, with the costs of creating and maintaining the exchange points typically shared evenly. Peering agreements may also take place at Internet exchange points (IXPs), specialized facilities and organizations where ISPs can connect to each other to exchange Internet traffic. To peer at an IXP, an ISP usually has to establish a connection and pay a membership fee, then it can use the circuit to exchange traffic with all other members of the IXP willing to peer with it. This multiple peering possibility at a single location makes peering at an IXP cheaper than establishing multiple direct bilateral peering exchanges each requiring a single physical connection. Being a member of an IXP also offers further advantages to an ISP: sharing of information and a free mutual technical help forum, possible elements towards forming insiderness of the virtual community of the exchange members. However, it is important to recall that, for an ISP, being a member of an IXP does not imply also being able to peer with all other members. Often, many ISPs are refused bilateral peering by other members of the same exchange. This refusal to peer also implies that only a partial bilateral connectivity structure takes place at an IXP. This is represented by a peering matrix, displaying a value equal to one when two members peer and zero when they do not.

In the following we focus on the specific bilateral peering decisions between ISPs at IXPs, trying to understand their main drivers and focusing on the question of whether or not geographical proximity among the ISPs is affecting their peering choices at the Internet exchange points.

11.3.2 The Peering Decision

Earlier work has identified several factors and problems that may affect networks' decisions whether, and with whom, to peer. A first, rather obvious factor is size. Peering requires establishing bilateral traffic exchange points, or peering points, which entail fixed and variable technological costs. It follows that a sufficiently intense traffic flow between the end users of the two networks is a necessary precondition for peering to be economically viable.

The larger two networks are, the more intense will be the traffic between their end users, therefore networks' size is necessarily a determinant of the peering decision. In fact, almost all large backbone networks peer with each other, the traffic being exchanged at several interconnection points homogeneously distributed on the relevant geographical areas. Somewhat smaller networks also peer with networks of comparable size, but typically have to supplement their interconnection with transit agreements with backbone networks. Since the costs of setting up and maintaining peering points are usually shared equally by peering networks, unbalanced traffic implies an unbalanced distribution of gains from peering against a balanced distribution of costs. Such unbalanced situations have developed in some cases, and have led to the discontinuation of the peering arrangement and to its replacement with a transit one. Finally, when two networks are peering and one of them is congested, the perceived speed of connection would not improve were the non-congested network to upgrade its infrastructure. And if the congested network chooses not to upgrade its infrastructure, it enjoys the full cost savings while it shares the reduced performance with all the networks it is peering with. This problem may, of course, induce caution in networks' decisions whether and with whom to peer.

11.3.3   AGGLOMERATION IN PEERING?

Little is known about the potential effects of ISPs' geographical location on their peering decision, the focus of our empirical analysis. Should we expect the geographical location of different ISPs to influence their peering decision? Of course, if two ISPs are very far away, building a connection from scratch would be very costly; hence one would expect that very far ISPs would not peer. However, consider a situation where there is an IXP where peering is cheaper, and that there is a number of ISPs, all of which are already connected to this IXP. Should we then expect the geographical location of these ISPs to matter in their choice of peering partners? Should agglomeration patterns be observed in the peering decision? The centrifugal force discussed before, softening competition through local differentiation, would not be active in this case, since the decision to peer at the IXP is independent from the location choice of the ISPs with respect to end users.

Some centripetal forces considered in the literature, such as knowledge spillovers obtained through interactions with peers, may be moderately active; and transport costs would be represented by the mile-cost of interconnection and the cost of reaching peers for joint activities and face-to-face interaction. Though, since we consider a population of ISPs that are connected to a given IXP, mile-cost of interconnection does not matter.

As discussed above, many features of a peering agreement are not able to be directly monitored, not to say verifiable/contractable. Hence peering agreements may require a great deal of trust and informal cooperation, in which case, face-to-face can be important.

11.4   AGGLOMERATION ANALYSIS: LINX, DE-CIX, AMS-IX

In this section we analyse the strength of agglomerating forces on the peering decision by constructing a series of maps. These are used to evaluate the existence of a possible relationship between the location of the IXP and the locations of its ISP members' headquarters. Moreover, the maps allow us to see if the geographical distribution of the number of peering agreements signed by each ISP shows clustering. We first focus on three especially relevant IXPs, selected with regard to both their geographical location and the number of participants for each: they are the LINX, AMS-IX and DE-CIX. We then provide summary results related to all the Euro-IX's IXP members.

11.4.1   LINX

Founded in 1994, the London Internet Exchange Ltd. (LINX) is one of the largest Internet exchange points in Europe. LINX is a totally neutral, not-for-profit partnership between Internet service providers. It was initially run on a voluntary basis by the founder members, then, in 1995, it became a company limited by guarantee. All members (at present 148), regardless of operational size, have an equal share of the company and equality in discussion and debate. Decisions are made by group consensus.[6]

Figure 11.1 below synthesizes the characteristics of LINX members (geographical position and number of peering agreements reached) and the features of the LINX peering matrix. Each ISP is represented by a bar, geographically positioned at the location of its headquarters, whose height directly depends upon the peering agreements signed by that ISP. The pairs of providers in peering relationships are joined by a line.

Figure 11.1 clearly shows a feature of agglomeration: LINX member ISPs are prevalently located in Europe, showing a 'proximity effect' between the ISPs and the IXP. While the ISP's location seems to affect the decision to join a certain IXP, no clustering characterizes the number of peering agreements reached; in fact, the heights of the bars seem to be random and not depending upon the geographical position within the area of interest. This conclusion is also supported by the Moran's *I* statistic of

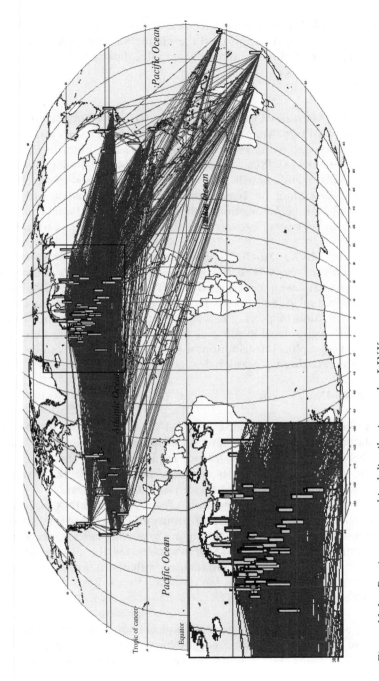

Figure 11.1   Peering geographical distribution at the LINX

323

spatial autocorrelation (see Table 11.1 below and Appendix A). There is thus strong evidence in support of the claim that the distribution of peering agreements follows a random geographical pattern.

11.4.2 DE-CIX

The Deutsche Commercial Internet Exchange (DE-CIX) founded in 1995 is located in Frankfurt (Main). This IXP handles about 85 per cent of all German peering traffic and is the third largest peering point in Europe. Currently, there are 141 ISPs connected to the DE-CIX. Similar to other exchange points, members will have to pay a one-time set-up fee and a monthly fee depending on bandwidth. This fee is recurrent with the membership fee for the Association of the German Internet Economy, thus promoting a higher level of organization and a higher lobbying capacity of the firms.[7]

As with the LINX, DE-CIX also shows a feature of agglomeration, having almost exclusively West European headquartered ISPs among its members: the relationship between which IXP to enter, and the ISP's location, is very strong. Again, Figure 11.2 above also shows that the geographical distribution of peering agreements at DE-CIX seems not to be influenced by geographical location of the ISPs. The randomness characterizing the geographical distribution of peering agreements is supported also by the standardized Moran's index, given by -0.066.

11.4.3 AMS-IX

The Amsterdam Internet Exchange (AMS-IX) was established in 1997. It has the largest ISP membership among European IXPs, over 200. Unlike some other IXPs, the AMS-IX has no requirements on the minimum number of peering partners of its members. Depending on the required service, members are charged a set-up fee plus monthly charges.[8]

Figure 11.3 above expresses very similar features to the LINX map, and thus the conclusions concerning the 'proximity effect' between the ISP and the IXP and the possibility of clustering in the peering agreements signed are the same. The standardized Moran's index for the distribution of peering agreements assumes the 'randomness' value of -0.157.

11.4.4 Other IXPs

To obtain a more complete picture of agglomeration in peering across Europe, we performed the same geographical analysis for each of the Euro-IX IXPs. Table 11.1 reports the spatial autocorrelation statistics

Table 11.1   Spatial autocorrelation statistics for the Euro-IX members

IXP	Moran's I Index	Theoretical I Index Under the Hypothesis of no Spatial Autocorrelation	Variance	z-value	Outcome
AIX	−0.0912	−0.07692	0.01087	−0.1369	random
AMS-IX*	−0.008	−0.00625	0.00012	−0.1569	random
BCIX	−0.0564	−0.07143	0.00501	0.21302	random
BIX	−0.0306	−0.02222	0.00147	−0.2196	random
BNIX	−0.0425	−0.02632	0.00209	−0.3553	random
CATNIX	−0.1197	−0.09091	0.01248	−0.2579	random
CIXP	−0.1005	−0.05556	0.00971	−0.4559	random
DE-CIX*	−0.007	−0.00794	0.00022	0.06605	random
ESPANIX	−0.1777	−0.04	0.00485	−1.9773	dispersed
FICIX	−0.0673	−0.07692	0.02584	0.05993	random
GIGAPIX	0.01981	−0.07143	0.01928	0.65701	random
GN-IX	−0.1898	−0.125	0.03914	−0.3274	random
INEX	−0.0681	−0.2	0.06038	0.53685	random
LINX*	0.00556	−0.0068	0.00019	0.89601	random
LIPEX	−0.0626	−0.025	0.00108	−1.1438	random
LIX	−0.1216	−0.11111	0.01544	−0.0847	random
LONAP	−0.0251	−0.02857	0.00163	0.08683	random
MADIX	−0.2096	−0.25	0.08067	0.14229	random
MIX	0.01394	−0.01754	0.00087	1.06691	random
MSK-IX	−0.0202	−0.00952	0.00025	−0.6725	random
NAMEX	−0.1527	−0.07692	0.00816	−0.839	random
NDIX	−0.1956	−0.25	0.03283	0.30044	random
NETNOD	−0.043	−0.02326	0.00138	−0.5323	random
NIX	−0.0329	−0.02439	0.00154	−0.2162	random
NIN-CZ	−0.0292	−0.02857	0.00253	−0.0131	random
PARIX	−0.0136	−0.03448	0.00762	0.23892	random
RONIX	−0.22	−0.05	0.00881	−1.8113	dispersed
TIX	−0.0267	−0.02222	0.00157	−0.1141	random
TOPIX	−0.077	−0.09091	0.00894	0.1466	random
VIX	0.07147	−0.01389	0.00061	3.45367	clustered
XCHANGEPOINT	−0.0407	−0.01266	0.00053	−1.2253	random

Note: *Although the maps represent the complete spatial distribution across the world, the spatial autocorrelation statistics are computed by taking into account the European headquartered ISPs only.

(observed Moran's index, theoretical Moran's index under the hypothesis of no spatial autocorrelation, variance and standardized Moran's index). Overall, we obtain a very consistent result, showing that the variable 'number of peering agreements for each ISP' follows an approximately

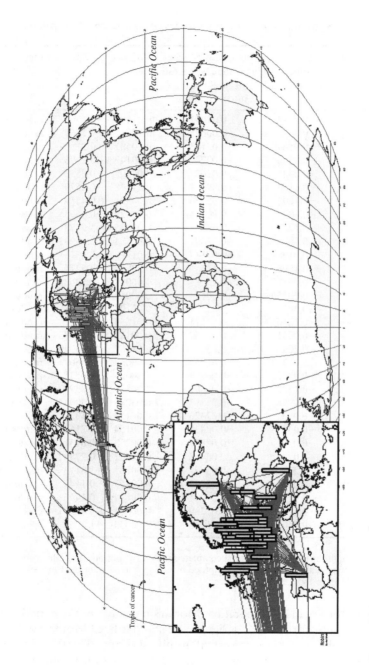

Figure 11.2   Peering geographical distribution at the DE-CIX

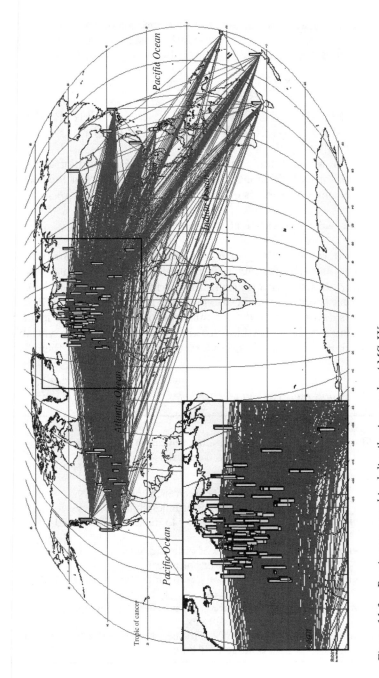

Figure 11.3   Peering geographical distribution at the AMS-IX

327

random geographical distribution. A noticeable exception is the case of Vix, whose distribution is very significantly clustered. Other exceptions are Espanix and Ronix, each of which shows a perceptible degree of dispersion.

11.5   AN ECONOMETRIC ANALYSIS OF THE ROLE OF AGGLOMERATION IN PEERING

In this section we give the results of estimating a probit model (see Appendix B) in order to highlight the possible determinants of the peering decisions, focusing on the cases of LINX, DE-CIX and AMS-IX.

11.5.1   Empirical Specification of the Probit Model

The dependent variable, the peering decision, is obtained from the IXP peering matrix, showing, for each pair or providers, whether or not they are in a peering relationship (peering = 1, not peering = 0) (see Table 11.2).

We introduce several variables to explain the peering decision. A first set of variables is devoted to model the influence of the geographic location on the peering decision. In this direction, we consider three variables involving each pair of Internet providers: the distance between them;[9] the

Table 11.2   Probit regression model variables

Dependent Variable	
Peering (dummy)	Assumes value 1 in case of peering between providers, 0 otherwise
Independent Variables	
Dist ISPs	Distance between each couple of ISPs (in thousands of miles)
Cum_Dist_from_IXP	Sum of distances to the IXP (in thousands of miles)
Diff_Dist_from IXP	Difference of distances to the IXP (in thousands of miles)
Common_IXPs	Number of European IXPs in which the ISPs are both present
Diff_IXP_Member	Difference in the number of memberships in European IXPs
Diff_Relevance	Difference in the betweenness value (in hundred thousands of units)

sum of their distances to the IXP; and the difference in their distances to the IXP.

For each Internet provider we derived its set of Euro-IX members. This information was used to devise a second set of variables. First, the possibility of reputation effects in peering decisions (Titley, 1997) and the technical element of the 'hot potato routing' are expressed by a variable indicating, for each pair of providers, how many IXPs they are both members of.[10] Second, we introduce a variable to model the asymmetry in the providers' size by considering the difference in the number of Euro-IX IXP memberships.

Finally, we devised a variable to model traffic imbalances. Although traffic flows are kept confidential, it is possible to determine a proxy for traffic imbalances by looking at the publicly available border gateway protocol (BGP) routing tables.[11] In particular, we calculated the following measure of betweenness centrality (Shimbel, 1953) for each Internet operator v:

$$B_s(v) = \sum_{s \neq v \neq t \in V} \sigma_{st}(v)$$

where $\sigma_{st}(v) = \sigma_{ts}(v)$ is the number of shortest BGP paths from the Internet operator s to the operator t on which the v lies on. High betweenness for v indicates that presumably a relevant quantity of traffic flows among that node.

11.5.2 Estimation Results

In the following we discuss the probit model estimation results (Table 11.3) for AMS-IX, DE-CIX and LINX.

For all the IXPs considered, the variables COMMON_IXPs and DIFF_RELEVANCE have the highest z-statistic and the same sign across the three models. This is indeed a very consistent result, offering useful insights on the determinants of Internet peering. First of all, the results strongly indicate that the mutual presence at many Internet exchange points positively affects peering. As we suggested before, at least two explanations are possible. The first relates to the technical element of 'hot potato routing': carrying traffic is costly and peering networks (that exchange traffic for free) try to minimize these costs by routing the data packets to the destination network relatively soon. The mutual presence at several IXPs makes this possible, thus enhancing the incentives for peering. A second explanation is suggested by Titley (1997). He argues that, if the mutual presence at several IXPs leads to several peering agreements being realized, the pairs of

Table 11.3   Probit estimated model results

	AMS-IX	DE-CIX	LINX
COMMON_IXPs	0.458	0.353	0.394
	(30.72)	(20.77)	(26.24)
DIFF_IXP_MEMBER	−0.022	−0.024	0.013
	(6.34)	(5.17)	(2.98)
DIST ISPs	−0.023	0.267	0.029
	(1.45)	(2.25)	(1.92)
CUM_DIST_FROM_IXP	−0.025	0.219	0.021
	(3.13)	(3.00)	(2.82)
DIFF_DIST_FROM IXP	0.006	−0.564	−0.072
	(0.44)	(5.85)	(5.41)
DIFF_RELEVANCE	−0.161	−0.165	−0.144
	(21.73)	(18.72)	(18.04)
CONSTANT	0.304	0.318	0.125
	(19.45)	(13.44)	(5.99)
Observations	18 145	9 316	12 880
Peering ratio	0.57188	0.630528	0.588898
Percentage correctly predicted	0.63918	0.666273	0.632376
Pseudo R-square	0.0685	0.0688	0.0609
Log-likelihood	−11 532.946	−5 714.3237	−8 191.56
Significance test statistic: LR chi²(6)	1 696.18	843.77	1 063.03

Note: Absolute value of z-statistics in parentheses.

providers enjoy a positive reputational effect, which enhances the likelihood of further peering being realized.

A second consistent result is related to the effect of traffic imbalances, represented by the proxy variable DIFF_RELEVANCE, on the peering decision. As argued on theoretical grounds, the model estimates suggest that traffic imbalances negatively affect peering.

The difference in the number of memberships among Euro-IX IXPs, DIFF_IXP_MEMBER, used as proxy for size difference among providers, seems to have contrasting effect on peering. In particular, it negatively affects peering within AMS-IX and DE-CIX, while it has a positive effect within LINX, although in the latter case the z-statistic is significantly smaller than the previous cases.

The role of geographical location follows two different patterns. On the one hand, it seems not to affect peering within AMS-IX, with only the sum of distances to the IXP being statistically significant and negatively affecting peering. On the other hand, all the three variables introduced to model location are significant for both DE-CIX and LINX, and come with consistent signs across the two IXPs. In particular, distance between headquarters seems to affect peering positively. A possible explanation for this result can be found in Foros and Hansen (2001), examining the role of spatial differentiation in peering: in this case two distant headquartered ISPs can perceive their services more as complementary than as substitute because of their horizontal-spatial differentiation. The sum of the providers' headquarters distances to the IXP also has a positive effect on peering. However, this result needs to be evaluated jointly with the imbalance in the distance to the IXP, which instead has a negative effect on peering.

A commonly used measure to evaluate the goodness of fit for the estimated models is given by the percentage of correctly predicted outcomes. This percentage is compared with the actual peering ratio. Indeed, in absence of a model, if we were asked to predict the interconnection regime between a pair of providers we would always choose 'peering is realized', since this is the most frequent outcome for all the three IXPs considered. The 'always predict peering rule', however, would be right in 57 per cent, 63 per cent and 58.8 per cent of cases for AMS-IX, DE-CIX and LINX, respectively. Table 11.3 shows that the estimated models lead to a significant improvement in the overall percentage that is correctly predicted.

11.6 CONCLUSIONS

In this chapter we investigated the possibility of geographical agglomeration in the bilateral peering decisions of Internet service providers participating at different European Internet exchange points, in particular at the LINX, DE-CIX and AMS-IX. We considered the wider issue of the effects of information and communication technology on geographical agglomeration forces and, in particular, on industrial districts, and we found that their governance requirements might explain the significance of geographical proximity in the specific case study analysed.

We discussed how ICT exerts two opposite effects on the agglomeration: a weakening of the centrifugal forces and a redesigning of the barycentre of the centripetal ones, focusing agglomeration around virtual locations. Peering decisions between ISPs contain substantial non-measurable aspects requiring trust and informal cooperation between peering partners. Our empirical analysis of the bilateral peering decision of the ISPs connected with the LINX in London, the DE-CIX in Frankfurt, the AMS-IX in Amsterdam, confirms that the peering decision is very complex and significantly influenced by several explanatory variables.

We obtained two very consistent results across the three models estimated. The difference in the traffic flows, represented by the proxy variable 'DIFF_RELEVANCE', turns out to be always strongly significant and having a negative impact on peering. Another significant variable positively affecting peering, represented by the proxy 'COMMON_IXPs', measures the possibility of early routing of traffic to the destination network, together with reputation effects and mutual knowledge.

The difference in size of providers seems instead to have contrasting effects on peering. The estimated models show that the variable 'DIFF_IXP_MEMBER' has a significant negative effect on peering within AMS-IX and DE-CIX, but positively affects peering within LINX, although in this case it is characterized by a lower z-statistic.

Finally, it is worth noticing that we find contrasting effects of physical distance on peering decisions. The variables introduced to model geographical location seem not to affect peering within AMS-IX, but they do play a role within LINX and DE-CIX. In particular, the results show that the likelihood of peering increases, ceteris paribus, when the distance between headquarters increases, too.

A second result shows, however, that there is no a clear geographical pattern in the distribution of peering agreements. For almost all the IXPs considered, the Moran's I indices of geographical clustering show that the distribution of peering agreements signed by the ISPs follows a random pattern. This result is also evident from the visual analysis of the maps provided.

Nevertheless, proximity matters. IXPs are still playing a crucial role in fostering the emergence of virtual communities, where ISPs tend to locate. This result is clearly underlined by the maps, indicating that ISPs tend to be members of nearby IXPs. We believe that this is due to the role that proximity still plays in reducing the transaction costs of monitoring and punishing deviant behaviour within an industry where cooperation is essential for efficient traffic exchanges as required for universal Internet connectivity.

A final interesting outcome arises when we consider the issue of agglomeration by looking at the location of all the ISPs that are members of at least one of the more than 30 IXPs constituting the Euro-IX. In this case the focus is not on peering, but on the strategic 'location' decisions. Figure 11.4 gives the number of ISPs headquartered at a given geographic location as the height of a bar, and this shows a very high ISP agglomeration in Amsterdam.

This can be thought as an interesting example of the Hotelling's (1929) principle of minimal differentiation.

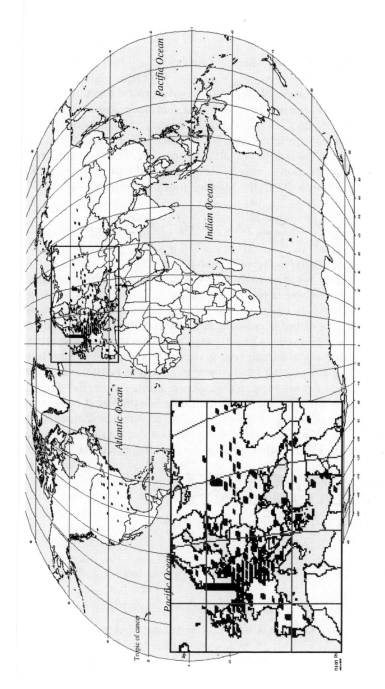

Figure 11.4   Europe-headquartered ISP distribution

APPENDIX A

Spatial Autocorrelation and Moran's *I* Index

Moran's *I* index (Moran, 1948) is often used to test the hypothesis of *no-clustering* for spatially distributed variables. This index, actually measuring spatial autocorrelation, is calculated by taking into account the value assumed by the variable under analysis at different locations. In particular, let N denote the total number of observations, let x_i be the value that the variable takes at location i, let μ be its average and let w_{ij} be elements of a spatial weights matrix. Then the Moran's index is given by:

$$I = (N/S_0)\sum_i\sum_j w_{ij}(x_i - \mu)(x_j - \mu)\Big/\sum_j(x_i - \mu)^2$$

where S_0 is a normalizing factor given by $S_0 = \Sigma_i\Sigma_j w_{ij}$.

The inference is based upon the analysis of the standardized z-value[12] of Moran's index: this is obtained by subtracting its expected value under the hypothesis of no spatial autocorrelation (in this case the expectation of I is $1/(N-1)$, see Upton and Fingleton, 1985) from the I-statistic and dividing the result by the observed standard deviation. The z-statistic is employed to test the hypothesis of no spatial correlation. Moreover the z-test also indicates the sign of the geographical clustering, if any (a positive value for the z-statistic suggests positive spatial autocorrelation – clustered outcome – while a negative value for the z-statistic suggests a dispersed one).

The sequence of images below (derived from ArcGIS software) shows the possible spatial autocorrelation outcomes, from a dispersed to a clustered pattern, going through a random (no spatial autocorrelation) pattern.

DISPERSED   RANDOM   CLUSTERED

APPENDIX B

The Probit Model

Let y be a binary variable, $\mathbf{x}$ be a $(1 \times K)$ vector of explanatory variables and $\hat{a}$ be a $(K \times 1)$ vector of unknown parameters. The probit model is derived from the following underlying latent variable model:

$$y^* = \mathbf{x}\hat{a} + e, \; y = 1[y^* > 0]$$

where e has a standard normal distribution[13] and is independent of the explanatory variables $\mathbf{x}$. Let Φ be its cumulative density function (cdf); then, it can be shown that:

$$P(y = 1|\mathbf{x}) = p(\mathbf{x}) = \Phi(\mathbf{x}\hat{a}).$$

We are interested in the effect of the explanatory variable x_k on the above response probability. In such a model, this effect is not entirely determined by $\hat{a}_j$: it also depends on the values assumed by the explanatory variables $\mathbf{x}$. In particular, if x_j is continuous:

$$\frac{\partial p(\mathbf{x})}{\partial x_j} = \phi(\mathbf{x}\hat{a})\hat{a}_j$$

where $\phi(z) = d\Phi/dz(z)$ is the standard normal density function. Instead, if x_k is discrete the partial effect of x_k going from c_k to $c_k + 1$ is given by:

$$\Phi[\hat{a}_1 + \ldots + \hat{a}_{k-1}x_{k-1} + \hat{a}_k(c_k + 1)] - \Phi[\hat{a}_1 + \ldots + \hat{a}_{k-1}x_{k-1} + \hat{a}_k c_k].$$

Hence, the partial effect of x_j on $p(\mathbf{x})$ depends on $\mathbf{x}$ through $\phi(\mathbf{x}\hat{a})$. However, since Φ is a strictly increasing cdf, the sign of the partial effect is determined by the sign of $\hat{a}_j$. It is worth noticing, finally, that since the latent variable does not have a unit of measurement, the magnitude of the $\hat{a}_j$ are not meaningful.

NOTES

1. As we will see later on in this chapter, Internet operators mainly exchange traffic through two different interconnection regimes: peering and transit. In a transit agreement, the downstream Internet operators buy traffic capacity from the larger upstream provider; in a peering agreement, instead, the two providers exchange the traffic directed to their final customers, usually without any monetary settlement.
2. Internet exchange points are specialized organizations where ISPs can connect to exchange their Internet traffic.
3. This process leads to claims of 'death of distance' whereby instantaneous communication made possible by the Internet leads to a collapse in space-time boundaries.
4. This so-called 'digital divide' refers to the fact that Internet access and use is distributed unevenly over social groups and geographic regions (see, for example, Warf, 2001).
5. The issue of the survival of geographical agglomeration when ICT becomes an efficient substitute for face-to-face dealings has been addressed by Santarelli (2004). In a panel data analysis of the long-term evolution of Emilia Romagna's industrial districts, he

found that spatial concentration is no longer the most crucial factor in agglomeration and the term 'multi-located' district describes recent forms of industrial agglomeration in a better way.

6. A very interesting development is taking place inside the LINX: ISPs can now connect to LINX from anywhere with no need to locally deploy routing equipment, pay collocation fees or negotiate housing contracts. A number of LINX members are in fact offering other ISPs private point-to-point Ethernet connections on their international networks. The connections terminate in a dedicated Ethernet port, with an individual IP address controlled by the customer ISP, on the member's router at LINX.

7. For more information see http://www.de-cix.net.

8. For more information see http://www.ams-ix.net.

9. We followed a two-stage process to calculate the distance: we first individuated latitude and longitude for each ISP's headquarters, then we used the 'great circle distance formula using decimal degrees' to calculate the distance between any couple of headquarters. The formula is given by $dist(P_1, P_2) = 3963.0$, where lat_i and lon_i are respectively the latitude and longitude of point P_i * arccos[sin(lat_1/57.2958) * sin(lat_2/57.2958) + cos(lat_1/57.2958) * cos(lat_2/57.2958) * cos(lon_1/57.2958 − lon_1/57.2958)].

10. In order to obtain the relevant variables from the initial set of data, given by the peering matrixes for the Euro-IX members, we created several visual basic routines.

11. The border gateway protocol (BGP) is a series of 'instructions' that govern the transmission of packets over the Internet. The BGP establishes the paths that data packets will take through connected networks. The BGP is itself data, and by design nearly always take the same paths; this method (in-band transmission) avoids the introduction of new false positive routing information: a non-existent link can not be traversed by routing data (Woodcock, 2002).

12. See Anselin (1992).

13. Another commonly used binary model is the logit, which is obtained assuming that e has a standard logistic distribution: the cumulative density function is given by $G(z) = \Lambda(z) = \exp(z)/[1 + \exp(z)]$ while the density function is $g(z) = \exp(z)/[1 + \exp(z)]$.

REFERENCES

Anselin, L. (1992), 'Spatial data analysis with GIS: an introduction to application in the social sciences', University of California, Technical Report 92-10.

Forman, C., A. Goldfarb and S. Greenstein (2002), 'Digital dispersion: an industrial and geographic census of commercial Internet use', NBER Working Paper 9287, National Bureau of Economic Research.

Foros, Ø. and J. Hansen (2001), 'Competition and compatibility among Internet service providers', *Information Economics and Policy*, **13**: 411–25.

Fujita, M. and J.-F. Thisse (2002), *Economics of Agglomeration*, Cambridge: Cambridge University Press.

Glaeser, E., H. Kallal, J. Scheinkman and A. Schleifer (1992), 'Growth of cities', *Journal of Political Economy*, **100**: 1126–52.

Hotelling, H. (1929), 'Stability in competition', *The Economic Journal*, **39**, 41–57.

Isaksen, A. (2004), 'Knowledge-based clusters and urban location: the clustering of software consultancy in Oslo', *Urban Studies*, **14**: 1157–74.

Krugman, P. (1991), *Geography and Trade*, Cambridge, MA: MIT Press.

Learner, E. and M. Storper (2001), 'The economic geography of the Internet age', NBER Working Paper 8450, National Bureau of Economic Research.

Marshall, A. (1890), *Principles of Economics*, London: Macmillan.

Miller, R. (2002), 'The economics of peering', *Web Host Industry Review*.

Moran, P. (1948), 'The interpretation of statistical maps', *Journal of the Royal Statistical Society, Series B*, **10**: 243–51.

Power, D. and M. Lundmark (2004), 'Working through knowledge pools: labour market dynamics, the transference of knowledge and ideas, and industrial clusters', *Urban Studies*, **41**: 1025–44.

Quah, D. (2000), 'Internet cluster emergence', *European Economic Review*, **44**: 1032–44.

Relph, E. (1976), *Place and Placeness*, London: Pion Limited.

Santarelli, E. (2004), 'Patents and the technological performance of district firms evidence for the Emilia-Romagna region of Italy', Max Planck Institute for Research into Economic Systems Papers on Entrepreneurship, Growth and Public Policy, No. 29.

Shimbel, A. (1953), 'Structural parameters of communication networks', *Bulletin of Mathematical Biophysics*, **15**: 501–7.

Spagnolo, G. (1999), 'Social Relations and cooperation in organizations', *Journal of Economic Behavior and Organization*, **38**: 1–26.

Titley, N. (1997), 'An analytical model of peering between Internet service providers', Release 1.

Upton, G.J.G. and B. Fingleton (1985), *Spatial Data Analysis by Example. Volume 1: Point Pattern and Quantitative Data*, Chichester, England: Wiley.

Warf, B. (2001), 'Segueways into cyberspace: multiple geographies of the digital divide', *Environment and Planning B*, **28**: 3–19.

Woodcock, B. (2002), 'BGP for bankers (white paper on transactions and valuation associated with inter-carrier routing of Internet protocol traffic)', Packet Clearing House.

12. Explaining the scarce returns of European structural policies from a new economic geography perspective

Andrés Rodríguez-Pose and Ugo Fratesi

12.1 INTRODUCTION

European regional support has grown in parallel with European integration. Every recent stage of the integration process has been accompanied by a renewal and an important increase in the funds aimed at tackling disparities within the European Union (EU). Overall, the funds targeted at achieving greater economic and social cohesion and reducing disparities within the European Union (EU) have more than doubled in relative terms since the reform of the Structural Funds in 1989, making regional development policies the second most important policy area in the EU, behind the Common Agricultural Policy (CAP). However, and despite a few successes, such as Ireland – that cannot be exclusively attributed to the impact of European structural policies (Barry, Bradley and Hannan, 2001) – almost two decades after the wholesale reform of the European Structural Funds, there is a growing number of voices that have started to question their capacity to deliver the objective of greater economic and social cohesion (Rodríguez-Pose, 2000; Vanhoudt, Mathä and Smid, 2000; Boldrin and Canova, 2001; Puga, 2002; Midelfart-Knarvik and Overman, 2002; Rodríguez-Pose and Fratesi, 2004). The grounds on which these criticisms are supported are related to the absence of regional convergence across Europe (Boldrin and Canova, 2001; Puga, 2002), the relative lack of economic dynamism of a large number of regions with the highest level of support – the so-called Objective 1 regions – (Rodríguez-Pose and Fratesi, 2004), and the conflict between Structural Fund objectives and other European policies and state aid (Midelfart-Knarvik and Overman, 2002). Most assisted regions seem to be caught in a poverty trap from which they are finding it difficult to escape.

In this chapter, we address why the returns of European structural policies have so far been below the ambitious goal of economic and social cohesion, using a new economic geography (NEG) theoretical framework as explanation. We find that the excessive emphasis on infrastructure and, to a lesser extent, on business support, may be contributing to a greater concentration of economic activity in the core at the expense of the periphery, a trend that does not seem to be compensated by the positive returns of investment in human resources in a period of low labour mobility.

In order to achieve this goal, the chapter is divided into five further sections. The following section presents an overview of the European regional policies, paying special attention to their evolution within the EU budget. Section 12.3 looks at the evolution of regional growth trends in the EU, focusing on Objective 1 regions, in particular. Section 12.4 analyses the allocation of European financial resources to the key structural policy axes, while Section 12.5 examines the economic returns of the European development effort in Objective 1 regions and the reasons for the relatively scarce impact on the economic trajectory of the assisted regions, using an NEG framework. The final section presents the general conclusions.

12.2   A VERY BRIEF HISTORY OF THE EVOLUTION OF THE EUROPEAN STRUCTURAL POLICIES

The political belief, fostered by some Southern European leaders such as Felipe González, Spanish socialist prime minister during the 1980s and first half of the 1990s, that European economic integration would fundamentally benefit the core at the expense of the periphery and hence fuel greater territorial inequality within the EU, has been the main driver of the massive expansion of European regional policies over the last two decades (Padoa-Schioppa, 1987; Emerson, 1990; European Commission, 1994). Each step towards greater economic integration has thus been preceded by a significant restructuring and expansion of the EU's territorial development effort. The introduction of the single market on 1 January 1993 had been paved by a comprehensive reform of the Structural Funds, implemented on 1 January 1989. This reform led to the coordination of the then three Structural Funds (ERDF, ESF and EAGGF-Guidance Section) around the principles of territorial and financial concentration, programming, partnership and additionality, that were later complemented by a principle of efficiency. European Monetary Union (EMU) was also preceded by the creation of the Cohesion Fund, whose original aim was to help prepare the transition to EMU of the four poorest EU member states at the beginning of the 1990s (Greece, Ireland, Portugal and Spain).

These reforms represented a huge budgetary boost for the EU development effort for its less developed regions and countries. In a period of barely 12 years, the EU expenditure on regional and national development went from representing a mere 16 per cent of the EU budget in 1986 (Table 12.1) to 35.5 per cent in 2004. Development policies now represent the second largest EU policy in budgetary terms, less than seven points behind the CAP, when in 1986 the gap was 46 points (Table 12.1). The recent enlargement towards Central and Eastern Europe – which has brought into the EU a group of countries with much lower levels of GDP per capita and greater development problems than previous member states – is only likely to boost the status of the Structural and Cohesion policies, barring a wholesale reform of the EU policy structure (for example, Sapir et al., 2004). In absolute terms, the increase has been even more apparent. The Structural Funds merely represented €13.6 per capita (measured in 2000 constant prices) in 1980 (Table 12.1). By 2004 this figure stood at €101, a more than sevenfold increase in 24 years.

The bulk of the expansion took place in the so-called Objective 1 regions, that is, the poorest regions of the then EU-15: those whose GDP per capita, measured in purchasing power standards in the three years before the implementation of a programme, was below 75 per cent of the EU average. Since 1989, Objective 1 regions have received more than two-thirds of all the Structural Funds spent in the EU and more than 61 per cent of all European development funds. This support represented on average 1.74 per cent of the GDP of these regions during the two first programming periods (Rodríguez-Pose and Fratesi, 2004). The reason behind the concentration of the development effort in the poorest regions of the EU is set up in Art. 158 of the EU Treaty, which states that the EU shall endeavour to reduce disparities between the levels of development of European regions and thus achieve greater economic and social cohesion in the EU.

12.3 THE EVOLUTION OF REGIONAL DISPARITIES IN THE EU

Has this increase in the EU's development effort paid off? Are we now closer to achieving greater 'economic and social cohesion' at a regional level than we were two decades ago? There seems to be no easy answer to these questions. In fact, despite the large number of works on the topic, scholars still do not entirely agree about whether we are witnessing greater convergence, greater divergence, or nothing at all across Europe. The consensus on the issue is limited to the starting points. First, it is accepted that there are significant disparities in the distribution of wealth across the EU. Second, it is also generally agreed that after World War II and until the early 1980s, regional convergence had been the norm, with a relatively slow

Table 12.1 Evolution of the EU development fund expenditure from 1980 onwards

	1980	1983	1986	1989	1992	1995	1998	2000	2001	2002	2003	2004
Percentages of EU out-turn in payments (commitments from 2001)												
General budget:												
EAGGF Guarantee Section	68.6	62.1	61.7	57.7	51.4	50.4	47.4	45	45.8	46.3	46.4	42.7
Development funds	11	16	15.8	18.8	30.2	28.1	34.7	34.6	33.7	33.4	33.3	35.5
of which: Cohesion Fund	0	0	0	0	0	2.5	2.8	3	2.8	1.8	2.8	4.9
of which: Structural Funds	11	16	15.8	18.8	30.2	25.6	31.9	31.6	30.9	30.6	30.5	30.6
Research	2.2	5.3	2.2	3.6	3.1	3.6	3.6	3.9	4.9	4.8	4.9	4.4
External	3.7	3.5	3	2.5	3.5	5	5	6	4.9	5.0	5.1	5.2
Administration	5	4.4	4.3	4.9	4.7	5.7	5.1	5.1	6.5	6.5	6.7	7.6
Internal												
Other Items	9.5	8.7	13.0	12.5	7.1	7.2	4.2	5.4	4.3	5.0	3.7	4.6
Total	100	100	100	100	100	100	100	100	100	100	100	100
Annual growth in nominal terms (%)	11.4	19.4	24.2	−0.5	10.6	11.3	1.2	8.6		3.6	1.5	13.0
Total Community expenditure (2000 prices) (EUR million)	32 533	41 759	54 527	55 974	73 159	77 446	87 133	92 253	95 532	97 944	98 433	108 770
Annual growth in real terms (%)	1.7	13.6	21.1	−5	9.2	7.7	−1.2	8.6		2.5	0.5	10.5
Community expenditure as % of public expenditure in member states	1.7	1.9	2.1	2	2.2	2.1	2.3	2.4				
Expenditure as % of Community GDP	0.8	0.94	0.99	0.94	1.09	1.04	1.09	1.09	1.1	1.1	1.1	1.1
Expenditure per capita (EUR)	62.7	93	110.8	129.5	175	183.2	219.3	244	257.3	266.1	268.5	301.6

Table 12.1 (continued)

	1980	1983	1986	1989	1992	1995	1998	2000	2001	2002	2003	2004
Expenditure per capita (EUR, 2000 prices)	124	152.7	168.6	171.4	210.4	207.4	231.6	244	253.0	258.9	258.8	284.2
Development funds per capita (EUR, 2000 prices)	13.63	24.5	26.66	32.21	63.55	58.28	80.35	84.52	85.2	86.5	86.1	101.0
Development funds on EU-15 GDP (%)	0.09	0.15	0.16	0.18	0.33	0.29	0.38	0.38	0.37	0.36	0.36	0.42

but steady process of catching up by the poorest regions in the EU (Barro and Sala-i-Martín, 1991; Armstrong, 1995; Cheshire and Carbonaro, 1995; Molle and Boeckhout, 1995; Tondl, 2001).

The evolution since the mid-1980s – almost coinciding with the reform of the Structural Funds and with the EU giving itself the goal of achieving greater economic and social cohesion – is, however, more controversial. First, national disparities have continued to decline throughout the 1990s and part of the beginning of the twenty-first century. Most of the countries in the periphery of the EU have performed better than the countries of the core. Ireland is the most spectacular case. With rates of real growth that exceeded more than 8 per cent per annum during the majority of the 1990s, the country went from being the third poorest member state in 1985 to the second richest – after Luxembourg – in a space of barely 20 years.

But Ireland has not been the only case of national convergence. Spain has narrowed its economic gap with the EU average since the mid-1990s, as did Portugal until the crisis that affected the country at the beginning of the twenty-first century. Greece, once regarded as a laggard, has also managed to catch up since the late 1990s. Overall, national disparities have declined by about 25 per cent since the reform of the Structural Funds (Puga, 2002). These national trends have led some researchers (that is, Leonardi, 1995) and, in certain documents, the European Commission (for example, 1999) to claim that the EU development effort has paid off by generating greater economic and social cohesion. In the Executive Summary of the 1999 *Sixth Periodic Report*, for example, it is stated that there is 'unambiguous' convergence in which 'the Structural Funds have also played an important part' (European Commission, 1999, p. 7).

The picture is, however, much more hazy when regional economic performance is considered. In this case there is little sign of the high levels of economic growth of peripheral countries, as the majority of peripheral regions have tended to perform below their national level. This is the case with most of the regions of the Italian Mezzogiorno, the former East Germany, Western and Northwestern Ireland, most of Portugal outside Lisbon, and much of Western and Southern Spain. According to Puga (2002), regional disparities in the EU increased by 10 per cent over the last two decades. This trend has also been identified by a host of studies that, taking into account factors such as the existence of spatial dependence in regional growth trends, highlight that the recent trend has been one of little change in regional disparities or outright divergence (Boldrin and Canova, 2001; Cuadrado-Roura, 2001; Fingleton, 2004; Magrini, 1999; Puga, 2002; Rodríguez-Pose, 1999; Rodríguez-Pose and Fratesi, 2004). Other scholars have underscored the emergence of convergence clubs (Neven and Gouyette, 1995; Quah, 1996; López-Bazo et al., 1999). From this perspective, despite a closing of the gap at the national level, the panorama at a regional level has been featured – when spatial autocorrelation is taken into account – by stability, lack of convergence and increasing polarization across the EU (López-Bazo et al., 1999; Puga, 2002). This lack of upward mobility of regions that have been supported at an average level of 1.74 per cent of their GDP casts doubts about the economic returns of the European development policies to deliver their goal of greater economic and social cohesion.

The failure of Objective 1 regions to rise above the threshold of assistance is a second factor fuelling questions about the efficiency of the Structural Funds. Of the 44 regions that were classified as Objective 1 in 1989, in 2005 43 remained within the Objective (Rodríguez-Pose and Fratesi, 2004) (Figure 12.1). Only Abruzzo, among the original 1989 Objective 1 regions, has managed to come fully out of the Objective before 2005 (Figure 12.1). Five others have been phased out at the end of 2005 and 2006. And, although vested interests in remaining below the threshold may have played a part in this lack of upward mobility, the economic performance of many Objective 1 regions has left a lot to be desired.

The stability in the original set of regions has not prevented the number of Objective 1 regions from increasing. For the programming period 2000–06, the number of Objective 1 regions was 67. German reunification brought the five *Länder* of the former German Democratic Republic and East Berlin into Objective 1. Burgenland became a member with Austrian membership. The remainder joined the Objective as a result of the revision of eligible regions before each programming period. Cantabria in Spain, Hainaut in Belgium, Valenciennes in France, Flevoland in the Netherlands and the Highlands and Islands and Merseyside in the United Kingdom joined Objective 1 in this way in 1994. South Yorkshire, West Wales and the Valleys, Cornwall and the Isles of Scilly (all in the United Kingdom) as well as six Scandinavian regions became Objective 1 in 2000 (Figure 12.1).

Enlargement in 2004 to ten mainly Central and Eastern European countries with lower GDPs per capita than the EU average is only likely to increase the number of regions and the protagonism of the EU's development effort in the future, with increasing competition between regions and countries in order to get funds.

12.4　THE ECONOMIC RETURNS OF THE KEY EUROPEAN DEVELOPMENT AXES

Given the above-described evolution of regional disparities within the EU, the potential impact of the EU development effort, in general, and of the Structural Funds, in particular, is controversial. On the one hand, the

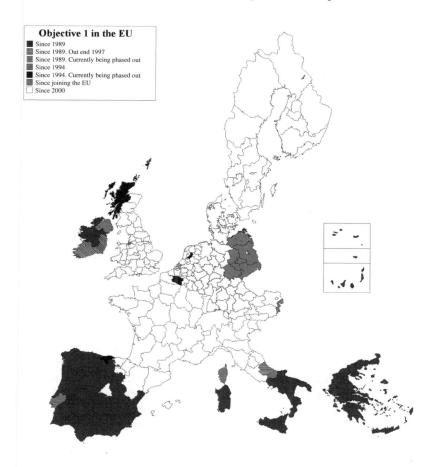

Figure 12.1   The evolution of Objective 1 regions in the EU-15

Structural Funds may have played a significant part in generating greater cross-country convergence. On the other, many of the supported regions have not performed particularly well and in some cases (for example, Spain) Objective 1 regions have tended to perform worse than regions outside the Objective (Rodríguez-Pose, 2000). The within-country divergence observed across the EU is another indicator of greater polarization that counters the objective of economic and social cohesion.

What are the potential reasons for the lack of an unambiguous positive impact of the European development effort? Successive scholars have pointed in several directions when trying to demonstrate why the impact of the European development policies has tended to be below expectations. The centripetal effects unleashed by European economic integration (Brülhart and Torstensson, 1996; Midelfart-Knarvik et al., 2000), the tendency of R&D and innovation to concentrate (Moreno, Paci and Usai, 2005), the decline in inter-European migration trends (Faini, 2003), or the significant drop of rural–urban migration in the periphery of Europe since the mid-1980s (Cuadrado-Roura, Mancha Navarro and Garrido Yserte, 1999) are some of the factors that have been identified as the culprits behind the lack of regional catch-up.

Other analyses have highlighted the role played by public policies in preventing a greater catch-up by peripheral regions. Midelfart-Knarvik and Overman (2002) have pinpointed the potential anti-cohesive impact of specific public policies implemented by national governments in order to protect and/or develop strategic sectors. The CAP has also attracted attention, as the main beneficiaries of the policy have tended to be large landowners and intensive farmers in the core of Europe (De la Fuente and Doménech 2001; European Commission, 2001).

The actual composition of the expenditure of the Structural Funds has deserved, however, much less attention. Yet the choice of development priorities in Objective 1 regions can shed light as to why the returns of the EU development effort have been below expectations, especially from an NEG perspective. And in the case of Objective 1 regions, the choice of development axes has been very uneven. As revealed by Rodríguez-Pose and Fratesi (2004), for the two first programming periods after the reform of the Structural Funds (1989–93 and 1994–99) the 1.74 per cent of GDP that the Structural Funds represented on average for Objective 1 regions, were very unevenly distributed. About half of the total expenditure (49.6 per cent) was devoted to the building of infrastructure and the environment. Slightly less that one-fourth (23.2 per cent) was aimed at the promotion of the local economic fabric, including tourism. Human resources attracted 12.3 per cent of the total, and 8 per cent went to agriculture and rural development. The remaining 5.9 per cent corresponds to entries that are difficult to classify under any of the above categories (Rodríguez-Pose and Fratesi, 2004, p. 100).

The priorities of different countries and regions, however, differed significantly from these statistical averages. At a national level, Portugal, Spain and, to a lesser extent, Greece, put the emphasis on infrastructure and the environment, in general, and on transport infrastructure, in particular. In these three countries, more than 50 per cent of expenditure commitments were aimed at the improvement of infrastructure. The share rose to more than 75 per cent in the cases of Spain and Portugal for the second programming period (Table 12.2). Business support was the preferred

Table 12.2 Structural Fund commitments in Objective 1 regions (percentage of nominal values)

Country	1989–93					1994–99				
	A	B	H	I	TOTAL	A	B	H	I	TOTAL
Austria	–	–	–	–	–	15.0	68.7	16.3	0.0	100
Belgium	–	–	–	–	–	0.0	66.2	17.2	16.6	100
France (except overseas dep.)	28.6	15.9	10.1	45.4	100	9.6	32.8	18.7	39.0	100
Greece	11.2	18.4	16.6	53.8	100	18.7	13.4	13.6	54.3	100
Ireland	14.7	33.7	26.4	25.2	100	0.0	54.7	3.8	41.4	100
Italy	14.4	35.0	1.9	48.8	100	21.0	21.3	27.0	30.7	100
Netherlands	–	–	–	–	–	22.2	20.4	21.0	36.4	100
Portugal	11.5	6.1	35.3	47.2	100	0.0	15.2	8.6	76.1	100
Spain	26.7	13.2	8.8	51.4	100	0.6	14.3	7.5	77.6	100
UK	10.5	38.1	20.9	30.4	100	12.2	25.0	33.1	29.7	100
Total	17.6	21.1	16.3	45.0	100	7.0	24.0	12.1	56.8	100

Notes:
The 5.9 per cent of total funds not easily ascribable to any of these categories has been omitted.
A   Support to agriculture and rural areas.
B   Business support and tourism.
H   Human resources.
I   Infrastructure and the environment.

Source: Rodríguez-Pose and Fratesi (2004, p. 101).

development axis in the cases of Ireland and in those of Austria and Belgium for the second programming period. Ireland committed around 45 per cent of the funds between 1989 and 1999 to this axis, while two-thirds of the commitments in Austria and Belgium were aimed at business support in the years 1994–99. The emphasis on human resources was highest – in relative terms – for the United Kingdom, Italy and the Netherlands, while support for agriculture and rural areas was a key priority for France in the first programming period and for the Netherlands, Italy and Greece, in the second (Table 12.2).

The balance between priorities also differed noticeably among countries. Whereas in the cases of Italy, the Netherlands, or the United Kingdom, there was a relative equilibrium in the volume of expenditure commitments among the four development axes countries such as Austria, Belgium, Greece, Portugal and Spain tended to prioritize one or two axes and to adopt very unbalanced development strategies, especially in the second programming period (Table 12.2).

National contrasts in development priorities are reproduced and exacerbated at the level of individual Objective 1 regions. There are huge geographical and chronological differences in the importance of each of the axes. Geographical differences tend to reflect national differences in regional development strategies, whereas chronological differences reproduce changes in those strategies between the two programming periods considered in the analysis. In Portuguese and Spanish Community Support Frameworks (CSFs), there was a strong emphasis on infrastructure, transport and the environment. During the second programming period, investment in infrastructure represented close to 90 per cent of the Objective 1 Structural Fund commitments in Portuguese regions (with the exception of the two archipelagos) and about 70 per cent of the commitments in the Spanish Objective 1 regions (with the exception of the Northern African enclaves of Ceuta and Melilla). This denotes an increase from the first programming period, where investment in infrastructure and related areas in both countries was around 50 per cent of the total. The heavy bias towards infrastructure meant that the remaining priority axes received limited support. In the Continental regions of Portugal, during the second programming period an average of 10 per cent of Objective 1 funds was targeted to business and tourism support, with almost no resources going into education and human capital or into support to agriculture and rural promotion. In the two archipelagos, more emphasis was put on human capital development, with around 18 per cent of the funds committed to that axis in the Azores and 28 per cent in Madeira. Support to agriculture and rural promotion, that represented slightly more than 10 per cent of the commitments during the first programming periods, almost disappeared from the Portuguese development priorities during the second programming period. In Spanish Objective 1 regions, and in spite of strong regional variations, about 15 per cent of all Structural Fund commitments were earmarked for business and tourism support. Human capital came third and support to agriculture and rural promotion, which was the second priority axis during the first programming period, fell to fourth place during the second period. Corsica has been another region whose development strategy has been fundamentally based on infrastructure. Around half of the funds committed during the two programming periods were aimed at improving the infrastructural endowment and the environment of the region. Support to agriculture and rural promotion constituted the second priority axis, whereas the remaining funds were equally divided between human capital and business support.

The breakdown of commitments in other Objective 1 regions has been substantially different. Two-thirds of the Objective 1 funds committed in Hainaut (Belgium) and Burgenland (Austria) went to business and tourism support. The remainder was spread fairly evenly between infrastructure and human capital in Hainaut and agricultural support and human capital in Burgenland. In Merseyside (United Kingdom), more than half of the funds were targeted at improving education and human capital, a quarter each at business support and infrastructure, with no money going to agriculture or rural development.

Greater heterogeneity in development strategies can be observed across Italian and Greek regions. In Italy, infrastructure was the main development axis during the first programming period in all Objective 1 regions, with the exception of Abruzzo and Basilicata. Business support came a close second, with more than one-quarter of all commitments in all Objective 1 regions – with the exception of Molise – and more than 50 per cent in Abruzzo. Support to agriculture was the third main development axis, amounting in most cases to between 15–20 per cent of total commitments, while the investment in human capital was the weakest axis, only surpassing 5 per cent in Basilicata. The structure of commitments in Italian regions changed radically and became more heterogeneous during the second programming period. Support to infrastructure suffered a decline in relative terms, to the benefit of human capital, whose share in the total Objective 1 commitments increased throughout Southern Italy. Commitments to this development axis ranged from 11 per cent of the total in Molise, to 37 per cent in Sicily and 38 per cent in Basilicata. Support for businesses declined in relative terms in all regions, bar Calabria, but remained one of the key development axes. Finally, there was greater divergence in support to agriculture and rural promotion during the second programming period. Whereas in Basilicata or Calabria this axis almost ceased to exist, in other regions – such as Apulia, Sardinia, Sicily and especially in Molise – its share grew.

In Greece the allocation of funds was closely related to the production structure of each region. As in other countries, infrastructure was the main axis, receiving around 50 per cent of Objective 1 funds in both programming periods. However, in the case of Attica this percentage grew to more than 90 per cent in the second period, coinciding with the selection of Athens as the host of the 2004 Olympic Games in 1997. Support to agriculture and rural promotion hovered between 25 and 40 per cent of all commitments in the heavily rural northern and central regions, whereas tourism and business support scored high in the Greek islands. Human capital and education attracted only between 10 and 20 per cent, with the exceptions of Attica and Crete, where its share was lower.

Finally the greatest balance across development axes is found in the UK regions of Northern Ireland and the Highlands and Islands, and in Flevoland (Netherlands). In Northern Ireland, business support represented the main development axis during the first programming period and was substituted by infrastructure, transport and the environment in the second period. However, the gap between these two axes and human capital support has been relatively small. Agricultural support and rural development also drew more than 10 per cent of Objective 1 commitments. In the Highlands and Islands, during the second programming period business support and infrastructure amounted to slightly less than one-third each of the total commitments, with 22 per cent going to agriculture and rural development and 15 per cent to human capital. In Flevoland, infrastructure represented more than one-third of the commitments with roughly equal proportions being allocated to the other three axes.

Year on year differences in the volume of expenditure commitments were also significant. Let us take three regions to illustrate this point. In Basilicata, in Italy, the Structural Funds commitments have ranged from less than 0.7 per cent of GDP in 1991 to slightly more than 3 per cent in 1997, with jumps of more than 1 per cent of GDP in the years 1992–93, 1993–94, and 1996–97. In the Spanish region of Extremadura, the gap between the year with the highest level of relative support (1999) and that with the lowest (1989) represents 4 per cent of GDP, and in the French region of Corsica the relative level of support in 1995 was eight times lower than in 1989. Basilicata, Extremadura and Corsica seem to be the rule rather than the exception, as considerable variations in Structural Fund commitments from one year to another are evident in almost all Objective 1 regions.

12.5 THE RETURNS OF THE EUROPEAN DEVELOPMENT EFFORT IN OBJECTIVE 1 REGIONS FROM A NEG PERSPECTIVE

The question that can be raised at this point is have these differences in priorities across countries and Objective 1 regions had an impact on development trends? Can the different trajectories of Ireland, on the one hand, and parts of the Italian Mezzogiorno, or some lagging regions in Greece, Portugal and Spain, on the other, be associated with their different priorities in development strategies? In this section we try to answer this question by regressing, using panel data analysis, the economic growth of the original Objective 1 regions on the financial commitments to each individual development axis, considered independently from commitments to other axes.

This regression uses the growth differential between a region and the country to which it belongs during the two first programming periods (1989–99) as a dependent variable. Some structural variables are added to the regression in order to reduce any 'omitted variables' bias. The structural variables include regional employment, youth unemployment, female employment and agricultural employment rates.

Table 12.3 presents the panel estimation of the impact of commitments in each development axis. The results are reported using up to six-year lags in order to give a dynamic picture of the potential middle-term impact of investment on different development priorities.

The results of the panel estimation highlight the scarce returns in terms of economic growth of commitments to the two main development axes. The coefficients of the commitments to infrastructure and the environment, and business support and tourism, which together represent around three-quarters of the total investment effort of the Structural Funds for

Table 12.3   Panel estimation of impact of commitments

Lags	Agriculture		Business		Human Capital		Infrastructure	
	Coeff.	Sig.	Coeff.	Sig.	Coeff.	Sig.	Coeff.	Sig.
No lag	2.64184	0.011	0.04080	0.946	0.96726	0.099	0.06571	0.830
Lag 1	1.07566	0.293	−0.00040	0.999	1.15333	0.044	0.37431	0.223
Lag 2	1.76516	0.127	0.45525	0.504	1.11696	0.067	0.28840	0.379
Lag 3	1.12091	0.401	−0.05990	0.942	1.68867	0.010	0.73076	0.040
Lag 4	1.30357	0.369	0.40540	0.702	1.09613	0.129	0.43997	0.289
Lag 5	−1.78680	0.286	0.14490	0.909	0.88395	0.251	0.63257	0.179
Lag 6	−0.46000	0.809	−1.71950	0.451	1.36230	0.111	0.24743	0.657

Objective 1 regions, are generally not significant. No association of the investment in these two axes with economic growth is observed for a period of up to six years after the original investment, with the exception of infrastructure in year three (Table 12.3). Investment in agriculture and rural support has a pattern of returns that is closer to that of income support policies, rather than investment policies: the returns on economic growth are highly positive and significant in the year of the investment, but that sort of investment loses its significance after one year and even starts becoming negative (albeit not significant) after five years (Table 12.3). Only investment in the training and redeployment of human resources has a positive and significant association with economic growth (Table 12.3). This association is also sustained in time.

NEG theories and models place particular importance on the analysis of transportation costs. The insights of these theories and models may thus help explain the observed patterns and the low returns of Structural Fund commitments, in general, and of investment in transport infrastructure, in particular. Unfortunately, different NEG models use different assumptions that sometimes lead to different conclusions. As a consequence, there is no integrated and/or univocal conclusion and NEG may be ambivalent about the potential impact of investment in transport infrastructure – and especially about where this impact is going to be felt – on economic growth.

First of all, the introduction of increasing returns to investment into economic models has shown the possibility of self-reinforcing agglomeration and multiple equilibria. In particular, starting from a situation of unstable equilibrium, even a small perturbation can lead the economy to move to different stable equilibria. When the starting situation of the economy is a stable equilibrium, in contrast, small perturbations result in temporary effects. Hence, in order to move an economy from the starting situation, the shock has to be larger than a certain threshold (Ottaviano, 2003). The question is whether past and current Structural Fund investment, especially in Objective 1 regions, has been higher than the required threshold to provoke sustained changes in growth patterns. It could be argued that Structural Fund expenditure, despite its greater magnitude, has so far remained below the threshold needed to trigger a significant change in regional growth trajectories across European countries.

Bearing this in mind, the impact of the modification of transport costs from an NEG framework on the location of economic activities has deserved special attention. As most Structural Fund expenditure has been devoted to transport infrastructure, in general, and inter-regional transport networks, in particular, these studies are particularly relevant in order to explain the lack of significant returns on this type of investment in Objective 1 regions.

The oldest model is the core-periphery model (Krugman, 1991). Using a bi-regional framework of monopolistic competition and worker migration, Krugman shows that the equilibrium is dispersed for high transport costs. When transport costs decrease, however, equilibrium with agglomeration become possible, until transport costs fall to 0, when the only stable equilibrium is agglomeration in one of the two regions. This conclusion is shared by many other models (such as Ottaviano, Tabuchi and Thisse, 2002, who develop an analytically solvable framework able to represent the same features). This would imply that decreasing transport costs has an agglomeration effect. The infrastructure policy of the EU may therefore be contributing to greater, rather than lower, regional disparities, as many of the supported transport schemes link the periphery of each country to its national core, and the periphery of Europe to its core (that is, the trans-European networks or TENs).

The results of the NEG models, however, are different depending on the framework used and the assumptions about the mobility of workers (Puga, 1999), of goods (Behrens, 2004; Alonso-Villar, 2005a) and the shape of transport costs (Alonso-Villar, 2005b). Venables (1996), for example, using a framework in which there is no worker mobility but vertical linkages between firms that provide the reason for agglomeration, shows that agglomeration is the stable output for intermediate transport costs. In the cases of high or low transport costs, in contrast, a dispersion of economic activities will be the most likely result. At the extreme, when transport costs fall to 0, the dispersion of economic activities becomes, once again, possible. The implications of Venables' model for the EU are that the lack of economic returns of infrastructure investment may only be temporary and that they could pick up in time, once sufficient investment has taken place. Venables' (1996) conclusions are shared by Krugman and Venables (1995) and Puga (1999), but only in the case of immobile workers. If workers are mobile, agglomeration remains the most likely outcome for low transport costs.

More sophisticated models have introduced a differentiation among types of infrastructure, so that the effects of regional policy depend on the type of infrastructure favoured by public expenditure. Martin and Rogers (1995) develop a model with domestic (that is, internal to the region) and international (that is, linking different regions) infrastructure. In this model, if domestic infrastructure increases, the lagging region univocally increases its income as well. The improvement in international infrastructure leads, in contrast, to potentially agglomerative effect. Using evidence from this model and confronting with the empirical evidence of decreasing national differences and increasing regional disparities, Martin argues that 'improving public infrastructure in a country and thus facilitating inter-regional trade increases its aggregate attractiveness but does not help convergence between regions as it may favour the richest regions of that country' (1998, p. 771). This may have been made more evident by the fact that the Cohesion Fund expenditure – exogenous to our regressions – has had a tendency to be concentrated in the core areas of the four Cohesion countries (Greece, Ireland, Portugal and Spain). Such investment would have thus contributed to the dynamism of Madrid, Dublin or Lisbon, often at the expense of more peripheral regions within those countries.

Lanaspa and Sanz (2004) add an additional twist by differentiating between export and import infrastructure. In their model, the location of firms in a given region is positively affected by the quality of domestic and international export infrastructure. Alonso-Villar (2005a), starting from a model similar to Venables (1996), indicates that regional convergence is best achieved by reducing transport costs between upstream and downstream industries, rather than by addressing those between firms and consumers. Martin (1999) analyses the issue of infrastructure and agglomeration in terms of growth dynamics. He concludes that infrastructure facilitating inter-regional trade fosters both growth and agglomeration, whereas the building of intra-regional infrastructure in the poorer regions decreases both agglomeration and growth. Improving innovation infrastructure leads to increased growth but also to decreasing regional disparities. This result is consistent with ours, as we observe that the expenditure in human capital within the region has been the only development axis to have persistent and statistically significant positive results.

The impact of the public sector for economic development has also been analysed. When the core-periphery model is extended to contemplate the presence of the public sector (for example, Lanaspa, Pueyo and Sanz, 2001) the relationship between transport costs and agglomeration is no longer monotonous and, more interestingly, regions with a lower tax-burden or a higher efficiency of the local public sector become more attractive for firm location. This process may reflect what has been happening across European regions. Many Objective 1 regions have much lower administrative capabilities than more advanced ones. Hence, the introduction of basic accountability requirements for the use of Structural Funds may produce positive effects in the longer term.

In summary, infrastructure is easily justified on the grounds of the scarce accessibility of many peripheral regions and of the potential by high returns of this type of investment, as indicated by the literature started by Aschauer (1989). Infrastructure is also popular among decision-makers because the population generally demands it. It is highly visible and tangible; it allows for high expenditure without having to design and implement comprehensive strategies; and it allows for ribbon-cutting right before elections (Rodríguez-Pose, 2000, p. 106). But, given the weakness of the economic fabric of many peripheral regions, investment in transport infrastructure may be favouring a greater concentration of economic activity in the core at the expense of the periphery, thus undermining the very objective of economic and social cohesion the Structural Funds are designed to achieve. These circumstances would explain the meagre returns of investment in infrastructure identified by recent studies (for example, Rodríguez-Pose, 2000; Vanhoudt et al., 2000; Puga, 2002).

Paradoxically, the emphasis on infrastructure could also partly explain the higher economic performance of peripheral countries as a whole. As mentioned earlier, the concentration of economic activities at the subnational level (Puga, 2002) is not happening yet at the European level, probably because of the imperfect economic integration at European level. Hence, the high growth of core regions within peripheral countries (regions that in the case of Madrid and Lazio, for example, are outside Objective 1) the main factor for the catch-up of Cohesion countries, has been fuelled in part by investment in infrastructure elsewhere in these countries.

In some cases, however, the emphasis on infrastructure and business support seems to have backfired. The regions that have used the Structural Funds in order to set up more balanced development strategies (that is, those that have tended to pay more attention to their local comparative advantages and shortcomings and designed the strategy accordingly, rather than splashing out on infrastructure investment) have performed better. Flevoland in the Netherlands and the Highlands and Islands and Northern Ireland in the United Kingdom, which became Objective 1 regions in 1994 and followed this pattern, have managed to come out of Objective 1 in a relatively short period of time or are currently being phased out. The regions that have placed the greatest emphasis on infrastructure or business support investment have, in contrast, not been able to narrow the economic gap with the core of Europe. This is especially true of regions, such as Asturias or Valencia in Spain, which is in spite of being relatively close to the 75 per cent of the EU GDP threshold in 1989 and in spite of a relatively high national growth during the period of analysis, have been unable to converge. Corsica has experienced relative economic decline during this period. A development strategy based fundamentally on infrastructure investment has left it exposed to other markets while devoid of the local firms or the necessary human capital to be able to compete in a more open economic environment. Similarly, many of the Southern Italian regions that invested heavily in local business support have been incapable of catching up, and the emphasis on agricultural and rural support in some Northern Greek and Spanish regions has equally not paid off.

12.6 CONCLUSION

This chapter has analysed the impact of EU development policies in inducing greater economic cohesion in the EU, with special focus on Objective 1 regions. The evidence that convergence has happened at country level, but that lagging regions have generally failed to catch up has been investigated with particular attention paid to the effects of Structural Fund expenditure. The results have highlighted that the Objective 1 commitments have been unbalanced towards infrastructure and business support, and that the economic returns of these development axes have been limited. New economic geography models – despite their diversity – provide some potential explanations for this. Investment in transport infrastructure, in particular, is contributing to greater economic agglomeration, making any change to the present equilibrium situation difficult. Moreover, the improvement of transport infrastructure can itself be a reason for increasing agglomeration and disparities. NEG models point out that infrastructure linking different regions usually tends to favour those regions endowed with a stronger productive fabric, and thus further reinforce agglomeration. This also contributes to explain why the expenditure in human capital, which goes in the direction of providing local economies with better skills to overcome some of the endowment shortcomings of the periphery, has been the only axis to provide significant and durable growth effects in Objective 1 regions.

REFERENCES

Alonso-Villar, O. (2005a), 'The effects of transport costs revisited', *Journal of Economic Geography*, **5**(5): 589–604.

Alonso-Villar, O. (2005b), 'The effects of transport costs within the new economic geography', Documentos de Traballo, Universidade de Vigo Departamento de Economía Aplicada.

Armstrong, H.W. (1995), 'An appraisal of the evidence from cross-sectional analysis of the regional growth process within the European Union', in R.W. Vickerman and H.W Armstrong (eds), *Convergence and Divergence Among European Regions*, Pion Limited, London, pp. 40–65.

Aschauer, D.A. (1989), 'Is public expenditure productive?', *Journal of Monetary Economics*, **23**: 177–200.

Barro, R.J. and X. Sala-i-Martín (1991), 'Convergence across states and regions', *Brookings Papers on Economic Activity*, **1**: 107–82.

Barry, F., J. Bradley and A. Hannan (2001), 'The single market, the structural funds and Ireland's recent economic growth', *Journal of Common Market Studies*, **39**(3): 537–52.

Behrens, K. (2004), 'Agglomeration without trade: how the non-traded goods shape the space-economy', *Journal of Urban Economics*, **55**: 68–92.

Boldrin, M. and F. Canova (2001), 'Inequality and convergence in Europe's regions: reconsidering European regional policies', *Economic Policy* **16**: 207–53.

Brülhart, M. and J. Torstensson (1996), 'Regional integration, scale economies and industry location in the European Union', *CEPR Discussion Papers*, 1435, London.

Cheshire, P.C. and G. Carbonaro (1995), 'Urban economic growth in Europe: testing theory and policy prescriptions', *Urban Studies*, **33**: 1111–28.

Cuadrado-Roura, J.R. (2001), 'Regional convergence in the European Union: from hypothesis to the actual trends', *Annals of Regional Science*, **35**: 333–56.

Cuadrado-Roura, J.R., T. Mancha Navarro and R. Garrido Yserte (1998), *Convergencia regional en España. Hechos, tendencias y perspectivas*, Madrid: Ediciones Argentaria/Visor.

De la Fuente, A. and R. Doménech (2001), 'The redistributive effects of the EU budget', *Journal of Common Market Studies*, **39**: 307–30.

Emerson, M. (1990), *The Economics of 1992*, Oxford: Oxford University Press.

European Commission (1994), *Fifth Periodic Report on the Social and Economic Situation and Development of the Regions of the Community*, Brussels: Commission of the European Communities.

European Commission (1999), *Sixth Periodic Report on the Social and Economic Situation and Development of the Regions of the European Union*, Brussels: Commission of the European Communities.

European Commission (2001), *Unity, Solidarity, Diversity for Europe, its People and its Territory. Second Report on Economic and Social Cohesion*, Brussels: Commission of the European Communities.

Faini, R. (2003), 'Migration and convergence in the regions of Europe. A bit of theory and some evidence', mimeo, University of Brescia.

Fingleton, B. (2004), 'Some alternative geo-economics for Europe's regions', *Journal of Economic Geography*, **4**(4): 389–420.

Krugman, P. (1991), 'Increasing returns and economic geography', *Journal of Political Economy*, **99**: 483–99.

Krugman, P. and A. Venables (1995), 'Globalization and the inequality of nations', *Quarterly Journal of Economics*, **110**: 857–80.

Lanaspa, L.F. and F. Sanz (2004), 'Regional policy and industrial location decisions', *Investigaciones Económicas*, **XXVIII**(I): 67–87.

Lanaspa, L.F., F. Pueyo and F. Sanz (2001), 'The public sector and the core-periphery model', *Urban Studies*, **38**(10): 1639–49.

Leonardi, R. (1995), *Convergence, Cohesion and Integration in the European Union*, Basingstoke: Macmillan Press.

López-Bazo, E., E. Vayá, A.J. Mora and J. Suriñach (1999), 'Regional economic dynamics and convergence in the European Union', *Annals of Regional Science*, **33**: 343–70.

Magrini, S. (1999), 'The evolution of income disparities among the regions of the European Union', *Regional Science and Urban Economics*, **29**: 257–81.

Martin, P. (1998), 'Can regional policies affect growth and geography in Europe?', *World Economy*, **21**: 757–74.

Martin, P. (1999), 'Public policies, regional inequalities and growth', *Journal of Public Economics*, **73**: 85–105.

Martin, P. and C.A. Rogers (1995), 'Industrial location and public infrastructure', *Journal of International Economics*, **39**: 335–51.

Midelfart-Knarvik, K.H. and H.G. Overman (2002), 'Delocation and European integration: is structural spending justified?', *Economic Policy*, **17**(35): 321–59.

Midelfart-Knarvik, K.H., H.G. Overman, S.R. Redding and A.J. Venables (2000), 'The location of European industry', *European Commission, Economic Papers No. 142*, Brussels: European Commission.

Molle, W. and S. Boeckhout (1995), 'Economic disparity under conditions of integration – a long-term view of the European case', *Papers in Regional Science*, **74**: 105–23.

Moreno, R., R. Paci and S. Usai (2005), 'Spatial spillovers and innovation activity in European regions', *Environment and Planning A*, **37**(10): 1793–812.

Neven, D. and C. Gouyette (1995), 'Regional convergence in the European Community', *Journal of Common Market Studies*, **33**: 47–65.

Ottaviano, G.I.P. (2003), 'Regional policy in the global economy: insights from new economic geography', *Regional Studies*, **37**: 665–74.

Ottaviano G.I.P., T. Tabuchi and J.-F. Thisse (2002), 'Agglomeration and trade revisited', *International Economic Review*, **43**: 409–36.

Padoa-Schioppa, T. (1987), *Efficiency, Stability and Equity: A Strategy for the Evolution of the Economic System of the European Community*, Oxford: Oxford University Press.

Puga, D. (1999), 'The rise and fall of regional inequalities', *European Economic Review*, **43**: 303–34.

Puga, D. (2002), 'European regional policies in light of recent location theories', *Journal of Economic Geography*, **2**(4): 373–406.

Quah, D. (1996), 'Regional convergence clusters across Europe', *European Economic Review*, **40**: 951–8.

Rodríguez-Pose, A. (1999), 'Convergence or divergence? Types of regional responses to socioeconomic change', *Tijdschrift voor Economische en Sociale Geografie*, **90**: 363–78.

Rodríguez-Pose, A. (2000), 'Economic convergence and regional development strategies in Spain: the case of Galicia and Navarre', *EIB Papers*, **5**(1): 89–115.

Rodríguez-Pose, A. and U. Fratesi (2004), 'Between development and social policies: the impact of European Structural Funds in Objective 1 regions', *Regional Studies*, **38**(1): 97–113, http://www.tandf.co.uk.

Sapir, A., P. Aghion, G. Bertola, M. Hellwig, J. Pisani-Ferry, D. Rosati, J. Viñals and H. Wallace (2004), *An Agenda for a Growing Europe: The Sapir Report*, Oxford: Oxford University Press.

Tondl, G. (2001), *Convergence after Divergence?: Regional Growth in Europe*, Berlin: Springer.

Vanhoudt, P., T. Mathä and B. Smid (2000), 'How productive are capital investments in Europe?', *EIB Papers*, **5**(2): 81–106.

Venables, A.J. (1996), 'Equilibrium locations of vertically linked industries', *International Economic Review*, **37**: 341–59.

Index

EBRD (European Bank for
Reconstruction and Development)
index 300
econometrics 250
economic activity, concentration of
101
economic geography 254
economies of distance 190–93
economies of localization 207
economies of scale
foreign direct investment (FDI)
281–3
and polarization 45–7
spatial transaction costs 183–5
transport costs 179–81, 192–3
economies of urbanization 207
educational attainment 77–93
efficiency, of labour 77–93
efficiency change 230–31, 234, 235–9,
241–6, 354
Egger, P., et al. 280
Ekholm, K. 280, 292, 293
elasticity of demand 12, 19–20,
191–2
elasticity of substitution
and agglomeration 117–18, 159–63
and break points 41
constant elasticity of substitution
(CES) function 12, 146–54, 156,
158, 159–63
correlation surface 35
and geographical allocation 154–6
and NEGG models 146–50
and wages 36
Ellison, G. 224
Elteto, A. 303
empirical analysis of spatial dynamics
260–73
empirical testing (NEG)
agglomeration and transport costs
111–15
background 98–9
interpretation of findings 115–21
limitations 121–5
testable hypotheses 102–4
wage equation estimate 104–11
employment
and capital distribution 256–60, 261
data 208–9
density 92, 219–21

and foreign direct investment (FDI)
305
specialization 205–10
epistemological adequacy 250, 253–4,
255–6
equilibrium
and agglomeration 44–7, 59–60
core-periphery (CP) model 56–7
long-run, application 32–47
in regional political economy 254,
256
short-run, application 25–32
spatial modelling 250–51
and symmetry 45–7, 59–60
Estrin, S. 300, 301, 302, 303
Estrin, S., et al. 301
Ethier, W. 286, 287
Euromoney 300
European Internet Exchange Points
Association (Euro-IX) 315,
324–8, 329–33
European Union (EU)
break points 115–21, 124
data 235
foreign direct investment (FDI) 277,
278
integration 295–7
NEG perspective 351–6
peering (IXPs) 322–4
regional disparities 340–44
regional productivity 230–31, 234,
235–46
specialization 214
structural policy 338, 340–50, 351–6
wage rates 74–5
Eurostat REGIO database 235
export-platform 294
exports, and foreign direct investment
(FDI) 286–94, 303

face-to-face contact 317–19
factor mobility 54–60 *see also* labour
mobility
Falzoni, A.M. 290
Fan, Y. 86
Färe, R., et al. 233
Farrell, M.J. 232
Farrell, R., et al. 290
FE (footloose entrepreneurs) model
factor mobility 54–60